BRITISH NAVAL
Swords & Swordsmanship

THE NAVY: VARIOUS

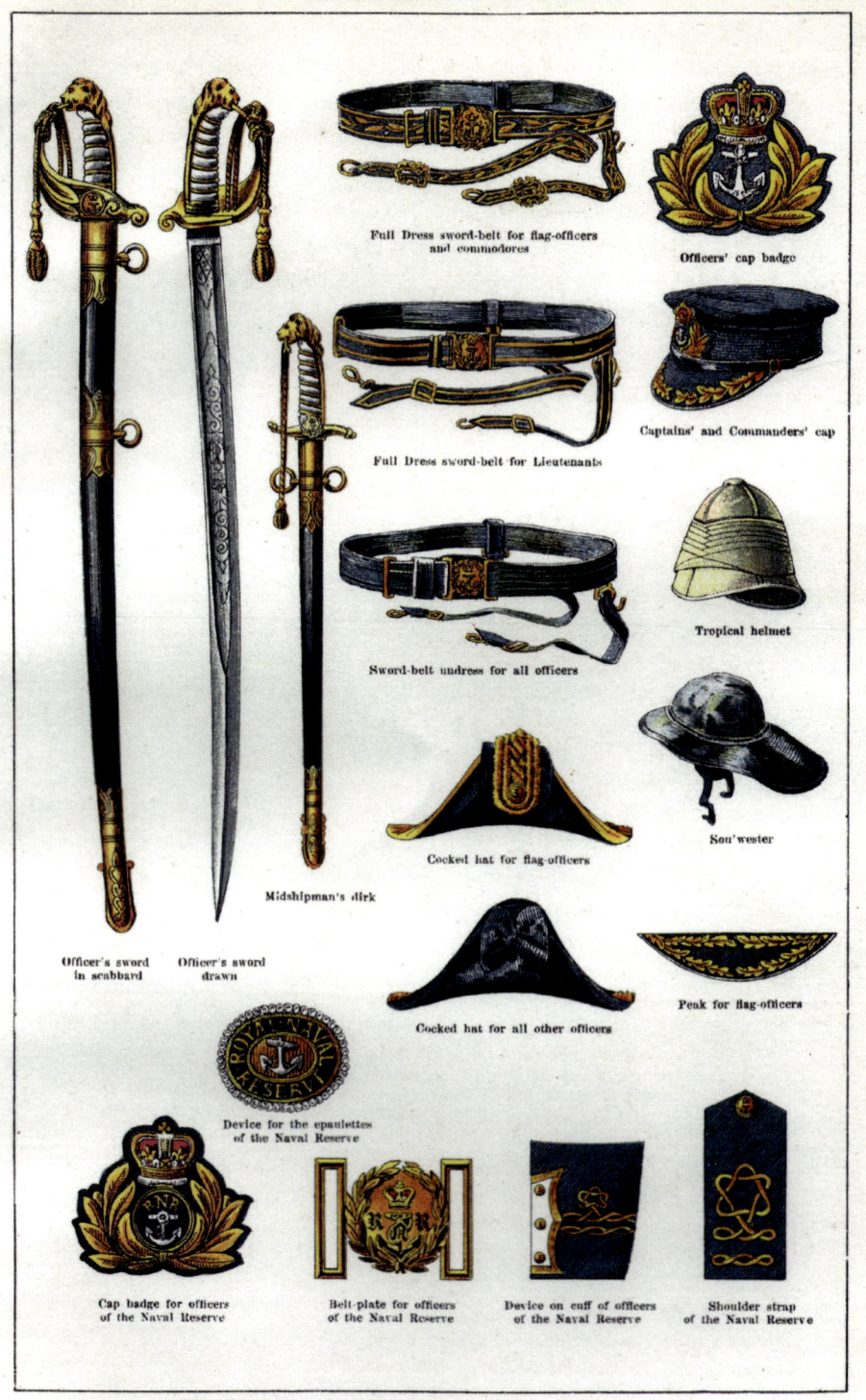

This plate gives some idea of the range of uniform items required by an officer in the RN or RNR in 1898.

BRITISH NAVAL
Swords & Swordsmanship

John McGrath & Mark Barton

Seaforth
PUBLISHING

Title page: A chromolithograph depicting 'A boarding party', from Charles Rathbone Low's book, *Her Majesty's Navy Including its Deeds and Battles*, published in 1890. *(Author's collection)*

Copyright © John McGrath & Mark Barton 2013

First published in Great Britain in 2013 by
Seaforth Publishing,
Pen & Sword Books Ltd,
47 Church Street,
Barnsley S70 2AS

www.seaforthpublishing.com

British Library Cataloguing in Publication Data
A catalogue record for this book is available from the British Library

ISBN 978 1 84832 135 9

All rights reserved. No part of this publication may be reproduced or transmitted in any form or by any means, electronic or mechanical, including photocopying, recording, or any information storage and retrieval system, without prior permission in writing of both the copyright owner and the above publisher.

The right of John McGrath and Mark Barton to be identified as the authors of this work have been asserted by them in accordance with the Copyright, Designs and Patents Act 1988.

Typeset and designed by Mousemat Design Limited
Printed in China through Printworks Int. Ltd.

Contents

Preface   6

1	The Naval Sword in Action	7
2	Cutlasses	26
3	Officers' Swords	35
4	Dirks	55
5	Swords of Officers of the Reserves, the Merchant Navy and Other Maritime Organisations	60
6	Presentation Swords	76
7	Nelson's Swords	82
8	Training in Swordsmanship	92
9	Transition to a Sport	100
10	Your Naval Sword	110

Appendix 1: Patriotic Fund of Lloyds – Swords Awarded   119
Appendix 2: City of London Presentation Swords   124
Appendix 3: Naval Service Awards of the Wilkinson Swords of Peace   125
Appendix 4: Service Champions and Trophies   126

Glossary   131
Bibliography   133
Notes   136
Index   142

Preface

The sword has long been a part of our professional and personal lives. As naval officers, we have wielded swords at numerous ceremonial occasions, both official and unofficial, from passing-out parades to weddings. As fencers, we have both been naval champions and have competed in international competitions. Naturally, as historians and collectors, we have gravitated towards British naval swords.

This book has come about because we have been approached many times over the years by friends and colleagues with questions regarding naval swords. There are several well-respected texts dealing with British naval swords, their evolution and history and it is not the intention to try to supplant these. This book instead addresses the questions that those books do not answer and sets the sword in the context of the social history of the Royal Navy.

Here, we explore the full historical period from the emergence of specifically naval swords to the present day. It is hoped that examination of this context will lead to a fuller understanding of the naval sword, which will no longer only be seen in isolation as a collector's item. It takes a swordsman, used to handling weapons, to appreciate the objectives and subtleties of the various schemes of fencing instruction and, to this, we believe we bring a discerning eye. The sword has long since ceased to be a combat weapon, now relegated to a purely ceremonial function, but, while this transition was taking place, swordsmanship itself evolved from combat training into a full-blown sport that encourages pugnacity, promotes physical fitness and maintains morale.

We freely acknowledge our great debt to pioneer authors, such as Commander W E May and P G W Annis, who put the taxonomy of the naval sword on such firm foundations. The passage of time has not altered the general structure but added fine detail. There are several areas of study where we hope we have added to their work. We also aim to correct some common misconceptions and myths held within the Service.

No work like this would be possible without the help of many individuals and we wish to offer our sincere thanks to Chris Allen, Matt Bowden, Keith Bowers, Sacha Brooks, Sim Comfort, Laura Dimmock, David Foster, John Grodzinski, Graham Hockley, Robert Hughes-Mullock, Graham Hunt, Andrew Lambert, Sue Martel, Russell Milne, John McAleer, Robert Pooley, Cormac Rynne, Bobby Thorn, Chris Walker, Peter and Robert Watts, Paul Willcocks, Admiral Sir John Woodward and Jenny Wraight. A particular debt of gratitude is due to Julian Mannering and Stephen Chumbley of Seaforth Publishing whose keen eye for detail and unfailing patience have done so much to improve our initial offerings. All errors are, of course, ours alone.

John also gratefully acknowledges the tolerance of his wife, Zena, who has lived with his obsession for all things associated with swords and swordsmanship for more than forty years. Mark would like to thank his fiancée, Jenny Keates, for encouraging his interest and the many happy hours working together on the text.

Unless otherwise acknowledged, all the images are from items that are in or have passed through the authors' collections. We believe we have obtained the requisite permissions from the copyright holders of the remaining illustrations and offer our apologies if there are any instances in which we have failed. If there are any such cases, please bring them to our attention.

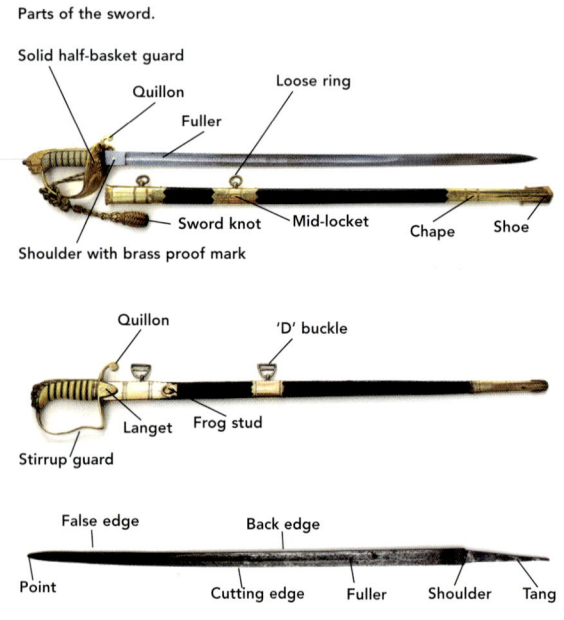

Parts of the sword.

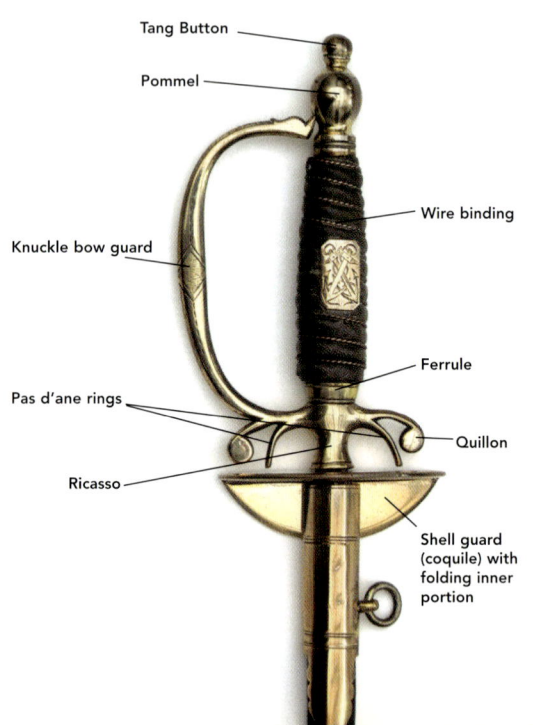

CHAPTER 1

The Naval Sword in Action

Sailors fought at sea with swords and other edged weapons for millennia, but misconceptions abound about how these weapons were employed by mariners, particularly from around 1650 until the beginning of the twentieth century. In this chapter, we discuss how sailors used swords and edged weapons in battle, both on shore and at sea, and in duelling. We also tackle the question of when swords were last used in action, and look at how they are used by today's naval officers.

The traditional image of sailors hacking their way aboard enemy vessels is far from the whole story; the majority of naval engagements throughout this period involved battles with cannon or were cutting-out expeditions, in which sailors would enter a harbour and capture or destroy enemy vessels or strongholds.

Five edged weapons were deployed at sea: the sword, the cutlass, the pike, the axe and the bayonet. Swords were personal weapons, owned by officers. Cutlasses and pikes were supplied to the ship's company as part of the ship's equipment. Axes were intended to be used to deal with damaged rigging such as ropes and spars, but were often used as weapons. Bayonets arrived attached to the muskets of the Marines in the seventeenth century and were later issued to the naval brigades in the nineteenth century. Sailors would also use whatever came to hand in the heat of hand-to-hand fighting, such as dirks, knives and marlinspikes. Most of what is described in this chapter applies not only to swords but also to these other weapons.

One of the main uses of swords was as part of boarding operations at the end of a gunnery battle. As one ship's fire slackened, the stronger vessel would come alongside and seek to board her if she had not already struck her colours. As Nelson phrased it: 'No captain can do very wrong if he places his ship alongside that of the enemy.' Unlike in earlier periods, when hand-to-hand fighting between vessels constituted the main naval tactic, from the seventeenth century, ships aimed to blast their opponents into submission using cannon fire. However, since the ships' hulls were typically 2ft thick[1] and built to resist roundshot, we should not be surprised that it was necessary to manoeuvre to close quarters. From the concept of the line of battle developed by Admiral Blake in 1653,[2] tactics for sea battles evolved with the aim being to reduce the enemy through a broadside duel.[3] However, this would often fail to force the enemy to strike his colours. In these circumstances, a captain would have to lay his vessel alongside and prepare to board and to repel boarders from the enemy ship. Since this would be almost certainly after an engagement with the great guns, it would be a desperate struggle and, as one might expect, techniques were brutal and relied on the sailors' stamina and strength.

The scale and ferocity of naval warfare meant that sword drill had to be simple so that men could fight instinctively. A First Rate ship of the line would mount a hundred or more guns and fire a broadside of some 2000lbs[4] of shot. At the battle of Waterloo, by comparison, British land forces had thirty-nine guns, able to fire around 276lbs of shot.[5] Furthermore, gun engagements at sea would last for many hours. At the battle of Barfleur in 1692, vessels engaged in

One of a series of coloured aquatints by George Cruikshank following the character Mr B, in this case with 'Mr B seeking the bubble reputation'. (Published by Thomas Maclean, 1 August 1835. © National Maritime Museum, Greenwich, London, PAD4725)

broadside duels for eleven hours. Even the battle of Trafalgar involved 4½ hours of broadsides and action. Unsurprisingly, sailors were issued with an extra ration of spirits prior to a battle, to anaesthetise them to the noise and the shock of constant bombardment and give them Dutch courage.

Long battles are exhausting. Michael Loades, the historical weapons expert, comments: 'Even the fittest of men will tire after several minutes of hard fighting. Delivering blows that are capable of severing limbs requires huge reserves of energy.'[6] A fighting sword of the period would typically weigh nearly 3lbs (1.36kg), a pound more than a modern ceremonial sword. The power of such blows should not be underestimated. During an attack on a fort in Muros Bay in Northern Spain, Lieutenant Yeo felled the fort's governor with a single stroke of the blade, but in doing so broke his own sword in two.[7] Since the age of chariots, warriors fighting on land had found ways to gain respite in the midst of battle. As Julius Caesar wrote in his *Gallic Wars*:

> [They] leap from their chariots and engage on foot. The charioteers in the meantime withdraw a little distance from the battle, and so place themselves with the chariots that, if their masters are overpowered by the number of the enemy, they may have a ready retreat to their own troops.[8]

However, in the close confines and crowded decks of a man of war there would be little opportunity to take a break until victory, surrender or the ships drifted apart. This is perhaps why the early cutlass drills involved exercising with both arms.

Boarding Actions

Three main types of action involved sword fighting – boarding, cutting out and landings. In 1813, the 350-strong crew of the 38-gun HMS *Shannon* boarded the USS *Chesapeake*. The men of the *Shannon* were armed with around 75 boarding axes, 100 boarding pikes, 150 cutlasses, 100 muskets and around 100 pistols with steel belt hooks. Each man in a gun crew had at least one secondary role, and half the gun crews were designated as boarders, three designated as first boarders and three more as second boarders. The first boarders were the assault party, and each would be issued with a cutlass and pistol. The second boarders were primarily the defensive force and would have pikes and axes.[9] Like modern sailors, the men prepared for close-quarters combat by tidying away loose ends of their dress – they would tie handkerchiefs around their heads and ensure their shirtsleeves were tucked up.[10]

This scale seems to be typical: when fitting out in 1805 for a crew of eighty-five men, the British whaler *Port-au-Prince*, which only intended to indulge in opportunistic privateering, was equipped with fifty small arms, fifty cutlasses, twenty barrels of gunpowder, twenty great roundshot and 50 hundredweight of small shot. The ship was 466 tons with twenty-eight guns (6, 9 and 12pdrs).[11]

Boarding was usually conducted when the enemy was on the defensive, having suffered a mauling by broadside.[12] However, this was not always the case. The usual tactic was reversed to good effect by Lord Cochrane and HMS *Speedy* in 1801 in a fight with the much larger Spanish frigate *El Gamo*. Whenever the Spanish were about to board, Cochrane would endeavour to pull away and fire on the gathered boarding parties. He eventually boarded the *El Gamo* himself, despite still being heavily outnumbered.[13]

A boarding would be a brutal and crowded affair. There was unlikely to be the room on a deck in the struggle that would give space for the elegant one-on-one combat loved by Hollywood. However, even contemporary accounts give rise to the man on man image, one French newspaper reporting[14] after the battle of Trafalgar how, apparently, Admiral Villeneuve offered Nelson a pistol so that they could fight fairly. The same report also declared it a complete French victory, and was sure their vessels had only been scattered by the subsequent storm.

Captain Selwyn RN commented at a Royal United Services Institute Lecture in 1862, that in the press of battle a sailor 'having got up his sword arm and being unable to get it down again, [had] to use the hilt of his cutlass, and knock his enemy's teeth down his throat'.[15] Captain Selwyn then commented on the habit of Lord Cochrane of arming his sailors for boarding with bayonets fastened to the outsides of their left arms with the points projecting 6in beyond the hand and then arming them only with cutlasses, telling them to attack. The bayonet formed a guard for defence as well as enabling attack. The responding lecturer, Mr John Latham, who ran Wilkinson's Swords at the time, commented this is effective and matched the Scottish method of fighting with a sword, dirk and targe; the targe being a small shield usually less than 20in in diameter. The dirk would be held in the same hand as the targe to help with defence (Lord Cochrane was, of course, a Scottish officer).

The preponderance of rigging and other obstructions added to the difficulty of fighting with swords during boarding. It should not be surprising that one notable difference between military and naval sword drills is the lack of over-the-head strokes in the latter, although there is a head defence. That this was probably common among most navies

Nelson boarding a Spanish launch in July 1797. (Oil painting by Richard Westall, 1806. © National Maritime Museum, Greenwich, London, BHC2908)

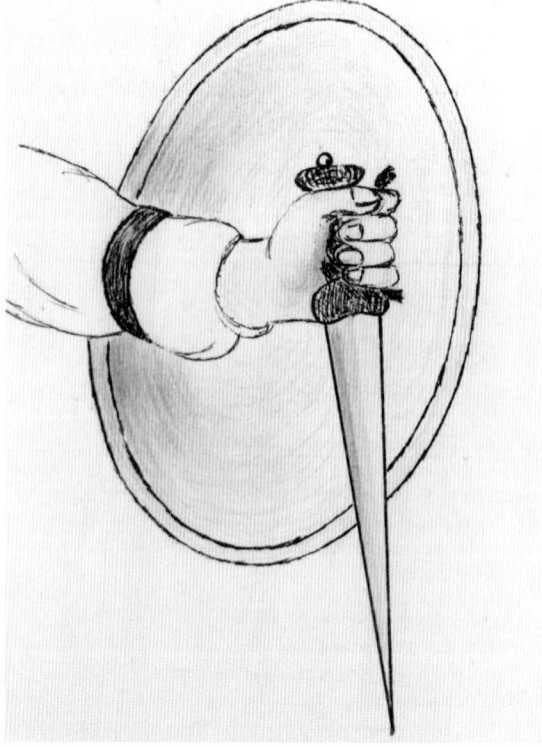

Holding a dagger behind a targe.

admiral, who deceased to his great honour and laud, than the advantage might have been of the winning of all the French galleys and their equipage.'[18]

British naval superiority in the Napoleonic period and Nelson's exploits in battles such as the battle of Cape St Vincent in 1797, when he captured the *San Nicolas* and then used her to capture the *San Josef* (a feat subsequently referred to as 'Nelson's patent bridge for boarding First Rates'), mean we often think of boarding as a British activity. But it is sometimes forgotten that boarding was a favoured French tactic.[19] The French government focussed on land campaigns and, following their successes ashore, believed that if they could bring revolutionary fervour into action at sea then victory would be achieved. To this end, they often carried soldiers on board, rather than marines, and would have a bigger crew than the average British warship. For example, in 1803, the brig *Racoon* fought three actions in short succession. On 11 July, she took on a French brig-corvette, then on 17 August she fought the brig *La Mutine*, which was carrying sufficient troops to form a long line on the shore, and on 14 October captured another brig *La Petite Fille*, which carried 180 additional troops, while accompanied by a cutter *L'Amelie* with seventy troops and a schooner with eighty troops *La Jeune Adele*.[20] Disparity of numbers was often evened up by different tactics: the British fired directly at the hulls to cause maximum casualties, whereas the French would fire at the rigging hoping to disable the vessel and affect manoeuvring. Edward Fraser describes how at Trafalgar the Spanish ships in the French-Spanish fleet were manned: 'To stiffen the new crews, and man the upper-deck guns and supply the musketry, and also to leave what trained seaman there were available, free for their own special work aloft strong drafts of soldiers were shipped.'[21]

Sir Edward Howard standing on the gunwale prior to being forced over the side. (*Navy and Army Illustrated*, 19 November 1897, p 60)

could be indicated by the fact that only the US Navy issued helmets to its personnel during the Napoleonic war. Although the defence was sometimes needed, as Captain Chamier comments, '. . . he made a desperate cut at me. My head, thick as it is, was defended by my cutlass'.[16]

It was important in any boarding action for the vessels to remain alongside, to enable reinforcement and facilitate retreat. When they did not, things could go very badly, as illustrated by the action at Conquet Bay on 25 April 1513. A squadron of French galleys had come round from the Mediterranean, under the command of the Chevalier Prégent de Bidoux, and had anchored in Whitsand Bay. An English council of war determined that they might be attacked. It was found that the galleys were drawn up close to the shore, in very shoal water, so the British admiral, Sir Edward Howard, resolved to cut them out with his boats and some small row-barges attached to the fleet. Howard ran his boats alongside the French and then leapt sword in hand along with seventeen crew on board the French vessel. The vessels separated again and, now trapped and unsupported, the British were forced back by pikes and sheer weight of numbers, and slowly pushed overboard. Sir Edward being the last, eventually ended on the gunwale. He threw his gold nobles and whistle that were his marks of office into the sea to prevent them falling into the hands of the French before he, too, was forced overboard and drowned.[17] Howard's death was felt as a national disaster. In a letter to Henry VIII, James IV of Scotland wrote: 'Surely, dearest brother, we think more loss is to you of your late

The preparations for battle also had to include mental preparation. Second Lieutenant Ellis of the *Ajax* provides an interesting insight into how the sailors behaved as they prepared to go into battle at Trafalgar.

> The men were variously occupied; some were sharpening their cutlasses, others polishing the guns, as though an inspection were about to take place instead of a mortal combat, whilst three or four, as if in mere bravado, were dancing a hornpipe; but all seemed deeply anxious to come to close quarters with the enemy.[22]

A remarkable boarding action

James Spratt was the Master's Mate on board *Defiance*, under Captain Philip Durham, at the battle of Trafalgar.[23] During the battle, finding the *Aigle*'s fire slacking but having drifted slightly away from the *Defiance*, he asked permission to lead a boarding party to *Aigle* by swimming. In his manuscript of the battle he describes it: 'I plunged over board from the starboard gang way with my cutlass between my teeth and my tomahawk under my belt and swam to the stern of *L'Aigle* where by the assistance of her rudder chains I got into her gunroom stern post alone.' He was by himself because:

> My men in the loud clamour of a general engagement not hearing what I said, or misunderstood me, did not follow, so I fought my way under God's guidance through a host of gallant French, all prepared with arms in hand, and through all decks until I got on her poop . . . I now showed myself to our ships crew . . . and gave them a cheer, with my hat on the point of my cutlass.

This painting shows the two fleets at the end of the battle of Trafalgar at about 5.00pm and is a bird's eye view from the south-east. In the foreground the most shattered of the British ships lie with their prizes. Beyond, the remaining ten enemy ships are making their escape. In the left foreground is the British *Tonnant*, in port-bow view, her topmast shot away, and astern of her the British *Defiance*, in port-bow view, having lost her main and mizzen topmasts. To the right of her is the French *L'Intrepide*, with her fore and mizzen topmast gone. (Painting by Nicholas Pocock © National Maritime Museum, Greenwich, London, BHC0549)

Later, after the ships had come alongside each other and more boarders had crossed over,

> . . . a grenadier from the starboard gangway with fixed bayonet thought to run me through, but I parried his thrust with my blade. He then retired levelling his piece at my breast, which I struck downwards with my trusty old friend the cutlass, so that the ball, which would otherwise have passed through my body shivered and shattered the bone of my right leg which was in advance, I felt something like an electric shock and dashed at him.

At this point his leg gave way and he had to depend on the others. This dramatic bid for promotion was successful as he made Lieutenant that year[24] but the injury ended his active career at sea as it did not heal[25] and he only made Commander on retirement from the active Navy List in 1838.[26]

With exertion such as this, it will not be surprising that after the battle the crew were exhausted. Lieutenant Nicholas, Royal Marines, describing the events at Trafalgar from his perspective on board the *Bellisle*, said:

> About five o'clock the officers assembled in the captain's cabin to take some refreshment. The parching effects of the smoke made this a welcome summons . . . still four hours' exertion of body with the energies incessantly employed, occasioned a lassitude, both corporally and mentally, from which the victorious termination now so near at hand, could not arouse us . . .[27]

The sword was so central to these actions that it was the weapon officers used to mark their surrender. The classic example was when the captains of *San Josef* and *San Nicolas* surrendered their swords at the battle of Cape St Vincent to the then Commodore Horatio Nelson. There were so many that he had to hand them to his bargeman William Fearney, who tucked them under his arm. But, it was not just captains of vessels that handed over their swords. The Dey of Algiers signalled the surrender of Algiers to Lord Exmouth after his bombardment on 27 August 1816 by sending his sword to the attacking warship.

Cutting-out Actions and Landings

From the 1750s to the end of the Victorian period, most naval swordfighting took place as part of cutting-out or landing expeditions. This was, though, building on tactics that had been used for several centuries. Following the lengthy, gruelling but indecisive battle of Barfleur in 1692, between the French fleet under Tourville and Admiral Russell's Anglo-Dutch fleet, the French had sought refuge at La Hougue where they would be under the protection of shore batteries and their soldiers. On 3 and 4 June, the Anglo-Dutch force attacked in longboats and, having deployed shore parties and fireships, burnt all twelve French ships of the line that had sought shelter there.

'Cutting out' involved taking the enemy's vessels from under the protection of shore batteries or other fortifications. Landing parties, on the other hand, attacked shore emplacements such as forts or telegraph towers and ventured further inland as naval brigades. Lieutenant G S Parsons describes several of these actions in his *Nelsonian Reminiscences* from his time at sea during the Napoleonic Wars. These were actions carried out by the squadron he was part of in the West Indies in 1805 and are typical for the period. In these accounts, the Commodore of the group would send his order across to all the vessels to provide a quota of volunteers '... armed with cutlasses, pistols and pikes'.[28] With valour in battle being a likely requirement for promotion for a lieutenant without the right connections, leading such expeditions was a sought-after position.

The volunteers would prepare for action, '... grinding their cutlasses, sharpening boarding pikes, and selecting pistols with good locks, well flinted'.[29] They may well also have fastened their swords to their wrists with a becket, a small loop of twine or cloth to ensure it was not separated from them.[30] As this was prior to the introduction of a uniform for sailors, in these particular skirmishes the attacking party also sewed a patch of white canvas on their sword arms so they could recognise each other. The Marines carried by the vessels would invariably form part of the attacking party, and they would be armed with muskets with bayonets fixed, while the Marine officers carried swords and pistols. Passwords and challenges would be issued; in one example, the words 'Church' and 'Chichester' as at the time they believed the 'ch' sound to be difficult for foreigners to pronounce.[31] In this particular squadron, their limited numbers enabled them to muster in a single ship to receive their orders prior to going ashore. To surprise the enemy, attacks were often made at night; the rowlocks would be padded to muffle the oars. Parsons described the fear and tension when, on one of these cutting out expeditions, they thought they might have been seen by a sentry.

An early cutting-out action, the battle of La Hogue. (Painting by George Chambers © National Maritime Museum, Greenwich, London, BHC0339)

> A discharge of grape and canister at this moment from the heavy guns would have swept us like a flash of lightening from the face of the ocean. Thank God! He drew back ... Each person drew his breath more freely; at least I can answer for myself, who felt as if a ton weight had suddenly been lifted from my breast. Every yard had now life or death depending on it. Yet we could not exert more speed without drawing on us the attention of our wary and vigilant foe. With us all was profound stillness and inactivity, far different from the bustle and noise of action; and I am confident many a good resolution was formed, and many a silent aspiration ascended to the throne of Heaven for mercy.[32]

A broadside from the target ship or a protecting battery on open boats could cause significant casualties and check any attack, as could volleys of musket fire from enemy infantry drawn up on shore. Any attack would be spearheaded by marines with bayonets fixed and the sailors, commanded by their officers, followed on behind, armed with their pikes and with swords and cutlasses drawn and pistols in their belts. Once the enemy was aware of their presence, they would give a loud battle cry. Captain Chamier, in his memoirs, confirms that these practices were still current when he describes a skirmish ashore in the US War of 1812.[33]

During the summer of 1801, three British frigates were watching the movements of the French and Spanish fleet lying within Brest harbour. In July, they discovered the 20-gun French corvette *Chevrette* at anchor under the batteries in Cameret Bay, and they resolved to cut her out. During the first attempt, the boats separated and not only failed to reach their target but were spotted by the French. The *Chevrette* ran further into the bay under the shelter of a stronger battery,

The cutting-out of a French brig, possibly *La Chevrette*. (Undated sketch by P J de Loutherbourg © National Maritime Museum, Greenwich, London, PAH8407)

A landing party armed with a variety of weapons on the beach during the attack on the capture of Fort Louis, Martinique, 20 March 1794. (By William Anderson 1795 © National Maritime Museum, Greenwich, London, BHC0468)

embarked some soldiers, prepared her guns and arranged a gun boat as a guard vessel at the entrance to the bay. She then issued a challenge by flying an English ensign beneath her own. This provocation riled the observing British. That night, 21 July, they dispatched fifteen boats with 280 officers and men. Lieutenant Lossack, the commander of the expedition, was distracted by the sight of another vessel and chased it with six of his boats, assuming it to be a lookout. The remainder, about 180 men, under Lieutenant Maxwell, proceeded. Despite timing their attack for after the moon disappeared below the horizon, they were still seen on approach and came under heavy fire. They pushed on regardless and, having somehow lost their firearms, the survivors boarded the *Chevrette* with cutlasses. The fighting on deck was intense but a prearranged group fought their way aloft to set the sails, while others cut the cable and thus they started to bring her out within three minutes of having boarded. Mr Brown, a boatswain, had managed to gain the taffrail of the *Chevrette*. When he saw Lieutenant Maxwell with a party further forward, he jumped up, waving his cutlass, and yelled 'Make a lane there, I'm coming!'

He cut his way through the French soldiers until he reached his friends on the fo'c'sle while H Wallis, a quartermaster, managed to cut his way to the wheel. So, finding their vessel sailing out of the harbour, many of the French abandoned ship or surrendered. However, others fled below and continued to fire up until they were threatened with no quarter if they did not desist, whereupon they, too, surrendered. Surprisingly, just ten British were killed, although fifty-seven suffered wounds, some of which proved to be mortal.[34]

The butcher's bill could be high in these cutting-out expeditions, as illustrated by the account in the *Naval Chronicle*[35] of the capture in 1803 of a different vessel called *Chevrette*, in this case a French corvette: 'Lieutenant Neville, of the *Urain*, immediately after boarding, ran aft to the quarterdeck, and discovering the French Captain, a combat ensued, in which the latter was presently vanquished, and fell lifeless near the wheel, having been run through with a cutlass'. This was in a battle that when the British '. . . got possession of the deck, when the carnage became more general, and the contest was kept up with great slaughter for about an hour and a half, until the deck of the vessel was literally filled with dead and wounded bodies.'

Like cutting-out actions, attacks by landing parties were part of the usual business of the Royal Navy during the Napoleonic Wars, projecting power and removing the threat of local batteries either as part of a larger action or to assist with cutting out expeditions. Preparation and tactics were very similar to those employed in cutting out.

Duelling in the Royal Navy

Not only was the sword a weapon for fighting with, it was also a mark of a gentleman's honour. In the days of Queen Elizabeth I, seafarers were as apt to settle their differences with the swords as were other members of society. The Elizabethan writer George Silver describes how two argumentative captains killed each other in a duel at Southampton. 'Two Captaines at Southampton even as they were going to shipping upon the key, fel at strife, drew their Rapiers, and presently, being desperate, hardie or resolute, as they call it, with all force and over great speed, ran with their rapiers one at the other, & were both slaine.'[36]

Duelling was illegal in Britain from the time of James I, but the habit spread particularly amongst military officers. This meant the winner of a duel may well have been subject to criminal charges such as murder. This trait of honour had a negative side as the Royal Navy, like so many other institutions, was not immune from the habit of duelling. In 1749 two Royal Navy Captains, Clark and Innis, had a disagreement and felt that the only way they could settle it was by duel. Clark killed Innis and was charged with murder. He was sentenced to death but luckily the King pardoned him.[37]

Many duels occurred involving naval officers, but most were with pistols. This is both because of when they occurred and the British custom in duels. Those naval duels identified by the authors nearly all date between 1740 and 1850 with the majority post 1780. The growth of the Royal Navy occurred in the late eighteenth century and by this time the wearing of side arms had ceased to be customary in civil society. In Britain at this time duelling was normally with pistols, as these were felt to suit the formality and to be fairer. Were a duel to be conducted with swords, being a skilled swordsman would have been an unfair advantage.[38] The 1770s saw the first manufacture of specialised duelling pistols, chiefly in Britain and the first comprehensive code to regulate pistol duels, known as the 'Irish Code' was published in 1777.[39] It would appear that, although they wore swords after society had stopped, for duelling naval officers followed fashion. This concentration on the pistol is a British trait and swords continued to be popular on the continent in Europe much later and even, with the German *schläger* tradition, continues today. McArthur, a naval author who wrote a manual of fencing in 1782, defended the art of fencing against the accusation of it leading to duels by commenting:

> But these objections are soon obviated, when it is considered, that the very few of the many who devote themselves to the practice of duelling understand a single movement in fencing; for pistols are the decisive weapons generally made use of on occasions of this nature. It must therefore be ascribed to the quarrelsome disposition, and perhaps too strict notions of honour, imbibed by duellists, and not to any knowledge that that might derive from acquisition of this art [fencing].[40]

Serious historical naval fiction matches reality. The duels in the Hornblower[41] and Lewrie's[42] books are with pistols. In Patrick O'Brian's series of books Maturin and Aubrey are involved in and report on several duels. These all involve pistols except in the incomplete twenty-first book, when Maturin is challenged by a Captain Miller. Miller wishes to use pistols, as he is a well-known, excellent marksman, but it is the aggrieved party, Stephen Maturin, who gets to choose the weapons. Stephen, sensibly, chooses swords. He disarms Miller and forces him to apologise – without hurting him.[43]

The last important duel fought with swords in England[44] was between Lord Byron (great-uncle to the famous poet), who held a Lieutenant's naval commission, and Mr Chaworth, his cousin. This was in 1765 and occurred in a dimly-lit room. Afterwards Byron hung the sword with which he had killed Chaworth on the wall at home earning himself the sobriquet the 'Wicked Lord'. The Royal Navy caused a famous duel in 1728 when Prime Minister William Pitt fought George Tierney MP over a bill introduced by Pitt to improve the conditions in the Royal Navy. Fortunately neither was hurt. As well as a claim to the last duel fought with swords, it was a member of the Naval Service, a Royal Marines' Officer, who took part in the last official recorded duel in England on the evening of 20 May 1845, near Gosport.[45]

Duelling was not rare, the *Naval Chronicle* in its report from Devonport for the summer of 1799 records three duels within a couple of weeks. While this might have been a peak, nothing in the wording indicates so and they would appear to be included more because it was a slow news period. Commodore Sir James Yeo who, when in command during the Canadian Great Lakes campaign of 1812–15, endeavoured to embarrass people from duelling by insisting the first pair fought by firing muskets from sentry boxes, set 80 yards apart, out on the ice.[46]

When noted, it seems the most common causes were honour and ladies. It was not just junior officers; it penetrated right to the top of the naval service. In 1799 Admiral Sir John Ord was arrested for calling out Admiral the Earl St Vincent, as he felt his honour had been slighted by not been given command of a detached squadron.

As naval officers often wore swords ashore, you would expect fights ashore with swords when tempers overflowed. It is clear from Captain Chamier's account of his first attendance at a duel – in this case as a witness to one with pistols – he had some experience of using the sword:

> [I] had once had a brush in the coffee room with a marine officer where we each drew our swords. Thanks to the fencing master at Durham House, I soon pinned my adversary's wrist to his breast, after which I returned on board as quickly as possible, quite satisfied that what is called 'satisfaction' is about the most unsatisfactory thing in the whole world.[47]

However, it is clear that, in the mind of the author, a distinction is drawn between his encounter and a formal duel. This is further reinforced in the *Tales of the Coastguard* where the author, clearly drawing on experiences of his own or others, has a former naval officer commenting that on receiving a blow he followed up '. . . .the outrage by drawing my sword and challenging him to instant combat. You may guess the sequel. I was immediately arrested by the guard, and tried a few days afterwards by court martial. Exmouth stood my friend, or I know not what sentence might have been passed, and I was dismissed the service.'[48]

A sailor warding off the bayonet of the enemy with his cutlass while firing his pistol at the same time. An illustration from *Instructions for training a ships crew in the use of arms in attack and defence*, by Lieutenant William Pringle Green, 1812. (Repro ID: F0948. © National Maritime Museum, Greenwich, London)

Why Swords/Cutlasses in Preference to Pistols and Other Edged Weapons?

Today, boarding actions are conducted with pistols and rifles. However, it took a long time for pistols to become a viable alternative to, rather than a useful addition to, the sword. At the time of the Napoleonic Wars the sea service pistol was a simple, crude arm, which could not be reloaded quickly in combat. So in close combat the sword remained effective while the pistol was nearly useless once fired, as it was unlikely there would be an opportunity to reload. The first flintlock revolver, allowing multiple shots, was not patented until 1818. It was not until the mid-nineteenth century that revolvers become common, Smith and Wesson producing the first cartridge revolver in 1856, which started to give reliability in firing and a reasonably quick reload time. For the Royal Navy, other than the Crimea campaign, this was not a period of conflicts against similar powers with the latest weapons but a period when most actions were against indigenous tribes or those conducting piracy and slavery. Therefore, it should not be surprising that it took time for new practices to develop.

While being a formidable short-range man-stopper, once fired a pistol was usually either cast aside or in some cases simply thrown at the opponent. Lieutenant Green, who went on to write *Instructions for training a ships [sic] crew in the use of arms in attack and defence*[49] and who had been a Master's Mate at Trafalgar in HMS *Conqueror*, before being promoted Lieutenant in 1806, commented that: 'It is a matter of notoriety in the Navy that when firearms are from necessity put into the hands of untrained men with inexperienced petty officers, the consequences are as fatal to their friends as their foes'. Captain Hoffman supports this recording in his journal from the attack at Dominique in 1794, that his sailors 'had thrown away their pistols after discharging them'.[50] Therefore, Lieutenant Green advised that instead of throwing the pistol away it should be used, for example, as a guard to deflect cutlass blows to the head. This battle-hardened officer advised that 'a man armed with a pistol ought to reserve his fire to the last extremity if his life is to depend on the discharge of his pistol killing the man opposed to him'.

Treatment of a Wound from a Sabre cut

Alex Jack, who was surgeon when HMS *Shannon* captured the United States Ship *Chesapeake* on 1 June 1813, off Boston, kept a very clear and detailed Surgeon's Journal.[51] This records the details of all the injuries received by the crew in the battle and although the majority are not from sword wounds, Captain Broke of the *Shannon* received a severe injury. This is what the surgeon recorded:

P B V Broke, Esq,. Captain.
Received a deep cut, from a sabre, on the left parietal bone, extending from the top of the head, in a direction towards the ear. Both tables of the skull are penetrated for at least three inches in length. There are also several contused wounds immediately above the left ear – and one on the right side of the head, inflicted by the butt end of a musket, the integuments are detached for some extent, but not exposing the bone. – These wounds were received on board the U.S. ship Chesapeake where they received a partial dressing: immediately after, Capt. Broke was removed to this ship, at which time he was very much exhausted, having lost a vast quantity of blood. Pulse very weak and small - said that his right arm was broken, but on inspection there was not the slightest appearance of injury. The sabre wound was cleaned, and closed by means of adhesive straps. Simple dressings applied to the wound on the right side. From the debility following the great loss of blood, bloodletting unnecessary. An opiate was given and the patient left to rest.

2nd Has not rested well during the night. A considerable discharge of blood has taken place, in the form of a constant oozing. The integuments of the scalp swelled and very painful. Headache. Pulse small and soft. Straps removed and simple dressings applied. A saline purgative given and low diet ordered.

3rd Remains nearly in the same state, except that the headache is increased. There is still a considerable oozing of blood from the wound. Dressings as before. Saline purgative repeated.

4th Some purulent discharge from the wound. Not much blood oozing now. Dressings as before.

5th Discharge tinged with blood, and increased. Less headache and swelling of the integuments about the wound. The debility is very considerable. Dressings as before. Saline purgative repeated.

June 6th Discharge diminishing and sores looking well. The parts contused are very much discoloured. There still remains a considerable degree of tumefaction about the scalp, with soreness to the slightest touch. Dressings applied as before. Weather calm.

PM we arrived in Halifax Harbour, when Capt. Broke was immediately removed to the house of Commissioner the Hon. P Wodehouse. The care of the case devolved upon Dr. Rowland, the Surgeon, Royal Naval Hospital; Mr Duncan, Surgeon to the Forces at Halifax and to myself.

Captain Broke did continue his recovery but never commanded a ship again. He subsequently was made a Baron for this action and received several other awards.

Lieutenant Green also discusses the other edged weapons in use at the time. About the pike, he comments: 'The pike well managed in the hands of a cool and resolute man is a very dreadful weapon. Armed with it, either for attack or defence he is to keep it on his right side, directed at the heart of the enemy.' However, because of its length and because it relies on being wielded by a group of men coordinated together for maximum effect, it works more effectively in preventing boarding rather than the mêlée that is being sought on boarding. They would perhaps more accurately be termed anti-boarding pikes. It was the vessel's boarding party that would be involved leading the attempt to prevent boarding as well as conducting a boarding. They also because of their length would be difficult to cross with going from one ship to another. The primacy of their use in defence is confirmed by John Nicol who, describing his adventures in the British Navy during the Napoleonic War, comments: 'I was one of the boarders. We were all armed, when required, with a pike to defend our own vessel should the enemy attempt to board; a tomahawk, cutlass and brace of pistols to use in boarding them.'[52] The techniques for using them seem to have been similar to that which was used for musket drill. Certainly by the 1850s the Naval instructions stated: 'A party of men, already trained to the Naval Cutlass and Rifle Exercise, may readily be taught the following system of Bayonet or Pike Exercise as it is based on the same principles.'[53] With respect to the axe or tomahawk Green comments that it was not such an effective weapon as it was 'a weapon that when sharpened is of great service in cutting rigging . . . inferior to thrusting weapons, such as the musket and bayonet, pike and cutlass'.

Post-Napoleonic War Sword Actions

After the end of 1812–15 war against America, the Royal Navy was the dominant maritime force until the end of the era of the wooden walls. This meant that action between the British fleet and others just did not occur. The Victorian era was a period which involved anti-slavery patrols and anti-piracy work both of which led to the Royal Navy conducting boardings, which were focused on stopping and searching small or merchant vessels, very much as the Royal Navy continues to do today.

In the anti-piracy campaign off Africa in 1881, while commanding HMS *London*, an old two-decker 90-gun ship being used as a depot ship on the East Africa Station, Captain Charles Brownrigg set off in a steam pinnace to patrol local waters. They were attacked by sword-wielding Arabs, who killed seven of his ten crew and, while the other three swam to safety, Brownrigg endeavoured to hold them off. Although falling with a final fatal shot, he had by then had several fingers cut off and received over twenty sword cuts. An interesting capture was made by three members of the *London*'s crew While sailing in the yacht *Victoria* during their spare time, Boatswain Richard Trigger and Gunners Stephen Quint and Stephen Hopes saw a becalmed dhow. Although it was some seven miles away, they pulled towards it in the yacht's dinghy for two hours. On arrival they were met with a hostile response, but with a cutlass in his teeth, Trigger boarded the vessel over the bows and cowed the opposition.[54]

The Naval Sword Ashore

Another feature of the Victorian period for the Royal Navy was the use of naval brigades in various land campaigns. The Boer War, which was commemorated with the Field Gun Competition at the Royal Tournament, is just the best known

The naval brigade in action in the Indian Mutiny 1857. (*Navy and Army Illustrated*, 25 June 1897, p 66)

The naval brigade in action in the Anglo-Japanese War of 1863–4. (Courtesy of the Naval Historical Collectors and Research Association)

of many such operations. The Royal Navy was involved in a series of wars[55] as varied as the 1857 Indian Mutiny and the Anglo-Japanese war of 1863–4, which included the last firing from a wooden-walled vessel (HMS *Conqueror*). Other, often forgotten conflicts, include: the 1864 New Zealand Wars where a naval brigade of 300 from HM Ships, *Pelorus, Eclipse, Harrier* and *Esk* attacked the Maoris at Gate Pah and PO Samuel Mitchell gained a VC; the Abyssinian War of 1868; the Ashanti War of 1873–4 and even a purely naval campaign against Brohemie[56] (modern Benin) in 1894. The author Captain Peter Hore, who discusses the significance of these campaigns in his book *Seapower Ashore*, identifies three advantages naval

The naval brigade in action in New Zealand, 1860–1. (*Navy and Army Illustrated* 25 June 1897 p 68)

Commander Wyatt Rawson leading the combined Army/Navy operation at Tel-el-Kebir in 1882. (MOD Art Collection)

personnel brought to land operations: a skill in improvisation (using science and muscle power); guns and resolve; and identity. It certainly seems true that the Navy brought ashore some of its fighting spirit. General Sir Colin Campbell, the Commander-in Chief during the Indian Mutiny campaign, commented that Captain Peel regained Shah Najif, a fortified tomb near Lucknow in Northern India, 'as if he had been laying the *Shannon* alongside a hostile frigate'. The Royal Navy also profited because many officers gained experience of fighting and command from these operations including Fisher, Jellicoe, Beatty and Cunningham.

It is noticeable that brigades were smaller then, typically 500, than the current Army brigade, being kept in groups from a single ship's company to maintain identity and loyalty.[57] The Army looseness with scale is noted by W H Russell, *The Times* Crimean correspondent who commented[58] with respect to the Light Brigade that 'The whole Brigade scarcely made one effective regiment, according to the numbers of continental armies'. A Brigade is now around 5000 personnel,[59] this not just a looser definition for the Navy but also applied to Army Brigades as well. The Light Brigade at the battle of Balaclava was 800-900 strong, 600 plus charged and 200 left behind.[60]

During this period, while ratings would usually be armed with rifles and bayonets, officers continued to carry swords as well as a pistol. In Egypt in 1882, the British army, supported by a naval brigade, was guided to the field of the battle of Tel-el-Kebir by Commander Wyatt Rawson, the naval aide-de-camp to Lieutenant-General Wolseley.[61] He navigated successfully using the stars but was mortally wounded while acting as guide to the Second Division as the army moved silently into position. At about 5.00am on 13 September 1882 they attacked and the battle lasted for about an hour. This had not been his first experience of a land campaign as he had also been mentioned in dispatches[62] for his contribution operations against the Ashantees in 1874 during which he had been wounded. It is even reported that the one Royal Naval person present at the British defeat at Isandlwana, Signalman 1st Class W H Aynsley, died trapped against a wagon slashing at the Zulus with his naval cutlass, succumbing when a Zulu went under the wagon and stabbed him in the back.[63]

The 1880s sword procurement scandal (see box feature) led to an incident involving Captain A K Wilson RN (later to become Admiral of the Fleet Sir Arthur Knyvet Wilson VC). Whilst fighting with the Naval Brigade at El Teb in February 1884 during the campaign in the Sudan, he reported that when attacking the enemy his 'sword broke against his ribs'.[64] This sword is held by the Royal Naval Museum at Portsmouth[65] and it shows a clean brittle fracture horizontally across the blade, indicative of incorrect tempering of the steel after it had been quenched. Captain Wilson of HMS *Hecla* had attached himself to a half-battery of machine guns, when Arabs attacked a separated group. Captain Wilson rushed to the front to relieve a Marine who was under pressure and was quickly attacked by five or six Arabs. After his sword broke he continued to fight using the hilt and his fists until some soldiers arrived to assist. Although he had received a scalp wound he remained with the unit and for this he was awarded the VC.[66]

Captain Wilson's description of the event is very modest. In his letter to Captain Markham of HMS *Vernon* he writes:

The papers have only arrived to-day, and I see they have been telling wonderful sensational stories about me. What really happened was this: When we got within thirty yards or so of the battery where the Krupp guns were, about a dozen of the 65th, evidently thinking the place was deserted, rushed forward out of the ranks, but they no sooner looked over the edge of the parapet than back they came with twenty or thirty Arabs after them. I stopped two or three of the soldiers, and made them turn round and face the Arabs, the greater part of whom were shot before they got to close quarters. One fellow got in close to me and made a dig with his spear at the soldier on my left. He failed to reach him, and left his whole side exposed, so that

Sword Procurement Scandal

In the 1880s there was a series of sword procurement scandals that led to headlines describing the weapons bought as 'utterly useless'[67] and went on to say 'somebody must surely be responsible for this disgraceful state of affairs, and no time should be lost in altering a rotten system under which not only mouldy biscuits, uneatable flour and stinking preserved meats are supplied to our gallant troops but even the weapons they fight with are useless'.

As a result of headlines such as these, the government set up an enquiry which quickly looked to explain what had happened. This committee found that several key factors were to blame, as the work had been passed out to sub-contractors in Solingen. The blades were delivered from Germany in an unfinished state, being over case-hardened and oversized, they then had to be subjected to considerable grinding and polishing to remove the corrosion and make them appear correct, this all left the blades very weak. The number of weak weapons was such that, when a retesting regime was introduced, it was found that for the two regiments about to deploy 'half of the swords . . . unserviceable' and for a support Corps about to deploy with them the situation was even worse with 'most of the weapons being found to be utterly useless'.[68] This led to some complete disasters in the field with Lieutenant Wormald of the 7th Hussars having his 'sword bent double' when he delivered a blow to a Dervish warrior.[69]

With the involvement of the Royal Navy in various land battles at the time, the experiences were felt by our Service in various campaigns as was described by Captain A K Wilson RN above and as was picked up by a *Daily Telegraph* correspondent.

> I have seen a blue-jacket's cutlass sword-bayonet at Tamai, as well as some of the battles up the Nile, bend into a semicircle, and remain in that shape, unfitting it for a second 'point'. The use it was put to did not justify the giving way of the weapon. The fact that it did not regain its form further proved the quality of the blade was of the poorest. What I have said of the bad quality of the cutlass applies equally to the sword-bayonet. Many a soldier at Abu Klea saw with dismay his bayonet rendered useless at the moment when there was no chance to load his rifle, and when he most stood in need of its services. There also I saw sword-bayonets bend and twist with the facility of soft iron rather than steel. After that fight you might have noticed brawny foot-guardsmen, herculean life-guardsmen, and the deft fighters of the mounted infantry, all of whom had stood shoulder to shoulder in the square, straightening their bayonets across their knee or under foot. Others there were who discarded their distorted weapons and picked up some dead comrade's from the field.'[70]

It was known that this lead to the deaths of several servicemen as 'thus disarmed the seaman was killed by another Arab'.[71]

These scandals were not just limited to swords as poor recognition of likely areas of conflict mean that the rifles issued for the Sudan campaign struggled as well: 'the lives of our men [were] imperilled by the jamming of the cartridges in the rifles' and by 'defects . . . from the accidental fouling of the breaches of the rifles by the all pervading dust of the Sudanese desert'.[72]

Captain Wilson at the battle of El Teb where his sword was to break during the action and for which he won a VC. (*The Graphic*, Vol. XXIX No. 757, Saturday, 31 May 1884)

> I had a cool prod at him. He seemed to be beastly hard, and my sword broke against his ribs. The man on my right was a plucky fellow, and collared him round the neck and tried to throw him. The Arab still held on to his spear, so I hacked at him in a futile kind of way with the stump of my sword, and while I was doing so a second Arab came up and hit me over the head with a sword. My pith helmet took the greater part of the blow, so it only just cut the scalp, and I hardly felt it. Both Arabs were shot and bayoneted on the ground almost instantly. If I could only have got a basin of water and washed my face I should have escaped notoriety, but I only had a little cold tea in my water bottle, and until we got to the wells there was no water to be got, so the blood ran all over my face, and the Correspondents spotted me. General Buller, who was close behind, congratulated me in his cheery way, and he has since recommended me for the V.C. It has been a wonderful piece of luck, as I only walked out in the morning as a loafer just to see the fight. The Admiral has, however, since put me down as accompanying him. Nothing was further from my thoughts than going in for distinction of any kind, but as I happened to stumble into a hot corner I could not possibly have done anything but what I did, unless took to my heels.[73]

Captain Wilson was presented with two swords to replace the broken one; the first by the Captain and Torpedo Officers of HMS *Vernon*, where he had served, and the second by the Ladies of Malta. The first had a broadsword blade similar to the one he had broken and both were inscribed as part of the presentation. Other than these minor differences they were standard naval swords of the time.[74]

Naval Swords in Peacetime

After the end of the Napoleonic Wars there were many actions in UK home waters, which have generally been forgotten by history. They were those of the Coast Blockade organisation and the Coast Guard into which it was eventually absorbed. The Coast Blockade department[75] was set up to try and combat the smugglers who had gained such a hold during the Napoleonic Wars. Initially aiming to keep the smugglers from the coast of Kent, it quickly established that it would have to act ashore as well as mount boat patrols. Based in various stations, usually making use of the Martello Towers, each station was commanded by a Lieutenant and the patrols ventured forth armed with pistols and cutlasses. The tightness of the blockade led almost to rebellion in some areas and several armed affrays. This campaign lasted thirty years and attracted its own butcher's bill.

Of course swords and edged weapons were not just used in action: as part of a gentleman's accoutrements during the Napoleonic period they could prove a useful resource when meeting with footpads as Captain Watkins found on 5 October 1799 when he was surprised and successfully used his sword to defend himself.[76] Captain Chamier also comments that while in a Mexican inn, they slept '. . . using saddles as pillows and with loaded pistols and drawn swords by their sides'.[77] Lieutenant Parsons tells tales of the Young Gentlemen, those under training destined to be officers, using their dirks at a ball to create mischief with some guards who had refused them access to one part of the event[78] and also the advantage it could have in keeping rats at bay when acting as guard commander on a de-stored ship.[79] They could also prove an occasional danger as seen in a freak accident on 18 June 1799 when a sailor aboard HMS *Saturn* in Plymouth fell from the rigging, landing on the gangway sentry's bayonet.[80]

Swords would also be used to give a very visible presence for security, and so when sixty-three wagons of treasure[81] were taken from the captured Spanish treasure ships *Thetis* and *Santa-Brigida* this was done with an escort including Midshipman armed with cutlasses.[82] One must wonder why it was felt that they needed to have the ship's set of cutlasses rather than use their own swords.

The Last Use of the Sword at Sea and in Action

Along with 'How old is this sword?' the question that always seems to be asked of the authors is 'When was the last use of swords in action by the Royal Navy?' This actually is a question almost impossible to answer definitively. Like so many naval traditions, there are times it is known to have happened and after that the problem is usually one of trying to prove a negative and deal with oral history. For clarity though the order withdrawing the cutlass from service was issued on 22 October 1936.[83] However, cutlasses were carried at sea after that and, indeed, sometimes still are, but only for ceremonial purposes. Furthermore, in the early days after the order, some vessels may have been quite slow in returning their holdings. It is

The death of Major Plumbe at the battle of Graspan, 25 November 1899. (Illustration from H Wilson, *With the Flag to Pretoria*, Vol I, p 151)

probable that the answer to the last use at sea and the last use by the Royal Navy in action are not the same and there is also a distinction between wearing a sword at a battle and actually using it.

In endeavouring to account for the last use at sea in action by the Royal Navy one could look at the last conventional naval action prior to the First World War. However, since the Victorian period when the Royal Navy ruled the oceans was dominated by small land campaigns and anti-piracy actions, it is necessary to go back a long time to find the conventional action when ships of the line came alongside each other in a boarding action. One possible candidate engagement would be the fourth battle of Cape St Vincent on 5 July 1833, which did include closing with enemy vessels and boarding with the subsequent hand-to-hand fighting. The squadron was commanded by a Royal Naval officer, Charles Napier, and the vessels were mostly ex-Royal Navy or East Indiamen and it was British naval officers who were largely leading the crews, but it was actually a Portuguese squadron commanded on behalf of Dom Pedro IV, regent for Queen Maria II. The last action between sailing ships for which the Naval General Service medal was awarded was for the action between HMS *Endymion* and the USS *President* on 15 January 1815 at the end of the War of 1812.

So it is necessary to look more to the small vessel actions of the anti-slavery campaigns, which continued up until the end of the nineteenth century. Lieutenant Frederick Fogarty Fegen, of HMS *Turquoise*, was detached from the corvette near the island of Pemba, off Zanzibar, to conduct a patrol in a pinnace. He had a crew of five sailors, one marine and an interpreter. On 30 May 1887,[84] he sighted a dhow and sent his dingy with two sailors and the interpreter to board her. The dhow greeted this inspecting party with a volley of shots and then aimed to ram the dingy. Fegen opened fire with his 9pdr and the dhow attacked, attempting to board. The report reads: 'The gallant Lieutenant shot two of them with his revolver, and ran a third through with a sword', but then would have been killed himself except that AB Pearson managed to stop his attacker '. . . with his cutlass'. Eventually the dhow broke away but was driven ashore by the continued attack from Lieutenant Fegan's crew and fifty-three slaves were rescued. Since similar operations of boarding suspect vessels continued for another couple of years in the same area, it is likely that they employed similar weapons and equipment, but without the heroic action recorded in this case, it is not possible to determine if any actually used swords in action.

The late Victorian period saw the considerable use of naval brigades ashore in support of the army and it is probable that it is one of these that accounts for the last use of a naval sword in action. The British cavalry were still issued with swords during the First World War, using a sword of a pattern that was first authorised for other ranks in 1908 and in a more decorative pattern for officers in 1912. The last British Army cavalry charge was at Dacca, India, in 1919 and it is thought that swords may well have featured in that action. For the Royal Navy one likely candidate would be the Second Boer War from 1899 to 1902. At the battle of Graspan (also known as Enslin) on 25 November 1899, the author H W Wilson, who wrote the semi-official history, says 'The naval officers of the brigade still carried swords and could be readily distinguished; they were the target of every Boer rifle'.[85] Unsurprisingly, they gave them up in favour of revolvers. There is an illustration of the death of Major Plumbe RM during this battle showing him charging into action waving his sword. It seems to have merited a picture because he was accompanied by his dog. During the attack, Commander Ethelston (HMS *Powerful*) was killed at about the same time as Major Plumbe and it is possible that he died sword in hand. Other naval officers were in charge of gun batteries and it is not known whether any of them would have used their swords in action or have just been wearing them.

The last confirmed use of a sword in action identified by the authors, comes from the campaign against the Boxer rebellion in China. This campaign involved a heroic attempt by Admiral Seymour, assembling the largest force that he could,[86] to rescue European citizens besieged in Peking. The Naval Brigade was a mixed-nationality force (British, German, Russian, French, American, Italian and Japanese) and was equipped with whatever weapons they had. It was a campaign that saw several officers who were to rise to the top of the

Two of the memorials in Victoria Park, Portsmouth, commemorating Royal Navy involvement in China in 1900. The first is to the crewmen of HMS *Centurion* killed at Peitsang, Hskiu, Peiyang and Tientsin in 1900 and the second to those killed from HMS *Orlando* at Tientsin, in Admiral Seymour's column and at the Legation in Peking. The original bell on this memorial was returned to China in 2005 and a replica has replaced the original.

Royal Navy establish their credentials. Admiral Beatty, Admiral Jellicoe and Admiral Sir Roger Keyes were all involved as junior officers. An article in *The Naval Review*, published under a pseudonym by a Midshipman involved in the campaign, comments that they had no khaki and all wore blue uniform with the officers armed with swords and the ratings cutlasses. It is clear that several elements of the Brigade saw action, including some very heavy fighting ending with bayonet charges,[87] but no mention is made of the swords or cutlasses being used in action and, clearly, most of those involved were armed with and used rifles and bayonets. However, in support of the campaign the destroyers *Fame* and *Whiting* were involved in attacking the Taku Forts and, as part of this action on 17 June 1900, they used their small boats to cut out Chinese destroyers. One of the commanding officers, a then Lieutenant Keyes, describes how as they were boarding the 'Chinese officer fired a couple of shots from his revolver, at a range of a few feet, at Tomkinson [Keyes's second in command] as he sprang over the side, but fortunately missed, and Tomkinson attacked him with his sword and drove him overboard'.[88] This was prior to the relief expedition to Tientsin and then Peking where Commander Craddock led the Naval Brigade. Actions took place up until mid-August in which it is likely that they also used swords. It is quite clear from Keyes's account that they were still a natural weapon for the officers

A Bruce Bairnsfather cartoon from the First World War: 'That Sword. How he thought he was going to use it – and how he did use it'.

and some of those involved had also been taken part in the events the previous year including the naval brigade at Graspan and the relief of Ladysmith. One of Keyes's photographs of the naval brigade shows a cutlass hanging happily at the waist of a petty officer and the naval officers in the columns wearing swords. Midshipman Guy would probably have been armed with a sword when rescuing wounded under fire, for which he would be awarded the Victoria Cross.

It is probable that the slightly later campaigns off China against pirates involved cutlasses and swords. This is strongly indicated by the writings of 'Taffrail', the pseudonym of Captain Henry Taprell Dorling DSO RN. He wrote numerous books about the period before and during the First World War. Although fiction, they are deeply rooted in his own experiences and those of his contemporaries. One book, *The Watch Below*, has in it a story entitled 'The Shameen Pirates'. This describes an incident where a young lieutenant is ordered to take a picket boat and hunt for pirates operating in the Hong Kong/Canton West River area. They run aground, set up ashore, are attacked by the pirates and beat them in a fight involving cutlasses, '. . . our men cursing and grunting as they slashed away with their cutlasses, and the Chinese screaming and yelling as they came. I saw the bayonets flashing and the reddened cutlass blades rising and falling in the firelight'.[89] Since the tale is not exactly complimentary to the author and the technical details appear to be rooted in personal knowledge it is probably based on a real incident especially as Midshipman Dorling was serving aboard the cruiser HMS *Terrible* on the China station in the period circa 1901.[90] While the incident referred to was an attack while they were ashore (as their vessel has grounded), the incident opens up the possibility of a use at sea in this period, as the vessel had been equipped to undertake boarding.

There are other candidates for the last use of a naval sword or cutlass ashore. In the Royal Naval Museum in Portsmouth is an example of a traditional naval sword, but in a brown leather Sam Browne scabbard, that was carried by an officer in the Royal Naval Division during the First World War (Accession no 2003.86/1), during which there were well-attested uses of the sword. For example, at the battle of Neuve Chapelle on 10 March 1915, the company commanders of 2nd Battalion Cameronians (Scottish Rifles) were left with choice whether they carried swords or not. Major E B Ferrers of B Company reportedly ordered his officers to do so and at least some did. Prior to this, during the first battle of Ypres at Meteren on 13 October 1914, Lieutenant Bernard Law Montgomery (Royal Warwickshire Regiment) led his platoon across waving his sword. He was awarded the DSO for this action although, in his memoirs, he recalls that he was not trained to use it. So it would be plausible that an officer in the Royal Naval Division did likewise. However, the sword in the Royal Naval Museum shows no sign of any such use, so more evidence would be needed for this to be a credible claim. The view that swords were probably not used by the Royal Naval Division is reinforced by Bruce Bairnsfather's cartoon with the caption 'That Sword. How he thought he was going to use it – and how he did use it.'

The Royal Navy continued boarding ships during the First World War. Douglas Fairbairn[91] describes in his biography, how he was placed in charge of a prize crew bringing in a Dutch trawler as part of the checks in the North Sea in 1915. His men were armed with cutlasses and he, as the Sub Lieutenant, was armed 'with a revolver as well'. This

A painting by Norman Wilkinson showing HMS *Cossack* going alongside the *Altmark* with the boarding party on the fo'c'sle ready to jump. (Courtesy of the Wardroom Mess President, HMS *Nelson*).

contrasts with a plan later in the war for a raid on German patrol trawlers, where the boarding equipment is carefully described but cutlasses do not feature.[92]

The *Altmark* incident is often claimed as the last use by the Royal Navy of swords in action; this is strongly disputed by the majority of the members of the vessel's association. It occurred on 16 February 1940 when the German tanker *Altmark* was returning to Germany with 299 British merchant sailors on board, prisoners of war who had been picked up from ships sunk by the pocket battleship *Admiral Graf Spee*. On her way from the southern Atlantic to Germany, *Altmark* passed through Norwegian waters where she was investigated three times by Norwegian vessels. These boarded her and carried out cursory searches but did not inspect the hold and allowed the ship to continue on her way. Having been spotted by a British aircraft, she was intercepted by the destroyer HMS *Cossack* (Captain Philip Vian RN) and sought refuge in Jøssingfjord. *Cossack* followed her in the next day but Norwegian naval forces blocked initial attempts to board. After the Norwegian forces refused to take part in a joint escort, reiterating that their earlier searches of *Altmark* had found nothing, Captain Vian stated his intention to board, inviting the Norwegians to take part, an offer they declined. In the ensuing events, *Altmark* ran aground and the British boarded late in the evening[93] of 16 February, successfully capturing her. While HMS *Cossack* certainly carried a few cutlasses (for ceremonial purposes) and certainly did board with bayonets fixed, it is thought the story originated either from over-enthusiastic reporters on her triumphant return or from the German sign at the site which says: 'Here on 16th Feb. 1940 the Altmark was set upon by British sea-pirates'.[94] The HMS *Cossack* Association makes it clear from its members' recollections that it believes this story to be incorrect, and that it was bayonets with blades about 18in (457mm) long, which was the pattern then in use (P1907 without quillon).[95] This is supported by Frischauer and Jackson in their study of the action[96] and recordings of as many personnel memories as they could. It has though been disputed by a minority of the crew.[97]

A similar explanation is likely to lie behind the tale in the obituary of Major Michael Stillwell, which appeared in the *Daily Telegraph*.[98] This records Stilwell being in a Motor Torpedo Boat in February 1944 with six of his men when they intercepted a German schooner. The marines concealed themselves until the schooner had come alongside and then attacked. The story reports that two of the sailors were armed with cutlasses. However, it appears very unlikely that a vessel, almost certainly built during the war, had been issued with cutlasses several years after the RN withdrew them from active service. It would seem to the authors that this may again by a case of confusion, this time between the long bayonet used in the Royal Navy and the short, 'pig-sticker' bayonet in general use in the Army.

Tantalisingly, the authors came across an article of reminiscences in 2009[99] referring to the issue of cutlasses in 1952 to a boarding party from HMS *Armada*. This article is the only reference to this event the authors have found and the date is certainly incorrect, as HMS *Armada* was in the Middle East in 1951[100] and since in the account the planned boarding was cancelled, there was no actual use.

With all of the myriad possibilities, ignoring the potential for any eccentric individual acts, the authors' conclusion is that the last use was probably in China around 1900, and it was most likely ashore although they remain open to further evidence coming to light which supports a later date.

The Sword in Naval Symbolism

Given their aggressive purpose, it is hardly surprising many warships together with naval operations and exercises have received names derived from aspects of swordsmanship.[101] The earliest was *Assault*, first commissioned in 1780, with other early names including *Fleche*, which was used for three vessels in the Napoleonic Wars, and *Gladiator*, which spent years being used for many of the most serious courts martial of the Napoleonic period.

The Second World War saw destroyers of the 'Weapon' class with names related to swords including *Claymore, Cutlass, Dagger, Dirk, Poniard* and *Sword*. Also a series of landing ships was temporarily renamed as *Empire* with a suffix, which included *Empire Broadsword, Empire Cutlass* and *Empire Rapier* There is a badge listed for HMS *Rapier* from 1944 although the vessel was never built. However, the name did appear for a submarine in the novel *Devil Flotilla* by Edwyn Gray.

Probably the best-known example of a naval codename featuring swords is the D-Day beach 'Sword'. This was shortened from 'Swordfish' – the other two beaches were originally dubbed 'Goldfish' and 'Jellyfish'. However, when abbreviated, 'Jelly' was deemed inappropriate and changed to 'Juno'. Two operations by X-craft midget submarines in the Far East were codenamed 'Foil' and 'Sabre'. Perhaps the most bizarre designation of this type was given to a series of exercises codenamed Sharp Foil. By definition a foil cannot be sharp, so the author of this name created a classic oxymoron.

The trend continues right up to the present day and the conflict in Afghanistan where 3 Commando Brigade named one of their operations 'Aabi Toorah' (Pashtu for 'Blue Sword') after the Brigade's symbol of a dagger. The Americans' first operation after their entry into Helmand was Operation 'Khanjar'. which is Pashtu for 'Sword Strike'.

Ships with names related to swordsmanship – Royal Navy: *Assault, Attack, Attacker, Blade, Broadsword, Claymore* (possibly also *Claymore II), Cocquille, Cutlass, Dagger, Dark Gladiator, Dirk, Excalibur* (submarine), *Fencer, Fleche, Forte, Gay Fencer, Gladiator, Poniard, Sabre, Sabreur, Scimitar, Sea Gladiator* (cancelled aircraft transport), *Sword, Sword Dance, Swordsman* (transferred with same name to Australian Navy), *Thruster*; Royal Australian Navy: *Attack, Swordsman*; Royal Canadian Navy: *Quinte*.

Once a ship, Naval Air Squadron or shore establishment has a badge, that badge is used for any further unit carrying the same name. The following badges contain a sword – Royal Navy: *Acute, Adamant, Algerine, Ameer, Avenger, Blackwater, Broadsword, Bulwark, Caldeon, Chatham, Clacton, Clare, Conquest, Defence, Defender, Dieppe, Encounter, Example, Excalibur, Fareham, Felixstowe, Fencer, Finwhale, Foyle, Gurkha, Hostile, Hussar, Kempenfelt, Lofoten, Mameluke, Marmion, Myngs, Onslaught, Paladin, Rajah, Rapier, Ravager, Reggio, Rinaldo, Sabre, Smiter, Swordsman, Tariq, Trenchant, Triad, Trouncer, Ultimatum, Ultor, Verulam, Visigoth, Vortigern*; Royal Fleet Auxiliaries: *Sir Bedivere, Sir Geraint*; Royal Naval Air Squadrons *1792, 1846, 737, 759, 800, 830, 857, 881, 887, 895*. It also featured in the badge of the former Admiralty Surface Weapons Establishment, Fareham.

The first HMS *Gladiator* in the Royal Navy was a Fifth Rate commissioned in 1783 which was used for a considerable number of Napoleonic War court martials. The third shown here was a Second Class cruiser of 1896 and sunk in collision with the liner *St Paul* during a blizzard on the night of 24/25 April 1908 off Yarmouth on the Isle of Wight. She was hit so hard that 50 feet of her hull plating was torn out. Although she was salvaged, she was scrapped a year later for less than the costs of her salvage.

The escort carrier HMS *Fencer* on convoy duty to Russia during the Second World War.

Admiral Beatty on the bridge of the destroyer HMS *Attack* at the battle of Dogger Bank 24 January 1915. This, the third HMS *Attack* in the Royal Navy, also served at Jutland before being sunk by a U-boat on 30 December 1917.

Photograph of POWs taken at Palembang, Sumatra in March 1942 prior to the movement of the Senior Officers to Japan. Captain Mulock is the officer on the right in the back row.

The Last British Naval Officer to Surrender his Sword to the Enemy

In February 1942, the night before Singapore surrendered, Captain George F A Mulock DSO, FRGS, RN, the Head of Extended Defences for Singapore, was the most senior naval officer remaining in the colony and in nominal command of what was left of the naval base. Known as 'Polar Mulock', he had served under Captain Scott during the Antarctic Expedition of 1903–4 and had been awarded the DSO during the Gallipoli campaign.[102] After the First World War he retired to work in the Far East, but in 1939, at the age of 60, returned to active service. Initially, given his age, Mulock had been ordered to remain in post to meet the Japanese and, having ensured his entire staff had been evacuated, he awaited his fate. However, late on the 14th, Mulock was asked to convey thirty-eight senior officers to safety, because they were considered likely to be executed by the Japanese if captured. They sailed shortly before midnight, aboard a 40-foot motor launch, the *Mary Rose*, the last vessel to escape, sheltering during the day and travelling at night. Two nights later, the *Mary Rose* was sailing up the Moesi River towards Muntok when they were spotted and stopped by the Japanese navy.

At dawn on 17 February, the *Mary Rose*, under the watchful eye of the Japanese, moved up river to Muntok, where dozens of captured British craft were tied alongside. Captain Mulock emerged from wheelhouse in his dress whites, wearing his sword.[103] The enemy lieutenant boarded *Mary Rose* and, in perfect English, ordered the passengers to disembark once they were alongside. The lieutenant saluted Captain Mulock and, after returning the salute, he unhitched his sword and offered it to the young Japanese officer, who accepted graciously.[104] Half of those thirty-eight men did not survive internment and Captain Mulock remained a prisoner until late 1945. He was probably the last naval officer to surrender his sword to the enemy.

Swords and Discipline

In the Napoleonic era when a rating was tied to the gratings to be flogged he would be guarded by the vessel's Master at Arms with his sword drawn and any embarked Marines with fixed bayonets.[105] Young gentlemen and midshipmen of the gunroom were much harder to formally punish. However, informal punishments were frequent, the most common being 'mast heading' where the young man was sent to spend some time at the top of one of the masts, the equivalent of the naughty step used by parents today. A more unusual punishment was 'cobbing' which involved being spanked with the scabbard of a sword or dirk. This punishment seems to have been administered within the confines of the gunroom itself as Midshipman Elliot found after he had rescued the schoolmaster of HMS *Goliath* when he fell overboard.

> For this action the plucky young midshipman was tried by his brother-midshipmen at a gun-room court-martial, and ordered to be punished. As there was no denial of the fact that, he was found guilty of the aggravated offence of saving a schoolmaster and sentenced to be 'cobbed'.[106]

Until recently, when an officer was tried by court martial, the officer's sword was placed on a table, facing across the court. After the court had reached its verdict, it was re-aligned. When the accused returned to learn the verdict, it was immediately apparent because if the accused had been acquitted the hilt was towards the officer, if guilty, then it was the point. This practice ceased in March 2004, the first court martial without swords being held in HMS *Drake* on 15 March of that year. Until that date, the members of the court had all worn swords as had all other officers, whether appearing as

A Royal Naval court martial from 1899, in this case of Captain Rice for the loss of HMS *Sultan* in March 1898. (*The Graphic*, 13iv, 1899)

accused's friend, prosecutor or witnesses. The accused, if an officer, was marched into the court by an escort armed with a drawn sword or, if a rating, by an escort with a drawn cutlass.

Following an appeal to the European Court of Human Rights at Strasbourg in 2003[107] the judgment made brief but non-committal comments on the use of swords. The discretion that the President of the Court had to relax swords during the course of the trial was covered and its helpfulness, particularly to the uniformed advocates, was mentioned. The instruction to the Clerk of the Court that, in the case of officers, following pleas or findings of guilt the tradition of the Service was to be observed and the point of the Accused's sword turned to face him was also raised. Following this judgment, changes were necessary with respect to the appointment of the Judge Advocate but, as there was no adverse comment on the part played by swords in the procedures, there seemed no reason to think that this would soon be challenged.

However, the solicitor involved subsequently wrote to the Secretary of State for Defence claiming that officers wearing swords could be intimidating for defendants and that could be a breach of human rights.[108] He likened the proceedings to a Gilbert and Sullivan opera and threatened to take the matter to the European Court if it happened again. Two weeks later the following exchange occurred in the House of Lords:[109]

Lord Thomas of Gresford:

My Lords, I beg leave to ask the Question standing in my name on the Order Paper. In doing so, I declare an interest as having appeared as an advocate in various courts martial.

His question was:

To ask Her Majesty's Government whether, in the light of their objections to the procedures proposed by the United States Government for Guantanamo trials, the practice of the escort accompanying a defendant in a British naval court martial with a drawn and brandished sword, and the wearing and display of sheathed swords by the prosecutor and members of the court martial, is to be maintained.

The Parliamentary Under-Secretary of State, Ministry of Defence (Lord Bach):

My Lords, the Royal Navy has determined, for reasons wholly unconnected with Guantanamo, that there is no longer a requirement for the escort accompanying a defendant in a naval court martial to carry a drawn sword, or for members of the court martial to wear sheathed swords. The first naval court martial to be held without swords was convened at Her Majesty's Ship *Drake* in Plymouth on 15 March 2004.

Later the Secretary of State for Defence replied to the solicitor stating that as part of 'a review of the naval court martial process' swords were no longer required.[110] The solicitor attributed this to acute embarrassment by the Royal Navy by the disclosure of its archaic methods, although no one seems to have mentioned that naval personnel, whether officers or ratings, are used to seeing officers wearing swords and are highly unlikely to find it intimidating. Indeed, they are much more likely to be disturbed by the unfamiliar figure of a barrister in wig and gown.[111]

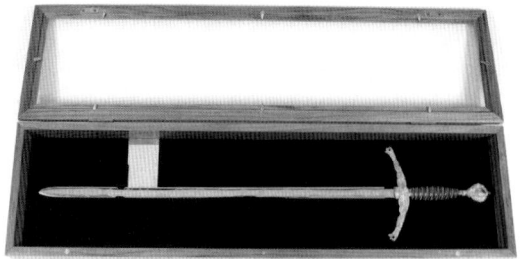

The Fleet Air Arm Sword presented by the Guild of Air Pilots and Air Navigators (GAPAN) to the Fleet Air Arm, to mark the centenary of naval aviation in 2009. (Courtesy Pooley Swords)

Current Annual Prize Swords

A current service pattern sword is presented each year to the unit of each of the Armed Services judged to have made the most valuable contributions towards establishing good and friendly relations with any community, at home or overseas. It was instituted in 1966 by Wilkinson and known as the Wilkinson Sword of Peace. A committee led by the Naval Secretary decides the winning unit. In 2005, the sponsorship for this prestigious award was taken over by Firmin & Son. This Birmingham based company has a long tradition as a supplier to the Armed Forces having provided swords, bayonets, cap badges, buttons, helmets and cuirasses to the services since 1677. The Swords of Peace are specially inscribed with the name of the unit concerned and the area in which it qualified for the award. They are, however, standard Service pattern swords so that they can be carried on parade. The winners are listed in Appendix 3 and the story behind the establishment of this prize is on page 79.

In 2011 a sword was given by the Guild of Air Pilots and Air Navigators (GAPAN) to the Fleet Air Arm, to mark the centenary of naval aviation in 2009. It was made and donated by Pooley Swords, the owner, Mr Robert Pooley, being a past-Master of the GAPAN. It is unusual in that it is not an engraved traditional naval sword, but a more mediaeval shape with a claymore blade, as well as therefore being very distinctive, it is also more representative of the wings of aviation and the blade makes a clearer space for the engraving.

HRH The Princess Royal presents the Queen's Sword at Dartmouth. (RN Press)

One face is decorated with the wings of pilot, observer and aircrewman with the name of the presentation and the other with a Swordfish aircraft and a Merlin helicopter with between them: 'In recognition of a century of outstanding courage, professionalism and technical innovation, 1909-2009' on the other. Pooley Swords are also providing annually a separate miniature 6in naval sword as an award for 'the finest feat of naval aviation in the year'; this was first awarded for the period March 2010 to 2011.

The Sword in the Royal Navy of Today

The sword remains very much in evidence on formal occasions in the Royal Navy today. Unlike some Navies, such as the Royal Norwegian Navy, the Royal Navy does not insist that every officer purchases a sword as part of the uniform. However, because swords are still required for ceremonial purposes, a stock is maintained from which officers can borrow swords when needed. Swords are worn at ceremonial divisions (parades) and are awarded, with great ceremony, to the best officers passing out from Britannia Royal Naval College (BRNC), Dartmouth. Officers distinguishing themselves in other phases of their training are, also, awarded swords. Dartmouth is not the only Training Establishment of the Royal Navy where swords are presented. Each year, the Officers' Association of HMS *Collingwood*, the Maritime Warfare School, awards one to the junior officer who has contributed most to leadership during the year. Naturally, these tokens of success are highly prized by the winning officers.

Another prize sword has been presented annually since 1987 to the Submarine Warfare Officer who is the top student[112] for the year from on the Advanced Submarine Warfare Course. In 2010 this course changed its name to be the Principle Warfare Officers Course (Submarines) (PWO(SM)). It is funded from a trust set up by Admiral C D Howard-Johnston in memory of his son, Sub-Lieutenant RG Howard-Johnston, who was one of the trainee officers on board HMS *Affray* when she was lost with all hands on 16 April 1951. The reason for the loss of *Affray* has never been fully explained but examination of the outside of the wreck indicates that possibly the submarine sank after being flooded through a large-bore hull valve which did not shut automatically after a failure of her Snort mast (the Snort mast is used to suck air into a submarine when it is running its diesels whilst submerged at periscope depth). This custom is, of course, not unique to the Royal Navy; Canada and Australia certainly give prize swords each year and Her Majesty the Queen gives a naval sword to the Ukraine Defence College as prize.

The tradition is still followed that at an officer's funeral, the coffin is draped with the Union Flag and the sword, together with cap and decorations, placed on the top. On a happier note, swords are used to form the arch for a newly-married officer and his bride when they leave the wedding service and, later, the groom's sword is used to cut the wedding cake. In a similar vein, when a ship is commissioned there is still a ceremony whereby a cake is cut. This is undertaken by the wife of the Commanding Officer (if married) and the most junior rating. They use the Commanding Officer's sword to cut the cake and, hopefully, will remember the corrosive nature of fruit cake and quickly wipe it afterwards.

Generally officers do not now purchase their own swords, preferring to rely on weapons drawn from a pool provided for ceremonial uses. Probably the best-known supplier of naval swords over the years, Wilkinson, is no longer involved in the market, having closed their sword manufacturing in 2005. The production was taken up by two companies: Weyersberg, Kirschbaum & Co (WKC), a firm based appropriately in Solingen, and Pooley Swords of West Sussex which acquired most of their tooling. Today, a new sword, scabbard, belt, knot and case costs around £1000, although a considerable mark-up is sometimes to be seen at both dealers and tailors. There are still tailors who arrange the assembly of a weapon from components supplied and badge it, just as they would have 200 years ago. There is, however, a healthy market in second-hand weapons. With intense pressure on defence expenditure, every item comes under closer and closer scrutiny and it may well be that, at some future date, it is decided that the cost of maintaining a loan pool of swords cannot be justified. That would be a great pity, as the sword still represents a clearly visible link to the history and traditions of the service, which contribute so much to the maintenance of its *esprit de corps*.

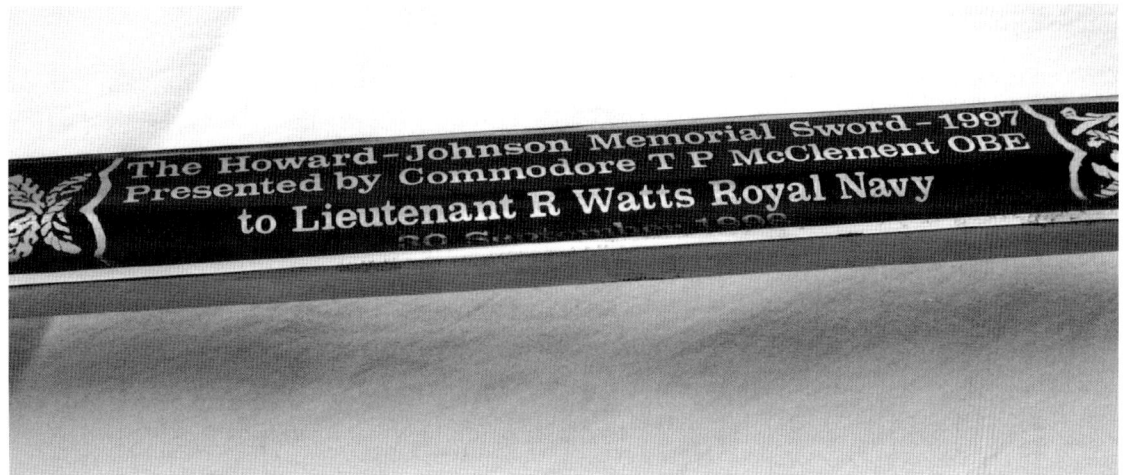

Howard-Johnston Memorial Sword presented in 1998 to Lieutenant R Watts RN. The engraver missed out the letter 'T' from Johnston but it was deemed too expensive to correct. (Commander R Watts Royal Navy)

CHAPTER 2

Cutlasses

The popular idea of the cutlass is coloured by pirate films and does not accurately reflect the true nature of this weapon. This chapter will show that cutlasses are as likely to be straight as curved and to be used for thrusting rather than cutting. With that in mind, the following definition is proposed:

> A short sword with a wide single edged blade that may be either straight or curved, flat or grooved; now esp. the sword with which sailors are armed.

It is believed that this gives a more accurate description of the physical characteristics of the cutlass without specifying the way in which an individual was taught or chose to use it.

The etymology given in the *Oxford English Dictionary*[1] derives cutlass from the French *coutelas*, an augmented form of *couteau* (*coutel*) meaning knife. There is a cognate Italian word *coltellaccio* that clearly shows its derivation from the Latin *cultellaceum*. Modern English words sharing this derivation are *cutler* and *cutlery*. Its first recorded appearance is in 1594 in a line from Kyd's *Cornelio* that reads: 'Arm'd with his blood-besmeared keen *coute-lace*'. This entry includes many true variations of this word as well as what it describes as 'perversions'. The other English name that is often used for short cutting swords of mariners of the seventeenth century is the hanger, in some texts of the period there seems to be a distinction between the hangar and the cutlass, in others they appear to be used interchangeably. The word also occasionally appears as *cutlash* and *cutlace*.[2]

Both May and Annis[3] and Gilkerson[4] make the point that the designation cutlass was never officially adopted by the Royal Navy. This is true as far as it applies to the design, procurement and issue of these weapons for which the preferred terms were 'Sword for Sea Service' and, later, 'Sword, Naval'. But this seems a very narrow interpretation, as cutlass appears in many official publications, e.g. A Manual of Gunnery for Her Majesty's Fleet, where the relevant sections are entitled 'Cutlass Exercise' and 'Inspection of Cutlasses'.[5]

Pre-uniformity

The evolution of the cutlass in the Royal Navy was slow. In the seventeenth century, short, curved, cut-and-thrust swords called hangers were used at sea and by the beginning of the eighteenth century we have records for orders being placed for them for use in ships. There were no official patterns for these swords, so we are left to draw our own conclusions from surviving weapons and from any other evidence offered by illustrations or writings. Hangers were relatively short, typically with a blade length of 25–28in (635–711mm), often with brass hilts. Some of these hilts were highly ornamented but it must be remembered that once the pattern had been made, which was a one-off charge, there was little difference in the cost of decorative or plain castings. Although brass offered superior resistance to corrosion than iron, it had the drawback of being easily damaged. Many brass-hilted swords show evidence of such damage, most often to the vulnerable protruding quillon or to the knuckle guard.

In parallel with these brass-hilted weapons, which bore many similarities to those used by armies all over Europe, versions with steel hilt furniture were in use. These were lighter and more rugged than their brass hilted contemporaries but, until cheap sheet iron and steel became available and mass production techniques such as drop forging introduced, were more expensive to produce. However, they overcame the weakness of the brass castings and, when improved methods of mass-producing items from sheet iron and steel, and from cast iron were developed, supplanted brass for hilting cutlasses. Around the middle of the eighteenth century, these ferrous alloys were selected by the Royal Navy for the guards and grips of its cutlasses. Once adopted, sheet ferrous metal was never supplanted for guards in the Royal Navy and it was not until midway through the following century that alternatives, such as leather, replaced cast iron for grips. Iron or steel guards required protection if they were not to rust and, for most of the patterns that followed, this was achieved by the application of black paint.

The first half of the eighteenth century seems to have been a time of experimentation with cutlasses and it is towards the end of this period that a weapon with a specifically British

Hilt of pre-1804 cutlass with cylindrical handle covered with sheet iron. While cheap, this would not have provided a secure grip for the user.

characteristic first emerges. This is a style of hilt known to today's collectors as the 'double disc' or 'figure of eight' guard. Some of the earliest specimens of this type of cutlass have grips of antler through which the tang of the blade passes to be secured over a pommel cap. Some examples of these weapons bear the name Hollier and are the work of Thomas Hollier, sword cutler and gunsmith. Operating in Whitechapel from 1700 to 1729, he sold 1000 cutlasses to the Board of Ordnance in 1726; he also rebladed naval cutlasses. An employee of his, Thomas Nelson, working at Armoury Mills, Lewisham from 1730 to 1754 also supplied naval swords to the Board of Ordnance in 1743.[6] Gilkerson[7] favours identifying Hollier as the 'most likely candidate' for the invention of this style of guard. Comfort, in whose collection there are several Hollier cutlasses. agrees with this suggestion.[8] This is entirely possible, but there is no documentary evidence to support this view, which remains an interesting theory.

What is clear is that the design was considered sufficiently successful to form the basis of the official pattern when the Royal Navy began the process of standardising its weaponry. Always interested in cost as much as effectiveness, the authorities replaced the antler grip with a cheaper version made of a sheet of iron wrapped around a wooden former that, in turn, allowed the pommel cap to be changed to a simple disc. Cheap and nasty, this style of grip must have been very slippery when held in a cold, wet hand. This weapon had either a straight blade or, more rarely, a curved blade between approximately 25in and 28½in (635 and 724mm) long with a groove, properly referred to as a fuller, running close to the back edge.

At various times, Ordnance stores were marked to indicate some or all of Crown ownership, manufacturer, quality assurance and date. During this first period, markings seemed to be dependent on the whim of the individual supplier, with no official scheme in place. Some were marked with the Royal Cypher, *GR*, and others, additionally, with a crown. The presence of a British maker's mark by itself does not guarantee that the weapon was supplied to the Royal Navy, as the same manufacturers were providing arms to both the merchant service and the emerging American market.

The 1804 Pattern

In 1804, the Royal Navy established its first official pattern sword, placing its first order for 10,000 Swords for Sea Service on 30 May of that year.[9] This may seem a lot of swords but the Naval Proportions Book for 1834 allocated 350 cutlasses, scabbards and belts to First and Second Rate ships and 280 to Third Rates. Add all those required for lesser warships and those kept in store for future issue and replacement of damaged weapons and numbers in the thousands are rapidly reached.[10] This cutlass retained the double disc form of guard with a simple roll of metal in lieu of a quillon. There was a slot for a sword knot. Like its predecessors, it had no pommel; the tang of the blade being directly riveted over the rear of the guard. The major change was the replacement of the smooth, sheet iron grip by one of cast iron that was shaped to fit the hand and grooved both circumferentially (usually eighteen grooves) and longitudinally (six grooves). This must have been a major improvement over the grip of earlier swords. The blade of the new weapon was straight, between 27⅞in and 29¼in (708mm and 742mm) long and 1¼in to 1½in (32mm to 38mm) wide. It was flat without the narrow fuller of many earlier weapons and had a rather obtuse point. Government ownership was indicated by the Royal Cypher and sometimes with other marks such as a small crown above a number. This latter was the mark placed by a Government viewer to indicate that it was passed as fit for service. These official markings are important aids to distinguishing RN weapons from those of the early American Navy, the 1814 Pattern Norwegian cutlass, and swords supplied to the merchant service.

This first official-pattern cutlass had some features that were to remain characteristic of most subsequent British cutlasses. The guard of sheet iron or steel has already been commented upon, as has the grooved cast-iron grip. This guard was pierced near the hilt with a slit for the attachment of a sword knot. This feature remained as the design of the guard evolved. The provision of a slot for a sword knot is a minor puzzle. There seems to be no mention of the use of sword knots and illustrations of ratings armed with cutlasses do not show sword knots in use. However, all uniform patterns of cutlass issued for naval service have such a slot. Procurement of naval weapons was in the hands of the Board of Ordnance until 1854 and the War Department thereafter. This meant a very large measure of Army control over naval weaponry and, as all Army swords were provided with sword knots, the authors suggest that this reflects a military input into cutlass design. Against this must be set evidence from written accounts that sailors fastened their cutlasses to their wrists when preparing for battle (see p 11). Along with these characteristics of the handle, went a blade that was straight or very slightly curved. The rather obtuse point of this first uniform pattern suggests a cutting rather than a thrusting weapon and it will be shown that this was reflected in the first cutlass exercise when it is discussed in Chapter 8. The blade was forged flat; a poor design for a thrusting blade, which should combine stiffness with lightness. The usual way to achieve this combination of properties is to employ a fuller. The groove both lightens and stiffens the blade in the same way that girder with an 'I' cross-section is both light and stiff. It may be that

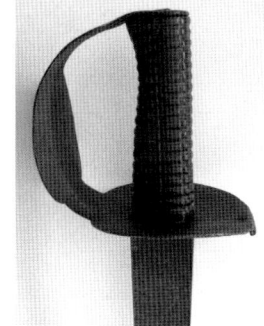

Above: 1804 Pattern cutlass, general view showing the broad, flat blade with a rather obtuse point.

Right: Hilt, showing figure of eight guard, cast iron handle, shaped to fit the hand, with longitudinal and circumferential grooving to provide a positive grip and the absence of a pommel.

this was done for cheapness, but it is possible that consideration was being given to the secondary role of the cutlass in cutting through nets and cordage to get at the enemy, severing cordage on which the enemy depended and cutting away fallen rope and canvas in one's own ship. Here the added weight of a blade without a groove would make it a more useful tool for these purposes.

This cutlass was carried in a brown leather scabbard with a brass chape. An interesting feature is the lack of a top locket, the brass frog hook being fitted directly into the leather of the scabbard. This would seem to be a weak arrangement and scabbards are sometimes found with this hook missing.

The 1845 Pattern

The end of the war with France in 1815 led to an immediate reduction in the size of the Royal Navy (from approximately 145,000 personnel to about 19,000) and, therefore, to a corresponding fall in the demand for new cutlasses. This did not dampen down experiments to develop an improved weapon and between that date and 1841 at least six different trial weapons were considered. None of these was manufactured in sufficient numbers to merit inclusion in the list of standard patterns.

During the early 1840s, several experimental swords were tested. In 1842, the Admiralty accepted a design proposed by Mr George Lovell, the Inspector of Small Arms,[11] and it seems that this formed the basis of the next pattern of cutlass issued to the Royal Navy. It is difficult to find a precise date for its adoption, a question made more difficult to answer following a fire in the Storehouse at the Tower of London where old cutlasses destined for alteration were stored. According to Ffoulkes and Hopkinson,[12] 10,000 cavalry swords were ordered to be altered to make up for this loss and in 1848 an additional 35,525 blades were ordered at 5s each. Whatever the precise series of events, bulk supplies became available around 1845 and this seems a useful date to employ when referring to this cutlass.

This new weapon was very different from its predecessor. The straight blade was replaced by a slightly curved, 29½in (750mm) long flat blade, which was to prove the longest blade fitted to RN cutlasses. Instead of a double disc, the new cutlass had a plain bowl guard with no quillon. This design of guard must have given far better protection for the user's hand. Either side of the slit for the sword knot, the new guard was folded outwards away from the grip, thus reinforcing an otherwise weak feature. This must have been a successful modification as all subsequent patterns of cutlass were treated similarly. Robson states that the guard of the 1821 Pattern Heavy Cavalry sword was the precursor for that on this pattern of cutlass.[13] While this is possible, there are major differences between the two, with the cavalry sword having a quillon and lacking the reinforcement around the slit for the sword knot provided for the cutlass by turning the metal outwards. These features seem first to have appeared in cavalry swords with the Pattern 1864.[14] The longitudinal cast grooves on the grip disappeared, leaving a grip with twelve circumferential grooves, and the elegant shaping to the hand of the earlier pattern was also discontinued. It seems likely that this grip was less efficient and it may have been adopted because it was cheaper to manufacture. A small pommel, technically described as a burr, was introduced with this design. Like its predecessor, this cutlass was carried in a brown leather scabbard with a brass chape and a brass frog hook fitted directly through the scabbard leather. This must have been an inherent weakness because, as in the example illustrated, the hook has been pulled out of the scabbard leather. This new pattern of cutlass had an acute point, well suited to thrusting and it will be shown in Chapter 8 that this is reflected in changes of emphasis in the official training regimes.

Close-up of the hilt of the 1845 Pattern cutlass showing the smooth bowl guard with the turned out reinforcement near the pommel. This illustration also shows the grip which is circumferentially but not longitudinally grooved and the small pommel (burr).

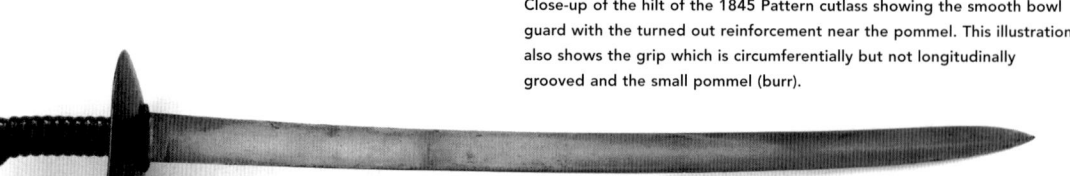

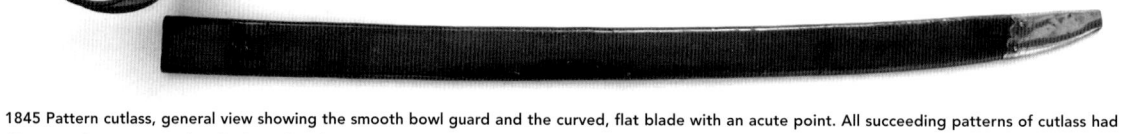

1845 Pattern cutlass, general view showing the smooth bowl guard and the curved, flat blade with an acute point. All succeeding patterns of cutlass had this type of point. Note that the brass frog hook has been torn out of the scabbard.

Modifications to the 1845 Pattern

In the years following the introduction of this pattern and its supersession by a completely new design in 1889, numerous minor modifications were suggested and tried. Many of the records pertaining to these weapons have been lost and, from those that remain, May and Annis have constructed a possible sequence of patterns and their distinguishing features. This is a bewildering variety of cutlasses which are very difficult to tell apart and some of which were probably only ever produced in short runs. At its simplest one can distinguish two varieties of the bowl guard. The first (Type A) is that introduced around 1845 in which the distance between the grip and the inner face of the knuckle guard was about 2¾in (70mm). With this guard came a grip that had a prominent swelling towards the pommel. The close-up of the guard and grip shows the key features for the 1845 Pattern. There is a variant of this hilt with an oval reinforcing washer riveted to the inner face of the guard between it and the grip.

In the second general type of hilt, introduced about 1859 (Type B), the distance between the grip and the guard was reduced to about 2⅜in (60mm), the swelling towards the pommel was much smaller and there was an oval washer between the guard and the grip. The top of this guard was also slightly turned over towards the blade. This hilt was mounted on a slightly curved blade 27in (686mm) long and 1¼in (38mm) wide at the shoulder. The 1870s saw two more patterns introduced both of which were manufactured by shortening the blades of earlier patterns to 26in (660mm) and straightening them. The two new patterns were those of 1871 with the Type B hilt and 1875 with the Type A hilt.

The problem for the Navy was not in the guards but in the blades. With tens of thousands of cutlasses in store and at sea, the temptation to make new patterns by altering old blades must have been very high. This would not have caused a problem had the profiles of the shorter and, sometimes, straight blades been achievable by simply grinding. However, this was not the case and, as a result, the blades needed to be hot forged to achieve the desired new size and profile. These straightening and shortening operations caused alterations in the microstructure of the steel that adversely affected its mechanical properties. These changes could only have been reversed by re-heat treating the blades. This was an expensive process involving soaking at a high temperature, quenching and then tempering at a lower temperature. It seems to have been overlooked or ignored, with the predictable result that these cutlasses were often of little use in combat. The inevitable failures on active service with the consequent deaths became public knowledge resulting in a series of procurement scandals.[15] Complaints improved the production regime and some later converted weapons were heat treated subsequent to modification. Blades treated in this way can be identified by a letter 'R' stamped into the metal.

It was not until 1887, when another cut-down version of the 1845 cutlass with its Type A hilt was introduced, that the new blade profile could be achieved without forging. Two years later a rigorous testing procedure was introduced for naval edged weapons and reported in *The Engineer* for 8 March of that year.[16]

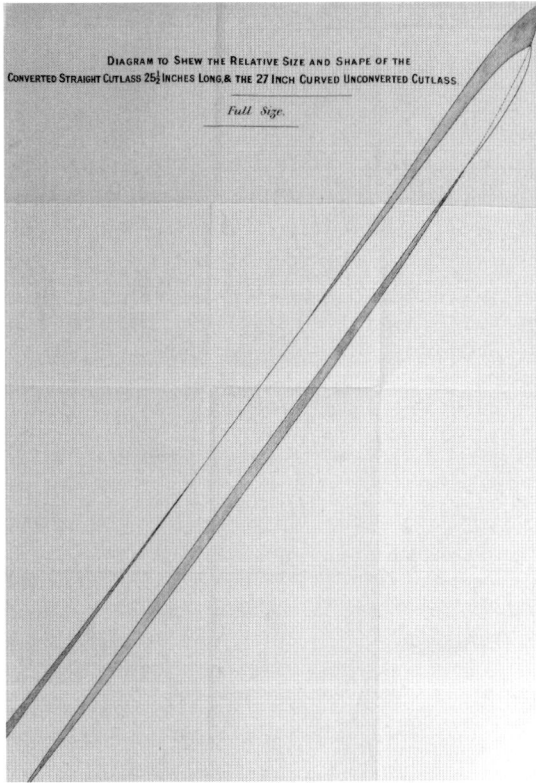

Published drawing of two blade profiles: that for the original 27in (686mm) weapon and that for the shortened 25½in (650mm) sword. The small area near the tip of the short cutlass could only be made from the longer blade by hot forging. Failure to heat treat the blades correctly after this conversion led to serious failures in service.

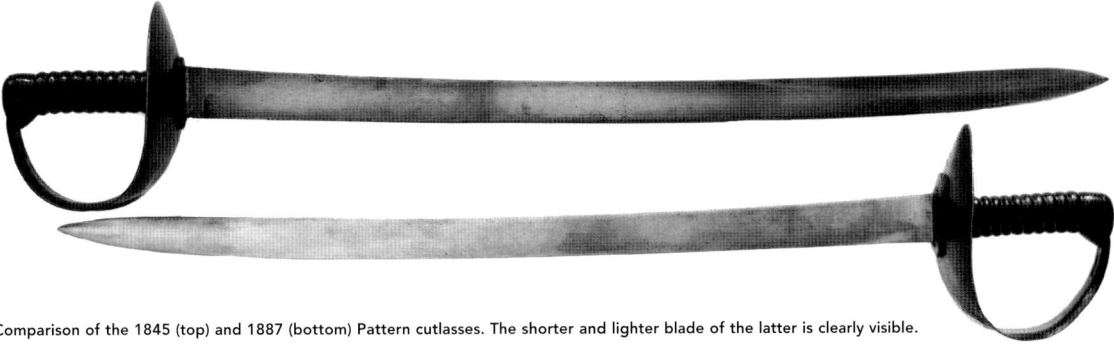

Comparison of the 1845 (top) and 1887 (bottom) Pattern cutlasses. The shorter and lighter blade of the latter is clearly visible.

The 1889 Pattern

Perhaps because older weapons were no longer available in sufficient numbers to make modification attractive, a new cutlass was introduced in 1889. This marked a complete break with the earlier designs. The new sword had a straight, flat blade with a spear point. The hilt consisted of a sheet metal guard, clearly modelled on the 1882 Pattern sword for cavalry troopers, and a cast-iron grip, which looks to be rather too cylindrical in cross-section to afford a really secure grip. Possibly the most innovative design element introduced during the whole time that the RN used cutlasses, the guard of this pattern had a pronounced everted rim to the forward-facing part of the bowl. Not only would this have provided added strength to the guard but it would have acted as a stop rib. This feature, a common element in the design of armours, was intended to catch the point of a weapon glancing off a curved surface and guide it harmlessly away. Despite the tensions that must have existed between the RN and the Army over the design and supply of cutlasses, this would seem to be an example where the Army input acted to the benefit of the RN. This sword was carried in a black leather scabbard with two steel mounts. The locket was fitted with a stud for use with a belt frog.

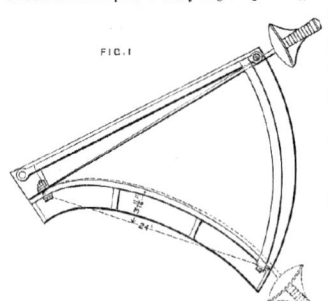

Right: Testing of naval edged weapons, article from *The Engineer*, 8 March 1889. In response to serious failures of cutlasses in service, these tests were introduced to ensure that weapons taken into store were fit for purpose.

Left: The design of the 1889 Pattern guard followed that of cavalry troopers' swords, reinforced by a turned edge which also acted as a stop rib to deflect a point away from the user. The cast iron grip is almost cylindrical.

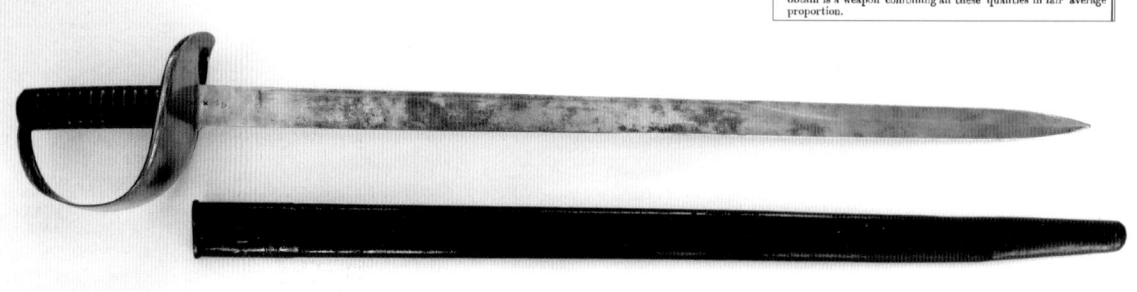

Below: The 1889 Pattern cutlass showing the straight, flat blade with an acute point.

Cutlasses 31

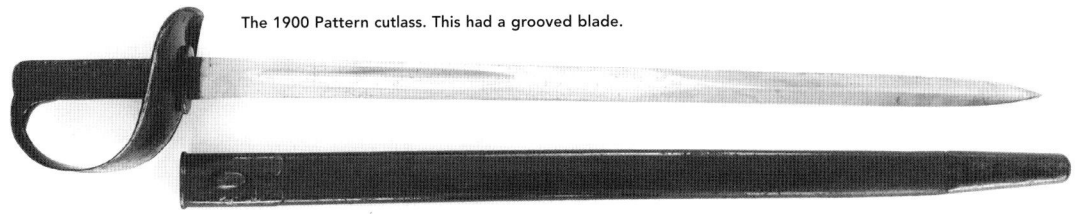

The 1900 Pattern cutlass. This had a grooved blade.

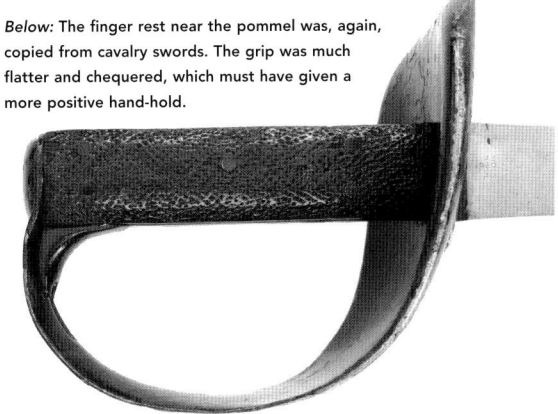

Below: The finger rest near the pommel was, again, copied from cavalry swords. The grip was much flatter and chequered, which must have given a more positive hand-hold.

The 1900 Pattern

1900 saw another pattern of cutlass introduced. Like its predecessor, this sword had a straight blade but this time there was a shallow fuller running along each face for about one-third of the blade's length. The bowl guard with the turned down rim was retained but the grip was markedly different. The smooth, almost cylindrical, cast iron guard was replaced by one with a much more rectangular cross section which was faced with knurled, black leather cheeks. An additional feature was a small concave insert between the heel of the grip and the guard where if joins the pommel. This finger rest which was intended to cushion the little finger of the sword hand was copied from the 1890 Pattern sword for cavalry troopers. The scabbard remained the same as for the previous pattern. This was to be the last pattern of cutlass in the RN. The order withdrawing the cutlass from service was issued on 22 October 1936.[17]

May and Annis state that these last two patterns were issued with bright steel guards. However, many examples of both these patterns are to be found with blackened mounts, including those chosen for the illustrations in Vol. II of their book.[18] 'Shiny cutlery' was certainly being used for ceremonial purposes as late as the start of the twenty-first century, so it is possible that both blackened and bright mounts were issued or that cutlasses were blackened on board to reduce the amount of cleaning necessary.

Some works on cutlasses include the pioneers' sword of 1856. This had a brass stirrup hilt and a saw-backed blade. Numbers of these weapons were transferred to the RN in 1903 but because there is little evidence of their use, they have not been included here.

The Enfield Cutlass Sword Bayonet, 1859

There were also two weapons which tried to be both cutlasses and bayonets. When the Enfield rifle of 1859, later converted to the breech-loading Enfield-Snider in 1867, was introduced, the RN seemed determined to have its own pattern of bayonet to accompany this, its first rifle, and duly came up with a cutlass sword bayonet.

This combination weapon had a flat, slightly curved, 27in (686mm) long blade terminating in a double-edged spear point. The hilt assembly consists of a sheet steel guard with a maximum width of 4.5in (115mm), tapering to ⅝in (16mm) where it enters the pommel. Close to the pommel it is pierced with a slot for a sword knot and folded outwards in reinforcement. The guard is sandwiched between a reinforcing plate on the outside and a muzzle ring/quillon on the inside. The internal diameter of the muzzle ring is ¹³⁄₁₆in (21mm).

The grip is leather-covered wood with six circumferential grooves and is secured to the tang of the blade by three rivets passing right through and by one additional rivet on the left hand face. A mortise for fitting this weapon to the rifle runs the length of the grip. The pommel has a catch operated by a leaf spring on the right hand side and a stud on the other. There is a small rounded plate forming the final part of the pommel assembly over which the tang is riveted. This is the earlier of two versions, sealed on 18 April 1859. This grooved grip must have been deemed too slippery as, less than a month later, on 1 May, another version with a knurled leather grip was introduced.[19] The scabbard for this cutlass sword bayonet was black leather with chape and locket of steel, the latter component fitted with a frog button.

Like most compromises, this weapon can hardly have been a pleasure to use in either of its roles. As a cutlass, the substitution of the muzzle ring for the upper part of the guard would have reduced the protection afforded to the hand, while its weight when fixed as a bayonet must have produced a very muzzle-heavy weapon.

Above: The Enfield cutlass sword bayonet of 1859; note the curved blade.

below: Close-up of the hilt showing the muzzle ring, the mortise groove and the thumb button for the spring catch which secured the bayonet to the rifle. The smooth, grooved grip (leather covering now missing) identifies this as an early specimen before the change was made to a chequered leather grip

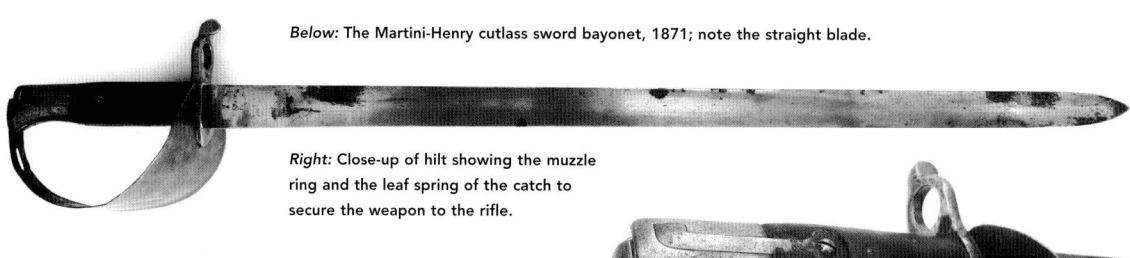

Below: The Martini-Henry cutlass sword bayonet, 1871; note the straight blade.

Right: Close-up of hilt showing the muzzle ring and the leaf spring of the catch to secure the weapon to the rifle.

The Martini-Henry Cutlass Sword Bayonet, 1871

The drawbacks to the Enfield-Snider cutlass sword bayonet suggested above cannot have been too serious, as when a new rifle, the Martini-Henry, was adopted in 1869, it was to be accompanied by a similar combination weapon. After trials of several proposed weapons, the result was the Pattern 1871 cutlass sword bayonet. It is perhaps noteworthy that this was lighter than its predecessor, so it is possible that user experience was taken into account when it was designed. This new weapon had a straight blade, 25½in (650mm) long and 1¼in (32mm) wide at the shoulder. Many of these were provided by straightening and shortening the 1859 Pattern and suffered from the same problems as the contemporary cutlasses. The specimen illustrated is one such, bearing 'S' stamps for manufacture at Solingen and 'E' stamps dating from its conversion in 1878. It is not stamped 'R' and therefore was not heat treated after conversion. Like its predecessor the scabbard was black leather with two steel mounts.

Specifications

Useful drawings of the following four patterns can be found in *The Swords and Records of Robert Mole & Sons 1835–1920*:[20]

Sword Naval 25½ inch Cutlass. Patt./ 71;
Sword-Bayonet Martini Henry Rifle, Naval. Patt.-/71;
Sword Naval, 27 inch Cutlass, with sharpened point;
Sword Naval 28 inch Cutlass. Patt.-/89.

These drawings give the dimensions of both the sword and its scabbard and the weight of the sword. The final drawing on p 73 is from the Royal Small Arms Factory specification and gives a good indication of the standard of dimensional accuracy expected of contractors.

The Coastguard Cutlass

In 1822, a rationalisation of a number of organisations led to the formation of the Coastguard which finally came under Admiralty control in 1856.[21] From this latter date until it passed to civilian control in 1923, ratings in this service would have been issued with standard naval weapons. However, shortly after its formation the Coastguard service adopted a pattern of cutlass of its own.[22] This is a short sword with a pronounced curve to the blade and a brass guard. The overall length of this sword is 29¾in (755mm) and the curved blade which is 25in (635mm) long measured in a straight line from the shoulder to the point of the back edge which curves by 1⅜in (35mm) from the straight. It is 1⁷⁄₁₆in (36mm) wide at the shoulder narrowing to about 1in (25mm) approximately 3in (76mm) from the very acute point. There is a single, narrow fuller running along each side of the blade from the shoulder to within 7½in (190mm) of the point. The outer face of the blade illustrated is completely plain and on the inner face towards the hilt are stamped: 'ENFIELD' and a crowned 'GR'. The brass guard consists of a stirrup hilt with a quillon. Additional protection is afforded to the hand by a loop on the outer side running from the mid-point of the cross guard to the most prominent part of the knuckle bow. On this specimen, a small letter 'C' is stamped on the cross guard just underneath the terminal of the quillon. There is no pommel and the knuckle guard is riveted directly to the pommel end of the cast-iron grip. The grip is shaped to fit the hand and has nineteen spiral grooves cast into its surface. The small countersunk hole drilled through the grip was probably made to facilitate mounting as part of a wall display. The scabbard for this cutlass was brown leather with a brass chape and frog hook.[23]

In the absence of any known surviving regulations, the markings on the weapon are important dating criteria. The Royal Small Arms Factory opened at Enfield in 1816 but the sword making facility was not operational until 1823. The combination of 'ENFIELD' and 'GR' stamps on the blade of this sword indicate that it was manufactured between 1823 and 1830 when William IV came to the throne. The letter 'C' indicates ownership by the Coastguard.

The date at which this pattern was superseded in the Coastguard service is not known. However, it appears that the hilts were re-bladed with straight blades, provided with black

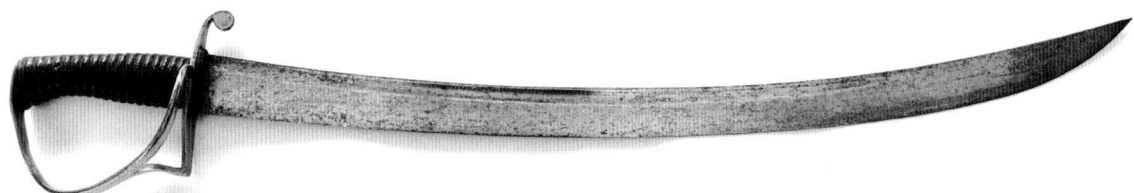

The Coastguard cutlass, ca 1825. This has a very curved blade with a narrow Fuller running close to the back edge and a very acute point.

Cutlasses 33

Close-up of the hilt showing the brass knuckle guard with additional side bar and the circumferentially grooved grip which is shaped to the hand. The countersunk hole in the grip was probably made to mount this weapon as part of a wall display.

leather scabbards with brass chapes and frog hooks and issued as sidearms for privates of the Army Hospital Corps in about 1857.[24] This date would fit well with the assumption of control of the Coastguard by the Admiralty in 1856.

Thames River Police

Formed in 1798 as a private concern funded by the West India Merchants but with Government approval, the unit of around fifty men was taken under Government control in 1800. In 1839 it was incorporated into the Metropolitan Police but maintained its distinct uniform and organisation, being based on the Royal Navy and hence having reefer jackets and boaters as hats. They continued to have rowing and sailing craft until the 1878 collision between the pleasure cruiser *Princess Alice* and the collier *Bywell Castle* which cost over 600 lives. This led to the purchase of two steam launches in 1884 with further powered craft being purchased from 1900. The unit is still in operation today.[25]

The sword of this organisation was a brass-hilted cutlass with a slightly curved, undecorated blade with a side single fuller along both faces. It is 27in (686mm) long and 1¼in (31mm) wide at the shoulder. The hilt is manufactured entirely of brass. It consists of a knuckle bow with a side guard and a single brass component for the grip and pommel. This component is cast with seven spiral grooves and engraved to simulate a back piece and ferrule. On the inside of the cross guard there is a press stud and spring catch which serves to secure the sword in its scabbard. This is black leather with two brass mounts, the locket being fitted with a frog stud.

Other Possible Government-issue Cutlasses

Cutlasses differing in a number of respects from the 1804 Pattern, while uncommon, are not rare and the example illustrated is fairly typical of the type. While it has the characteristic double disc guard, it has the primitive sheet iron grip replaced in 1804 by cast iron. However, the main difference is in the blade which is short, 24¾in (630mm) long, has a pronounced curve and a shallow fuller close to the back edge which runs the whole length from shoulder to point. The outer face of the blade is stamped 'GR' in block capitals. The Royal Cypher on naval cutlasses is in a cursive style but Government-issue firearms are marked in block capitals. It will be recalled that the Coastguard cutlass had a short, strongly curved blade. It is suggested that these characteristics may well have been retained from the cutlasses of its precursor service, the Revenue Service, thus pointing to the Revenue as the source of this style. It is, of course, impossible to verify this suggestion, which is offered only as a possible explanation for these swords.

The Merchant Marine

Although there is no doubt that many merchantmen were armed, especially during times of war or when trading in areas infested with pirates or populated by unfriendly tribes, identifying cutlasses used in these ships is difficult. Weapons similar to the standard patterns but not carrying any Government marks may well have been carried in merchantmen but, equally, they could have been produced for sale abroad. Cutlasses were from time-to-time sold out of service as newer patterns were adopted and these again could have been used either in British or in foreign merchant ships. A sword sold in 2012 may well be a rare example of such a weapon sold from Government stores and used on a merchant ship.[26] With a hilt identical to the Coastguard cutlass and a straight blade converted from an 1804 Pattern naval cutlass, this could easily be mistaken for the sword of a private in the Army Hospital Corps, ca 1860.[27] This pattern of Army sword is believed to have been issued from stocks made surplus to requirements when the Coastguard ceased to use them. What distinguishes this cutlass is the name *Pleiad* engraved on the knuckle guard. Macgregor Laird had been one of three survivors of an expedition to try to open up the River Niger to trade which had been mounted between 1831 and 1834. In 1854, he obtained Government support to mount another expedition up the Niger under the command of Dr William Baikie, this time in the small steamship *Pleiad*, built by the family firm. This expedition pioneered the use of quinine as a prophylactic for malaria and as a result no European died of fever during this 118-day voyage which resulted in the establishment of several trading posts.[28] This is exactly the type of voyage for which a ship would have needed to carry arms and these cutlasses had become surplus to Government requirements at about the same date. We know from Baikie's account that the vessel was 'armed with a 12

Cutlass of the Thames River Police with its solid brass hilt.

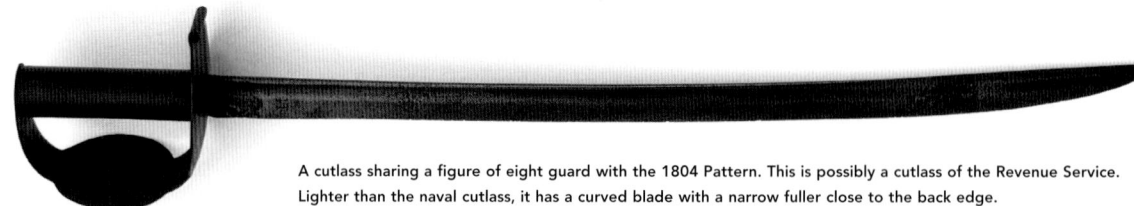

A cutlass sharing a figure of eight guard with the 1804 Pattern. This is possibly a cutlass of the Revenue Service. Lighter than the naval cutlass, it has a curved blade with a narrow fuller close to the back edge.

pounder pivot gun, four swivels, Minié rifles and double barrelled guns for the officers, muskets for the crew'. The National Maritime Museum has a pair of flintlock pistols from the same expedition inscribed with the ship's name on their trigger guards.[29] This sword would seem to be a rare example of a cutlass definitely used by a merchant ship and a survivor from an important expedition.

Markings on Cutlasses

Before 1804, the marking of cutlasses was usually restricted to the names of the manufacturers. Among those recorded are Craven, Gill, Harvey, Hollier, Osborn, and Woolley. Cutlasses of the 1804 Pattern are marked on the flat of the blade with the Royal Cypher, 'GR', in a cursive script accompanied by a crown. Some blades also bear an inspection mark in the form of a crown above a numeral. The manufacturer's name is often stamped on the back edge and, not surprisingly, many of those in the list above continued to supply these weapons. Among the names to be found are: Bate, Cooper, Craven, Dawes, Gill, Hadley, Osborn, Reddell, and Woolley.

As the nineteenth century progressed, the inspection and acceptance regimes became more formalised and the simple engraved Cyphers were replaced by stamps indicating government ownership, place of inspection and the identity of the inspector. Each of these marks consisted of three elements. At the top there was a crown, below this a single block capital letter and, at the bottom, the inspector's number. The letters are '**B**' for Birmingham, '**E**' for Enfield and '**S**' for Solingen. Difficulties with both the quantity and quality of cutlasses supplied by English cutlers had led to supplies being sought from Solingen in sufficient quantity to justify setting up an inspectorate in Solingen. To these, later, was added '**W**' for Wilkinson. In the account of the development of the Wilkinson firm, there is mention that while most cutlasses were assembled in Birmingham the blades tended to come from Solingen.[30] The identities of the owners of the individual numerical marks are unknown.

Before 1854 arms for the Royal Navy were procured by the Board of Ordnance and bear their '**BO**' mark. After that date, the role was taken over by the War Office and the mark replaced by '**WD**'. Government ownership is also often indicated by a stamped broad arrow. Swords withdrawn from service usually have another arrow stamped with its point touching the first arrow's point. Weapons produced for naval use often bear the stamp '**N**'.

Towards the end of the nineteenth century, it became customary to indicate the date of manufacture by stamping the last two digits of the year preceded by an apostrophe, e.g. ''**00**'

for 1900. When a weapon was converted from an earlier pattern, this was indicated by the letter **C**, e.g. '**C/'88**' for the 1887 Pattern converted from that of ca 1845 in 1888. Converted weapons often have the viewing marks of two different inspectorates, representing the quality assurance of both the original and new patterns. The mark '**R**' refers to blades that have been re-tempered. The final official mark found is an '**X**' indicating the face of the blade that had been convex during the compression test which formed part of the quality assurance process. This is sometimes confused with the withdrawn from service stamping described above.

Other types of marking can also be found. The first of these is the rack number found on the guards or pommels of many cutlasses. These indicate the position of a weapon in its stowage and, sometimes, the place of stowage as well, e.g. QD7 indicating a cutlass stowed in a rack on the quarterdeck. Enfield cutlass sword bayonets were not interchangeable between rifles, so individual cutlasses were paired with specific rifles and numbered to match the firearms.

After the arrival of uniform patterns of cutlasses in 1804, the number of manufacturers involved expanded. There is no complete list but these have all been recorded as supplying cutlasses.

Aston	Hadley	Reddell
Bate	Harvey	Reeves
Chavasse	Heighington	Robinson
Clauberg	Höller	Robinson & Watts
Cooper	Kirschbaum	Salter
Craven	Klönne	Shnitzler & Kirschbaum
Dawes	Lawrence	Swinburn
Enfield	Mole	Weyersberg
Gill	Moxham	Wilkinson
Greaves	Osborn	Woolley

Other suppliers of individual components are also known but these have not been included.

Scabbards, especially the later patterns, are also marked. Typical markings stamped into the leather on the reverse side would be: ENF, N, crown over 70 over E. These indicate manufacture at Enfield, naval use, and the inspector's stamp respectively. Simple numerical stamps also appear on the top locket, usually at the mouth or on the frog stud.

In cases where earlier weapons have been converted or refurbished, these markings on the sword and scabbard can be used to trace the history of an individual weapon. This adds considerably to the interest of individual examples.

CHAPTER 3

Officers' Swords

Unlike cutlasses, which were plain workmanlike tools issued by the Government, officers' swords have always been privately purchased. Because of this a sword often reflects the wealth of its owner and sometimes his own idiosyncrasies regarding its design. An officer might well own more than one sword; a heavy-duty one for fighting and a lightweight dress version for ceremonial occasions being a common combination. Uniform swords have also been used to reinforce distinctions in rank, with the swords of senior officers being more highly ornamented. This chapter will start back in the time of Henry VIII when there were no features to identify a sword as specifically naval. This means that only a good provenance will connect a sword to naval service. There are few such weapons, so the progress to the latter half of the eighteenth century when naval symbols such as the fouled anchor and the naval crown became increasingly common is rapid. Then the range of weapons used before standardisation will be explored and finally all the uniform patterns until the present day will be described. The accoutrements associated with swords, the scabbards, belts and sword knots, will also be looked at in detail.

From the Tudors to the Mid-Eighteenth Century

Henry VIII is often cited as the father of the Royal Navy and when his flagship, *Mary Rose*, sank in 1545 and was buried in the mud of the Solent, many weapons were preserved *in situ*. Among these is one complete sword and this is the earliest sword with an impeccable provenance of maritime use. The choice of the word 'maritime' is deliberate because there is no way of telling whether this weapon was owned by a sailor or a soldier. All we can say is that it is a typical basket-hilted broadsword of the period. Its overall length is 41½in (1050mm) with a hilt is forged from ¼in (6mm) iron bars. The blade is of poor quality, being of iron faced with a thin layer of steel which would soon have been sharpened away in use. It has been decided to place this with officers' swords rather than with cutlasses because although there is a very complete inventory of the Government stores held on board the *Mary Rose* in 1514 there is no mention of swords.[1]

This lack of differentiation between swords used on land and at sea is very clearly seen with the sword attributed to Sir Francis Drake. This is claimed to be the sword used by Queen Elizabeth I to knight Drake on board the *Golden Hind* on 4 April

Above: Mary Rose sword. This is the earliest English sword with an undisputed maritime provenance. (Courtesy of the Mary Rose Trust)

Below: Sword of Sir Francis Drake. This is a typical good-quality fighting sword of the mid- to late sixteenth century. Its attribution rests on family tradition. (Courtesy Wardroom Mess President HMS *Drake*)

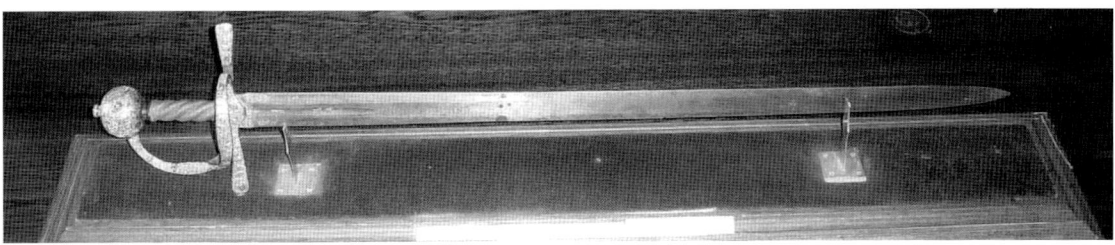

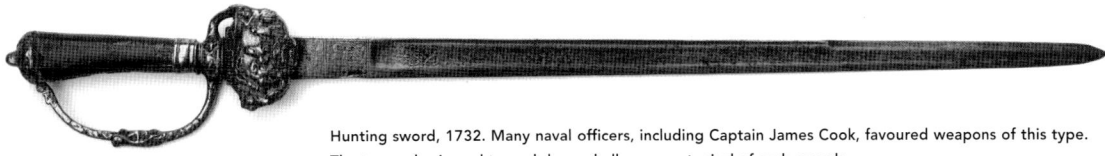

Hunting sword, 1732. Many naval officers, including Captain James Cook, favoured weapons of this type. The tapered grip and turned-down shell are very typical of such swords.

1581. It was definitely used by Her Majesty Queen Elizabeth II to knight Sir Francis Chichester in the grounds of the Royal Naval College, Greenwich, after his return from his single-handed circumnavigation of the world in 1967. It is a typical fighting sword of the mid- to late sixteenth century, albeit of much higher quality than the *Mary Rose* sword, with no specific naval characteristics. The engravings on the blade with details of Drake's voyages were probably added later, in the seventeenth century.

During the Interregnum which followed the defeat of Charles I and lasted until the restoration of Charles II and which saw the First Anglo-Dutch War, Admirals became Generals-at-Sea, so it is hardly surprising that military and naval swords were indistinguishable and this lack of specific naval characteristics continued well into the eighteenth century. In the first half of the eighteenth century, the most popular style of fighting sword for naval officers seems to have been the hanger or hunting sword. This was exactly the same type of weapon as any civilian gentleman might choose to carry in less formal circumstances, such as when travelling. Few bear any clear evidence of naval ownership so, unless a weapon comes with some provenance, it is impossible to ascribe it with certainty to a naval source. The main evidence for the popularity of these weapons comes from the frequency with which they are seen in portraits of naval officers of this period. They had relatively short blades, often curved but sometimes straight, and a simple guard, which frequently incorporated a decorative down-turned shell and a knuckle bow. A typical example has a straight, 22in (559mm) long blade that is single-edged for all but the 7¼in (185mm) closest to the point where it becomes double-edged. The brass guard, which is decorated with hunting scenes, has the characteristic shell, knuckle guard and pommel cap features. The leather covered grip tapers from the pommel to the guard, another common characteristic of these weapons. The blade is inscribed with the Latin motto *Quis separabit nos nil nisi mors* ('What shall separate us, nothing but death'), the martial nature of which suggests that it was owned by a naval or military officer. The blade is dated 1732. A silver-hilted sword of this type, also with a straight blade, which belonged to the great explorer Captain James Cook is preserved in the State Library of New South Wales. Perhaps in these short swords we can see an early stage in the development and adoption of the dirk. It has been suggested[2] that the curved hanger may well be the lineal ancestor of the curved dirk while, in a similar vein, the straight-bladed swords of this type evolved into the straight fighting dirk which was, in the late nineteenth century, to become the uniform weapon of the Midshipman (see Chapter 4).

The Later Eighteenth and Early Nineteenth Centuries

During the last quarter of the eighteenth century, several other styles of sword were prominent. The first of these, the slotted hilt sword, was popular with both naval and military officers. It was a simple hanger with a curved, single-edged blade. The hilts of these swords are of gilt brass with simple knuckle bow guards supplemented by a narrow loop on each side. Additional support for these loops is by a short bar through each at its widest point. Grips were often of ebony, either longitudinally reeded, as in the example illustrated, or with a spiral groove. The pommel was commonly globose, although other shapes can be found. Usually quite plain, these swords were practical fighting weapons and completely undecorated,

Above: Slotted hilt sword. Swords of this type were popular with both naval and military officers towards the end of the eighteenth century. This specimen is unmarked but some have devices such as fouled anchors incorporated in their decoration which identifies them unambiguously as naval.

Below: Drawing of a sword with double 'S' bar. A very practical type of fighting sword offering greater protection to the hand than the slotted hilt sword.

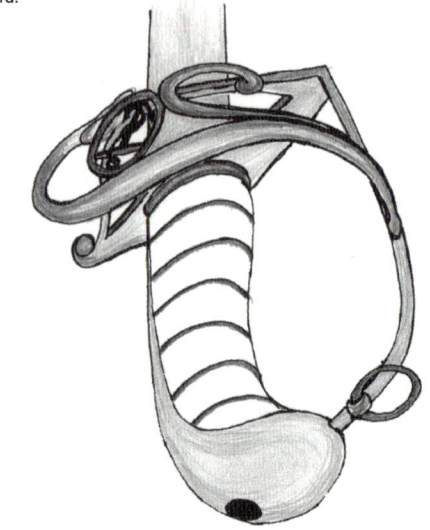

Officers' Swords 37

Oval side ring sword. This style, very much associated with Nelson, combined the attributes of both fighting and dress swords in one weapon. (Graham Hunt)

Naval version of the 1803 Pattern Army sword with a fouled anchor in the knuckle guard. (Graham Hunt)

making it impossible to know whether the weapon was naval or military in origin. However, some are to be found that have clear naval symbols of fouled anchors engraved on the pommel, blade or both and others have fouled anchors inset into the slots.

A heavier version of this curved fighting sword had a stirrup hilt enhanced by a loop on the outside which was further reinforced by one or two 'S'-shaped bars on the outside protecting the back of the sword hand. The pommels of these swords are either of the plain, rounded variety or in the form of a lion's head. The curved blades are sometimes quite substantial. Most of these swords date from the last decade of the eighteenth century or the first few years of the nineteenth. A very fine example of this type of sword, with the fouled anchor replaced by a lion trampling over a prostrate wyvern (a legendary winged reptilian creature with a dragon's head, the hindquarters of a snake or lizard with two legs or none, and a barbed tail) presumably representing Britain triumphing over France, is on display in the Museum of Castle Cornet in Guernsey. It was presented to Captain James Le Bair of the privateer *Mayflower* for his capture of the French privateer *Troisiéme Ferailleur* on 9 April 1800. This sword is important in providing an accurate dating reference.

While the slotted hilt sword was the continuation of the custom of wearing some form of hanger as a fighting sword, the oval side ring sword seems to have been a compromise between the practicality needed of a fighting weapon and the decorative appeal necessary in a dress sword.[3] British naval swords were generally fitted with the straight, single-edged backsword blade of the form known as a spadroon that was popular with military officers around the end of the eighteenth century. The main feature of this style of sword is the way the loop on the outside of the main knuckle bow is reinforced with an inner loop joining it back to the cross. Grips were bound with a combination of metal tapes and wires and pommels were ovoid. A feature of all these swords is a cup or plate designed to act as a seal over the mouth of the scabbard.

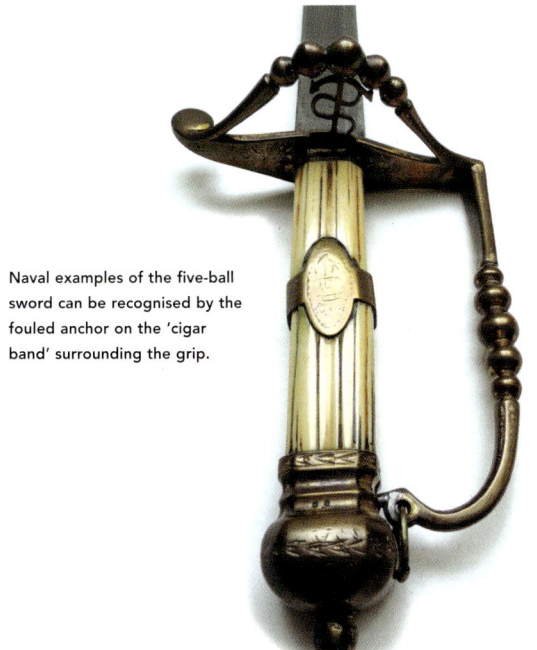

Naval examples of the five-ball sword can be recognised by the fouled anchor on the 'cigar band' surrounding the grip.

Five-ball sword. Named after the beaded decoration on the knuckle guard and side ring, these swords were used by both naval and military officers.

Swords of this type can be found with both brass and silver-gilt hilts. Lieutenant Walter Lock of HMS *Hebe* was presented with an oval side ring sword with a silver gilt hilt in 1786. The donor was the future King William IV. The oval side rings are among the less common swords of this period and it is only rarely possible to state specifically that such a sword is naval, as it is unusual for there to be any decorative elements of a maritime nature or the provenance to affirm its status.

Another of the styles popular with officers of both services at the turn of the century was the five-ball sword. These swords were generally fitted with the single-edged, cut-and-thrust spadroon blade. The amount of decoration on the blades is variable but usually incorporates patriotic and naval symbols. The hilt is formed around the basic stirrup form with an additional side loop. Both the knuckle guard and side loop are decorated with a group of five graduated beads or balls, after which feature collectors have named the sword. In the naval version, the hilt mountings are of gilt brass and the side loop is often supported by an inset fouled anchor. The grip is usually of square cross section, made of ivory and longitudinally reeded. Around the middle is a gilt brass band with an oval cartouche engraved with a fouled anchor, sometimes crowned. The cushion shaped pommel shown in the illustration is typical but examples are found with an Adam-style, urn-shaped pommel. Close to its junction with the pommel, the knuckle bow is fitted with a loose ring for the attachment of a sword knot.

In 1803 the Army introduced a new pattern of sword for officers of the infantry, light companies and grenadiers. This had a broad, markedly curved blade and a knuckle-bow guard incorporating the Royal Cypher. Light companies and grenadiers each had their own specific symbols of a bugle and a grenade. A variant of this weapon is sometimes found with a fouled anchor replacing the military symbols on the guard. May and Annis believed that these were more likely to have been swords of Royal Marine rather than RN officers. However, a sword in the Sim Comfort collection, which is of this type,[4] bears the name of Lieutenant Street RN on the top locket of the scabbard confirming that at least one of these swords was the property of a naval officer. In this period, immediately before uniformity was introduced, the authors believe it is probable that both RN and RM officers used this design of sword and only a clear provenance will permit an individual sword to be ascribed definitively to one or other of these services.

Small-swords

Throughout the eighteenth century, officers ashore (especially senior officers) would have worn a dress sword similar in style to that worn by every gentleman. This type of sword, known to collectors today as the small-sword, was a lightweight dress weapon descended from the earlier and heavier rapier and would, in turn, evolve into the court sword of today. Clear evidence that this fashion had already been adopted at the very beginning of the eighteenth century comes in the form of a small-sword hilt recovered from the wreck of HMS *Hazardous* which sank off Bracklesham Bay, near Portsmouth, in 1706.[5] As with hunting swords or hangers, many are indistinguishable from contemporary civilian weapons but, presumably because they were being worn ashore and by people proud of their profession, some are decorated with naval motifs. One such has a silver hilt, without hallmarks, that shows typical characteristics of small swords from about 1780. These are the flat,

Silver hilted small-sword. Dress swords of this type would have been worn on occasions of ceremony. The naval provenance of this sword is clearly indicated by the tiny fouled anchors inset in the *pas d'âne* rings.

oval shell, vestigial *pas d'âne* rings, double quillons and an urn shaped pommel. The tiny fouled anchors set into the *pas d'âne* rings discreetly proclaim the naval calling of its owner. These are very similar to those found on some City of London presentation small-swords of about the same period. The blade is of the characteristic, evenly tapered, triangular form, 28.1in (714mm) long and the sword is carried in a black leather scabbard with three silver mounts, the top two having loose rings for its suspension from the sword belt. With the pattern of rays on the guard which are echoed in the design of the other elements of the hilt, this is an elegant weapon which speaks plainly of the restrained good taste with which its owner drew attention to his profession. Small-swords with naval emblems are scarce, suggesting that they were luxury items, specially commissioned by wealthy officers.

There is a sword in the Sim Comfort[6] collection that shares many design features with the weapon illustrated, differing only in being made of gilt bronze and lacking the tiny fouled anchors in the *pas d'âne* rings. It carries a label attributing it to Vice Admiral Sir Patrick Campbell KCB. Comfort argues that this sword came from the French frigate *Desiree* captured by Commander Campbell in 1800 during a daring cutting-out expedition. The present authors dispute this, seeing no reason to consider this sword as anything other than Campbell's dress weapon. Even after the introduction of the uniform weapons to be described shortly, some officers continued to wear small-swords. For instance, a portrait of Vice Admiral Sir George Cockburn in full dress painted in 1820[7] shows him wearing the small-sword given to him by Nelson in 1797 (see Chapter 7).

While there is no doubt that small-swords were dress weapons worn on ceremonial occasions, the question arises whether or not they were ever used in battle; small-swords were, after all, regulation weapons in both the French and Spanish navies. Some clues in answer to this question can be found in portraits of flag officers of the period. As a general rule, those with battle scenes in the background show the officers armed with drawn fighting swords while those with peaceful seascapes have the officers wearing small-swords. But is this the whole story? Specifically, did officers ever elect to wear their small-swords in battle? If Spanish and French officers were wearing small-swords in action, surely, some British officers may have chosen to do likewise. Most of these portraits of naval officers wearing or carrying small-swords show them with their swords sheathed but there is at least one exception. On 17 April 1780,

Officers' Swords 39

Admiral Sir George Brydges Rodney, 1780. This engraving shows Rodney wielding a sword with many features in common with the silver hilted small-sword described above.

a French fleet commanded by De Guichen and a British fleet under Sir George Brydges Rodney met off Dominica in the West Indies. The action, although vigorous, was not decisive and Rodney himself was less than happy with the conduct of his subordinates. However, both the British and French governments claimed a victory. By the beginning of June, an engraving of Rodney by V Green after a painting by Hugh Baron was published. In this portrait, Rodney appears holding a small-sword and standing in front of a scene representing the recent battle. The sword is naked and he seems to be using it to give directions. In detail, the guard of his sword is seen to be decorated with a radiating design remarkably similar both to that of the sword illustrated and to the one described above in Sim Comfort's collection.

After distinguishing himself under a succession of commanders, Rodney had left the Royal Navy following the Treaty of Paris which had ended the Seven Years War between Britain and Portugal against France and Spain on the 10 February 1763. Rodney then went to France to escape from his creditors and it is possible that interaction with his contemporaries from the French Navy led him to wear a small-sword in battle. However, it is difficult to believe that, in an age where fashions in weapons transcended national boundaries, there were no other high-ranking British officers who adopted this style.

The 1805 Patterns

Despite there being no uniform dress for ratings, a standard pattern of cutlass had been introduced in 1804 (see Chapter 2). Officers, however, had been given uniforms in 1748 which reflected the fashions of the times but made no provision for uniformity of swords. There was to be a 57-year delay before this matter was addressed. The Army had started to regularise its swords in the 1780s and had had a flurry of sword design activity at the end of the eighteenth and beginning of the nineteenth centuries. For example, 1796 saw the introduction of pattern swords for officers of the infantry, the light, and the heavy cavalry while in 1803 a new pattern for light company and grenadier company officers was promulgated. The RN must have been reluctant to fall too far behind the Army in regulating all items of dress and weaponry.

The original orders of 1805 promulgating these first naval patterns and the pattern swords themselves, which would have accompanied them, no longer exist but correspondence from the latter part of that year makes it clear that this is the crucial date. Two patterns were introduced at this time: an ornamented sword for officers of commander's rank and above, and a plain sword for lieutenants, and those officers who held warrants rather than commissions, including midshipmen and mates.

The ornamented sword

The ornamented sword for officers of commander's rank and above had a straight, single-edged blade of the spadroon form already seen with the five-ball sword. Although the spadroon is by far the commonest style of blade, swords will also be found

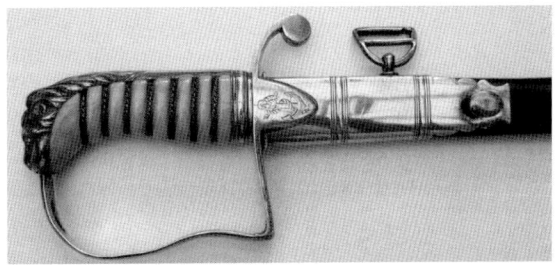

Details from an 1805 Pattern, Ornamented sword. Note it has a knuckle bow guard, a grip of white ivory and a pommel in the form of a lion's head. Note also the 'D' buckles, which are features of early swords of this type, later swords having the conventional loose rings.

1805 Pattern, Ornamented. This was the sword for officers of commander's rank and above.

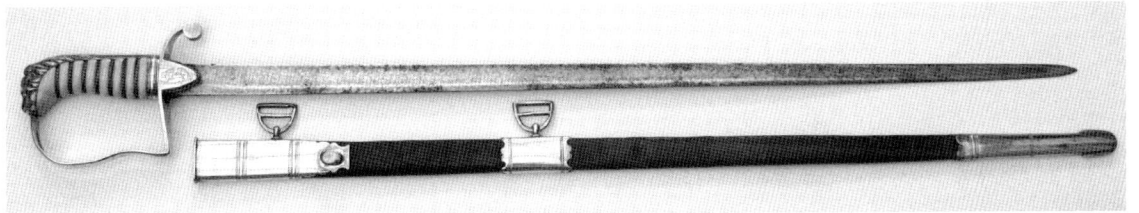

Above: A fine example of the blue and gilt that would originally have been on most 1805 Pattern swords. (Private Collection)

Below: Another example of an 1805 Pattern, Ornamented sword, this one with a double-edged blade. (Private Collection)

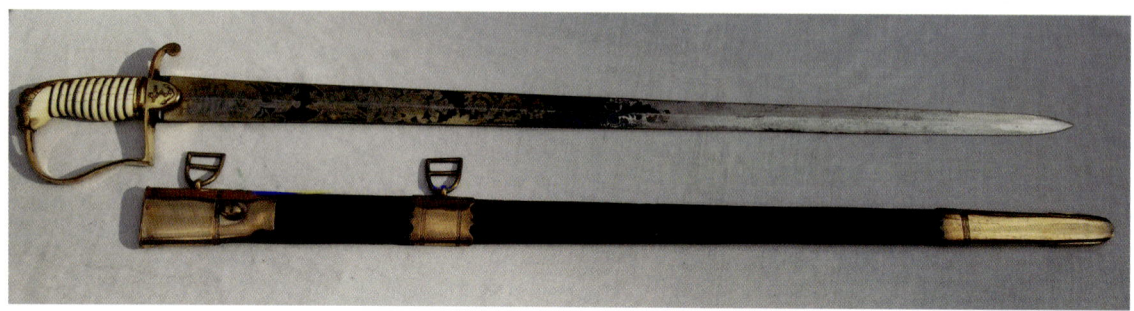

mounted with double-edged blades of flattened, hexagonal cross-section. The blade was usually decorated with emblems such as the Royal Cypher, the Royal Arms and naval trophies of arms. On many blades, this decoration was enhanced by gilding and often by blueing as well. However, it is not surprising that approximately two centuries of wear and tear have taken their toll on many fine blades and these are now, sadly, rubbed and corroded. The guard was of a simple stirrup form with langets displaying a fouled anchor, sometimes surmounted by a crown. Most of these swords had a slot for the sword knot close to the pommel but a few were fitted with a loose ring. The grip was made of white ivory, shaped to fit the hand and bound with gilt wires. The pommel, in the form of a lion's head, and the back piece were combined into a single component. In by far the majority of cases, the mane of the lion's head extends only a short distance down the back piece. Adjacent to the cross part of the guard, a gilt ferrule securing the grip and back piece together completed the hilt assembly.

The scabbard was black leather with three gilt mounts, the top two carrying loose rings for suspension from the familiar two slings of unequal length. On some early scabbards 'D' buckles take the place of the familiar rings, as in the sword illustrated. In designing this sword, it seems that the Admiralty selected certain characteristics from several patterns of Army sword. The blade came from the 1796 Infantry Pattern, the stirrup hilt and grip shaped to the hand from the 1796 Pattern

Sir George Cockburn in the undress uniform of a Rear Admiral in about 1817. He is shown holding an 1805, Ornamented sword with a beautifully blued and gilt blade. (Oil painting by John Halls © National Maritime Museum, Greenwich, London, BHC2619)

Straight stirrup hilt (left) and stirrup hilt (right). There is a debate about the significance of these two variants but, as there seems to be a continuum of style between the two extremes, the authors do not believe the difference to be important. The left hand image shows the hilt of the 1805 Pattern, Plain. This was the sword specified for lieutenants and warrant officers. It had a knuckle bow guard, a grip of black fish skin and a plain, stepped pommel.

Officers' Swords   41

Drawing of 'Light Cavalry Type Hilt'. These swords had curved blades mounted in a hilt very similar to that of the 1796 Pattern Light Cavalry sword. They can be distinguished by the inclusion of naval symbols in their decoration.

Light Cavalry Sword, and the lion's head pommel from the 1803 Grenadier and Light Infantry Sword.

There is an on-going debate about some features of these swords. It is sometimes maintained that the presence of a crown above the fouled anchor is indicative of a date after 1812 when this device was adopted for uniform buttons. However, this overlooks the fact that many earlier swords, especially of the five-ball type, bear the crown and fouled anchor in their decoration. It seems likely that the crowned and fouled anchor became more popular towards the end of the period 1805 to 1827 but its presence is an unreliable guide to dating. May and Annis distinguish between two forms of this hilt: the stirrup hilt and the straight stirrup hilt. They deduce that the latter was introduced when regulations were clarified with the publication of the first illustrated version of the dress regulations in 1825. However, there seems to be a continuum of shapes between these two extremes suggesting that both varieties and all the intermediates were in use throughout the lifespan of this pattern. Distinguishing between them seems to be more a feature of the desire of collectors to classify than of differences in regulation patterns.

The plain sword

The plain pattern for Lieutenants and below had a similar spadroon blade but this was not usually blued and gilt; its decoration being restricted to engraving of the conventional symbols of Royal Cypher, Royal Arms and naval trophies of arms. The guard was of the same stirrup form with langets embellished with a fouled anchor which is sometimes crowned. Instead of ivory, the wire-bound grip was covered with black fish skin. The combined back piece and pommel was much less elaborate consisting of a simply fluted back piece and a plain, rounded and stepped pommel. As with the ornamented sword, this component and the grip were secured together by a ferrule adjacent to the cross guard. Once again the scabbard was of black leather with three gilt mounts but these tended to be plainer than the equivalent mounts of the ornamented sword. In 1825, all commissioned officers were instructed to wear the ornamented sword leaving the plain sword for midshipmen and warrant officers.

Midshipman in 1823 wearing an 1805 Pattern sword. Despite the fact that young gentlemen went to sea at a very early age, they were not promoted to midshipman until they were in their late teens or even older. This suggests that very few needed especially small weapons. (Lithograph by F W Ommanney © National Maritime Museum, Greenwich, London, PW3721)

As always, individual officers came up with their own interpretations of the regulations, which seem mainly aimed at producing superior fighting weapons. A splendid example of this independence is a sword that once belonged to Lord Exmouth.[8] This is mounted with a broad 1⅝in (38mm), double-edged blade without a fuller. Perhaps this reflects the independence of thought and action which brought him to prominence as a frigate captain earlier in his career and enabled him to secure active appointments as an Admiral. Some officers had regulation hilts mounted on curved blades. Others opted for smooth back pieces and pommels which May and Annis refer to as the 'Light Cavalry Type Hilt'. Most of these curved swords are fitted with flat-backed blades but one in the Sim Comfort collection[9] is fitted with a pipe-backed blade (for a description of this type of blade see the section on the 1827 Pattern swords).

1805 Pattern, Plain, small version of the sword alongside a full-size sword. The differences in dimensions of these two versions of the weapon are quite clear. There is some debate about whether these were dress weapons or if they were those of young midshipmen.

Dress swords

With the introduction of uniformity in the swords worn by naval officers, the wearing of small-swords on dress occasions ceased. They were replaced by smaller versions of the regulation weapon, many of which were elaborately decorated. Such a dress version of the senior officers' weapon was sold by John Salter, Sword Cutler & Jeweller to HRH the Duke of Sussex, a tradesman working at 35 Strand, London, with whom Nelson also did business.[10] The polished and gilded blade is only 28¼in (718mm) long compared with about 32in (813mm) for a typical full-size sword and its overall length is 32¼in (820mm) compared with about 36½in (927mm). It has a very elaborate hilt. The ivory grip is beautifully knurled and secured near the cross guard with a ferrule decorated with the Greek key pattern. The knuckle bow of the stirrup guard is ornamented with a spiral design of leaves and berries, presumably laurel. The cross guard and langets are edged with foliage and the quillon terminates in foliate scroll. The design on the langets consists of a crown and fouled anchor, the latter having the stock set at an angle. A typical flattened lion's head acts as the pommel and the lion's mane extends some distance down the back piece. The three mounts on the black leather scabbard are also elaborately decorated. This is one of a series of fine weapons associated with this supplier.

There are two possible explanations for similar small-scale swords of the plain pattern. It is likely that many were the dress weapons of lieutenants, a view supported by the observation that many are of superior workmanship to the full-size swords. However, it has been pointed out that at this date midshipmen were instructed to wear swords of a size compatible with their height. This has led to the belief that most such small-scale swords belonged to midshipmen. It has been overlooked that, although aspiring officers went to sea at around the age of twelve, they would not have been rated as midshipmen until late in their teens by which time they would have been almost fully grown and not have needed a miniature sword.

Swords with black grips and lion's head pommels

A further complication is the hybrid sword with black grips and lion's head pommels that is generally accepted to have been unofficially adopted by lieutenants sometime between 1805 and 1825, at which later date the wearing of the decorated pattern was extended to them. This is sufficient explanation for those swords that have the crown and fouled anchor badge, where the presence of the crown argues strongly for attribution to the Royal Navy. However, those swords with just a fouled anchor could have equally well have belonged to a privateer or other officer in the merchant service, as will be illustrated in a later section.

Lieutenants were not the only officers to interpret the regulations loosely. The sword taken by Captain (later Rear Admiral Sir) William Parry in HMS *Hecla* on his voyages to find the North-West Passage, in the Museum of the Royal Navy, Portsmouth,[11] is an 1805 Pattern Plain sword with a loose ring for the cord of the sword knot and a crowned and fouled

1805 Pattern, Ornamented, dress sword by John Salter. This beautiful weapon by one of the principal sword cutlers of the day shows all the features expected in a dress weapon. It is lighter than a fighting sword, the guard and scabbard mounts are elaborately decorated and the chequering of the grip is very fine.

Sword with black grip and lion's head pommel with the grip made of horn. Such hybrid weapons are generally interpreted as those of lieutenants wishing to show their status as commissioned officers.

anchor on the langets. Parry was promoted to Lieutenant on 6 January 1810, supporting the viewpoint expressed above that the presence of a crown above the fouled anchor is not reliably diagnostic of a date after 1812. He clearly chose not to upgrade this sword on promotion to Commander on 4 November 1820, although he may well have had another weapon for more formal occasions.

The 1825 Pattern for the Civil Branches

The three civil branches were secretaries to admirals, pursers and medical officers. In 1805 physicians and surgeons became entitled to wear officer's uniform[12] and a letter dated 28 April 1805 includes the key sentence: 'All Medical Officers to wear the sword established for the Navy'.[13] Although this makes it clear that from then onwards medical officers were expected to wear regulation swords, it does not say whether these were to be the ornamented or the plain pattern.[14] All was to change in 1825 when the first illustrated dress regulations (as opposed to descriptions) were published. It included swords, sword knots and sword belts and a commercial copy also went on sale.[15] At this time it was decided that the civil branches, of which the medical branch was one, were to wear 'a small-sword, with plain brass handle with the appropriate device'. This anachronistic sword with its gilt brass hilt, flat oval shell, small *pas d'âne* rings and double quillons was a flash back to the late eighteenth century. It was, presumably, thought to reflect the roles of these officers better than a fighting sword and may also have been intended to emphasise the point that these officers had no executive authority. On some of these small-swords, the inner part of the shell guard is hinged to allow it to fit more closely to the side of the wearer.

The three branches were distinguished by the appropriate badge engraved on a tablet mounted on the grip. These badges were: for the Secretaries, a crowned and fouled anchor, the badge of the Navy Office; crossed fouled anchors for the Pursers, the badge of the Victualling Office and the Medical Branch had a snake entwined around an anchor, the badge of

the Sick and Hurt Office.[16] The sword illustrated has the crossed anchors of the Purser and was supplied by I (John) Symons of Devonport. The town of Plymouth Dock became Devonport in 1823 following a successful petition to King George IV and from that date to 1830 Symons was trading at number 74. This sword, therefore, dates from between 1825 and 1830. This pattern of sword was superseded in 1832.

The Solid, Half-basket Hilt with Pipe-backed Blade, 1827–1846

In 1822 the Army introduced a new pattern sword for infantry officers. It had a gilded, openwork, half-basket hilt in the Gothic style. Five years later, the RN took advantage of a major redesign of the uniforms of officers to follow suit. The style of hilt introduced with this change is still in use today. Unlike the infantry sword, the half-basket guard of the naval sword was solid with a crowned fouled anchor replacing the Royal Cypher in the cartouche. This may have been a response to the inadequacies of the brass, open-basket which was later to be described by John Latham as 'so flimsy as to be no protection for the hand and . . . made of bad metal badly tempered'.[17] The grip was white fish skin and the combined lion's head pommel and back piece was retained. The mane

RN officer's sword, 1827 Pattern.
a. This pattern had a hilt with a solid, half-basket guard in gilt metal, a grip of white fish skin and a pommel in the form of a lion's head. The blade was pipe backed. Except for the blade, the sword has changed little since.
b. The top locket with a hook for suspending the sword from a frog attached to a cross belt.
c. Characteristic tip of the pipe-backed blade showing the rib extending to the point and the false edge above it.

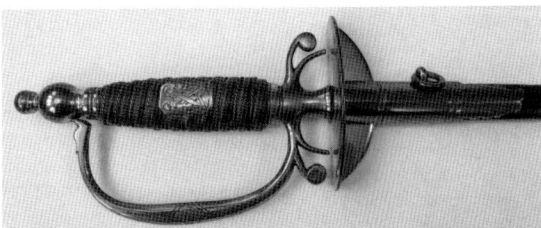

Small-sword of the civil branches, 1825–32, Purser's pattern. These throwbacks to the eighteenth century seem designed to emphasise that their wearers had no executive authority.

Badges of the civil branches. (a) Purser with crossed fouled anchors; (b) Secretary to an Admiral with a crowned, fouled anchor and (c) Surgeon with a snake entwined around anchor.

The ring fixed to the ferrule just inside the guard for the attachment of the sword knot is characteristic of early examples of 1827 Pattern swords.

As well as the blade, there were other differences from today's naval officer's sword. The scabbard had only two mounts as it was worn in a frog on a shoulder belt. The authors have seen an example of one of these in a collection attributed as belonging to Lord Collingwood. However, this great admiral, second in command at Trafalgar and administrator of the Mediterranean in the years following, died at sea on 7 March 1810 just one day into his voyage home to retirement, seventeen years before the introduction of this pattern of sword.

The sword knot had twelve individual bullions rather than the barrel shaped moulding used today and this new type of sword knot had an additional length of the cord inside the hilt. To accommodate this cord, early swords of this pattern were provided with a ring mounted on the ferrule on the inside of the grip. In later swords this feature is replaced by two holes from the lion's head pommel never seems to extend for more than a short distance down the back piece in these swords with their pipe-backed blades. This follows a design feature remarked upon as common in 1805 Pattern Ornamented swords. A ferrule adjacent to the inner surface of the guard secured the grip and back piece together. This sword was fitted with a type of blade which is described as pipe-backed, ramrod-backed or quill-backed by today's collectors. The features of this blade design are a rib running along the back of the blade all the way to the point and a characteristic flare of the blade as the point was approached to give a prominent back edge. This gives the blade a rather eel-like appearance. It was supposed to be an effective design for both cutting and thrusting but, although it was very stiff and a good thrusting weapon, it proved to be useless for cutting because the reinforcing rib along the back edge hindered effective penetration of clothing and flesh.

Right: John Lucas's painting of Captain Sir William Peel VC at the relief of Lucknow in 1858 clearly showing him using a pipe-backed sword. This is twelve years after the official pattern was changed. Captain Peel had already won his VC at the battle of Inkerman in the Crimea. When in command of HMS *Shannon*, he was diverted from his passage to the Far East to help deal with the Indian Mutiny. Landing at Calcutta, he formed an effective naval brigade of 450 men. He was severely wounded at the second relief of Lucknow, and died shortly afterward of smallpox contracted while being treated. (© National Maritime Museum, Greenwich, London, BHC2943).

Below: Two pipe-backed swords, one full size and the other rather smaller. The smaller of the two may have been either the sword of a midshipman or a lightweight dress sword.

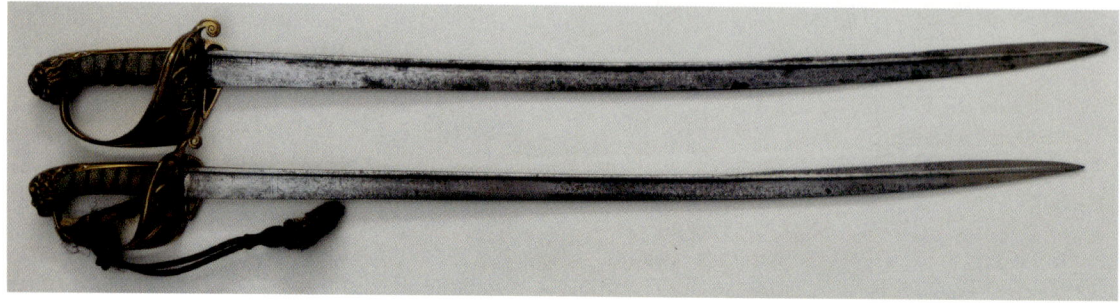

drilled through the guard just below the edge of the blade.

As usual with these early dress regulations, there were ambiguities. Midshipmen wore the 1827 Pattern with the white grip and lion's head pommel but it is uncertain whether masters, mates and warrant officers wore this sword but with a black fish skin grip and plain pommel. The ambiguity was resolved in 1832 when gunners, boatswains and carpenters were specifically ordered to wear the sword with the black grip and plain pommel with the blade not blued and gilt.[18] Also in 1832, the civil branches gave up their distinctive small swords and adopted the solid, half-basket hilted sword with the pipe-backed blade. It seems that 1832 was a key date as, in this year, the scabbard also returned to the familiar three mounts, with differences in decoration for flag officers, captains and commanders, and below.

Like its predecessor, the 1805 Pattern, this sword is found in both standard and small sizes. The lower specimen illustrated is a small version that may have been bought by a midshipman as, at that date, they were still wearing a sword rather than a dirk. However, an order of 18 December 1827,[19] restricting the wearing of dress swords to the drawing-room, makes it much more likely it was a light dress weapon equivalent to the small versions of the 1805 Patterns.

Good or bad, this sword was to be the naval officer's weapon in hand-to-hand combat for many years and there are several good paintings of them in action. The painting chosen is of the naval hero Captain William Peel during the Indian Mutiny, still using his pipe-backed sword twelve years after it had been superseded by the flat-backed pattern.

Sword with open half-basket guard and pipe-backed blade. Such weapons may have been manufactured before the regulations of 1827 were properly understood. (NMM WPN1150, Image E 1289)

Open Half-basket Hilts

Occasionally swords will be found fitted with an open half-basket hilt of the type introduced by the Army in 1822. There are several explanations offered for these; one is that they were made incorrectly before the regulations were properly understood. It was only in 1825 that the Admiralty introduced images for its uniforms rather than depositing a set of patterns at a naval base and, throughout this period, uniforms relied more often on the *Gentleman's Magazine of Fashions* than the Admiralty patterns. The sword of Captain George Bohun Martin in the National Maritime Museum[20] which was made by Lambert and Maclaurin, a company that went out of business in 1828 shortly after the introduction of the 1827 Pattern, is probably such a weapon. This sword also has a grip of knurled ivory, again suggesting that it was made before the change to white fish skin was properly understood. The design in the cartouche on the guard is unusual, consisting of a crowned and fouled anchor surrounded by a wreath of laurel. On swords with solid half-basket hilts, such a design is associated with a much later and unofficial flag officers' sword retailed by Gieves. However, Martin was promoted to Captain in 1828 by which time the regulations should have been well promulgated, so it seems equally possible that he was just making an individual choice of weapon.

Another sword in the same collection with an open half-basket guard[21] has a white fish skin grip and the badge in the cartouche is a fouled anchor. This hilt has been fitted to an earlier broad, curved blade. Perhaps significant is that on each of these swords the lion's head pommel is of the flattened form more usually associated with the 1805 Pattern rather than the more naturalistic form typical of the 1827 sword. Were the suppliers just selling swords made up using components to hand at the time?

A third sword with an open half basket hilt[22] has the black grip and the acanthus pommel used on Army swords. The black grip may suggest a junior officer and as this is a small weapon with a narrow blade it could be interpreted as the sword of a midshipman. However, 1827 was the date when the use of the white grip was extended to midshipmen. This could be a simple case of misinterpreting the rules but there are other possibilities to be considered. Perhaps they were worn by Royal Marines officers. This sword was the standard infantry weapon from 1822 to 1837 and, with a different blade, until 1892 and some officers may have chosen to have a fouled anchor in the cartouche rather than the Royal Cypher. Another possibility is that they were Coastguard swords with a fouled anchor replacing the letters *CG* in the cartouche. What is certain is that, whether they were accidental aberrations by the maker or examples of officers' individuality, they are interesting swords posing unresolved questions of interpretation.

The Mameluke-hilted Sword for Flag officers, 1842–1856

In 1831, the army introduced a completely new pattern of sword for general officers which was based on the eastern weapons that had become fashionable following the Egyptian campaign in the Napoleonic Wars. Again the Royal Navy was late in following this example and it was not until 1842 that a similar weapon was authorised for optional wear by flag officers. The main differences between the flag officers' pattern and that worn by general officers were the badge on the ecusson of the guard, which is a fouled anchor instead of crossed sword and baton, the terminals of the cross guard

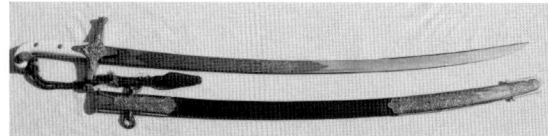

Mameluke-hilted sword for flag officers, 1842–56. (Private Collection)

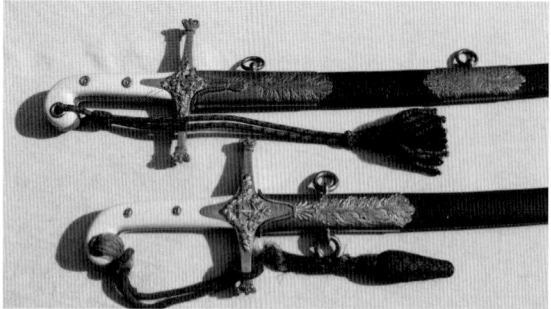

Above: Two Mameluke-hilted swords, the upper with the scabbard fastening that entered service in 1856. The swords knots are the two variants in use from 1827. (Private Collection)

Admiral of the Fleet Sir Charles Keppel wearing the Mameluke-hilted sword in 1896, some forty years after it had ceased to be a regulation weapon.

which are in the form of crowns rather than spheres. General officers had two different scabbards; a brass version for wear in the field and a black leather one with three gilt mounts for levee wear. The naval sword had just one scabbard of black leather with two elaborate gilt mounts.

It was, of course, a dress weapon and a flag officer would have maintained his ordinary uniform sword for less formal occasions and to wear in action. This may have accounted for the lack of popularity which saw it withdrawn in 1856. However, as late as 1896 Admiral of the Fleet Sir Charles Keppel, who did not reach flag rank until 1857 the year after they were withdrawn, was photographed wearing one.[23] This is an interesting weapon as its scabbard has three gilt mounts instead of the two which it had until 1856. This implies that not only did Keppel really want to wear one of these swords, but that he went to the trouble of having a scabbard specially made to conform to the dress regulations then current.

The Solid Half-basket Hilt with Flat-backed Blade, 1846 to the Present Day

The Army replaced the thoroughly unsatisfactory pipe-backed blade with the Wilkinson designed flat-backed blade in 1845 after twenty-three years' service[24] and the Royal Navy made the change a year later after suffering from this inadequate weapon for nineteen years. Today's swords remain substantially the same as those resulting from this change, differing in only minor details which will be discussed in due course. Also, the extent to which the mane extends down the back piece is now much more variable with some swords retaining the short mane of the pipe-backed sword, while on other specimens the mane extends for the full length of the back piece.

When this sword was introduced in 1846, the design of the scabbard with three gilt mounts with loose rings fitted to the mid- and top lockets for suspension from a sword belt with two unequal slings remained unchanged from its pipe-backed predecessor. Just one year later this changed with the scabbard now having only two mounts, a chape and a locket, the latter fitted with two loose rings, one either side, to suspend the sword vertically from two, short, equal slings. For all officers the locket was 4in (102mm) and the chape was 7½in (190mm) long. In the case of flag officers, the locket was decorated with acorns and the chape with oak leaves and honeysuckle. The scabbard mounts of all other officers were

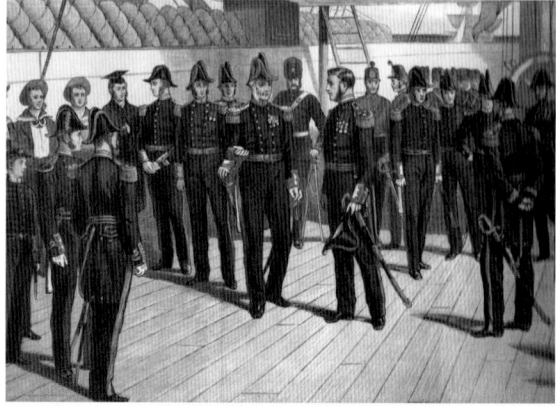

A gathering of officers showing the variety of sword belts in use around 1900 from the *Boy's Own Paper*.

Scabbards for Naval Officers' Swords, 1805 to the Present

Date	Ranks	Top locket	Mid-locket	Chape
1805	All officers	Loose ring/D buckle, lines	Loose ring/D buckle, lines	Lines
1825–32	Civil branches	Loose ring, lines	Loose ring, lines	Lines
1827	All officers (civil branches after 1832)	4in (102mm), frog hook, lines		6in (152mm), lines
1832	Flag officers	4in (102mm), loose ring, oak leaves, acorns	3½in (89mm), loose ring, oak leaves, acorns	7½in (191mm), oak leaves, acorns honeysuckle
	Captains	4in (102mm), loose ring, lines, flutes, volutes	3½in (89mm), loose ring, lines, flutes, volutes	6½in (165mm), lines, flutes, volutes
	Commanders and below	4in (102mm), loose ring, lines	3½in (89mm), loose ring, lines	6in (152mm), lines
1842–56	Flag officers, optional pattern	5¼in (133mm), two loose rings, V, shell, oak leaves, acorns		9in (230mm), shell, oak leaves, acorns two intertwined dolphins
1847	Flag officers	4in (102mm), two loose rings, oak leaves, acorns, volutes		7½in (191mm), oak leaves, honeysuckle, volutes
	Captains and below	4in (102mm), two loose rings, lines, flutes, volutes		7½in (191mm), lines, flutes, volutes, honeysuckle
1856	Flag officers (post-1960 this was reserved for Admirals of the Fleet and in 2003 this was extended to also include First Sea Lord)	4in (102mm), loose ring, oak leaves, acorns, volutes	3½in (89mm), loose ring, oak leaves, acorns, volutes	7½in (191mm), oak leaves, acorns, honeysuckle, volutes
	Captains and below	4in (102mm), loose ring, lines, flutes, volutes	3½in (89mm), loose ring, lines, flutes, volutes	6½in (165mm), lines, flutes, volutes, honeysuckle

decorated with fluted threads and scrolls. However, like many such regulations these minutiae of scabbard ornamentation were often ignored.

In 1856, there was a return to the two unequal slings and a 6in chape for all officers below flag rank. This year also saw the adoption of the dirk as the sidearm for the midshipman.

The table above details the changes in scabbard patterns from 1805 to the present day. These changes can sometimes be followed in the scabbard mountings of a sword, which were modified to conform to the latest dress regulations. For example, the pipe-backed sword started life sometime after 1832 when scabbards had three gilt mounts. In 1847, the design of the scabbard was changed to one with two gilt mounts, the top locket bearing two loose rings for suspension from two short equal slings. Rather than purchase a new scabbard for his sword, the owner had the top locket modified by the addition of an extra loose ring. This shows up both because the ring is of a different diameter from the two originals and because it is less expertly soldered into the locket. The sword with the flat-backed blade was converted the other

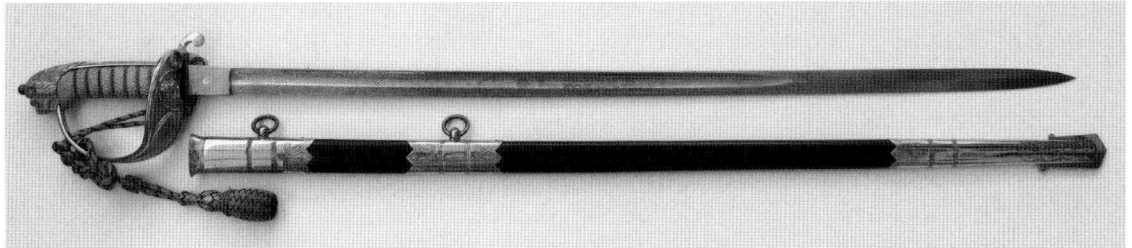

1846 Pattern sword with flat-backed blade. This wedge-shaped blade with broad shallow fullers on each face replaced the earlier unsatisfactory pipe-backed blade.

The top locket with two loose rings was introduced in 1847; this suspended the sword vertically beside the wearer.

way, having originally been provided with a scabbard with two rings on the top locket; the 1847 pattern. The new mid-locket and ring are good matches but the engraving on the mid-locket is rather coarser than on the original top locket. It was added to conform to the 1856 dress regulations.

Since 1832, the scabbards of flag officers' swords have been decorated with designs incorporating oak leaves and acorns. This scabbard went into abeyance at the outbreak of the Second World War, but after the war it was re-introduced for Admirals of the Fleet only.[25] Then in 2003 Admiral Sir Alan West (now Lord West of Spithead), who was Chief of the Naval Staff, sought and received permission for officers serving as First Sea Lord or Chief of the Defence Staff to wear the scabbard ornamented with the oak leaves.[26] Since then it has been extended and now also goes with the positions of Commander-in-Chief Fleet and the Second Sea Lord and also by the Defence Services Secretary if a Naval Officer holds that position. Currently, it is more economic to provide an entirely new scabbard than change the mounts and chape.[27]

Until about 1880, no precautions were taken to secure the sword in the scabbard but around that time, the familiar system with a peg on the top locket engaging with a hole on the turned down inner guard became common.[28] However, there is evidence that its introduction began rather earlier.[29] A possible transition stage to the full blown 'peg and hole' system is seen on a sword with an additional single hole in the upper part of the inner guard. This is positioned in such a way that it could not possibly have engaged with a peg on the top locket. It is surmised that the purpose was to secure the sword in the scabbard with a piece of thin twine passing through this hole and the upper loose ring. If the sword were needed, this could easily be broken by a sharp tug. It is unknown if this was a design feature introduced by the sword's manufacturer, Silver & Co, or was an idea of its original owner. Wilkinson supplied some swords where the weapon was not retained in the scabbard by a peg and hole but by a spring thumb catch like that found on the midshipman's dirk. This style of sword did not have a folding inner flap to the guard, but the catch passed through a hole in a solid guard.

As well as the sword with a white grip and lion's head pommel, the sword with the black grip and plain pommel was retained for warrant officers and masters-at-arms when the flat-backed blade was introduced. In 1918, warrant officers and chief warrant officers were given the same sword as commissioned officers leaving only the master-at-arms with the black grip and plain pommel. Warrant rank was abolished

a. The scabbard of this sword with a pipe-backed blade was originally made with three gilt mounts in accordance with the 1832 dress regulations. The top locket was later modified by the addition of a loose ring to the top locket to conform to the 1847 dress regulations. Note the larger diameter of the rod used to make the new ring and the soldering of the new boss to the socket.

b. The scabbard of this sword with a flat-backed blade was originally made to conform with the 1847 regulations with just two gilt mounts, the top locket and the chape. The top locket was fitted with two loose rings. It was later modified to match the 1856 dress regulations by the addition of a mid-locket with a loose ring. This new scabbard mount is of a different colour and the engraving is coarser. In particular, note that the small design on the central point of the locket, which is repeated on the chape, is missing from the newer mid-locket.

c. Flag officer's scabbard; the band of oak leaves and acorns decorating the top locket is repeated on the other two mounts.

d. The peg and hole method of securing the sword in the scabbard.

Officers' Swords 49

In this possible transition to the peg and hole system, a hole in the upper part of the folding inner guard is positioned so that the sword could be secured in the scabbard by a piece of thin twine passing through the hole and the loose ring on the top locket. This hole could never have engages with a peg on the locket.

A sword secured into its scabbard by a thumb catch in a manner identical to that used on many dirks.

Sword of master-at-arms, George V; note the black fish skin grip and the plain, stepped pommel.

Comparison of the St Edward crown (left) and the Tudor crown (right). The form taken by the St Edward crown is very variable.

in 1949, when warrant officers became branch officers, and re-introduced in 1970 with the creation of Fleet Chief Petty Officers (FCPOs). In 2004 the position of Charge Chief Artificer was made into the substantive rank of Warrant Officer Second Class (WO2), with previous warrant officers becoming Warrant Officers First Class (WO1). Only WO1s are mentioned in the regulations as carrying swords and, when required, the correct sword for the WO1 has the black grip with plain pommel and back-piece.[30]

Other changes have been small. The blade width was reduced to between ⅝in and ⅞in (16mm and 21mm) in 1929 and, finally, made straight in 1937. The crown changed from St Edward's to Tudor in 1901 and back again in 1952. Contrary to popular belief, these are not 'Queen's crown' and 'King's crown', as the choice of regnal crown is the monarch's. It will be interesting to see which crown will be chosen by the Prince of Wales when he ascends the throne. In recent years some suppliers have been manufacturing the blades of their swords from stainless steel rather than the traditional carbon steel. This will, no doubt, reduce the instances of corrosion on the blades but it remains to be seen if it will be a sufficient defence against the corrosive properties of wedding cake left on a blade after the cake-cutting ceremony.

It was not only the scabbard which changed over time but the other accoutrements of sword knot and sword belt also underwent changes. During the period 1800 to the present day there have been six different sword knots, which are listed in the table below and some of which are illustrated. Sometimes

Sword Knots from about 1800 to the Present Day

Date	Pattern
Ca 1800	Blue & gold ribbon, flat tassel embroidered with fouled anchor, fringe blue with gold bullions
Ca 1825, white hilt	Blue & gold ribbon, round tassel with embroidered fouled anchors, gold fringe with 17 bullions
Ca 1825, black hilt	As above but with blue silk tassel with a gold fringe (no bullions)
1827, white hilt	Blue & gold cord and knot, no anchors, fringe of 12 gold bullions
1827, black hilt	As above, gold fringe, no bullions
1891	Blue & gold cord with blue & gold barrel-shaped moulding

Some sword knots. Left to right: a hybrid between the 1825 and 1827 Patterns with the seventeen gold bullions of the former but, like the latter, lacking the anchors embroidered on the moulding; the 1827 Pattern with twelve gold bullions; a hybrid between the 1827 Pattern and the 1891 Pattern with the bullions fastened down to the barrel-shaped wooden core; and the 1891 Pattern with barrel-shaped wooden moulding covered with a woven design in blue and gold.

The two-part sword knot.

a hybrid version is found such as a knot with seventeen bullions but no embroidered anchors.

As well as these standard patterns there is a rarely-encountered design which is a transition between the 1827 and 1891 knots. In this knot, a large number of gold bullions are gathered together around a solid wooden core identical to that used in the 1891 pattern. The bottom of this knot is finished off with a coil of bullion material. A knot of this type is fitted to the hilt of the sword broken by Captain Arthur Knyvet Wilson at the battle of El Teb where he won the Victoria Cross in 1884.[31] However, this style of knot was persistent, as another is on the post-1901 sword of an RNR officer who was not commissioned until 1912.

Another style was adopted by some Flag Officers for wear with the Mameluke-hilted sword of 1842. This terminated in a moulding of the acorn form used on Army sword knots but in the naval colours of blue and gold. Examples of this can be seen on one of the swords illustrated and in the photograph of Admiral of the Fleet Sir Charles Keppel. Another Mameluke sword with this type of knot was sold at auction in 2012.[32] This form of sword knot was also used by the Royal Dockyard Battalion (see Chapter 5).

Since the 1827 Pattern sword, the cord of the knot has been made in two parts. The part with the knot itself is joined to the plain cord with a reef knot. The cord then passes through the slot in the guard near the pommel and through either a ring close to the inner surface of the guard (a feature of early swords with pipe-backed blades) or through two holes in the guard just below the cutting edge of the blade. The ends are then joined and the joint concealed with the Turk's Head slider. This design is unusual, it is certainly not found with Army or Royal Air Force swords and may, indeed, be unique to naval services. This extra length of cord inside the guard always looks a bit untidy and seems to serve no purpose that could not be achieved by a slightly longer main cord. The present authors assume that, at the date of its introduction, there must have been some logic behind this idiosyncratic design but they have been unable to discover it.

If the variety of scabbards and sword knots seems puzzling, then the bewilderment of sword belts will only deepen the confusion. These are outlined in the table opposite and some examples are illustrated.

Round slings from a sword belt of the 1856 Pattern.

An order promulgated in 1832 stated that the wide black leather shoulder belt, which had been worn beneath the waistcoat was to be replaced by a gold embroidered waist belt worn outside the coat, flag officers' belts to decorated with oak leaves and acorns, those of captains and commanders with three gold straight lines and those of lieutenants with two.[33]

Uniform Sword Belts, 1805–1939

Date	Rank	Order of Dress	Pattern
1805	All officers	All	Narrow black leather waist belt, S-hook connection, two unequal slings, sling buckles with lions' heads
	Senior	Dress	As above but with gold embroidery, an unofficial pattern
1825	Lieutenants & above	Full dress	1½in (38mm) white silk waist belt, two unequal slings, anchor on belt buckle anchors on sling buckles
		Undress	1½in (38mm) blue silk or black leather waist belt, two unequal slings, anchor on belt buckle, anchors on sling buckles
	Other officers	All	1½in (38mm) blue silk or black leather waist belt, two unequal slings, anchor on belt buckle, anchors on sling buckles
1827	All officers	All	2¼in black patent leather shoulder belt with frog.
1829	All officers	Frock coat	Black patent leather waist belt with frog. An addition to the 1827 pattern.
1832	Flag officers	Full dress	1½in (38mm) black leather waist belt embroidered with gold oak leaves and acorns, two unequal slings
	Captains and commanders	Full dress	1½in (38mm) black leather waist belt embroidered with three gold lines, two unequal slings
	Lieutenants	Full dress	1½in (38mm) black leather waist belt embroidered with two gold lines, two unequal slings
	All officers	Undress	1½in (38mm) black leather waist belt, two unequal slings
	Warrant officers	All	1½in (38mm) black leather waist belt, two unequal slings
1847	Flag officers	Full dress	1¾in (44mm) black leather waist belt embroidered with gold oak leaves and acorns, two equal 7in (179mm) slings
	Captains and commanders	Full dress	1¾in (44mm) black leather waist belt embroidered with three gold lines, two equal 7in (179mm) slings
	Lieutenants	Full dress	1¾in (44mm) black leather waist belt embroidered with two gold lines, two equal 7in (179mm) slings
	All officers	Undress	1¾in (44mm) black leather waist belt, two equal 7in (179mm) slings
	Warrant officers	All	1¾in (44mm) black leather waist belt, two equal 7in (179mm) slings
1856	Flag officers	Full dress	1½in (38mm) black leather waist belt embroidered with gold oak leaves and acorns, two unequal round slings
	Captains and commanders	Full dress	1½in (38mm) leather waist belt embroidered with three gold lines, two unequal round slings
	Lieutenants	Full dress	1½in (38mm) black leather embroidered with two gold lines, two unequal round slings
	All officers	Undress	1½in (38mm) black leather waist belt, two unequal round slings
	Warrant officers	All	1½in (38mm) black leather waist belt, two unequal round slings
1891			As for 1856 but with flat instead of round slings

This change in the belts led to the changes in the fittings of the sword scabbards.[34] A year later, in 1833 the gold-embroidered morocco leather of the flag officers sword belt was changed from black to blue. The buckles of belts after 1847 all have a crown and anchor motif and the style of crown changes from St Edward's to Tudor depending on the Sovereign's choice of regnal crown.

With the outbreak of the Second World War, swords were put into abeyance and with their re-introduction after the end of the war came some changes. The undress belt was the first to return worn underneath the uniform reefer jacket. The frock coat was never re-introduced and so this belt is never seen worn outside the coat. Admirals of the Fleet were permitted to wear the belt embroidered with oak leaves and acorns with full dress uniform, while other Flag Officers were to wear the belt with three gold lines of embroidery.[35] The rank of Admiral of the Fleet was put into abeyance in 1996, seemingly leading to the gradual disappearance of the oak leaf belt until its reintro-

Sword belts of the 1891 Pattern:

a. The full dress belt embroidered with oak leaves and acorns between two gold lines. Also note the elaborate two-part, circular waist buckle and the ornate buckles on the sword slings. The St Edward crown on the waist buckle indicates that this is a Victorian sword belt. This belt originally conformed to the 1847 Pattern with two, equal, short slings. It was later modified by lengthening the after sling with a strap of plain leather. The construction of the belt in three parts seems to have been confined to the 1847 Pattern, later belts being in one piece.

b. The full dress belt embroidered with three gold lines. Despite having the pre-1952 Tudor crown on the buckle, this belt belonged to Rear Admiral Sir R J Trowbridge, KCVO (1920–2003) who was not promoted to flag rank until 1970, illustrating how such expensive items of uniform are passed down among officers.

c. The full dress belt with embroidered with two gold lines.

d. The plain black undress belt.

duction in 2003 for officers serving as First Sea Lord or Chief of the Defence Staff.

From 1846 to 1856, midshipmen continued to wear swords not dirks but few, if any, miniature versions of the sword with the 1846 blade exist. This reinforces the view that such swords were dress weapons rather than those of midshipmen. Fashion seemed to have changed at about the time of the introduction of the flat-backed blade and officers requiring a lightweight dress sword favoured weapons that were the same length as the 'fighting' weapon but with a narrower blade and a hilt in proportion. This resulted in a light-weight weapon sometimes referred to as a 'levee sword' by collectors. With the 1929 regulations on blade width, all swords became dress or levee swords.

Variations from the Regulations

Officers have always treated the regulations governing swords as guidance rather than prescription and, as a result, they have often been liberally interpreted. Indeed John Nicol describes how officers took advantage of being in Canada in 1776 to have scabbards made of snake skin.[36] Between about 1870 and 1880, a few officers chose to wear swords with non-uniform blades, such as those mounted with straight, double-edged,

Comparison of full-size (fighting) sword and lightweight (levee) sword. The fashion for lighter weight swords continued with a weapon having a narrower blade and hilt in proportion. The weight difference was considerable. Two swords, one made in 1918 and the other two years later, illustrate this. The full size sword weighs 2lb 11oz (1219g) in the scabbard and 2lb 1oz (936g) by itself. In contrast, the levee sword weighs just 1lb 15oz (879g) with its scabbard and 1lb 7oz (652g) alone.

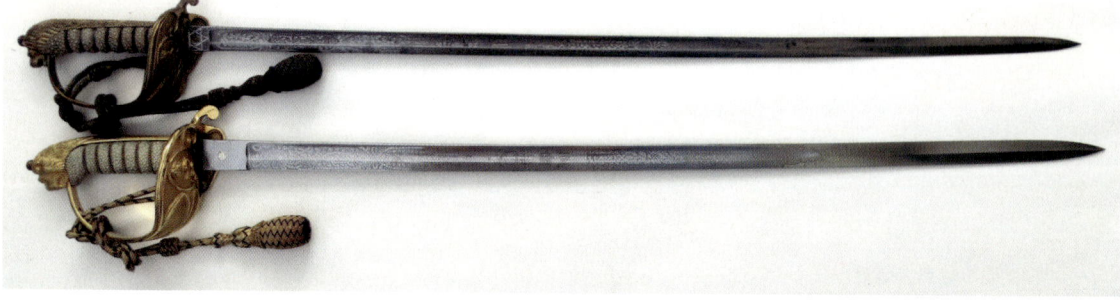

Chinese officer wearing a sword described in Keyes's letters.

Another instance of non-conformity to regulations, this sword on the right has a grip covered in white leather. It is compared with a sword having the uniform grip covering of white fish skin which would give a much more positive hold.

broadsword blades with two narrow fullers on each face, similar to those fitted to the broadswords carried by officers of Highland regiments. It is possible that these were chosen by Scottish officers. Another uncommon blade is the Toledo type with a rectangular section for about half its length from the hilt, changing to a spear point. There is also a hybrid blade which has a pipe-backed point on a flat-backed type of blade. Occasionally a blade with a flattened oval cross-section, similar to those used on some court swords, was used. Flag officers also took liberties and purchased swords supplied by Gieves where the crowned and fouled anchor in the cartouche was surrounded by a laurel wreath. Sometimes the fish skin grip is replaced by another material such as white leather or, even, white painted canvas.

Two swords illustrated in this book, those of a master-at-arms and an RNR officer, were sold by Royal Navy officers on their retirements. They had worn them throughout their careers without attention ever having been drawn to their inappropriateness. Another wore a sword of the Chinese Maritime Customs, which had belonged to his grandfather who had served in that body, throughout his naval service.[37] He was in good company because Admiral of the Fleet Sir Roger Keyes commented on a Chinese officer who had been executed by the Boxers:

> So I kept his full-dress sword (made by Wilkinson of Pall Mall), which was just like ours, except that that it had an Imperial Dragon instead of a lion's head on the hilt, and was engraved with a dragon entwined round an anchor on the blade. I have worn the sword ever since.[38]

Yet another officer wore an East India Company sword. At a wedding in the late 1990s, a member of the guard of honour, a female officer, was wearing a sword of the United States Navy with which she had been presented on completion of an exchange job in the States.

Below: Some officers asserted their individuality by having their swords mounted with non-uniform blades. Among these the straight broadsword blade with its double edge and two narrow fullers along each face was popular.

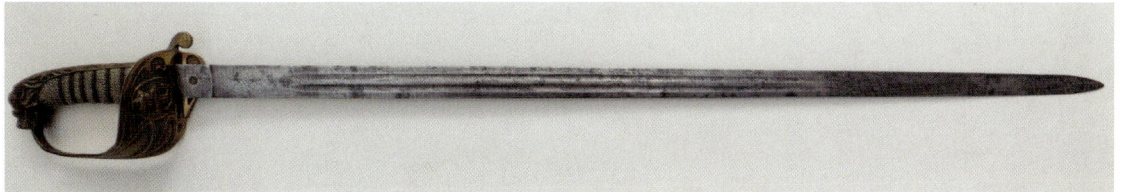

Officers of the Royal Navy have always treated the regulations governing swords in a cavalier manner; it is only collectors who worry about the minutiae. Just because a sword appears to be earlier than a name engraved upon it does not mean that the naming is incorrect. The officer may well have personalised a second-hand sword. Nowadays, even some presentation swords with their very specific inscriptions are refurbished second-hand weapons. Anyway, such irregularities are one of the attractions of collecting.

The Irish Naval Service

At the outbreak of the Second World War, the Irish Marine Service and Maritime Inscription were formed. These evolved into the Irish Naval Service, a constituent formation of the Irish Defence Forces, in 1947. However, having roots and traditions drawn from the Royal Navy, it was not until 1973 that it adopted the use of a ceremonial sword in line with the other two services. This was at the behest of the Flag Officer Commanding the Naval Service, Commodore McKenna, who also oversaw the introduction of current rank insignia and uniforms. The sword introduced was a completely new design.[39] Details of this weapon were first promulgated in the *Defence Force Magazine*.[40] Unlike most naval services which had at one time been under British influence, this sword with its canted pommel and pommel cap was decidedly American in design, a style which in its turn owes much to nineteenth-century Continental European styles. The gilt metal guard is of half-basket form with an ornamented quillon and the badge of the Irish Defence Force displayed in the centre of the guard, surrounded by a pierced design of oak leaves and acorns. The same badge appears on the pommel cap. The white fish skin grip is bound with gilt wire. So far, nothing would indicate that this is a naval weapon but this aspect is covered by the presence of a fouled anchor in the etched decoration of the blade. In another divergence from British practice, the sword knot consists of a flat tape of gold and silver lace terminating in a flat bullion tassel formed around a navy blue core. The scabbard is of black leather with three gilt metal mounts. Raised bands simulating 'Figure of Eight' knots supply the attachments for the loose rings fitted to the top and mid lockets and indicate the naval character of the sword as does the sea serpent decoration to the drag. The black leather sword belt is fitted with two unequal slings and fastens with a gilt metal buckle bearing the Army badge. The belt is fitted with a hook adjacent to the forward sling. As well as serving to hitch up the scabbard when the sword is drawn, this is an important fitting as the members of the Irish Naval Service wear their swords on the hip via a slit in the reefer jacket. The hilt faces forward on ceremonial occasions and aft on liaison or other informal duties.[41]

At the time of its introduction, there were only about thirty officers in the Irish Naval Service. Ten swords were ordered by the Naval Service and three were privately purchased. They were all manufactured by Joseph Starkey of London and supplied by Gieves, who also supplied the belts and fittings. All ten of the official swords are still held by the Naval Service and just one of the three privately-purchased swords has appeared on the open market; this formerly belonged to Commodore McKenna.[42] Only one other sword has appeared for sale. As the sale of Irish military uniform items or accoutrements on the open market is strictly prohibited, an investigation took place which determined that, although the sword offered resembled the official pattern, it was in fact made up of parts purchased privately on closure of Wilkinson's Sword manufacturing facility in 2005.

Since the initial purchase, the Irish Naval Service has moved to using a pattern closely resembling the standard Royal Navy sword but without the lion's head pommel. This was necessitated in the first instance by the closure first of Starkey and then of the Wilkinson's facility in 2005 and the sale of tooling and most residual parts to WKC Stahl- und Metallwarenfabrik of Solingen. The current pattern of scabbard supplied is identical to the RN pattern.

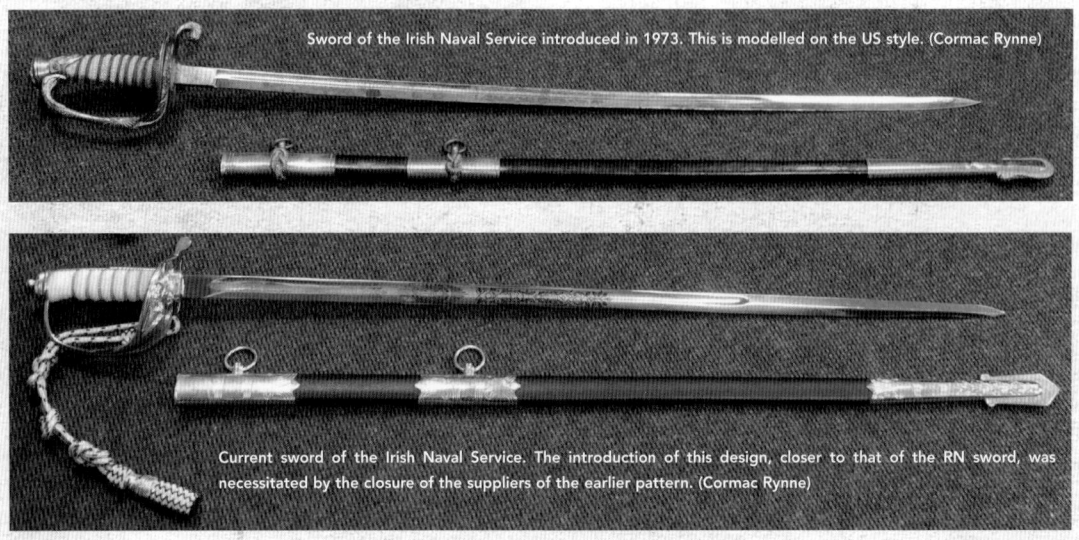

Sword of the Irish Naval Service introduced in 1973. This is modelled on the US style. (Cormac Rynne)

Current sword of the Irish Naval Service. The introduction of this design, closer to that of the RN sword, was necessitated by the closure of the suppliers of the earlier pattern. (Cormac Rynne)

CHAPTER 4

Dirks

In addition to the well-known use of the term dirk for a short Scottish weapon, the *Oxford English Dictionary* gives its meaning as 'a small sword or dagger formerly worn by junior naval officers on duty'.[1] It offers no etymology for this common word. As will be shown below, the definition is rather restrictive in its scope with the naval dirk being used at different times in its history by officers of all ranks and for a range of functions.

Early Days

The theory that dirks, both curved and straight, originated in the hangers and hunting swords popular during the earlier part of the eighteenth century has already been mentioned, so this account can begin in the latter part of that century. Dirks came in a great range of designs and sizes reflecting the uses to which these items could be put. The very small ones were simply items of cutlery used at the table or as the basic working tools of a seaman. Larger and more elaborate dirks could well have served these same purposes but also acted as an indication of an officer's status. It must have been far more convenient to wear a dirk than a sword for much of the time. Then there are very substantial weapons, 18in (457mm) or more long, which could well have been used in action. Some dirks have decorative elements which clearly point to their naval provenance but others lack these. Although often described as naval by both auction houses and dealers, they need to be treated with some caution as dirks were also worn by army officers and the possibility that they were owned by officers in the merchant service should not be overlooked. Even the country of origin of many of these weapons is uncertain. Also, these same sources often ascribe such dirks to midshipmen. They may well have been owned by such gentlemen but it is equally probable that they were the possessions of commissioned or warrant officers. There were no dress regulations so how could one know? Senior officers certainly wore and had their portraits painted wearing dirks, as the portrait of Vice Admiral George Darby painted by George Romney between 1783 and 1786 makes clear. From the other perspective we have the young Alexander Hood, aged 14, writing to his father Samuel Hood in 1772 and specifying a sword when ordering his uniform.[2] That they were viewed as badges of rank is made clear by the description of the funeral service for Lieutenant Lawry in 1794. At this service 'his uniform hat, his sword and dirk' were placed on the coffin.[3] The difficulties of both identifying and dating naval dirks were mentioned by May and Annis[4] and the problems have certainly not got any fewer in the intervening years. As naval dirks from this period are desirable, expensive items, it pays to be alert to the background of these weapons. Unless there are definite indications of naval provenance in the form of maritime symbols, such as Neptune, anchors or masts of ships, all such weapons are best treated with suspicion. Just as with swords, this lack of regulation engendered countless designs and from these the authors have tried to select some of the more typical.

Vice Admiral George Darby by George Romney, 1783–6, showing him wearing a dirk. (© National Maritime Museum, Greenwich, London, BHC2643)

From the series following the adventures of Mr Blockhead, here fitting out prior to joining his first ship and playing with his dirk. (© National Maritime Museum, Greenwich, London, PAD4721)

It is important to recognise the dates which are important in the study of dirks. Until 1805, there were no regulations but those introduced in that year and the subsequent set in 1825, both made it clear that the uniform weapon of the midshipman was a sword. Although this may seem surprising, it is important to realise that midshipmen were not the young boys of fiction. For example in HMS *London* in 1791, the youngest midshipman was 18 years old and the oldest was 47 and their average age was 23½ years.[5] Given these statistics, even the idea that small versions of the 1805 Pattern Plain sword were necessarily owned by midshipmen is questionable. The 1825 regulations state that midshipmen in consideration of their height will have a sword 'of such a length as may be convenient'.[6] Between 1827 and 1846 dirks were the uniform weapons of Volunteers 1st and 2nd Class but there were no uniform designs for these dirks. With the 1856 dress regulations, the dirk became the midshipman's weapon and a uniform pattern was specified.

Despite the clear evidence provided by portraits of the Napoleonic period that dirks were worn by senior officers, the misconception that they were the weapons of midshipmen clearly dates from an early period. The author C G Sloane-Stanley describes how, when his father was outfitting him in 1850 as a midshipman, they had expected to buy a dirk and were surprised to be told that midshipmen wore swords.[7]

The routes by which young men seeking to become officers in the Royal Navy have joined the service have changed with time and could well have contributed to confusion of just who did or did not wear a dirk. From Pepys's time, to become a midshipman required two years' service at sea and this service could not begin until the age of 13 except in the case of the sons of naval officers in which case it was 11. However, these rules were often bent and only started to decline following the court martial of Captain Isaac Coffin in 1788 for 'knowingly signing a false register'[8] which eventually led to the tightening of regulations. An order in council of 16 April 1794 started the process of regularising officer entry with the introduction of Volunteers 1st and 2nd Class with Class 1 to 'consist of young gentlemen intended for sea service'.[9]

That these volunteers wore dirks is made very clear in the memoirs of Captain Frederick Chamier. He tells how, when aged 12 and having been kitted out for sea, he went to his school for a final time and that 'my cocked hat was fitted on every head; my dirk was withdrawn and sheathed while I paraded about'.[10] As he was preparing to join in the Autumn of 1793 Captain Frederick Hoffman recalls, that his friends who came to say goodbye envied his finery and in particular

Dirk, ca 1790, with a single-edged blade with a narrow fuller running close to the back edge.

Close-up of the cushion-shaped pommel and reeded ivory grip with a 'cigar band' with a crowned and fouled anchor in the cartouche which are very similar to those found on contemporary five-ball swords.

Dirk, ca 1790. This is a type sometimes referred to by collectors as a 'propeller' dirk. It has a narrow two-edged blade with a central fuller which still retains some traces of the original gilding.

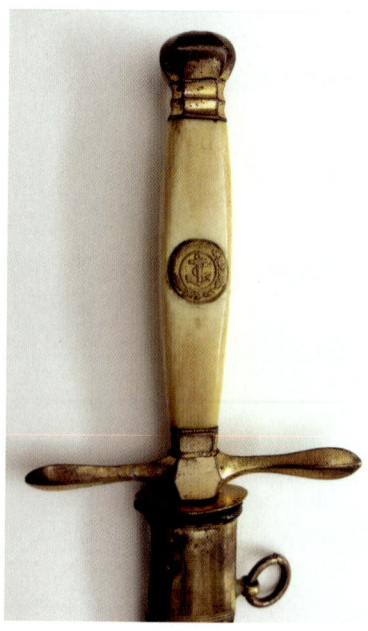

The contemporary uniform button inset into the ivory grip leaves no doubt that this is a naval weapon. Note the metal plate acting as a cover to the mouth of the scabbard.

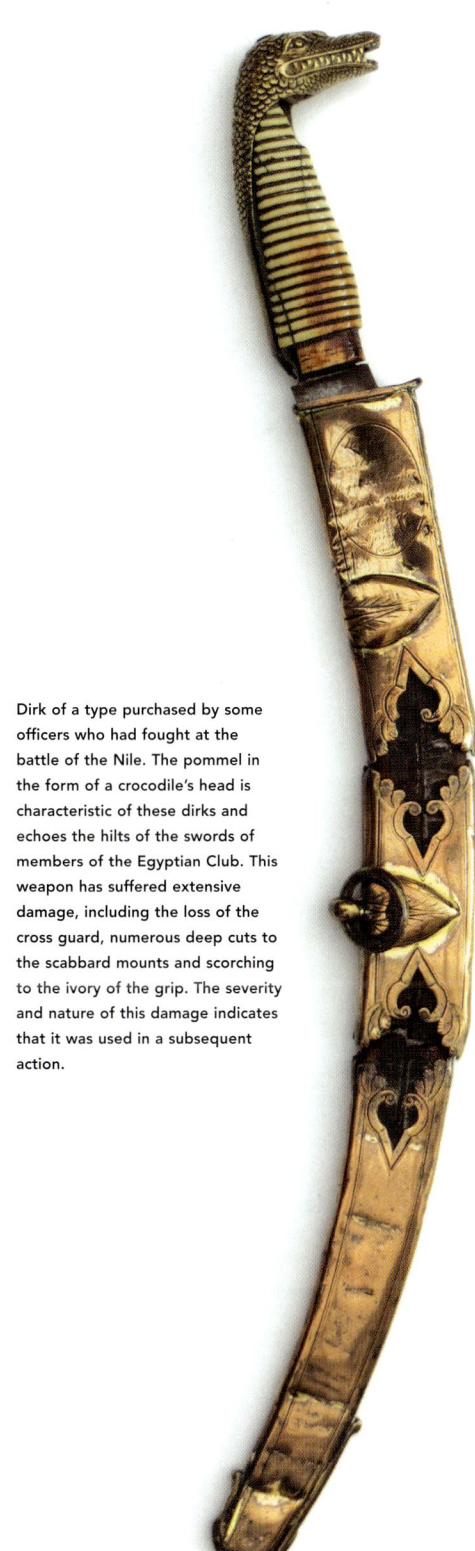

Dirk of a type purchased by some officers who had fought at the battle of the Nile. The pommel in the form of a crocodile's head is characteristic of these dirks and echoes the hilts of the swords of members of the Egyptian Club. This weapon has suffered extensive damage, including the loss of the cross guard, numerous deep cuts to the scabbard mounts and scorching to the ivory of the grip. The severity and nature of this damage indicates that it was used in a subsequent action.

'my dirk, which they examined so often that I began to think they would wear it out'.[11] Admiral Jervis, Lord St Vincent, recorded a similar tale in that when he went to be introduced to the Captain who was to allow him to start his time at sea that he was dressed with a 'dirk and gold-laced hat'.[12]

Hoffman also records the experience of one of the Young Gentlemen purchasing a new dirk after he lost his overboard then meets the Rear Admiral in the dockyard. Since the youngster does not have the money to provide a replacement, the Admiral Sir Isaac Montague offers to not only provide directions to the sword cutler but also provides a letter to guarantee the payment. When asked what type of dirk he wants, the youngster replies 'a good one . . . one at about forty shillings'.[13] Unfortunately for the Admiral, the youngster is sent abroad prior to being able to pay and thus the Admiral ends up with the bill.

During the later years of the Victorian period and into the twentieth century, officers entered as cadets and when they became midshipmen wore the dirk established in 1856. It is from this period that the universal association of midshipmen with dirks seems to date; an association reinforced in by fiction and film. It is clear that the first time of acquiring a dirk as part of the uniform was highly symbolic. Lieutenant Commander Fairbairn in his biography from his service from 1907 to 1924[14] describes with pride how when he joins his first ship in 1912 as a Midshipman he is no longer at BRNC that he can now wear a dirk. He makes a similar reflection on his promotion to Acting Sub-Lieutenant and his receiving his commission and therefore the right to wear a sword.

In this period before regulation, many dirks closely followed the styles of contemporary swords. The example illustrated with its single-edged, 15¾in (400mm) long blade is typical of this type. It has a reeded ivory grip of flattened octagonal cross section with a gilt brass band around the centre bearing an oval cartouche engraved with a crowned and fouled anchor pointing to its naval origin. This grip and the octagonal, cushion-shaped pommel are clearly related to the same components of a five-ball sword. In this case the guard is shaped as a flat, elongated oval but other dirks of this type have a five-balled side loop to the guard.

Another dirk has a 14¼in (362mm) straight blade of the more typical flattened elliptical cross section with a central fuller. There are traces of engraving and gilding still remaining. The shape of the cross guard of this weapon leads to its popular description as a 'propeller'-type dirk. Like the previous example, there is no doubt about its naval provenance, in this case proclaimed by the contemporary naval button set into the ivory of the grip. Complete with its leather scabbard with three gilt mounts, this an excellent example of a genuine naval dirk. It is worth remarking that the scabbard mounts were designed for the dirk to hang from the belt like a sword. This would have made it very easy for the owner to unclip his sword and clip on a dirk in exchange or *vice versa*.

On the night of 1 August 1798 and the following morning, a squadron of British ships commanded by Rear Admiral Sir Horatio Nelson fought the French fleet under Vice Admiral François-Paul Brueys d'Aigalliers in the Bay of Aboukir a few miles from Alexandria in Egypt. This is now known as the battle of the Nile. To mark this success Nelson's agent, Alexander Davison, had a medal struck and the surviving captains formed The Egyptian Club and subscribed to buy Nelson a sword with a gold hilt formed in the likeness of a crocodile. Other captain present at the battle had copies of this sword made with hilts of gilded base metal. However, many other officers not eligible for membership of this exclusive club felt that they would also like to mark their participation in this action. They achieved this by purchasing dirks with hilts incorporating the crocodile motif associated with the battle. The dirk illustrated is one of these. The common feature of these dirks was a pommel in the form of a crocodile's head. In some example the cross guard also incorporated a crocodile in its design[15] while other specimens had simple recurved quillons. This cross guard is missing from the weapon illustrated, so it is impossible to know its exact form. The knuckle guard was almost certainly a chain. The blade measures 14¼in (362mm) around the outside of the curve and is a substantial 1⅛in (29mm) wide at the shoulder. Some of these dirks have blades decorated by bluing and gilding but, like many others, this blade shows no signs of ever having been decorated but has definitely been sharpened. It retains its badly damaged leather scabbard with three elaborate gilt mounts. In an oval cartouche on the top locket is the name and address of the supplier:

Reddell
Sword Cutler to their
Royal Highnesses
The Dukes of Sussex
& Cambridge
138 Jermym St
London

This was clearly an item purchased from a prestigious sword cutler.

Uniform Dirks

In the absence of a prescribed pattern for the dirk which was the uniform weapon of Volunteers between 1827 and 1846, it is necessary to rely on pictorial evidence. The engraving of a Volunteer 1st Class shows a curved dirk but other pictures show a straight dirk. It is, of course, possible that a young man would just choose whatever he fancied or the naval tailor persuaded him to buy. Unless some new evidence comes to light, this question must remain unresolved.

Once 1856 is reached and the dirk becomes the uniform weapon of the midshipman, the picture becomes much clearer. There is no known pattern weapon, so the details of the design can only be deduced from surviving examples. It had a straight blade about 13½in (340mm) long and 1⅛in (29mm) wide and simple recurved quillons terminating in acorns. Like the uniform sword, the grip was made of white fish skin and the

Volunteer 1st Class wearing a curved dirk. (Detail from a lithograph published November 1828 by Engleman, Graf, Coindet, & Co, © National Maritime Museum, Greenwich, London, PAF4198)

pommel was in the form of a lion's head. The dirk was carried in a black leather scabbard with two gilt mounts, the upper of which carried a frog stud. There is a rarely encountered variant of this dirk with a shorter (12¼in, 310mm) and broader (1⅜in, 35mm) blade which is decorated with etched designs.[16]

In 1879 the dirk blade was lengthened to 17¾in (451mm) and was blued and gilt. It also acquired the oval medallion incorporating a crowned and fouled anchor in the centre of a laurel wreath which decorates the cross piece. The locket of the scabbard no longer had a frog stud but two loose rings, so that the dirk could be suspended from two short slings attached to the waist belt. The regulations were re-issued in 1891 with a few clarifications and it is after this date that the decoration on the blades is etched rather than blued and gilt. This matched the decoration on contemporary swords. This new variety of dirk also had a mechanism for securing the weapon in its scabbard, reflecting the adoption of such an added security feature by swords at about the same date. Early versions of this dirk have a spring clip operated by a button on the reverse side of the grip but before 1900 this had changed to a thumb catch passing through the upper quillon.

The illustration clearly shows that after 1891 the dirk knot was essentially a miniature version of the contemporary sword knot. The waist belt for the dirk was similar to that for the sword but slightly narrower at 1¼in (32mm) and with two 9in (229mm) long slings which are ¾in (19mm) wide.

The association with midshipmen was probably reinforced by the custom at HMS *Britannia* and subsequently at the Royal Naval College, Dartmouth, of awarding dirks to some of the

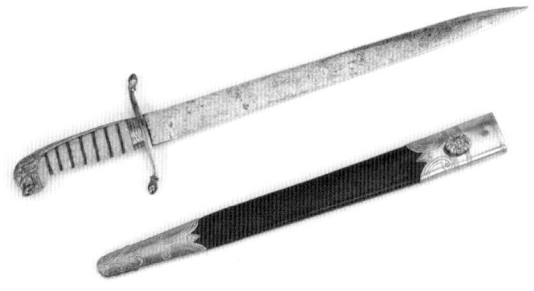

Dirk believed on the evidence of surviving examples to be the 1856 Pattern. This has a frog stud for wear with a cross belt. (NMM WPN1152, Image E1192)

Dirks 59

Dirk of post-1879 Pattern. This example dates from the reign of George V and has the etched blade which became the standard form after 1891. The owner of this dirk was a Midshipman in HMS *Superb* during the battle of Jutland.

Cadets as prizes. In the *Britannia*, from at least 1867, the two Chief Cadet Captains in each term were recipients of these dirks. After naval education was reformed in the early 1900s, the period in the training cruisers was also reflected in the award of dirks which were inscribed with the name of either *Cornwall* or *Cumberland*, the training ships. In 1923 the King took over the presentation of these dirks from the Admiralty and the inscriptions on them reflect this change. These presentations ceased in 1942.

The dirk illustrated, awarded by King George V in 1934 to Chief Cadet Captain John Brackenbury, is identical to the uniform weapon except for the Royal coat-of-arms in silver on the outer face of the top locket and the inscription on the blade. Brackenbury was born on 28 January 1917 and qualified as a submariner, later becoming an anti-submarine officer. He retired from the Royal Navy on 1 October 1947 in the rank of Lieutenant Commander.

The dirk was put into abeyance at the outbreak of the Second World War and has never been re-introduced.

Dirk belt. Note the two 9in (229mm) slings from which the dirk hung vertically by the wearer's side.

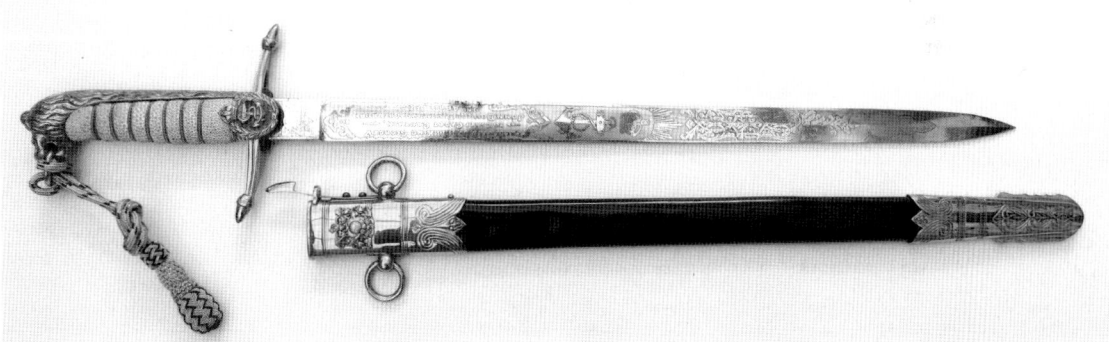

Above: Dirk awarded by King George V to Chief Cadet Captain John Boileau Fabian Brackenbury on 2 April 1934. The Royal Coat of Arms in silver on the outer face of the locket indicates the status of this weapon as a Royal presentation dirk.

Below: Inscription on the blade of the dirk. Brackenbury trained as a submariner and later became an anti-submarine officer. He was awarded the MBE for his services in the Arctic convoys and retired from the RN in 1947 in the rank of Lieutenant Commander.

CHAPTER 5

Swords of Officers of the Reserves, the Merchant Navy and Other Maritime Organisations

Over the centuries, many arrangements have been made to increase the size of the fighting fleet in times of danger. Once a permanent Royal Navy had become established and as the design of warships increasingly diverged from that of merchant ships, it was no longer possible to rely on seamen plucked from their peacetime employment to fulfil this role. This created a niche for reserves trained in the necessary skills and whose finance and training were under the control of the Royal Navy. The section which follows takes these reserve forces in chronological order of establishment.

The Sea and River Fencibles

Among the earliest naval reserves were the bodies of men known as the Fencibles, who were originally raised in 1798 as the threat of French invasion grew. Disbanded after the Peace of Amiens (1802), they were rapidly reformed in 1803 at which date the River Fencibles were also established. Other volunteer units were also formed at this date including the Trinity House Artillery Volunteers, with William Pitt as Colonel, and the Harbour Volunteer Marines. These units were all disbanded by the end of the Napoleonic Wars. The Sea Fencibles were a coastal protection force and came under the control of the Admiralty while the River Fencibles, who patrolled large rivers such as the Thames, were under Army control. However, both bodies were recruited from professional seamen or watermen and were essentially naval in character. Unsurprisingly, there seem to have been no official regulations governing their swords but it can be expected that they closely followed naval practice, being indistinguishable unless a strong provenance exists. A rare example is the sword of Captain William Brownfield of the London River Fencibles.[1] This is a stout fighting weapon with a curved blade and a hilt with a stirrup knuckle guard with double 'S' bar side guard that contains a fouled anchor. It has a plain pommel.

The Royal Dockyard Battalion (RDB)

Despite the victories at Trafalgar and Waterloo, Britain faced a perceived threat from France throughout the remainder of the nineteenth century. These years were punctuated by a series of alarms and, in 1847, one of these resulted in the raising of a volunteer force to defend the naval installations. This was the Royal Dockyard Battalion which was recruited from among the employees of the dockyards. According to the National Maritime Museum,[2] the idea for this body of men was first advanced in 1846 by Lord Ellenborough, who was the First Lord of the Admiralty. Continued support led to the appointment of Captain Bartholomew Sulivan RN as Colonel and Chief of Staff of the organisation. Recruitment was authorised, and some 10,500 men were enrolled, divided between infantry and artillery specialisations. Battalions were raised in Deptford, Devonport, Chatham, Pembroke, Portsmouth, Sheerness and Woolwich. Most have the date of appointment of their adjutants in April 1847,[3] but in the case of Deptford this did not occur until two years later.[4] Abroad, an artillery battalion was raised in Malta but records of its adjutants do not appear in Hart's Army Lists. With the exception of these adjutants, the battalions were officered by senior civilian employees in the dockyards. The force seems to have been disbanded in about 1858, as the adjutants do not appear in Hart's for the following year.[5] Sulivan went on to become an Admiral with a knighthood.

This outline is supported by the history of the 8th Battalion at Pembroke Dock which mentions that the Pembroke Battalion was still functioning in 1857. It lists

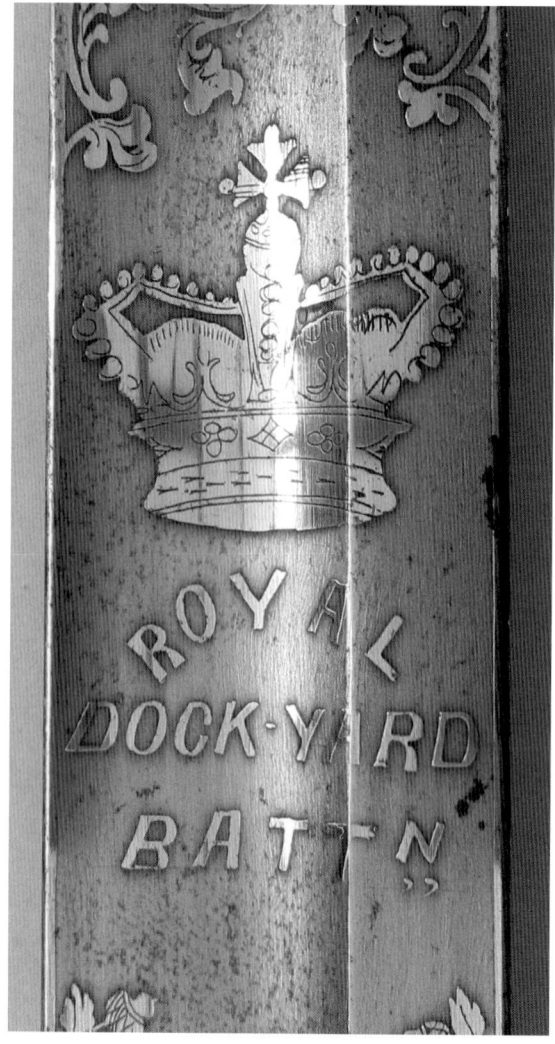

All the swords of the Royal Dockyard Battalion have identical blades manufactured by Wilkinson. The name of the organisation is incorporated in the etched decoration on the outer face of the blades.

Swords of Officers of the Reserves, the Merchant Navy and Other Maritime Organisations   61

fourteen officers, gives details of the preparations made at the time of the Crimea War and describes some of the exercises which they conducted.[6]

With the man placed in overall charge, Captain Sulivan, being designated the Colonel and with subordinate ranks of Major, Captain and Lieutenant, the organisation was clearly military rather than naval in its structure. This status is emphasised by the lack of the word 'naval' in its title (cf the later Royal Naval Artillery Volunteers) and the use of 'battalion' rather than the more naval 'brigade' or 'division'. Henry Wilkinson was awarded the contract to equip the force.[7] The headgear adopted was a shako, again highlighting the military nature of the battalions. Some battalions were Infantry, e.g. Devonport, and wore a red coat while other battalions, e.g. Pembroke and Malta, were artillery and wore blue coats with red facings. With this background in place, it is time to look at the swords carried by officers of the RDB.

These swords reflect both the naval and military aspects of this organisation. Not surprisingly given that Wilkinson had the contract to equip the RDB, all the swords have identical, flat-backed blades manufactured by that firm. The outside face of the blade is etched with the words 'ROYAL DOCK-YARD BATTN', together with a crowned and fouled anchor and the brass proof mark of Henry Wilkinson is inset on the shoulder. The inner face bears the crowned Royal Cypher and the name Henry Wilkinson and address of Pall Mall, London. Most of these blades are fitted with the hilt of the type in naval use at the time. This consisted of a solid, gilt brass, half-basket guard with a crowned and fouled anchor in the cartouche, a white fish skin grip bound with twisted gilt wires, and a back piece with a lion's head pommel. All the components of the hilt match those of other contemporary Wilkinson swords in the authors' collections. The only variability seems to be in the colour of the fish skin but it is believed that they all started out white but many have become darkened by dirt in the intervening years.

The real differences come with the variety of scabbards in which these swords can be found. The commonest is the black leather scabbard with two gilt mounts introduced in the RN in 1847, the date of the formation of the RDB. The inner faces of the lockets on these scabbards bear heater-shaped shields carrying the legend 'Wilkinson, Gun & Sword Maker, Pall Mall, London'. In this scabbard, the sword looks identical to the contemporary RN weapon and is only distinguishable by the etching on the blade.

The sword which belonged to Lieutenant T P Rickord of

Three swords of the Royal Dockyard Battalion, from left to right: Sword in a leather scabbard of the 1847 RN Pattern which has been modified to conform to the 1856 RN Pattern by the addition of a mid-locket – the tassel section of the sword knot is probably not original; Sword in a military-style steel scabbard – swords such as this are sometimes found in the brass scabbard of a field officer; Sword with an open, half-basket guard in the military style and with a military-style pommel and back piece in a steel, military scabbard.

Sword belt of Lieutenant T P Rickord of the Royal Dockyard Battalion of Artillery, Malta. Unlike the vast majority of naval sword belts, this is made in three sections and has a rectangular rather than circular buckle.

the Royal Dockyard Battalion of Artillery, Malta, is displayed in the Malta Maritime Museum, located in the former Royal Navy bakery on the water's edge in Vittoriosa. This display adds considerably to our knowledge of the accoutrements that accompanied these swords. The sword belt is divided into three lengths joined together by circular, brass rings. Unlike naval sword belts where the buckles are circular with a circumferential laurel wreath, the buckle on the RDB belt is rectangular, a shape it shares with many military buckles from the same period. The main device is a crowned, fouled anchor surrounded by a wreath of oak leaves, not laurel. The wreath is enhanced by a stand of arms in the background. The border of the buckle plate is roped. This more elaborate design is possible because of the extra space afforded by its rectangular shape. The sword knot is a blue and gold cord, terminating not in the gold bullions of the contemporary naval sword but in a blue and gold acorn mould similar to that used by the Army. Not only that but it does not have the extra loop inside the guard of the naval sword and, as a consequence, there are no piercings through the guard of this sword to take this component. Some other Royal Dockyard Battalion swords examined also lack these piercings through the guard, although one sword has been examined which does have these holes. Perhaps they were added later, possibly when the sword was being used by an officer in the RN.

Rectangular buckle from Lieutenant Rickord's sword belt. The design is more elaborate than that on an RN belt.

Next commonest are swords in steel Army-pattern scabbards. It might be concluded that these are cases where a sword had been inserted in an incorrect scabbard. However, in all cases the fit is snug and the authenticity of such a combination is supported by a sword with a steel scabbard in the NMM collection which belonged to Lieutenant Ebenezer Wood.[8] Wood was a shipwright, who was a Lieutenant in the Devonport Battalion with a seniority of 1 June 1848 and was promoted to Captain with a seniority of 3 May 1849.

As well as steel military-style scabbards, at least two other swords have been sold in brass scabbards.[9] Infantry officers of field rank carried their swords in brass scabbards but officers of captain's rank and below used scabbards of steel. Of the fourteen officers listed for the Pembroke Battalion only two were majors and would have been entitled to the brass scabbard. Infantry officers also wore their swords in leather scabbards for levee purposes but, unlike the naval pattern, these had three gilt mounts with a loose ring on each of the top and mid-lockets. The design of the RDB sword belt described above would have made it a simple matter to change the after sling from short to long and *vice versa* as required. It is suggested that all the variations in scabbards can be accounted for by the military nature of the RDB and the variety of scabbards in use in the Army at the time. An alternative is that individual battalions interpreted whatever regulations there were very loosely and slightly different swords resulted.

All the swords described so far have standard naval hilts but the final sword to be examined, which was sold by Taylor's auction house in 2010 is completely different. A casual glance would dismiss it as a standard infantry officer's sword with the gilt, openwork, Gothic, half-basket hilt introduced in 1822, the black fish skin grip with twisted wire binding, and the stepped pommel decorated with acanthus foliage on the back piece. The device in the cartouche is the Royal Cypher ('*VR*') and not a crowned and fouled anchor. However, it has a blade inscribed to the Royal Dockyard Battalion, identical in all respects to those mounted in the naval style hilts described above. It is in a black-painted steel scabbard into which it fits too tightly. Both the tip of the blade and the shoe region of the scabbard have matching damage, suggesting that the sword and scabbard have been united for some while. It is uncertain whether the paint is contemporary or later. Conforming to the regulation pattern sword for a junior officer in the infantry,[10] this would seem to be a very appropriate sword for such an officer in one of the infantry battalions and one wonders why this is not the pattern most commonly encountered.

One possibility is that such a sword belonged to the adjutant of one of the battalions. Unlike the other officers, who were drawn from among the dockyard staff, these were all Lieutenants, Royal Marines, on half-pay. Such an officer may well have had a blade inscribed to the Royal Dockyard Battalion mounted in the hilt of his service sword. If the original sword had been supplied by a manufacturer other than Wilkinson, a bad fit between the blade and the scabbard could well have resulted. There were seven battalions in the UK and one, Portsmouth had two adjutants (Cary followed by Long). There was a Battalion at Malta but it is not known if their adjutant was also a Royal Marines officer on half pay. That means that a maximum of nine such swords should exist if all Adjutants had one. As all the adjutants were below field rank, no swords of the RDB with army-style hilts should be found in brass scabbards.

The only common feature of all the swords to the RDB is the blade, always supplied by Wilkinson to the same dimensions and with identical etched decoration. Without supporting dress regulations or other documentation, the explanations suggested for the range of scabbards and hilts must all remain very speculative and the swords of the RDB provide an opportunity for further research and discovery.

Guard of a sword of the Royal Naval Artillery Volunteers with the initials 'RNAV' in the cartouche of the guard.

Hybrid between an officer's sword and a cutlass of a type also used by the Royal Naval Artillery Volunteers. Unlike a rating's cutlass, the steel guard is provided with a quillon and it is pierced below the blade to accept the two part naval sword knot. The knot attached to this sword is the 1891 RN Pattern. The Royal Naval Artillery Volunteers were disbanded on 1 April 1892, so although this knot may be original, this is by no means certain.

The Royal Naval Artillery Volunteers (RNAV)

The Royal Naval Artillery Volunteers were authorised by Act of Parliament on 5 August 1873, at the prompting of Thomas Brassey, MP. Their function was to man coastal guns. There were Brigades formed in London (1873), Liverpool (1876), Bristol (1881) and the Clyde (1886). They were disbanded on 1 April 1892 when there was a proposal to place them under the control of the Army. This body was a precursor to the Royal Naval Volunteer Reserve.

The sword of the RNAV illustrated has the initials 'RN' and 'AV' displayed either side of the fouled anchor in the cartouche of the guard and also between the crown and the fouled anchor on the broadsword blade. None of the three swords of the RNAV in the National Maritime Museum (NMM) has any indication on the guard that it belonged to an officer of this body. On all these weapons, this information is confined to the blade, either in the form of initials or the whole title. A candlestick manufactured from the hilt of a sword with RNAV in the cartouche has also been seen by one of the authors. Of the swords in the National Maritime Museum, one also has a broadsword blade. Naval swords were sometimes mounted with such blades which are most closely associated with the swords of Scottish regiments.

One of the swords in the NMM collection[11] provides some details of the sword knot worn with this weapon. This sword was sold by Wilkinson in January 1877 to Sidney Crowley who appears in the 1882 Navy list as a Sub-Lieutenant RNAV and was promoted to Honorary Lieutenant in 1889. The knot attached to this sword has the conventional blue and gold rope and tassel but has a fringe of blue and gold threads rather than the twelve gold bullions which might have been expected (see Chapter 3).

A pattern of cutlass associated with the RNAV is a hybrid between an officer's sword and a naval cutlass. This weapon has the 29½in (750mm) blade of a cutlass but etched as for an officer's sword with a design incorporating the initials RNAV. The hilt consists of a steel cutlass-style guard which differs from a rating's cutlass by having a quillon. This is combined with a black fish skin covered grip bound with gilt wire and with the lion's head pommel and back piece of an officer's sword. A sword of this design in the NMM[12] was supplied by Silver of London and another, almost identical weapon, sold by Bonhams[13] was retailed by E M Davies of James Street, Liverpool. Despite the similarities in the weapons, the scabbards are markedly different with that of the NMM sword having just two gilt mounts while the other sword has three. It is not known if this was a rating's cutlass, as suggested by the dimensions of the blade and the form of the guard, some variant officer's sword, as indicated by the etching on the blade and the pommel, or the weapon of a warrant officer, for which the black fish skin of the grip would be appropriate.

The Royal Naval Reserve (RNR) and the Royal Naval Volunteer Reserve (RNVR)

The RNR was founded by Act of Parliament in 1859 but it was not until 1861 that officers were first recruited. The source of recruits for the RNR was mainly the merchant service. The RNVR was established in 1903 and recruited its members from amateur sailors. There was also the short-lived Royal Naval Volunteer (Supplementary) Reserve (RNV(S)R) formed in 1936 and disbanded at the end of the Second World War. These two reserve forces were amalgamated as the Royal Naval Reserve in 1958.

Many officers of these reserve services wore the standard naval sword (see Chapter 3), and only a name engraved somewhere on the weapon indicates its owner's status as a member of the reserves.[14] However, some officers chose to display their membership of one of the naval reserve forces by purchasing a specific sword with the initials 'RNR' across the shank of the fouled anchor. On some swords these initials are repeated in the decoration of the outer face of the blade. On swords belonging to officers in the Royal Naval Volunteer Reserve the initials 'RNV' are used, rather than 'RNVR' which might be expected.

Sword of the Royal Naval Reserve with the initials 'RNR' in the cartouche of the guard.

Buckle of sword belt to the Royal Naval Reserve. This is in two parts with the initials 'RNR' on the centre, male section.

Sword of the Royal Naval Volunteer Reserve with the initials 'RNV' in the cartouche of the guard.

The RNR sword belt carries the organisation's initials across the shank of the anchor which appears on the buckle. Many belts to this body have a two-piece buckle with the badge on the central, male portion and the surrounding laurel wreath as the female component.

Like their RN counterparts, some RNR officers seem to have worn the sword knot which is in transition between the 1827 pattern with its individual gold bullions and the 1891 pattern with its blue and gold barrel-shaped moulding. Two such knots belonging to RNR officers have been observed. One is on a sword in the Trinity House in Leith and the other on the sword of Lieutenant John George Spencer RNR who served in the RNR between 1912 and 1923. During his service with the RN in the First World War, Spencer was appointed to be the First Lieutenant of the 'Q' ship *Prince Charles*. She was the first such ship to sink a German U-boat (*U36*) unaided by an RN submarine on 24 July 1915.[15] Spencer was in charge of the 'panic party' which simulated the crew abandoning ship before she was sunk by gunfire. This may seem a less dangerous role than remaining on board to fight but, once in their boat, the panic party could be caught between two fires or machine-gunned by the U-boat. The Trinity House, Leith, sword was supplied by G Kenning of Liverpool while the supplier of Spencer's sword is unknown.

Just like their colleagues in the RN, officers of the RNR sometimes chose to wear unconventional swords. One such, known to one of the authors, wore a Spanish naval sword throughout his long and distinguished service.

The Royal Naval Air Service (RNAS)

The Royal Naval Air Service was created on 1 July 1914 from the Naval Wing of the Royal Flying Corps. On 1 April 1918 it once again amalgamated with the Royal Flying Corps, this time to become the Royal Air Force. The Royal Navy Air Service wore naval uniform with an eagle replacing the anchor below the crown on: the cap badge, epaulettes, buttons and sword belt[16] as well as on the sword cartouche itself. In the National Maritime Museum, there is a sword of the RNAS that belonged to Wilfred Henry Dunn.[17] He was commissioned as a Flight Sub-Lieutenant on 28 January 1915 and promoted to Flight Lieutenant on 1 April the next year. He was further promoted to Flight Commander on 30 June 1917 and transferred to the RAF on its formation. He rose to become an Air Commodore. The officer's sword of the RAF combines elements from the swords of its parent services. The military parentage is reflected by the sheet metal guard and the blade with its dumbbell cross section while the naval heritage shows in the white fish skin grip and animal head (eagle) pommel.

The Royal Naval Division (RND)

At the start of the First World War, the Royal Navy had a surplus of about 20,000 reserves even after the Fleet had been fully manned. Reserve personnel from the Royal Naval Reserve, the Royal Fleet Reserve, the Royal Naval Volunteer Reserve, a brigade of Royal Marines, Royal Navy and Army personnel were brought together at Crystal Palace in September 1914 to form the Royal Naval Division. This was commonly known as 'Winston's Little Army'. After fighting at Antwerp in 1914 and at Gallipoli the next year, it was sent to France in May 1916 and transferred to Army control in June of that year. Supplemented by a number of army units, it was then known as 63rd (Royal Naval) Division. After an address by the Prince of Wales, it was demobilised in France in April 1919 and disbanded in June 1919 after a final parade.

Sometimes a standard naval sword may be encountered in an army-style Sam Browne scabbard. Such a weapon with its mixed naval and military characteristics may well have been the sword of an officer in the Royal Naval Division and may possibly be offered for sale as such. However, in the absence of any other information about its provenance, such a sword should be treated with suspicion. A sword in the National Maritime Museum[18] is an interesting hybrid weapon. The hilt consists of the steel half-basket guard bearing the Cypher of George V, steel back piece and pommel, and black grip of the Infantry Officer's Pattern 1892 sword. The blade is the typical, slightly curved naval variety complete with the words Royal Navy and the design of a fouled anchor. It has a brown leather Sam Browne type of scabbard. In the catalogue entry it is

Badge of the Royal Naval Air Service.

An incident involving the Coast Blockade Service as depicted in an article by Commander The Honourable Henry N Shore RN in *Navy and Army Illustrated*, 21 January 1898, p 216.

Sword presented to Lieutenant Dobbin of HM Revenue Cutter *Diligence*. From this photograph, the sword can be seen to have a broad, curved blade with a single, wide, shallow fuller on each face. The etched inscription is not clear enough to read in this image. The tooled leather scabbard has three plain mounts, decorated with simple incised lines. The hilt is magnificent. It is of open half-basket form with a fouled anchor in an oval cartouche. Decoration in the form of roses and thistles fills the panels between the bars of the hilt. It is difficult to tell from this photograph, but no shamrocks seem to be incorporated in the design, which dates it to before the 1801 Union with Ireland. The back piece and pommel are a single component and the pommel portion is plain.

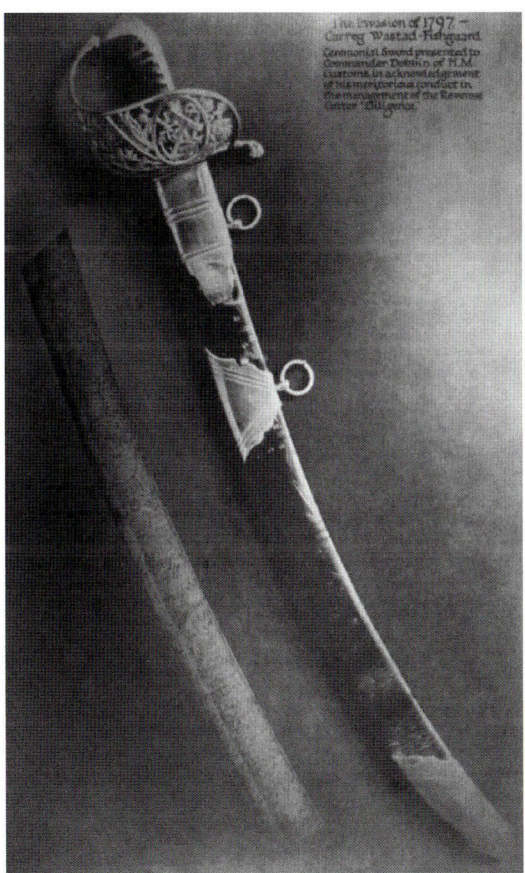

admitted that there is no incontrovertible proof that this was indeed the sword of an officer in the RND but it is considered the combination of features makes this likely.

Customs and Coastguard Services

A brief look at the common heritage of these two services[19] will make it clear why their swords should be considered under a common heading. The Coastguard[20] service originated from developments in the Revenue service at the start of the nineteenth century. The waters off the coast were patrolled by Revenue cutters and ashore there were Riding Officers. The Preventative Waterguard formed in 1809 added a third layer of surveillance between the other two. In the Kent area, Captain Joseph McCulloch, RN proposed uniting these under one system of command and, in 1816, the Coast Blockade was established under McCulloch's command to patrol the region from South Foreland to Dungeness. Clearly, with all these systems operating simultaneously, there was considerable scope for confusion and a committee was set up to recommend improvements. The result was the formation in 1822 of the Coastguard Service by the amalgamation of all the previous entities with the exception of the Coast Blockade, which remained with the Admiralty. The new service came under the control of the Board of Customs. The Coast Blockade was incorporated in 1831 and at the same date the Coastguard became a reserve for the Royal Navy. Officers for the service were recommended by the Admiralty. The Admiralty took full control under the terms of the Coastguard Service Act, 1856.[21] It remained that way until 1923 when control passed into civilian hands and it has stayed that way except for the period 1940–5.

At 5pm on 22 February 1797 a French force began disembarking at Carreg Wastad (Flat Rock) Bay a few miles from Fishguard in Pembrokeshire. The last invasion of mainland Britain had begun. It was also the occasion for recognition by the local commander, Lord Cawdor, of the services of two Revenue cutters, *Speedwell* and *Diligence*. Although mentioning the landing of her guns and their transport for 27 miles by Lieutenant Hopkins and the crew of the *Speedwell* as worthy of praise, he is less specific in the case of the other vessel. In her case, his letter of 14 March to the Board of Customs refers to: 'the conduct of Lieut. Dobbin of the *Diligence* cutter, to whom I think the Service highly indebted for exertions that do credit to the profession to which he has the honour to belong, and which will ever call for my grateful remembrance'. A letter from the Secretary to the Board stated that it 'would be giving urgent consideration to the manner in which the officers should be rewarded for their zeal'.[22]

Five-ball hilted sword with the badge of the Customs House on the cartouche, ca 1790. (NMM WPN1221, Image E1250).

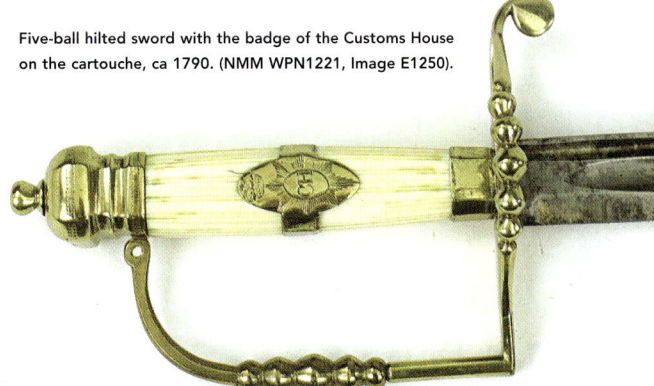

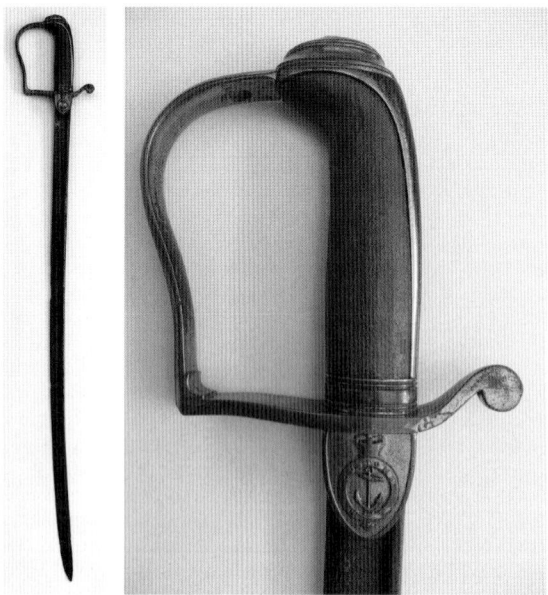

Above left: Sword of the Customs Service, possibly dating from between 1822 and 1840. This is a hybrid weapon with the stirrup hilt of the 1805 RN sword and the pipe-backed blade of the 1827 Pattern. Although the blade is very badly corroded, it is just possible to determine details of the maker, William & John Rigby, 19 Suffolk Street, Dublin. At the time of the Great Exhibition of 1851, this firm was trading at 24 Suffolk Street, so this sword dates from rather earlier.

Above right: Hilt of Customs Service sword. Note that the anchor in the design is not fouled and the belt surrounding it bears the word 'CUSTOMS'. The wooden grip is now missing its covering, which was probably of black fish skin. There is no evidence that this grip ever had a wire binding. The grip of a similar sword in the NMM (WPN1194) retains its covering of black fish skin and, again, there is no evidence of a handle binding. The backwards slope of the quillon is the result of damage.

The reward came in the form of a splendid sword. An image of Dobbin's sword is displayed in the Town Hall at Fishguard. This is one of the earliest swords known to the authors that can definitively be attributed to the Customs service. However, no claim is made that this presentation weapon is representative of the sort commonly worn by officers of that service.

That these officers seem to have followed the fashion of the day as described in Chapter 3 is quite clear from a five-ball hilted sword in the National Maritime Museum[23] which belonged to a Captain Walker. The straight blade of this sword has two fullers on each face and was originally blued and gilt. A diamond shaped insert replaces a fouled anchor as a support to the side loop. Its association with the Customs service is made clear by the badge of the Customs House engraved on the cartouche which is part of the band which encircles the grip. The badge consists of a crown above a star containing the letters 'CH'. This practical weapon is contemporary with the presentation sword described previously. Its scabbard is black leather with three gilt mounts, each of the two lockets having a loose ring.

The first uniform sword for officers of the Customs that the authors have been able to trace is a typical 1805 Pattern of the type specified for officers of Commander's rank and above in the Royal Navy. It had the usual stirrup hilt, white, wire-bound grip and lion's head pommel. The difference was in the badge engraved on the langets, which consisted of an anchor (not fouled) surrounded by a belt bearing the word 'CUSTOMS' and surmounted by a crown. Although it is difficult to be precise using the photographs that appeared on the dealer's website, it would appear from differences in colour that this weapon had had its original naval pattern langets cut out and new langets engraved with the Customs badge inserted in their stead. As Revenue officers were often drawn from Royal Navy officers on half-pay, a modification such as this to indicate a change of service would have been simple to effect.

The foundation of the Coastguard in 1822 coincided with the adoption of the pipe-backed blade by the Army, while in 1827 the Royal Navy changed its officers' sword from the stirrup-hilted spadroon to a weapon with a solid, half-basket guard fitted with a pipe-backed blade. The Customs and Coastguard services seem to have taken one or other of these changes as an opportunity to introduce their own pattern of sword. The designers of this weapon seem to have adopted a pick-and-mix approach, selecting elements from several existing patterns and adding some new features. This hybrid form is clearly seen in the combination of the stirrup hilt and the pipe-backed blade. As with the naval swords of 1805, there are two types of this weapon, one with an ivory grip, presumably for senior officers, and the other with a grip covered in black fish skin, probably for junior officers.

In both these patterns, the langets are decorated with an anchor (not fouled) surrounded by a belt bearing the word 'CUSTOMS' and surmounted by a crown. This design is an integral part of the hilt casting. This device may also be etched on the blade. The back piece and pommel form a single unit and the latter is plain, rounded and stepped. This design, taken from the 1805 Pattern naval sword for those of Lieutenant's rank and below, is common to both the sword with the white ivory grip and that with the grip of black fish skin.

Two swords with white ivory grips, both by John Salter, have black leather scabbards with three gilt mounts with the lockets each fitted with a loose ring for suspension. These mounts have only a minimal amount of decoration in the form of engraved bands.[24] The trading addresses of Rigby and Salter which appear on these swords suggest a dating bracket of between 1827 and about 1840 for their manufacture.[25] It would appear that swords had ceased to be worn by Customs Officers by 1868, as the *Customs Officers Manual* of that date makes no mention of swords in the section on uniforms.[26]

Turning now to the Coastguard service, it also had a sword with a stirrup hilt, pipe-backed blade, plain pommel and black fish skin grip, but with 'COAST GUARD' replacing 'CUSTOMS' in the belt around the anchor in the emblem on the langets.[27] However, some time before 1856, when the Admiralty took full control, officers of the Coastguard were already beginning to follow naval practice in the matter of swords, differing from the naval model only in the replacement of the crowned and fouled anchor device by the letters '*CG*' in the cartouche on the guard. One such sword has a white fish skin grip and lion's head pommel and is mounted with the flat-backed blade introduced to naval service in 1846. The letters '*CG*' are clearly separated from each other. The top locket of the scabbard has the two loose rings introduced a year later when the Royal Navy adopted a sword belt with two short, equal slings. The scabbard has been altered by the addition of a mid locket with a loose ring for wear with a sword belt having

Two Coastguard swords; these are similar to the contemporary RN officer's sword but with the letter 'CG' replacing the crowned and fouled anchor in the cartouche on the guards and also etched on the blades. The top locket of the weapon on the left suggests that it dates from the period 1847 to 1856. This sword has the white grip of an RN officer's weapon. The sword on the right has a black fish skin grip and the scabbard mounts are much more simply decorated. The scabbard with three mounts suggests a date after 1856 for this sword. No explanation is offered for these variations in design.

two unequal slings. This change, which took place in the Royal Navy in 1856, is evident because the engraved lines on the added mid locket are coarser than those on the original top locket and chape and the lose ring has a slightly greater diameter than that of the two originals.

A similar sword has a black grip with a lion's head pommel and the letters 'CG' are intertwined. The scabbard mounts are much plainer. This and the black grip may indicate that its original owner was a junior officer. It has a flat-backed blade and shows no evidence of alteration to the black leather scabbard which has three gilt mounts. This sword was supplied by Lambert and Brown of Regent Street who traded at No. 236 from 1835 to 1858.[28] Because this scabbard was clearly manufactured with three mounts, the only dates in which it could have been made by Lambert and Brown before they ceased trading were 1856, 1857 or 1858.

This would all be quite tidy were it not for the existence of Coastguard swords based on the 1822 Pattern infantry officers' sword. These have the pipe-backed blade, open half-basket guard, black fish skin grip and stepped pommel with acanthus decoration of the infantry sword, differing only in having the initials '*CG*' replacing the Royal Cypher in the cartouche on the guard and etched on the blade. The initials are almost separated in the cartouche and clearly separate on the blade. The Army replaced the pipe-backed blade with the flat-backed model in 1845, so this weapon may be contemporaneous with the sword with a stirrup hilt and a pipe-backed blade. The Army-style hilt suggests the possibility that this sword may have belonged to a shore based officer of the Coastguard. Support for this idea comes from the Irish Revenue Police (1832–57), a land-based force tasked with the suppression of illegal stills, which used a sword based upon the Army model but with its own badge in the cartouche.[29] To add further confusion, there is also the case of a sword with a flat-backed blade, an army-style brass scabbard and open work guard, black fish skin grip and a lion's head pommel. This is identifiable as a Coastguard sword only from the sales records of the Wilkinson Sword Company.

It is not known when a specific pattern of sword for Coastguard officers ceased to be worn but their scarcity suggests that many officers simply wore their RN or RNR weapons. Confirmation of this suggestion can be found with two swords in the NMM. One presented to Mr George Read on his retirement from the Lytham Coast Guard Station in 1862, where he was the Chief Boatman in charge of the station, is a standard uniform sword for a commissioned officer in the RN below flag rank.[30] The other belonged to Chief Officer F W Hyde.[31] Dating from after 1901, it is the regulation sword for a Warrant Officer RN and must have been purchased by Hyde while serving in the Coastguard as a Warrant Officer Boatswain between 1886 and 1907. In 1907

Right: Hilt of Coastguard sword modelled on the 1822 Pattern Infantry Officers' sword. This has the pipe-backed blade, open half-basket hilt, black grip and stepped pommel of the contemporary infantry officer's sword, differing by having the letters 'CG' in the cartouche of the guard and etched on the blade.

Below: Coastguard sword with an open half-basket hilt with the Royal Cypher in the cartouche, the brass scabbard of a field officer and a black grip; all features of the infantry officer's sword. However, it has the lion's head pommel of a naval officer's sword. This hybrid design is only recognisable as having belonged to an officer of the Coastguard from the sales records of Wilkinson.

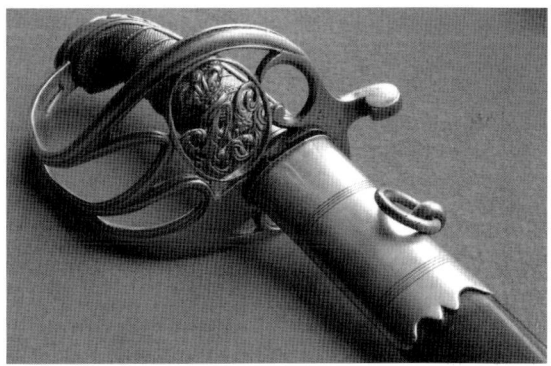

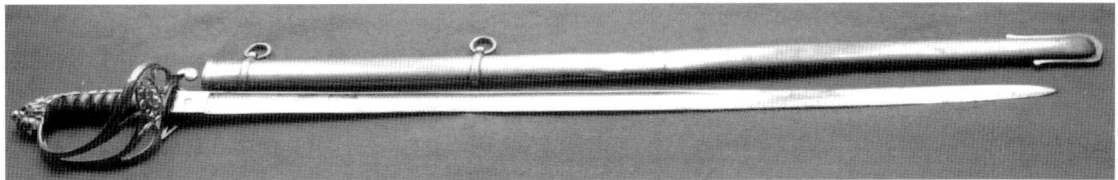

Chief Officer Parkes with the Gravesend and Tilbury crews. Illustrations of Coastguard officers wearing their swords are uncommon but this example appeared in the *Navy and Army Illustrated*, Vol II, 2 October 1896. This shows a sword of the naval pattern with a white grip, lion's head pommel and post-1891 sword knot. The resolution of the halftone block makes it impossible examine the badge in the cartouche on the guard.

Above and below: A Chinese Maritime Customs sword: (a) the pommel in the form of a dragon's head, and (b) the cartouche on the guard with dragon wrapped around the fouled anchor (Lieutenant Commander M Bowden, Royal Navy)

he was promoted to Chief Officer and continued to serve in that rank until 1913. He clearly chose not to update his sword on promotion.

To summarise, the following patterns of sword identified as being worn by officers of the Coastguard are listed in the table below. The dates are those provided by known examples and are, therefore, only indicative.

The Chinese Maritime Customs Service

This service, which was under the control of the Chinese authorities, had many British officers. It was founded in 1854 and lasted until the resignation of the final foreign Inspector-General in 1950. Although its original purpose was simply the collection of taxes, it became involved in many aspects of the Chinese administration. From a maritime perspective, the most important of its functions were customs and postal administration, the meteorological service, the management of harbours and waterways, the prevention of smuggling and the provision of lights on the coast of China and along the Yangtze River.[32] The uniform was modeled on that of the RN and the sword was very similar differing only in having the head of a dragon for the pommel and a fouled anchor and dragon device in the cartouche of the guard. Like all such weapons there are several variants and, as well as the type with a dragon for a pommel and incorporated in the design on the cartouche, there is a version with the pommel in the form of a lion's head[33] and another with a dragon's-head pommel but a simple

fouled anchor in the cartouche.[34] The weapon illustrated originally belonged to William Donald Fraser who joined the service in November 1904 as a Probationary Third Officer and retired in October 1939 as a River Inspector. This sword was later worn by his son-in-law, an officer in the RNR in Hong Kong, and his grandson, an officer in the RN. Its broadsword blade reflects Fraser's Scottish background. Swords of the Chinese Maritime Customs Service are also found with the standard flat-backed naval blade.[35] Chinese Maritime Customs dirks may also be encountered.[36]

Swords Worn by Officers of the Coastguard Service

Date	Design
After either 1822 or 1827	Stirrup hilt, pipe-backed blade, plain pommel, Coastguard badge on langets
Between 1822 and 1845	Infantry officer's sword, pipe-backed blade, 'CG' in cartouche, leather scabbard
Between 1845 and 1891	Infantry sword, flat-backed blade, brass scabbard, but with lion's head pommel, identifiable only by serial no
After 1847	As for RN commissioned officer but with 'CG' in the cartouche
After about 1858	As for RN commissioned officer but with black grip and 'CG' in the cartouche
After 1856	As for RN commissioned officer
After about 1901	As for RN warrant officer

William Donald Fraser in the uniform of the Chinese Maritime Customs and wearing the sword illustrated. (Lieutenant Commander M Bowden, Royal Navy)

The Inspector-General had a court dress, similar to that of an ambassador, with which was worn a court sword with an elaborate gilt hilt and mother of pearl grips.[37] It was carried in a black leather scabbard with two gilt mounts, the locket having a frog stud. The sword belt was of black silk with a black felt frog and was fastened by an 'S' buckle.

The East India Company (EIC) and later Indian Naval Services

The East India Company had a large and successful trading fleet and also had its own naval services to protect its interests in its sphere of operations. With this maritime duality, it forms a convenient bridge between the naval forces of the Crown and the Merchant Navy, which will be the subject of the next section.

In 1612, the first base of the Indian Marine, more formally known as the East India Company Marine, was established at Suvali near Surat. It continued as the Indian Marine until 1686 when, following the transfer of most of the Company's assets to Bombay, it changed its name to the Bombay Marine, a title it kept until 1830. From that date until 1858 it was styled the Indian Navy. There was also a smaller force operating under the Company's banner from about 1690 to 1858 called the Bengal Marine but little seems to have been written about that component of the Company's forces. As well as these formal naval forces, the East India Company's merchant ships were also armed.

In 1858, following the Indian Mutiny, the Company's forces were taken under Crown control, initially as Her Majesty's Indian Navy. The name changed again in 1863 to the Bombay and Bengal Marine. Queen Victoria assumed the title Empress of India in 1877 and this year saw yet another change of title, this time to Her Majesty's Indian Marine, a designation kept until 1892 when it became the Royal Indian Marine. Then in 1934 it became the Royal Indian Navy, a title it kept until independence in 1947. With independence, there was a partition into the Royal Indian Navy, which changed its name to the Indian Navy in 1950, and the Royal Pakistan Navy which became the Pakistan Navy in 1956. The Ceylon Naval Volunteer Force, formed in 1937, became the Ceylon Royal Naval Volunteer Reserve after the Second World War. In 1950 it became the Royal Ceylon Navy and in 1972 the Sri Lankan Navy.

It is against this complex background that swords of the Indian naval services must be assessed. Before the change of control in 1858, swords bearing one or other of the Company's devices could well have been from either the naval or mercantile arms. However, the comparative scarcity of these weapons argues strongly that they were worn by few of the Company's officers which points to the naval forces as their main source. Identification of these swords is by the EIC devices used in their decoration. Such swords will be attributed to the EIC but it must be remembered that this includes Company's naval force current at the time.

In the days before uniform swords were introduced to the RN, officers of the EIC wore similar swords to those of their contemporaries in the RN. A five ball sword in the NMM[38] is identical to the contemporary RN weapon in all except the badge on the band around the grip. This is the lion rampant, holding a crown in its forepaws, and standing on a heraldic wreath of the EIC. Another sword in the same collection, thought to have belonged to Captain Archibald Hamilton of the EIC is a substantial curved fighting sword with a hilt based on that of the 1805 pattern but with plain langets.[39] Were it not for the evidence of its provenance, this sword would, undoubtedly be classified as RN.

Two swords in the Sim Comfort collection indicate their association with the EIC by the presence of another device associated with the Company, namely a heart shape.[40] This is a simplified form of the bale mark which was used to mark the Company's goods and coinage. The full mark has the initials 'VEIC' (United East India Company) inside a heart shaped cartouche, which is crested with the numeral 4. One has a curved, single-edged blade with a crowned Royal Cypher, 'GR', on the outer face. This blade would seem to be equally at home in an RN sword. It is mounted in a hilt with a plain, gilt stirrup guard fitted with two side loops. In each of these is set a heart-shaped inset in the place of the anchors commonly found on RN swords. The rest of the hilt consists of a reeded ivory grip and a faceted urn-shaped pommel. The top locket has a heart shape cut out on the outer face to reveal the black leather of the scabbard. The other sword also has a curved, single-edged blade but undecorated. It also has a stirrup guard but this time only a single side ring on the outside. This is supported by a beaded, heart-shaped insert. The grip is reeded ivory and the pommel is the cushion style found on many five-ball swords. Comfort dates both these swords to before 1800 and, except for the EIC hearts, these could well have been RN swords.

It is necessary to sound one cautionary note about such swords. Although they are catalogued by Comfort as naval, there is no incontrovertible evidence that they are in fact naval, as such swords were also worn by military officers of the EIC. It needs clear naval symbolism such as fouled anchors or stands of arms embodying naval items (anchors, buoys, square-rigged masts and ships' sterns) to confirm such attributions. This is a fact of which Comfort is well aware[41] but the form and context all support his attribution to the EIC marine service.

By the time of the appearance of the 1805 Pattern sword in the RN, officers of the EIC seem to have settled on the Company's crest as the identifying design feature of their swords. The sword illustrated is typical of one of these 1805 Pattern swords to the EIC. This one is unusual in having the lion rampant facing to the heraldic left (sinister) rather than the right (dexter). One sword in the NMM shows that some EIC officers even followed the fashion for lightweight dress swords.[42] Another dress sword, now in the possession of Trinity House, which will be discussed later, is only attributable to the EIC by its provenance. A curved fighting sword in the Sim Comfort collection[43] has the stirrup hilt and langets, decorated with the EIC crest, of the 1805 Pattern but with an additional side loop to the guard, indicating that the Company's officers were just as likely to display their

Sword with the crest of the East India Company riveted to the guard. This sword conforms to the 1827 Pattern for the RN with a pipe-backed blade and a scabbard with two mounts and a frog hook on the locket. In the RN, this pattern of scabbard was superseded in 1832 by one with three mounts. The sword also has the early feature of a ring for the sword knot attached to the ferrule just inside the guard.

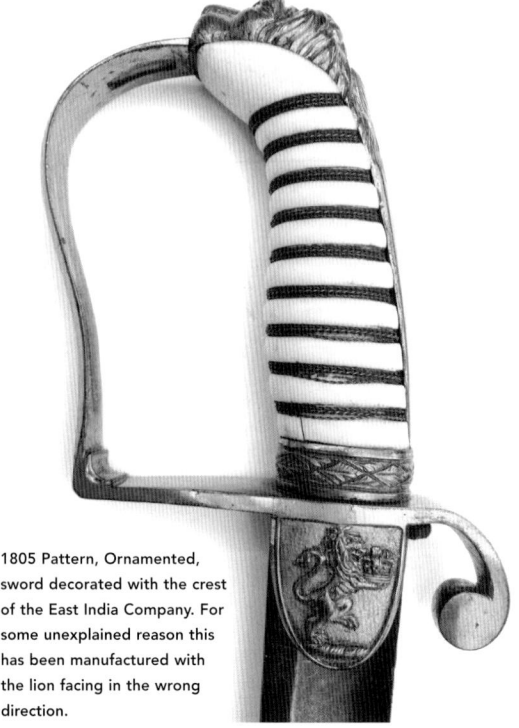

1805 Pattern, Ornamented, sword decorated with the crest of the East India Company. For some unexplained reason this has been manufactured with the lion facing in the wrong direction.

individuality in sword design as their RN colleagues. The scarcity of these weapons combined with the evidence from the sword of Hamilton and the Trinity House weapon suggests that many EIC officers just wore typical swords of the period with no EIC embellishment.

In 1827, the RN adopted its new pattern sword with the gilt solid half-basket guard in Gothic style carried in a black leather scabbard with a frog hook on the top locket. The EIC followed suit but with its crest appearing in the oval cartouche. On the sword illustrated, the crest is a separate casting riveted into place in the cartouche, suggesting that it was manufactured before the supplier had had time to create a mould for this new design. It also has the ring just inside the guard for the cord of the sword knot, considered to be diagnostic of an early example. Some of these swords have the EIC crest etched on the blade. One massive sword has the complete achievement of arms of the Company together with the motto (Auspicio Regis et Senatus Angliae) and the letters 'EIC' etched on the obverse and the Company's crest on the reverse.[44] This was also an early sword with the 1827 scabbard

Swords of Officers of the Reserves, the Merchant Navy and Other Maritime Organisations 71

This sword illustrates the difficulties of precise attribution. With its open, half-basket guard with an inset silver plate bearing the Company's arms and the letters 'EIC' in Gothic script and its black fish skin grip, it could be classified as military in nature. However, the lion's head pommel suggests that it could also be naval. We shall probably never know the sword's true origin but it would fit equally well in a collection of either naval or military swords.

A sword with the crest of the East India Company on the guard and etched on the blade. This sword with its flat-backed blade conforms to the 1846 Pattern for RN officers. The scabbard with three mounts was reintroduced into RN service in 1856, shortly before the East India Company lost its dominance of India following the Mutiny. This was supplied by Goy & Co, a firm which did not trade under this name until 1861, three years after the EIC maritime forces had become Her Majesty's Indian Navy. This is a very early example of the use of the peg and hole to secure the sword in its scabbard.

Sword of the Royal Indian Marine (1892–1934). Note the crown which differs from both the St Edward and Tudor Crowns and represents the Imperial State Crown. The background is the Star of India and the initials 'RIM' are placed across the shank of the fouled anchor.

Sword of the Royal Indian Navy (1934–50). This is similar to that of the Royal Indian Marine but lacks the letters 'RIM' across the anchor.

and a sword knot ring inside the guard. In both cases, the crest and anchor were aligned.

Keeping in step with RN uniform regulations, the EIC adopted the flat-backed blade when it was introduced in 1847 and this design of sword continued in use until the demise of the Company following the Indian Mutiny. With these later swords, the anchor is set at a definite angle to the crest. However, as usual, all is not quite this straightforward. The sword illustrated was supplied by Goy & Co of 36 Leadenhall Street, London. It was not until 1861, that the firm adopted this style and continued using it until after 1874,[45] the year in which the EIC was finally wound up by Act of Parliament. This sword could, therefore, have either been that of an officer in the EIC Mercantile Marine or of an officer in Her Majesty's Indian Navy using an obsolete pattern. It is noteworthy that this sword is secured into the scabbard by the hole and peg method, much earlier than Bosanquet suggested that it was introduced.[46] A similar sword in the NMM,[47] which was retailed by Grindlay & Co, a firm which traded under that name at a number of different addresses in London from 1844 to 1860, also has the hole and peg feature. Did this useful design improvement originate with the EIC? This sword is catalogued as belonging to the Indian Navy but the supplier's founder, Captain Robert Melville Grindlay, is recorded as purchasing arms and swords for the EIC.[48] It would seem that the Indian Navy to which the NMM is referring is the naval arm of the EIC.

From 1858 to 1892, officers of Her Majesty's Indian Navy, the Bombay and Bengal Marine, and Her Majesty's Indian Marine must all have had swords but there is no evidence of any specific patterns. Perhaps they just wore the current RN pattern. Officers of the Royal Indian Marine, from 1892 to 1934, wore a sword modelled on the RN pattern but with a different device in the cartouche on the guard and etched on the blade. This consists of a fouled anchor surmounted by a crown, set against the Star of India and with the letters 'RIM' across the anchor. The 'I' can be difficult to make out because it is part of the shank of the anchor. The crown is neither the St Edward nor the Tudor crown but a depiction of the Imperial State Crown and did not change following Queen Victoria's death in 1901. With the final change of name under British rule to the Royal Indian Navy in 1934, came the final pattern of sword, which was similar to that of the RIM but without any letters across the anchor.

The Merchant Navy (MN)

Although the title Merchant Navy (was not awarded to Britain's merchant fleet and its seamen until King George V did so in acknowledgement of the sacrifices made in the First World War, during which over 7.75 million tons of shipping were lost and more than 14,000 mariners killed, it is a convenient description for the British Merchant Service throughout its long and distinguished history.

Despite the fact that merchant ships were, in the past, routinely armed to provide some security against piracy and privateers, only two companies can be shown on the evidence of surviving weapons to have adopted patterns of swords specific to themselves. These were the East India Company, the swords of which have already been discussed, and the Peninsular and Oriental Steam Navigation Company (P&O). Reports of the officers of other companies wearing swords do occur and these will be discussed later.

Before 1805, officers of the RN were free to wear any type of sword they thought fit. The same freedom was, of course, also exercised by officers of the MN. At this date the MN would also have embraced privateers, some of whom would have been half-pay RN officers who were free to migrate from one service to the other. It is entirely possible that some swords catalogued to the RN belonged, in fact, to MN officers. It is also highly probable that MN officers favoured styles popular with their contemporaries in the RN and they would often have used the same tailors and cutlers to supply their requirements; these would have been only too happy to advise on what the well-dressed officer was wearing. Therefore, a doubt must always exist for swords without a precise provenance. With this as a background, the few swords with impeccable provenances to MN officers are particularly valuable in pointing to the types of swords used by these officers.

The stout fighting sword with a curved blade and a hilt with a stirrup knuckle guard with double 'S' bar side guard that contains a fouled anchor which belonged to Captain William Brownfield has already been mentioned in the section on Sea and River Fencibles. A similar but more elaborate sword presented to Captain James Le Bair of the privateer *Mayflower* in 1800, also described earlier, provides additional evidence that swords of this type were equally popular with MN officers as with their contemporaries in the RN.

Another curved sword with its langets engraved with anchors would definitely be classed as belonging to an RN officer, possibly a lieutenant because of the combination of

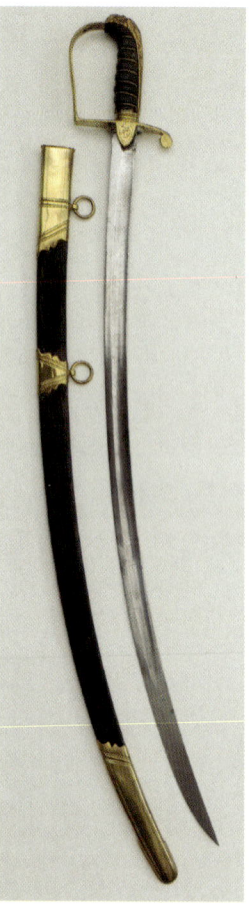

The sword of William Bodill Esq. This has the stirrup hilt associated with the 1805 Pattern RN sword, a lion's head pommel, black fish skin grip and a curved blade.

William Bodill's name etched on the blade; he was not a commissioned officer in the RN.

black grip and lion's head pommel. Swords such as this, based loosely on the 1805 pattern but with curved blades are not that uncommon and certainly some RN officers favoured them as fighting weapons. However, the blade of this sword is etched with the owner's name, William Bodill Esq, who was never an officer in either the RN or the EIC. He was, clearly, a seafarer and could, possibly, have been a privateer. Adding weight to this is that a Captain William Bodill was in command of the merchant sailing ship *Berengaria* when she sank in 1884 and seafaring was often a family tradition. Further research may, one day, unravel his story.

The EIC had lost its trading monopoly in India in 1834 and when P&O was incorporated as a company by Royal Charter in 1840 it soon began to challenge the EIC in its traditional sphere of influence. Perhaps because of this overlap, at least some P&O officers wore swords of a distinctive pattern. This is very similar to the contemporary RN weapon but with the Company's crest, a rising sun on a heraldic wreath replacing the crown in the badge on the guard. The company's crest does not appear in the decoration of the blade which includes a fouled anchor without a crown on each face. These

Sword of the Peninsular and Oriental Steam Navigation Company. The crown above the fouled anchor of an RN sword is replaced by the company's crest of a rising sun.

The Hamish Ashley Ripper Memorial Award of the Warsash Maritime Academy. This Sword of Honour is presented to the Deck or Marine Engineer Cadet who has demonstrated exceptional motivation, effort and determination to bring the cadetship to a successful conclusion. (Warsash Maritime Academy)

swords are very scarce and this particular sword is made even more intriguing by the owner's initials, 'TB', etched among the decoration on the blade. The supplier of the sword was Silver and Co, London & Liverpool, a firm which ceased trading in Liverpool in 1856.[49] Swords belonging to P&O officers are rare, suggesting that it was an option exercised by very few. Perhaps some officers, particularly masters, felt that a sword was needed for the formal calls necessary in some of the foreign ports visited. The Officers' Registers for P&O are held on loan at the NMM and consulting these yielded a short list of two possible candidates.[50] Of these, Thomas Beasley did not get his first command until January 1860 four years after Silver had ceased trading in Liverpool. That leaves Captain Thomas Black, who joined the company in 1846, aged 19, already qualified as a 1st Class Master. By 1853 he had gained his first command, *Norma*. He was in England from May 1857 to February 1858 and this would seem to match the post-1856 scabbard mounts of the sword and be close enough to Silver's dates in Liverpool for the address still to appear on the blade. He continued to command P&O ships until his record ends in October 1864 at Bombay.

P&O officers are the only ones where actual weapons prove that they sometimes wore a sword of a pattern specific to their company. However, as has been mentioned above, these swords are very scarce and it is possible that following the start of recruitment for officers into the RNR in 1861, most would have worn their RNR or RN pattern weapons when necessary. The tradition of P&O swords is kept alive by the cruise component of the modern company. On the inauguration of a new cruise ship, the Master is presented with a sword; complete with RN-style sword knot and this stays with the ship and is displayed on board.

When the Royal Mail Lines restarted its transatlantic operation in May 1921 an article in *The New York Times*[51] stated that, in earlier times: 'The officers, when in full dress, wore swords and carried pistols.' The authors know of no sword to this line suggesting that the officers wore RN pattern swords with their uniforms. There is, however, the intriguing possibility that swords to this company are out there awaiting discovery. Another shipping company where there are hints that swords were worn is White Star.[52]

After 1864, vessels of the merchant fleet wore Red Ensigns. The exception to this rule was when a ship was commanded by an officer of the RNR in possession of a Government warrant and had a certain proportion of retired naval personnel or members of the RNR in her crew. In these cases, the vessel would wear a Blue Ensign and certain shipping companies had a policy for all their ships to be Blue rather than Red Ensign vessels. In those cases, the officers would almost certainly have worn their RN or RNR swords on appropriate occasions of ceremony. This would account for the apparent absence of any company specific designs other than that of P&O.

Warsash Maritime Academy awards an annual Sword of Honour, the Hamish Ashley Ripper Memorial Award. This is made to the Deck or Marine Engineer Cadet who has demonstrated exceptional motivation, effort and determination to bring the cadetship to a successful conclusion. Unlike such awards in the RN, it is not retained by the winner but treated rather more as a trophy. This trophy was the sword of Captain Angus Brown RNR, who was the uncle of Hamish Ripper. During the 1914–18 war he served in a number of His Majesty's Ships including the *Ark Royal*. He flew as observer on many bombing raids in the Dardanelles campaign with Viscount Carrington as pilot. They were shot down twice, once on land where he and his pilot were able to avoid capture by the Turkish troops, walked back to the shore, stole a dinghy and rowed back to the *Ark Royal*. On another occasion the bomb-release mechanism jammed over enemy territory and he managed to climb out of the cockpit and released the bombs by hand for which he was decorated. Between the wars he served as Master of a number of merchant vessels and at the start of the Second World War he offered his services to the RN again. The Navy said he was too old so he promptly volunteered for the RAF and served as captain of a trawler recovering torpedoes on a practice range in the North Atlantic near the Shetland Islands.

Trinity House

With a history extending back to at least 1514 when Henry VIII granted a charter to the Guild of the Holy Trinity, which empowered them to 'regulate the pilotage of ships in the King's streams', it is hardly surprising to find that there are swords associated with this body. The earliest sword with a Trinity House provenance is that of Captain Sir John Woolmore, Knt, KCH, FRS (1756–1838) who was the Deputy Master of Trinity House from 1825 to 1834. Woolmore spent much of his time at

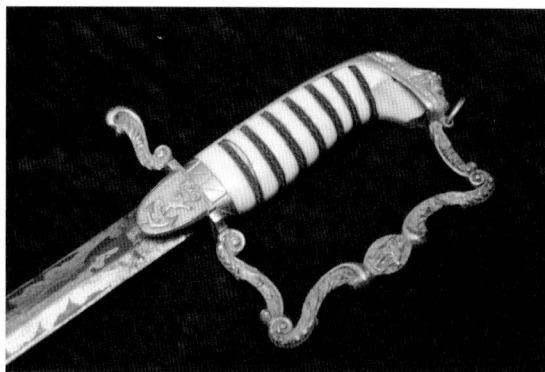

The sword of Captain Sir John Woolmore, Deputy Master of Trinity House from 1825 to 1834. Based on the 1805 Pattern RN sword, it has a straight, richly blued and gilt blade. On the guard, the langets have cast decoration in the form of a crowned and fouled anchor and the simple knuckle bow of the uniform sword has been replaced by a design of four 'S' curves with a central oval medallion. The pommel is also unusual as it is in the form of a recumbent lion rather than the more common lion's head. The scabbard, which has been repaired, is black with three ornate gilt mounts. The top locket is decorated with a stand of arms and bears the name Odell. (The Corporation of Trinity House)

Portrait of Captain Sir John Woolmore by Sir Martin Archer Shee. (The Corporation of Trinity House)

sea in the service of the Honourable East India Company until he came ashore in 1790. He remained connected with seafaring as part owner of several vessels and on 6 June 1803 he was elected as an Elder Brother of Trinity House. He was one of the driving forces behind the construction of the East India Docks and both Woolmore Street, London E14, and the school which stands in it are named after him.

His very ornate sword is based on that ordered in 1805 for officers in the Royal Navy of Commander's rank and above. It has a straight, double-edged blade which is richly blued and gilt. The pommel is unusual as it is in the form of a recumbent lion rather than the more common lion's head. The top locket of the scabbard is decorated with a stand of arms and bears the name Odell. Three companies of this name traded in London in the post-1800 period. These were J & B Odell, with premises at 114 New Bond Street. The partners went their separate ways in 1803. John Odell continued at the New Bond Street address before moving to number 85, then to 4 Pall Mall and, finally, to 57 Piccadilly. He ceased trading in 1810. Bennet Odell commenced business at 6 Mill Street and then moved, briefly, to 9 Lower Brook Street. From here he went to 4 Pall Mall, followed by 17 Old Bond Street and, lastly, Burlington Arcade. The firm became Odell and Atherly in 1834. There is a bit of a mystery over the 4 Pall Mall address as Bennet Odell traded here from 1806 to 1810, while John was here from 1807 to 1808.[53] It seems that these competitors were using the same address. It is not possible to determine which of these businesses supplied this sword. Perhaps the most interesting aspect of this sword is that symbols for neither the EIC nor Trinity House figure in the decoration of the sword or its scabbard. It is probable that, at this date, Elder Brethren would have owned swords worn during their service at sea and would have continued to wear these after election to the Brotherhood. This lack of either EIC or Trinity House symbols supports the proposition advanced earlier that many such officers just purchased standard RN swords.

There now seems to be a complete break in swords attributable to Trinity House, as the next precisely dateable example found so far dates to the early twentieth century. This is the sword of John Poyntz Spencer, Fifth Earl Spencer, which dates from his election as an Elder Brother in 1905. It resembles the uniform RN sword of the period but with the badge in the oval cartouche on the guard replaced by the arms of Trinity House, a cross of St George with a sailing ship in each quarter. This badge is repeated on the outer face of the blade, which, unlike the standard naval weapon, is straight and not slightly curved. The Spencer device of six intertwined letters 'S' appears on the outer face of the blade, surrounded by the collar of the Order of the Garter which he had been awarded shortly after his generous gift of Wimbledon Common to the Nation. The scabbard is the standard naval pattern of black leather with three gilt mounts and the sword knot is the 1891 Pattern with a blue and gold cord and barrel shaped moulding.

Unlike several of his ancestors, this Earl Spencer was not a distinguished naval officer but a Liberal politician who was twice Viceroy of Ireland. When the Liberal Party returned to power in 1892, Spencer was given the post of First Lord of the Admiralty which he held until it lost power in 1895. The first innovation he made was to retain the professional members of the Board of Admiralty (the Sea Lords) who had been appointed by the previous administration, thus introducing a degree of continuity into naval policy. A battle over the Naval Estimates in 1893/4

Sword of John Poyntz Spencer, 5th Earl Spencer, an Elder Brother of Trinity House. The arms of Trinity House appear in the cartouche of the guard and are also etched on the blade.

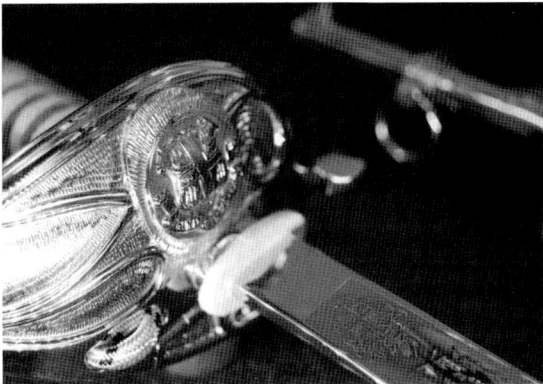

Trinity House, The Master's Sword presented to HRH the Duke of Edinburgh on 31 May 2007. (The Corporation of Trinity House)

Inscription on The Master's Sword. (The Corporation of Trinity House)

The Spencer device of intertwined letters 'S' and the Collar of the Order of the Garter on the blade of Earl Spencer's sword.

during which Spencer supported the demands of the Sea Lords against the Chancellor of the Exchequer led to a showdown with Gladstone which ended in his resignation as Prime Minister. Spencer continued to serve under Gladstone's replacement, Lord Rosebery, until the Liberals again lost power in 1895. It was this time as First Lord of the Admiralty which led to his election as an Elder Brother in 1905.

Other swords of Trinity House are similar with some minor differences. The sword that belonged to Walter Runciman, First Viscount Runciman (1870–1949),[54] who became an Elder Brother in 1936, also has a straight blade but etched with designs including the bow of a sailing ship and a fouled anchor. Representations of ships do not usually figure on blades of the Royal Navy at this period but occur on those of the Imperial German Navy. The shield of Trinity House appears in the oval cartouche on the guard. Unlike Spencer's sword on which this emblem is cast in high relief, it appears that the conventional crowned and fouled anchor has been ground out and replaced by a smooth plaque engraved with the arms of Trinity House. A peculiar feature is the sword knot. Instead of terminating in the barrel-shaped moulding introduced into the Royal Navy in 1891, it ends in a tassel of individual gold bullions. This is the pattern of sword knot used in the Royal Navy from 1827 to 1891. Why this sword should be fitted with this anachronistic sword knot is a mystery. The sword of Sir Donald Anderson (1906–73) who became an Elder Brother in 1965 was supplied by Gieves.[55] It has the Royal Arms and Royal Cypher, 'EIIR', etched on the blade. In 1952, the year of the accession of Queen Elizabeth II, HRH the Duke of Edinburgh was elected as an Elder Brother and in 1969 he became the Master of Trinity House. His distinguished service was recognised by the presentation of a sword on 31 May 2007. The blade is etched on its outer face with a design incorporating the Royal Cypher, an inscription and the full arms of Trinity House including the helm, crest, wreath, mantling and motto. The etched inscription reads:

The Corporation of Trinity House
The Master's Sword.

As well as the shield of Trinity House, the motto also appears in the oval cartouche on the solid, half-basket hilt. Unusually, the design is set against a background of rays filling the remainder of the oval space. A distinguishing feature of this sword is the form of the scabbard mounts. In addition to the standard engraved lines and volutes and the usual anthemion motif on the chape, each mount has a band of embossed oak leaves. In the case of the two lockets these are associated with the suspension rings. This is the pattern worn by Admirals of the Fleet, of whom HRH is one. The buckle of the black leather sword belt carries the shield of Trinity House.

The Lord Warden of the Cinque Ports

The incumbent of this appointment wears a naval style sword with the appropriate escutcheon in the cartouche: Per pale gules and azure three lions passant guardant Or conjoined to as many ships' hulls Or. The sword knot is the RN pattern and the sword belt is embroidered with four lines of gold thread.[56] Many holders of this ancient appointment have been distinguished naval officers and they probably continued to wear their service swords.

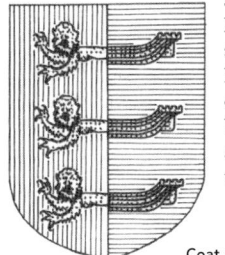

Coat of arms of the Cinque Ports.

CHAPTER 6

Presentation Swords

Since ancient times, swords have been presented as marks of appreciation or in gratitude for services rendered. These have varied from uniform swords with simple inscriptions to magnificent pieces of jewellery. However, while they might have had extra decoration and greater craftsmanship, they were swords designed for fighting. The presentation of a sword decorated purely as a gift or prize seems to date from the middle of the eighteenth century, with the recipient slowly moving down the social scale and the practice seeming to move from the colonies to Britain. In Britain, presentation swords arrive when the wearing of small swords as a fashion item began to decline. To differentiate these swords from other presentation weapons, they probably should be referred to as display swords. Wolfe uses the wider term 'presentation swords' and then draws a distinction between these ornate weapons and those given based on a regulation sword.[1] She points out that when the US Congress ordered some swords in 1785 for commendable actions in the US Revolutionary war, they were ten silver-hilted small swords, a fancy version of a fighting sword. Only one of these was awarded to a US naval officer – Commodore John Halewood. This book follows Wolfe's terminology and this chapter refers mainly to the former group of ornate weapons.

Early presentation swords tended to mark specific events and to be given by companies or groups of merchants or planters. The first known naval example, presented to Captain Middleton (later to become Lord Barham and First Lord of the Admiralty in 1805), was presented by the Assembly in Barbados for keeping down the privateers while he was serving on that station. The Victoria and Albert Museum[2] holds a sword that they attribute as probably Middleton's Barbados sword; such a heavily-jewelled weapon would not be practical for action. Presentation swords were also not necessarily for victories. Lieutenant Popham (later to become Admiral Home Popham, famous for developing the signal code used at Trafalgar) received a sword in 1786 from the East India Company for work on surveying. A naval sword was presented as a mark of victory by the Senate and People of Jamaica to Admiral Sir Samuel Hood in 1791, when he was a captain[3] and this was followed by a further four swords given by a committee of planters in the West Indies for the suppression of privateers between 1793 and 1797, with some further officers receiving silver plate. King George III presented the first known sword to be given outside the corporations with one to celebrate the Glorious First of June and Lord Howe's victory

Henry Perronet Briggs's painting from 1828 showing the visit of George III accompanied by Queen Charlotte to Howe's Flagship, the *Queen Charlotte*, on 26 June 1794 to present a diamond-hilted sword to mark his victory at the battle of the Glorious First of June 1794. (© National Maritime Museum, Greenwich, London, BHC0476)

off Ushant in 1794, a diamond-hilted sword valued at 3000 guineas as well as other marks of honour.[4]

Swords were a popular gift and much sought after by naval officers during the Napoleonic period. This is clear from the number chosen in preference to gifts of plate or cash (when such alternatives were on offer) and the willingness of officers to contribute to the cost of swords. After the battle of the Nile, the captains clubbed together to buy a sword to commemorate the battle as a gift for Admiral Nelson; several of them and at least one other officer present also had a sword or a dirk made for themselves with similar features, particularly a crocodile, featuring on the handle. This desire for presentation swords was not just a British phenomenon; Arthur Sinclair, a US officer involved in the skirmishes on the Great Lakes in the War of 1812, comments in a letter on the lack of recognition for his endeavours in the conflict on Lake Ontario moaning

Admiral Sir Samuel Hood's sword. (NMM Accession Number WPN1549)

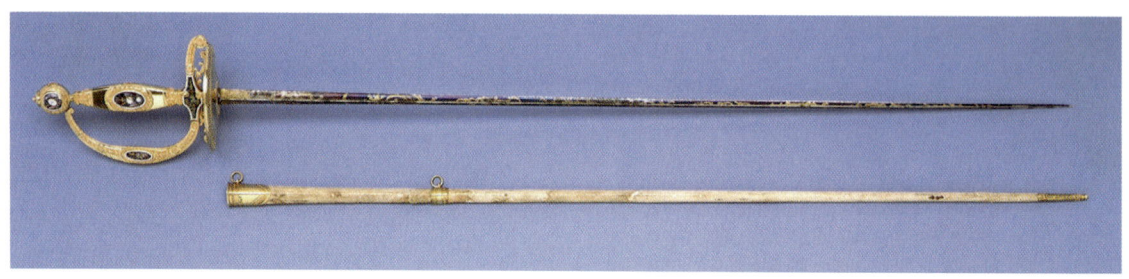

that he had got less 'than many who have received publick [*sic*] thanks – freedom of the citys [*sic*] in gold Boxes – swords and dinners and lord knows what'.[5]

For British swords of the Georgian period, there are three suppliers whose work remains best known. These are Richard Teed who was based in Lancaster Court, The Strand, in London, John Salter also based in The Strand, and John Prosser who was based around the corner in Charing Cross. All three of these were cutlers and would employ a wide variety of craftsmen and companies to make parts for swords.

Swords of the Patriotic Fund

However, probably the best known presentation swords are those given by the Patriotic Fund, which figure in many works of fiction about the Royal Navy in the Napoleonic Wars. This was a national fund established mostly by merchants and underwriters of the City, attracting more than 1500 initial subscribers, administered from the offices of Lloyd's of London. Its opening address made clear its purpose: 'When our very existence as a great and independent nation is at stake, it only becomes necessary to point out any means by which the exertion of our native spirit, and the application of our powerful resources may receive an additional stimulus.'[6]

The fund aimed to stimulate British military forces by two methods: financial support for widows and men injured in action, and awards for gallantry. The fund still supports service people and their families. These swords are often erroneously referred to as coming from Lloyd's Patriotic Fund, rather than the Patriotic Fund at Lloyd's. The awards for gallantry took the form of swords, plate and cash. Where a sword or plate was awarded cash was usually offered as an alternative, the exception being a couple of awards that had elements of all three.

These swords were awarded by the fund between 1803 and 1809. Commencing these awards in 1803 is logical because that could be considered the nadir of British fortunes in the Napoleonic era. The collapse of the Peace of Amiens that year was a bitter blow, raising a terror of French invasion, inspiring numerous schemes and militias aimed protecting the country. This was against a background fear of a French-style revolution. Only that year, there was an uprising in Ireland, the 1797 Fleet mutinies at Spithead and The Nore were still vivid memories, and the cost of living had been rising steeply since the 1790s.

The time was ripe, therefore, for a popular fund to capture the mood and encourage the Royal Navy to greater exertions. Why the fund stopped in 1809, six years before the war ended, is much less clear. However, In 1809 the campaign in Spain started to make headway and the Royal Navy had won command of the sea. Trade was growing and insurance rates were dropping. The City now had a realistic expectation of eventual victory, although these expectations were to falter later especially with the entry of America into another war with Britain in 1812. None of the concerns for final victory were enough to re-establish the presentation of the awards for valour, although the pension work continued.

While the majority of these swords were given to naval officers, seventeen were awarded to officers of the Honourable East India Company (HEIC); all for a single action. A mixed convoy of sixteen East Indiamen and various other merchantmen, without naval escort but with an HEIC brig, were returning from Canton to India when they were met by a squadron of French warships under Contre Admiral Charles-Alexandre Durand Linois. The convoy, by its aggressive behaviour, convinced the French it was too well defended and so drove them off. A few swords also went to army officers. These were all for actions that involved expeditionary forces that had been landed by the Royal Navy or for the capture or defence of sea ports around the world.

The Fund granted 205 awards where the recipient was offered a sword, although only 151 of these opted for a sword. The remainder taking the cash alternative or a piece of plate instead, which usually would be a vase. There were two exceptions to this: Captain Codrington asked that the money be used for those injured in the battle of Trafalgar and Lieutenant Boyd died prior to receiving his award and the family asked for the money instead.

The swords came in three values: £100, £50 and £30, and although some collectors classify the Trafalgar swords as a separate group, they were all worth £100. All were made by Teed. The Fund made around 222 gifts, if the vases, tankards and a medal are included, with a significant number of people either only being offered or opting to take cash instead. The Fund would only offer plate for a number of reasons: the awards were either too high or too low in value; made posthumously; the recipients were not officers (one secretary and one surgeon) or the award was for an event that took place outside the heat of battle. Two officers got a sword and vase for the same action and five already had a sword and then opted for a vase for their second award. Interestingly, one Royal Marines officer, Edward Nichols, opted for two swords – the first one worth £30, as a lieutenant, and then a £50 one, when he was a captain. After the awards of swords ceased, pensions and monetary awards continued, and in this period ten officers applied and were granted permission to have swords made, one even managed to get his through the traditional funding route until it was made clear to Teed that it had ceased. Mr Sutherland, who was only offered plate, clearly subsequently persuaded the Fund to make a sword instead as it passed through the Funds accounts being made by Teed. One officer, Lieutenant Menzies, was initially awarded a £30 sword but wrote to the Fund and asked that this be upgraded to a £50 sword which the Fund duly did. Furthermore, at least three unofficial swords exist; one to Lieutenant Thomas Sherlock Cox RM (Isle de France 1810),[7] one to Lieutenant James Arnold (Capture of Suriname 1804) and the other to Major Edward Fleming (battle of Albuera 1811).[8] Each of these officers received an award of money from the fund and since all were in the period when the fund was granting permissions for the monetary awards to be spent on swords, they should be considered in keeping with both the intent and spirit of the fund.

The importance of valour was reflected in the whole design of the swords, as explained on a label mounted inside the presentation box:

> The ornamental design for the hilts of the swords Presented from this Fund in reward of British Valour imports that NATIONAL UNION (figured by the Roman Fasces) produces HERCULEAN EFFORTS (of which the club of Hercules is emblematic) which, aided by WISDOM (denoted by the Serpent) lead to VICTORY (implied by the skin of the Nemean Lion – the proudest of that Hero's Trophies). The Wreath of Laurel denotes that REWARDS Await the brave who shall successfully Wield their Swords in the Cause of their Country, in Defence of British Security, Independence & Honour.

Patriotic Fund Sword of £100, presented to Captain Bolton of HMS *Fisgard* for the action off Curaçao, 1 January 1807. (Courtesy of the Wardroom Mess President, HMS *Raleigh*)

All the swords had the same hilts, the different values being distinguished by the degree of elaboration of the scabbard and the amount of blued and gilt decoration on the blade. The example illustrated is of a £100 sword and has inscribed on the blade:

> From the patriotic fund at Lloyd's to William Bolton Esq Captain of HMS *Fisgard* for the conquest of Curacao by a daring coup de main on the 1st of January as recorded in the London Gazette of the 27th Feb 1807.

The swords came with a sword knot of gold bullions attached to a blue and gold cord and a blue sword belt elaborately embroidered with gold oak leaves and furnished with gilt mounts. If awarded to an army or Royal Marines officer then it was a red sword knot.

While the main battles of the period are still remembered, the many smaller naval actions and the daring of the captains are often forgotten. Take the action in which the Royal Navy seized Curaçao, in the West Indies (a 38-mile-long island near Venezuela), on 1 January 1807 as an example. The Patriotic Fund honoured all four captains and they chose either vases or swords. In late 1806 it was reported that the citizens of the Dutch island of Curaçao were keen to make an alliance with the British. A squadron of three ships under Captain Charles Brisbane set sail for the island on 29 November. The *Anson*, *Latona* and *Arethusa* reached the island of Aruba on 22 December, anchored and were joined by *Fisgard* on the 23rd. Weighing anchor on the 24th they aimed to arrive on New Year's Day and to take advantage of the tradition that 'every

Sword belt and sword knot of a £100 Patriotic Fund sword. (Courtesy of the Wardroom Mess President, HMS *Raleigh*)

loyal Dutchman makes it a point to steep his senses in strong drink' on that day.[9]

The main town, St Anne, was well defended both naturally and with fortifications, having a narrow harbour entrance surrounded by hills, with the heavily fortified Fort Amsterdam atop the nearest peak. A Dutch frigate, the *Kenau Hasselaar* (36) was moored at the harbour entrance. Fort Republeik overlooked the bottom of the bay, keeping the harbour "within grapeshot distance" and the Dutch corvette *Suriname* (22) was in the harbour. Brisbane determined to catch them completely by surprise. At 1am on 1 January 1807 they sighted the east end of the island. Making full use of the prevailing south-east trade wind they sailed straight in.

Arethusa entered first under a flag of truce with *Latona*, *Anson* and *Fisgard* following in that order. The Dutch ignored the flag and opened fire. Initially matters did not go according to plan as a shift of wind checked the *Arethusa*'s progress and caused *Fisgard* to ground temporarily. However, minutes later the wind shifted again enabling the rest of the squadron to take up position. *Arethusa* by now had her jib boom over the town wall. Calmly, under fire and using the capstan as a desk, Brisbane wrote a summons to the governor: 'Sir, The British Squadron are here to protect, and not to conquer you; to preserve to you your lives, liberty, and property. If a shot is fired at anyone in my squadron after this summons, I shall immediately storm your batteries. You have 5 minutes to accede to this determination.'[10] The governor ignored the letter, continuing to fire. Pulling down the flag of truce and firing broadsides, Brisbane boarded *Kenau Hasselaar* and *Lydiard* took *Suriname*. Achieving this by 7.20am, all four crews rowed ashore and stormed Fort Amsterdam, carrying it within 10 minutes. Then, having quickly seized in turn the citadel, minor fortifications and the town, they returned to their ships and opened fire on Fort Republeik. By 10.00am it too had fallen and by noon the whole island had submitted.

See Appendix 1 for a full list of Swords awarded and made. The currently most accurate list of the further awards of plate appears in Gawler's 'Britons Strike Home' and the latest location of Patriotic Fund swords is maintained online.[11]

City of London Swords

Although the swords of the Patriotic Fund are best known, they are probably not the best artistically. That distinction should go to some of those awarded by the Corporation of the City of London. Unlike the Patriotic Fund, the City of London has continued to mark distinguished service by the presentation of swords. The first was awarded to Admiral Sir John Jervis in 1797 following his victory at Cape St Vincent, although the Corporation had already given presentation boxes to Jervis and Nelson (a commodore at the time) for the same battle and Admiral Howe and Jervis for the battle of the Glorious First of June, 1794. A total of sixty-three swords have been presented, of which twenty-six have gone to naval officers. Until the outbreak of the First World War, these weapons were of two values. Swords of 200 guineas were given to those in superior command while 100-guinea swords were for those second-in-command or for a single action. These swords have been of many styles, varying from highly-enamelled small swords to ornate sabres.

After the First World War, all the swords awarded were of 100 guineas. Admiral Beatty's sword[12] from this time is recognisable as a very ornate modern-style naval sword. Inflation was allowed for after the Second World War, when of

Presentation Swords

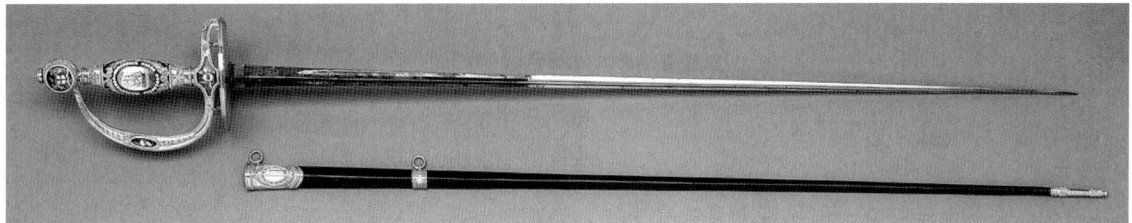

The small-sword presented by the City of London to Admiral Sir John Jervis, Lord St Vincent (1735–1823). This was the first sword to be presented by the City of London and was the style followed for many up until the First World War. (NMM Accession Number WPN1439)

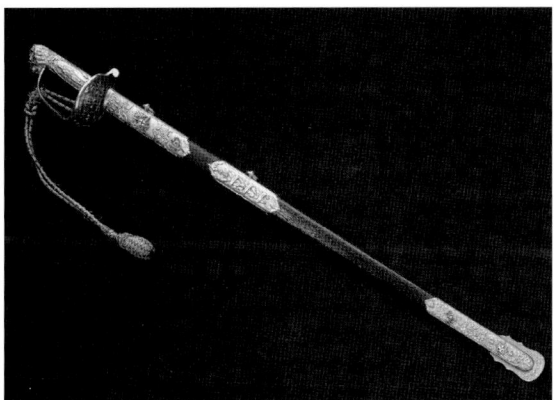

the eight swords awarded, six had a value of about £500. The two swords awarded following the Falklands Conflict in 1982 were £898 each including that to Admiral Sir John Woodward. These are the only two of these swords that were not accompanied with the gift of Freedom of the City. There was a march through the City of London on 12 October 1982, after which a dinner was held in the Guildhall. The City authorities decided on 21 September that this event should be marked with the presentation of swords. At this time the Corporation decided to procure two swords already made and get them engraved, rather than commission a specific manufacture. A list of the City of London Swords presented to naval officers is in Appendix 2.

The sword presented by the City of London to Admiral Beatty for his contribution in the First World War. (NMM Accession Number WPN1581)

Lieutenant Snook and the Sword of Peace

The Award of the Wilkinson/Firmin Sword of Peace to each service as described in Chapter 1, commemorates an event in 1799 when Lieutenant Samuel Snook, an officer in the Bombay Marine, helped return a small group of Pelew Islands[13] women refugees to their home after they had been stranded in Bombay from 1793–7 without friends or means of supporting themselves. Snook supported them out of his own slender pay and in 1797 travelled with them on the *Warley* but bad weather meant that they went straight to Macao, not stopping at Pelew. In Macao, Snook purchased a small vessel, the sloop *Diamante*, at an overall cost of £4200[14] to the East India Company to take them back to their home in the Philippines. After being forced to stay in harbour by bad weather they eventually reached the Pelew Islands in safety and Snook restored the women to their families. This improved local relations and facilitated the use of the Islands as staging posts for the East India Company ships in the Pacific. It also enabled Snook to return five Malay and one Chinese employees of the Company back to Macao. In recognition of this, the East India Company Court of Directors presented him with a special sword.

This sword was purchased at auction in 1965 by Wilkinson who then presented it to the National Army Museum. The blade is curved and highly decorated with gilding, bluing and engraving, including the dedication; it has a gilt stirrup guard with an ivory grip, ornate cross guard and a pommel in the form of a helmet and either gilt feathering or scales overlaid onto the base of the handle; the cartouches on the scabbard show Britannia in various images; the decoration is the work of the goldsmith Thomas Hamlet. The blade is inscribed:

'PRESENTED BY THE COURT OF DIRECTORS OF THE UNITED EAST INDIA COMPANY TO LIEUT SAMUEL SNOOK OF THE BOMBAY MARINES AS A MARK OF THE COURT'S APPROBATION OF HIS SERVICES WHEN AT MACAO IN THE YEAR 1799.'

In many ways it is very similar in design to a Patriotic Fund at Lloyd's sword. The sword was ordered by the East India Company in 1805 and presented on 22 February 1806, so after the Patriotic Fund started and rather than the earlier date mentioned in the award. In style and value, it equated to one awarded by the Patriotic Fund to a Captain at the battle of Trafalgar. Lieutenant Snook also received many subsequent promotions in the company prior to retiring to England.

Lt Snook's sword which is held by the National Army Museum. *(Pooley Swords Image from Wilkinson Archives)*

Other Presentation Swords

From the Napoleonic period and shortly afterwards, a variety of organisations made gifts of one-off naval presentation swords, which would provide splendid additions to any collection. Many similar weapons were also presented to army officers of this period and officers leading local militias. Georgian presentation swords remain highly collectable with appropriately expensive auction prices.

Other nations and colonies continued to award swords for incidents important to them. Sir Edward Hamilton, who cut out the *Hermione* – whose crew had mutinied and defected to the Spanish in October 1799 – was awarded a sword of 300 guineas by the House of Assembly in Jamaica. The city of London voted him a gold box to the value of 50 guineas for the same event.[15] Even insurance companies presented swords, with Captain Fairfax Moreseby of HMS *Wizard* receiving one from the British Insurance Company at Malta in 1807 for the protection of trade to and from Malta.[16]

At the other end of the scale, we come to uniform swords with a simple inscription on the blade. The example illustrated was given to Geoffrey Durham Stokes by his parents when he was promoted lieutenant in 1920. The inscription on the blade, etched using a mask prepared from the handwriting of one of his parents (probably his father), recalls his service in the great fleet action of Jutland on 31 May 1916. At that time, he was a 16-year-old midshipman serving in HMS *Malaya*. This ship fired 215 rounds from her 15in main armament. In return, she was hit seven times by German 12in shells, which killed sixty-three of her crew and wounded another sixty-eight. Phillip, the eldest son of Mr and Mrs Durham Stokes had died in France in 1917, aged 20. Geoffrey Stokes's parents must have been very grateful that this son returned safely from the war and the inscription on the blade of this sword encapsulates their feelings of both pride and relief.

As has been discussed in Chapter 1, both naval swords and dirks have traditionally been presented as prizes to naval officers for individual excellence in training, and this continues to today. Similarly, the authors have already mentioned in Chapter 3 the female officer presented a USN sword on completion of an exchange job in the United States.

Inscription on sword presented to G D Stokes RN by his parents to commemorate the battle of Jutland.

The battleship HMS *Malaya* in which Stokes served at Jutland.

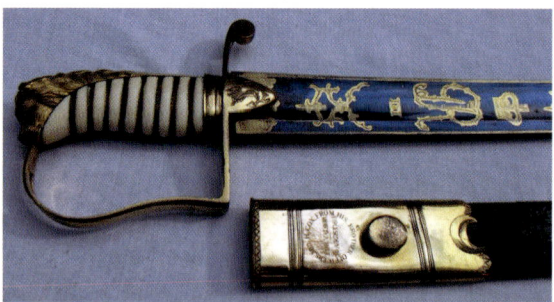

A presentation sabre presented to Midshipman H Cox for valour on 14 August 1813 from his brother officers. This was for the action when HMS *Pelican* captured the US sloop *Argus*. Later in his career he received a second presentation sword from London Underwriters for his work in commanding a Coast Guard station. (Private Collection)

A gilt copy of Admiral Sir William Cornwallis' silver gilt small-sword. Inscribed '21 June 1805 His Majesty's Ship Wasp'. (Private Collection)

Detail from the copy of Admiral Sir William Cornwallis' small-sword. (Private Collection)

A sabre presented to Lieutenant George Prettyman from the Petty Officers and Crew of His Majesty's Ship *Salisbury* as a token of their regard. He served in HMS *Salisbury* in the East Indies from 1818 to 1821. (Private Collection)

Detail from Lieutenant Prettyman's sabre showing the winged victory knuckle guard. (Private Collection)

Presentation Swords 81

58/6255
THE LATE ADMIRAL SIR HOUSTON STEWART, G.C.B.

Admiral Sir Houston Stewart GCB. (Private Collection)

Sword of Captain Fane, an officer who had a meteoric rise from Lieutenant in 1801 to Post Captain in 1804, no doubt helped by his relationship through marriage to Admiral Lord St Vincent, who was First Lord of the Admiralty at this time. Fane became a prisoner of war in 1810 and never saw active service again. The sword has the Latin phrase on the hilt 'Libus undis virtutis verae custos rigidusque satelles' which is the second half of a quote from Epistles Book 1 Number 1 lines 16 and 17 and would have started 'Nunc agilis fio, et mersor civilibus undis' meaning 'In the tumults of public affairs I am the guardian of true virtue and its stern companion'

the family motto 'ne ville fano' meaning 'from the towns shrine' and mounted with the family symbol the Bull. The blade is inscribed 'Intaminatis fulgeat honoribus' which means 'Let him shine with unstained honour' Odes Book 3 Number line 18. Both are quotations from the Odes of Horace. (Private Collection)

Above right: Detail from Captain Fane's sword showing the crossed anchors within the guard and the Latin inscriptions. (Private Collection)

Above and below: Two swords presented to Admiral Stewart: (a) presented to him as a Captain by the Midshipmen of HMS *Menai* in January 1825, and (b) presented to Captain Stewart for his work in the area by John Lynch of the Island of Jamaica where he served from 1815 to 1817. (Private Collection)

CHAPTER 7
Nelson's Swords

The cachet of Nelson's name, along with the word 'Trafalgar', adds value to anything linked to it. No sword, however, can definitively be said to be the one Nelson used in action, thus creating a fertile area for claims and counter claims for provenance. He would have used weapons of his choice throughout his career, because an official pattern naval sword was only established in 1805, just months before he died. Indeed, he could have used several swords over the years. Furthermore, while Nelson was very frequently portrayed in artworks, with great attention paid to the correct depiction of his uniform, rarely was such care taken over the depiction of the weapon he was carrying.

The Lure of the Name

Any weapon linked to Nelson or Trafalgar may command a considerable premium, compared with other similar swords. For example comparing the sale of two Patriotic Fund £100 swords, both including the original case and in comparable condition, one – awarded to Captain Charles Tyler of HMS *Tonnant* – sold at the Trafalgar 200 Anniversary sale for £179,200, while the sword awarded to Captain Jahleel Brenton for a single-ship action in 1810 sold in November 2008 for £84,000.[1]

The name adds marketing value despite very weak provenance, as demonstrated by an example from 2012 of a sword being sold by an auction house abroad. While the auction house was careful to put appropriate caveats in their online advertisement, the sword was nonetheless described as:

> **Admiral Lord Nelson Interest: An 1805 Pattern Naval Officer's Sword:** the 32.25 inch fullered and blued blade with lion, unicorn, crown, anchor and military trophy engraved and gilt decoration, the gilt hilt with ivory grip, lion pommel, the knuckle guard engraved 'Used by Lord Nelson and presented by him, to Lieutenant Edward Gascoine Palmer.', in gilt mounted leather scabbard bearing similar inscription and monogram HN, length 38" – 96.5 cm.[2]

The date of Nelson's death alone makes this claim unlikely, since Nelson did not receive his own 1805 sword before he set sail for his final voyage. Furthermore, according to O'Byrne's *Dictionary of Naval Biography*, Lieutenant Palmer had only just joined the Royal Navy at that date, and never served in the same vessel as Nelson, although he was in the same squadron. His vessel was not present at Trafalgar, and Palmer did not become a lieutenant until four years later. It was unusual to engrave weapons or scabbards. Therefore, any engraving or decoration on blades of the period was probably done later, by either a subsequent owner, by someone genuinely wishing to record an association, or, potentially, from the more base motive of attempting to deceive.

The problem of the manufacture of Nelson relics was identified early by Sir Nicholas Harris Nicolas, a biographer of Nelson, who wrote in a letter published in *The Times* in 1846 of 'the manufacture of Nelsonian relics, swords and buckles &c., seems so profitable a speculation in certain curiosity

Nelson's Column. (Paul Lilly)

dealers, and the folly of persons who can be imposed on by such things is so glaring'.[3]

Indeed, the Palmer sword mentioned above is one of several associated with Nelson recorded by May and Annis that are of a 'most doubtful nature'.[4] May and Annis also identified a dirk associated with Lieutenant Palmer. They further list: a Turkish scimitar with the initials 'NB' ('Nelson and Bronte') and a coronet; a general's sword; a flag officer's sword from 1854; a small-sword; a sword similar to the 1805 and a 1825 sword all with the initials 'HN' and on some a crest/coronet. Lastly, they also draw attention to an 1805 Pattern sword of that for lieutenants or below, which is acknowledged by the inscription that it was Nelson's sword when he was a 'mate'. However, Nelson was a vice admiral by the time this pattern of sword was introduced.

Since then a further item has also appeared on the market, coming from the estate of Nelson's prize agent, Alexander Davison. A silver-mounted combined sword-pistol,[5] it was made by H.W. Mortimer of London sometime in 1805-06.

The Confirmed History of Nelson's Swords

In the midst of all the debate and conjecture surrounding Nelson's swords, certain facts remain, and any sword claiming Nelsonian provenance needs to fit those facts.

Nelson was very much the popinjay and enjoyed all the outward show that he could muster. He would often appear sporting all his decorations and awards, (as was common practice among officers of the period). However, at times he lacked the funds to support this display. This occasionally led to him breaking up decorative elements of his swords, such as jewels, to liquidate into cash.

After the loss of his right arm at Tenerife on 25 July 1797, which ended his days of conducting cutting-out and boarding operations, he continued to wear his sword on the left, as all the portraits show. To get it out of the scabbard easily, therefore, he would have needed a short blade. He might have bought a new sword, had the blade shortened, had a new shorter blade fitted or accepted that he would have difficulty drawing it. Any of these alternatives are possible.

After returning from chasing Villeneuve to the West Indies on 18 August 1805, Nelson is known to have visited his sword cutler, Salter, at least once before sailing again on 15 September, because he ordered some silver for his daughter Horatia on 21 August. He could, therefore, have ordered a sword of the new pattern.

At Trafalgar, he did not put his sword on but left it in his cabin. When Captain Hardy packed up the contents of Nelson's cabin to take to Lady Hamilton at Merton, those contents included two swords. May and Annis record that these were said to be a dress sword of 1795 and a fighting sword of the 1805 pattern, which are the arms you would expect, but the authority of that statement is unknown.[6]

It is known that in 1811 Lady Hamilton had some dealings with Salter (see Chapter 6), where she disposed of some jewellery and plate and had some other pieces repaired. Among her purchases were a naval sword with knot and belt, a naval dirk and a gold sword. The low price she paid for the gold sword is somewhat mysterious, because it does not reflect any realistic price from the time – even if it were assumed to be gilt – unless it was for a repair or alteration, and much the same is true for the dirk. Two theories are put forward for this: firstly, that Nelson had ordered but not collected and paid for a sword in 1805 and Lady Hamilton decided to honour the purchase. The second theory is that the payment was, in fact, for work to remove jewels or other elements from the sword, rather than to purchase the weapon.

In 1813, Lady Hamilton sold most of the contents of Merton to Alderman Joshua Smith, the bill of sale for which included a sword and a sabre. The contents of Merton seem to have been packed up after her death in 1815 and later transferred to a Mr John Kinsey, the Constable in the Town Hall of Southwark, probably in 1831. Thereafter, the clarity of ownership runs cold and the intrigue begins.

The Galfridus Walpole-Suckling Sword

In 1711, Captain Galfridus Walpole of the *Lion* lost his arm in an action against four similar French ships at Vado Bay near Genoa. He died in 1726, just after the birth of Maurice Suckling, who had a distinguished naval career, with a meritorious action in the *Dreadnought* (60) off Cape François and ended up as Comptroller of the Navy in 1775. Suckling was Horatio Nelson's uncle, and provided the interest to enable him to go to sea and progress his early career. Legend runs that Captain Walpole left the sword he had worn at Vado to Maurice Suckling, who either gave it or bequeathed it to Nelson, and that Nelson treasured it. James Stanier Clarke and John McArthur, who wrote *The Life and Services of Admiral Lord Nelson* in 1809, commented on a sword that Nelson valued greatly and that had come from Galfridus Walpole. The *Naval Chronicle* for 1805[7] records a tale that, in an earlier part of his life, Nelson had received a small-sword with a strong injunction that he was 'never to part with it but with his life'. The *Chronicle* goes on to tell that in the attack at Tenerife when Nelson was hit in his right arm this sword, understandably, fell to the ground but that he managed to recover it with his left hand and keep hold of it while being returned to his ship. These publications, which are the only primary sources for these stories, are by the same men, Clarke and McArthur, who edited and published the *Naval Chronicle*.

The Suckling Family Sword

In 1971, the Suckling family still held a sword that is presumed to be Galfridus Walpole's. This weapon, a hunting sword, the silver hilt hallmarked 1752, has an earlier cut-down German blade. There are several problems with the provenance of this sword, however. First, Maurice Suckling had other relatives who served in the Royal Navy at the same time as Nelson, so why Nelson should have been singled out so early in his career to be the recipient is unclear. Second, if this is the sword, there is no provenance known to the authors as to how it got back to the Suckling family. Suggestions have been made that it was handed to Lieutenant Maurice William Suckling who was going home in the *Agamemnon* in 1796 when Nelson moved from the *Agamemnon* to the *Captain*, in which case it could not have then been carried at Tenerife. A second suggestion is that it was handed over for an unclear reason when the same Lieutenant Suckling visited Nelson and the Hamiltons when they landed at Yarmouth in 1800. A third is that it was still in Nelson's cabin in *Victory* at Trafalgar and was subsequently carried home by Midshipman Benjamin William Suckling. However, although a member of *Victory's* crew, Midshipman Suckling was not on board at the time of Trafalgar.

Further problems occur with the will of Galfridus Walpole, which does not mention the sword. The will was written a week before Maurice Suckling was born and Walpole died three weeks after the birth. It seems unlikely that Walpole gave a sword to a newborn baby.

Furthermore, Walpole's estate did not descend to the Sucklings but stayed with his widow and then went to his brother Robert, 1st Earl of Orford. The 3rd Earl inherited the estate in 1751, which would tie in with the date on the hilt. Cutting down the blade and adding a new hilt would have been considered an update to a useful tool. The 3rd Earl did not die until 1797, so at some point the sword must have been passed across, quite possibly as a present, when his cousin Mary married Maurice Suckling in 1764.

It seems more credible that, if Nelson owned the sword, that the legend regarding the requirement to keep it safe is a gloss put on by Clarke and McArthur, perhaps because they could not resist the tale that the same sword fell twice with severed right arms.[8] If Nelson owned it, then it is entirely plausible he felt it right to give it to Lieutenant Suckling as he returned home in the *Agamemnon*, because the lieutenant had unexpectedly become the Suckling heir. This, of course, would mean that it was not used at Tenerife.

Nelson's Oval Side Ring

Nelson must have been an enthusiast of the oval side ring style of sword, since it appears in the portraits in preference to any of the grand swords he received to mark his victories. It also has credibility as the candidate for the sword that he was given by his uncle Maurice Suckling. It is the style of sword that McArthur and Clarke, in their biography of

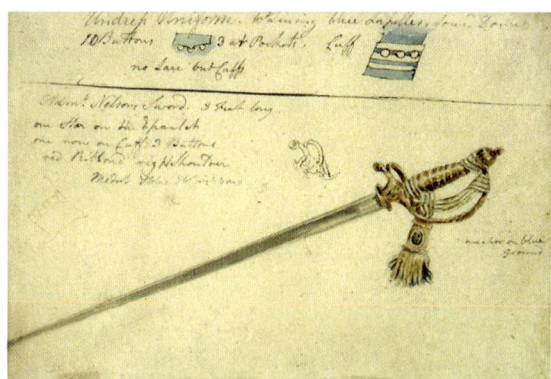

Watercolour sketch of Lord Nelson's oval side ring small-sword as drawn while with his lace makers, Barrett, Corney and Corney, in September 1805. (Nelson Museum, Monmouth).

Nelson, show him using in action; McArthur had known Nelson and even commissioned a portrait of him by Lemuel Francis Abbott. May and Annis say that Nelson is believed to have purchased one with a short blade after losing his arm in 1797.[9] As this type of sword is clearly designed for right-handed use, with the side ring protecting the outside of the hand, this seems an odd choice of weapon for a man who was, by necessity, left-handed. It is possible that he had already ordered the weapon prior to the battle of Santa Cruz de Tenerife (22–25 July 1797) and was honouring his contract to purchase. However, he certainly owned a sword of this type in 1805, because, in September that year prior to departing, he left it with his lace makers, Barrett, Corney and Corney, to have a new sword knot made, along with some adjustments to his uniforms. While the sword was in their hands, a sketch was made, which also contains the notation that the sword is three feet long. This shows that this sword was not shortened to accommodate the loss of his right arm. The location of this sword is not known. A similar weapon is illustrated in Chapter 3. A silver-gilt copy of the sword was made by the manufacturers Prosser in 1797 and auctioned at Sotheby's in 1969. The location of this sword is also unknown.

The Starbuck Sword

The Starbuck sword first appeared in 1843 and was owned by Reverend F F Starbuck at the time of the Royal Naval Exhibition of 1891, where it was described as Nelson's first sword, and as the sword Nelson took to sea in 1770, the tale being that it was given to a Mr Dennington in 1843 by a servant of Nelson's family. This sword was sold in 1917 at Christies and then in 1961 presented to Commander-in-Chief, Portsmouth, by Lieutenant Colonel and Mrs A C Whitcome of Seaview, Isle of Wight. It was intended for Commander-in-Chief (Portsmouth) and his successors to display. It was initially displayed in HMS *Victory* and was recorded as still there by May and Annis in 1971. The sword, however, is a stirrup-hilted dress sword with crown and fouled-anchor langets and therefore probably dates from after 1805 and possibly after 1812. By 1961, the sword had become associated with a dirk also described as having belonged to Nelson, in this case from his time in the *Raisonnable* in 1771. This dirk was not part of the Christie sale and is now in storage at the Royal Naval Museum (accession number 1961/65). It has a small oval leather patch sewn on to the scabbard with the words '*Horatio Nelson Raisonnable 1771*'. The donor believed it to have belonged to Nelson because a relative of his wife's family was in service with the Nelson's at Burnham Thorpe. Both of these weapons were considered surplus and disposed of in 1984 by the Royal Navy Trophy Centre[10] and the dirk was transferred to the Royal Naval Museum. The Navy sold the sword, probably as a standard 1805 Pattern sword, through Portsmouth auctioneers' Nesbitts. The publication in the 1970s of data on Napoleonic sword manufacturers means it was likely to have been confirmed as made after Nelson's death.

Sword Inscribed to Captain Suckling as Presented to Midshipman Horatio Nelson

This hanger in the National Maritime Museum has engraved inside the knuckle-guard 'CAPT. SUCKLING COM^G H.M.S. TRIUMPH' and then has a gilt band around the grip inscribed 'To HORATIO NELSON Mid^n'. The sword itself is one of a style that came into fashion after 1785 and the band did not appear on grips until the 1790s, with the use of the abbreviation 'H.M.S.' appearing about the same time. However, Captain Suckling was captain of *Triumph* from 1771 to 1774 and Nelson was a midshipman at this time. So it would seem extremely unlikely that the sword belonged to Captain Suckling and certainly could not have previously belonged to Galfridus Walpole, who died in 1726. The sword came from the Walter Nelson collection that was lent to the museum, during its creation in 1935, and subsequently acquired.

Sword Presented by Admiral Lambert to the Royal United Service Institute (RUSI)

In 1860, Vice Admiral Sir George Robert Lambert presented a sword to the RUSI Museum as the sword worn by Nelson at St Vincent and Tenerife. Admiral Lambert had served in the Napoleonic Wars and became a post captain in 1825. When the RUSI Museum closed in 1960, the sword was transferred to the National Maritime Museum. However, this sword is of a light cavalry type, which did not come into use until the 1790s, so could not have been given to Nelson in time for St Vincent and Tenerife and is unlikely to have been given to or purchased by Nelson later. It is held in storage at the National Maritime Museum.[11]

Sword engraved as presented to Midshipman Nelson by Captain Suckling of HMS *Triumph*. Captain Suckling was captain from 1771 to 1774 but the sword probably dates from the 1790s. (NMM Accession number WPN 1063)

Sword presented to RUSI by Admiral Lambert originally claimed to have been from Nelson's early career, although it dates from the 1790s. (NMM Accession number WPN1256)

The Evans-Nicolas Sword

In 1844, Mr John Kinsey, a constable of Southwark, acting for the wife of Alderman Smith who had possibly acquired the contents of Merton Place (see 'The Confirmed History of Nelson's Swords' above) got in touch with an antiques dealer called Thomas Evans and in one of the crates was a uniform and a small-sword. Evans approached a collector called Sir Nicholas Harris Nicolas and offered him the items. Nicolas then managed to circumvent Evans and directly approached Mrs Smith and also involved Mrs Horatia Ward (née Nelson). This set off a feud between Evans and Nicolas. The uniform coat was established as the one worn at Trafalgar when Nelson was killed and was purchased by Nicolas directly from Mrs Smith. The Prince Consort was then persuaded to purchase it and donate it to the Royal Hospital at Greenwich, and thus to the National Maritime Museum, where it is still on display. Evans assumed the sword with the coat also belonged to Nelson and, as such, offered it to the Prince Consort. It was stated that this was not only the one left in the cabin but also the one placed on the coffin at the state funeral. A series of correspondence occurred back and forth in *The Times* between November 1846 and January 1847 and eventually a libel action reported in June 1847.[12] The sword was purchased from Evans by an unknown patron who presented it to Admiral Sir Robert Stopford, the Admiral in Command of the Royal Hospital at Greenwich. Despite a sworn affidavit that it was remembered by the boatswain who looked after the body

existence of which Kinsey kept quiet in 1844. But a sketch of a sword in his possession, dated 1847, provides some credibility and it could have been the sabre referred to in the original inventory of Merton. It is reputed to have eventually found its way to Lady Llangattock of Crickhowell, whose collection forms the basis of the Nelson Museum at Monmouth.

An elaborate 1805-style sword with the initials 'HN' engraved on the top locket of the scabbard is in a private collection. However, without a traceable provenance, it remains established just as an attractive sword of the early nineteenth century.

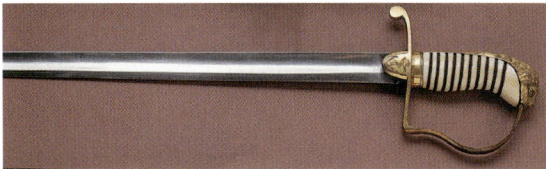

An 1805 Pattern sword but with a curved blade and a knurled ivory grip and the langets replaced by gold medallions with embossed naval trophies featuring the initials 'HN' long thought to have been a Nelsonian relic (Private Collection)

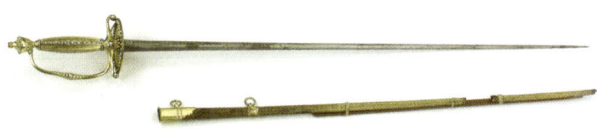

This weapon featured as part of a libel case in 1847 over its claim as having belonged to Nelson. Now attributed to Joshua Smith, although Sir William Hamilton is also a credible original owner.

while it was lying in state, it was established that there was no sword on the coffin. In *The Naval Officer's Sword* Captain Bosanquet suggests this could have been Alderman Smith's sword, although equally credible is that it was Sir William Hamilton's, as it was from Lady Hamilton's property and could have been placed there prior to coming to Alderman Smith. The sword also appeared to have had jewels removed and replaced with silver studs – giving more credence to the second of these possibilities, given the known involvement of Lady Hamilton with the jewellers mentioned earlier. This sword is currently in the National Maritime Museum collection, attributed to Alderman Joshua Smith.[13]

Nelson's 1805 Pattern Sword

Nelson possibly purchased a sword of the 1805 pattern from John Salter before departing for Trafalgar. It is possible that this is the fighting sword that remained in his cabin at Trafalgar and was returned to Lady Hamilton. The Nelson Museum in Monmouth, Gwent, holds an 1805 Pattern with a blade that is 6in (152mm) shorter than the norm, probably to allow it to be drawn from its scabbard by the left hand. This particular sword is also purported to have, as described previously, passed to Alderman Smith and then to a servant, John Kinsey, who tried to sell it via a newspaper advertisement in 1847, and the

An 1805 Pattern sword attributed as being bought by Nelson just prior to sailing for his final voyage. (Nelson Museum, Monmouth)

Admiral Tryon's Nelson Sword

It is known that the Victorian Admiral George Tryon procured a collection of Nelson artefacts, but the knowledge of its whereabouts died with him when he went down with HMS *Victoria* after she sank following a collision in 1893. The wreck has recently been discovered off Lebanon and the divers who found her claim to have found Tryon's collection and have brought a couple of artefacts to the surface as evidence of their claim. They reported that they have located and identified Nelson's sword but that it remains on the wreck. The wreck is a declared gravesite and as such may not be disturbed or salvaged, so it is neither known what type of sword this is nor how credible the claim.

Sword Presented by Nelson to Captain Cockburn

The National Maritime Museum holds a small-sword that is engraved 'Presented by Commodore Nelson to Captn George Cockburn of His Majesty's Ship la Minerve in commemoration of two gallant Actions fought on the 19 & 20 Decr 1796'. Captain Cockburn was Nelson's flag captain at this action in which the frigate *Minerve* (38), in company with the *Blanche* (32), each captured a larger Spanish frigate. In the *Minerve*'s case, this was 'after a brave resistance of two hours and fifty minutes, during which she lost her mizenmast, and had her fore and main masts shot through in several places, the Spanish 40-gun frigate *Sabina*, Captain Don Jacobo Steuart, struck her colours to the *Minerve*, whose masts, although none of them had been shot away, were, as well as her rigging and sails, much wounded'.[14] With the ending of the Cockburn baronetcy in 1880, the sword was sold but then recovered by a relative to keep it in the family. It descended through the family and, on the death of Lieutenant George Cockburn Yorke in 1948, was presented to the National Maritime Museum where it is on display.[15]

Nile Swords

After the battle of Nile, Nelson received a number of presentation swords. Three days after the battle, the fourteen surviving captains of the fleet inaugurated the 'Egyptian Club' to present a sword to Nelson and have a portrait painted. This sword was the one used by Nelson when he was involved in the investiture of his second-in-command at Copenhagen, Rear Admiral Thomas Graves, as a Knight of the Order of the Bath.[16] The sword descended into the Bridport family through the second Baron, who married Nelson's niece and inherited the Bronte estate, which was permitted to be passed by lineal primogeniture through the female line. This hilt was also auctioned in 1895, the blade having disappeared, and then exhibited in the Painted Hall at Greenwich from where it was stolen in 1900 and never recovered. The grip and pommel of this sword were formed into the shape of a crocodile. Some, if not all, of the captains had copies made. Two of the copies are in the National Maritime Museum, that belonging to Captain Hood (HMS *Zealous*)[17] and one whose original owner is unknown.[18] A further one, belonging to James Saumarez (HMS *Orion*), who was Nelson's second in command at the Nile, is in the Castle Cornet Museum in Guernsey. Any of the fourteen captains could have ordered a sword. As well as the captains, Lieutenant Cuthbert – who took over from Captain Westcott (HMS *Majestic*) – had a presentation sword with a crocodile handle made with his reward money.[19] It is possible Lieutenant Thomas Capel,[20] who was given command of the brig *Mutine* to bring the news home, ordered a commemoration weapon. Two pieces of evidence support this conjecture: firstly, the captain of HMS *Pickle*, who brought the news back of Trafalgar, received a sword for his services, and the Fund minutes treated it as nothing unusual. Capel was also

Sir William Beechey's painting of Sir George Cockburn proudly wearing the sword he was presented with by Nelson. (© National Maritime Museum, Greenwich, London, BHC2618)

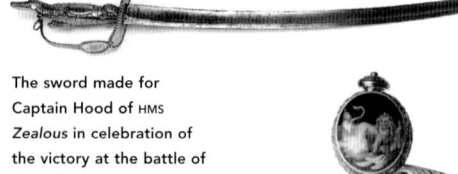

The sword made for Captain Hood of HMS *Zealous* in celebration of the victory at the battle of the Nile. (NMM Accession Number WPN 1550)

The sword presented to Nelson by the City of London for his victory at the battle of the Nile. (London Museum Artefact Number 11957)

at Trafalgar, then as a captain, but opted for a vase instead of a Patriotic Fund Sword, which suggests that he may already have had an ornate sword.

Two more of these Nile swords are known. One was presented to the Duke of Clarence, later to be William IV. Finally, Alexander Davison, a friend of Nelson who secured the appointment of Prize Agent for the Nile, and who made the arrangements for the swords, had at least one made for himself. A further dirk in a private collection with a crocodile head pommel is known.[21]

The further gifts of swords to Nelson for the Nile are:

- From the King of the Two Sicillies – this was a small-sword with a gold hilt and studded with diamonds. It had one diamond stolen when Nelson wore it at a fête in Hamburg.[22] He willed this to his brother to pass as part of the Bronte estates in Sicily and thus it descended into the Bridport family. The Bridports removed the remainder of the diamonds to make a necklace. The necklace and the hilt were sold at auction in 1895. By this time, the blade had disappeared. Lady Llangattock of Crickhowell later acquired the hilt, which featured in a Richard Dimbleby programme in 1953 and was then stolen a few nights later and has never been recovered.

- From the Sultan of Turkey – this was a scimitar and was bequeathed in Nelson's will to his agent, Alexander Davison. Somehow the scimitar and its scabbard became separated. The scabbard was passed to the National Maritime Museum from Greenwich Hospital. It was bequeathed to Greenwich by Alexander Davison's son, along with the two other items mentioned in Nelson's will as bequeathed to Davison. At this stage, however, the scabbard was with a different scimitar, which has a hilt that does not belong to it but appears to be one from an Egyptian Club sword with the enamels replaced with engravings. The sultan's scimitar was found in the private collection alongside several other Nelsonian relics of another descendent of Alexander Davison in 2002. This sword sold at Sotheby's on 21 October 2002 to a private collector for £366,650.

- The City of London sword – the inscription states that, at a council meeting in the Guildhall on 16 October 1798, the City resolved to purchase a sword for 200 guineas as a 'Testimony of the high esteem they entertain of his Public Services and of the eminent advantages he has rendered his country'. The City paid Robert Makepeace £210 for it in 1799, although the sword was made by James Morisset. The gold hilt has a series of translucent, blue enamel plaques. The grip shows the coats of arms of the City of London and Lord Nelson. The guard has 'Nile' and '1798' written in diamond studs between depictions of crocodiles. On either side of the pommel are illustrations of Britannia and a lion trampling the French flag. On the shell is a scene with a bust of Nelson being crowned by Britannia in the presence of Hercules and Minerva. This sword was made with a left-hand grip because it post-dated the loss of the arm at Tenerife. It was auctioned in 1928, bought by Lord Wakefield who presented it back to the City of London, where it is now on display at the City of London Modern Galleries.[23]

A contemporary memoir of Nelson[24] relates that, for the battle of the Nile, the Island of Zante awarded him a gold-headed sword set round with all the diamonds the island could furnish and a cane. This was 'for having, by his victory, preserved that part of Greece from the horrors of anarchy'. Nelson is said to have responded 'No officer . . . had ever received from any country a higher acknowledgement of his services'.[25] It would appear that the memoir records it incorrectly because the two items – the sword and the cane – appear to be one and the same. No further trace of a sword can be found, but the cane is clearly recorded being loaned by Nelson descendants to the RUSI museum and then the National Maritime Museum, before being sold at Sotheby's in 2005.[26] It fits the description in being gold-headed and set around with jewels.

Other Swords Presented to Nelson

The Nelson Museum in Great Yarmouth holds a presentation sword similar in style to those of the Patriotic Fund of Lloyd's, commissioned by Marquis Circello, the Sicilian Ambassador to London, as a gift for Nelson. It is dated 9 October 1805, meaning Nelson never received it and possibly never knew about it. The archive at the National Maritime Museum contains a letter from HRH the Duke of Clarence in 1805 to Collingwood[27] congratulating him on the battle of Trafalgar. In this letter, the Duke mentions that he had presented both Earl St Vincent and Lord Nelson with a sword in their hour of victory.[28] No other record of this sword is known but from the way the letter reads it is also possible that it was not a gift from the Duke but one that he had presented on behalf of an organisation. The authors have also seen statements that a sword was given by the City of London to Nelson for the battle of Cape St Vincent in 1797. This is incorrect: only one sword was given and that was presented to Admiral Sir John Jervis, later Earl St Vincent. Nelson received a presentation box for this battle, which contained his Freedom of the City.

Edward Fraser,[29] who used various written sources around the centenary of Trafalgar to record a significant quantity of information on Nelson but without modern referencing, refers to Cardinal York being given passage by Nelson on board *Agamemnon*. Cardinal York was brother to the Young Pretender and the last Prince of the House of Stuart at the time, and Fraser records him as presenting Nelson with a sword or dirk as a mark of his thanks. At the time Edward Fraser was writing, the weapon was preserved at Trafalgar House, the seat of Earl Nelson. It has not been possible to trace this weapon.

The Swords Surrendered to Nelson

Nelson received the swords of the officers of opposing ships as a mark of surrender on several occasions, as depicted in the famous scene when the captains of *San Josef* and *San Nicolas* surrendered at the battle of Cape St Vincent to the then Commodore Horatio Nelson. Nelson handed the swords to his bargeman, William Fearney, who tucked them under his arm.

Both Sim Comfort's collection (EW56) and the Wallace Collection (A695) have Spanish broadswords that are inscribed as having been captured at Cape St Vincent. The former is inscribed 'SWORD TAKEN OUT OF ONE OF THE SPANISH MEN OF WAR AT THE BATTLE OF CAPE ST VINCENT BY VICE ADMIRAL WALDEGRAVE 14 FEBr 1797' and in the second case 'San Josef Feby. 14 1797'. The provenance of the first is supported by one of the letters written by Nelson, which comments that he is sending an account of the battle and 'also the Sword of one of the Officers (I believe Second Captain of the *San Nicolas*) with which he killed one of my seaman'.[30]

Two paintings showing Nelson receiving swords, after the battle of Cape St Vincent on 14 February 1797: (*above*) the surrender of the *San Josef*, and (*right*) the surrender of the *San Nicolas* (© National Maritime Museum, Greenwich, London, Daniel Orme BHC0493 and Richard Westall BHC2909)

The swords of the three French and Spanish Admirals, Villeneuve, Cisneros and Alava, who fought at Trafalgar were surrendered to Admiral Collingwood, being delivered by Don Francisco Riquelme of the *Santa Ana* (as well as his own) and remained in the Collingwood family until sold in auction in 1899 by Christies.[33] The sword belonging to Admiral Gravina, who escaped from the battle, is held at the Museo Naval Madrid.

As the custom of the time was so strong, there would have been other swords offered in surrender to Nelson, although whether he kept any is unknown. It is clear from those already mentioned that he may have passed them to his officers or returned them to the surrendering captains.

Nelson Statues and Paintings

Caution needs to be exercised when drawing conclusions from representations of swords in depictions of Nelson. Many of the portraits are posthumous and the swords thought to be appropriate by the artist are not necessarily correct. For example, the statue in Trafalgar Square shows him wearing a sword with a crude cross-shaped hilt that is clearly an anachronism. This is probably because the statue was completed in 1843 and the sword is similar to the shape of the Mameluke-hilted pattern sword that was introduced in the previous year. Interestingly, this does not match the maquette of the statue that sits in the entrance hall to the Old Admiralty Building. On the maquette, he is holding what appears to be an 1805 Pattern sword. Various explanations have been put forward for this: one is that the statue was struck by lightning in either the 1880s or 1896 and the sword then replaced with an incorrect one. The alternative view is that, for some reason, the sculptor E H Bailey changed the sword between the maquette and the main statue, perhaps for ease of manufacture. The evidence for this being the correct explanation rests with the image in the *Illustrated London News* of the statue prior to it being placed on top of the plinth, which clearly shows this crude, incorrect sword present on the original statue.

The east face of the plinth shows Nelson after the battle of St Vincent in 1797. Here, he is also wearing a sword, which is a stylised weapon rather than an accurate depiction of any particular weapon of the period.

The Board Room in the Old Admiralty is dominated by the 1799 painting of Nelson by Leonardo Guzzardi. Believed to have been commissioned by Sir William Hamilton himself, it shows Nelson ravaged by age and war, and is thought to be

Nelson presented a further sword, previously belonging to Captain Don Tomas Geraldino, to Captain Ralph Miller of the *Captain*. This sword was known to be in the family in 1825 but is now untraced. Lastly, the sword of Admiral Don Francisco Xavier Winthuysen of the *San Josef* was presented by Nelson to the City of Norwich and is on display at Norwich Castle.

The National Maritime Museum also held a brass-hilted small-sword purported to be the sword of Don Miguel Tyrason who was in command of a barge captured by Nelson off Cadiz in July 1797. This was said to be one of two swords given by Lady Nelson to her cousin and then descending through the family to Colonel Seddon who loaned it to the museum. It is now back in the family's private collection.

Lieutenant Parsons in his memoirs[31] records Nelson being presented with the sword of Rear Admiral Perrés of *Le Généreux* after the action against the *Northumberland* and the *Success* (Captain Berry). No trace has been found of this sword. Similarly, Edward Fraser records that when Captain Berry of the *Spartiate* captured the *Aquilon* at the Nile, he sent the boarding party across under a Lieutenant Galwey who accepted the surrender and that Captain Berry then passed the French captain's sword on to Nelson.[32]

The last-known of these swords is that surrendered by Rear Admiral A S M Blanquet du Chayla at the battle of the Nile. This is held by the City of London at the Museum of London.

Photograph of the maquette for the statue on Nelson's Column. This is located in the entrance hall in the Old Admiralty Building, showing a crude 1805 Pattern sword.

The statue of Nelson as it was shown to the public in Trafalgar Square prior to being placed on top of the plinth as captured in the newspaper at the time. (*The Illustrated London News*, 4 November 1843, p 289)

Often claimed as an accurate painting of Nelson, showing the man worn down by his injuries and age, with an oval side ring sword. It adorns the Admiralty Board room and is by Leonardo Guzzardi. (MOD Art Collection)

the most accurate portrayal of Nelson. This picture shows him with an oval side ring sword.

Blackfriars Hall in Norwich holds a painting by Sir William Beechey, who was a friend of Nelson and a member of the Royal Academy. The picture is thought to be one of the last portraits of Nelson, painted in 1802, and also shows him carrying an oval side ring sword. Interestingly, a much more ornate second sword appears in the picture, which is an accurate depiction of that of Admiral Don Francisco Xavier Winthuysen of the *San Josef* discussed above. Beechey produced a second version of this painting, now located in the Court Room at Drapers Hall in London. Nelson received the Freedom of the Drapers' Company in 1798 and the Company's Court of Assistants commissioned it 10 December 1805, paying 200 guineas.

Numerous engravings and pictures exist based on the paintings above and, as copies, do not add further evidence. The weight of evidence from these pictures makes it likely that the oval side ring was Nelson's weapon of choice.

Other evidence muddies the picture, however. An early portrait of Nelson, by Jean Francis Rigaud, begun when Nelson was a lieutenant and completed in 1781 when he returned from the West Indies as a captain, shows him holding a sword that is clearly a slotted hilt. Also, the effigy at Westminster Abbey made by Catherine Andras shows him carrying a five-ball sword. While claimed by Emma Hamilton to have been a good likeness, the effigy even has the wrong eye damaged. It is known that it was given a genuine sword in 1806, but there is no evidence that it was one of Nelson's own swords or meant to represent such. The effigy appears to be based on Hoppner's painting, as the pose is identical. What is different from the painting are some of the awards and the

Sir William Beechey's painting of Nelson which shows him carrying an oval side ring sword and with the sword of Admiral Don Francisco Xavier Winthuysen of the *San Josef* sat as a trophy. (NWHCM : Civic Portrait 17 Norfolk County Council or via Drapers' Hall)

Paintings Showing Nelson with a Sword[34]

Sir Guy Head painting of Rear Admiral Nelson receiving the sword of Rear Admiral A S M Blanquet du Chayla after the battle of the Nile	Shows a Midshipman bringing du Chayla's sword and Nelson wearing an oval side ring sword
Oil painting by John Rising (1801)	Oval side ring
1797 Robert Laurie mezzotint based on the Leghorn miniature sent to Fanny Adams in 1794 (although since the original miniature is circular it does not travel this far down)	Shows part of the handle of a sword which also appears to be an oval side ring but could be a small-sword
Pencil and ink drawing by Henry Edridge 1797	Oval side ring
Pencil and ink drawing by Henry Edridge 1802	Oval side ring
Oil painting by Abbott face and top half and Barnard who broadened the field adding the legs and sword.	Oval side ring
Oil by John Hoppner 1801	Not possible to determine but the handle and scabbard shape match an oval side ring but it appears to have an additional flat hilt piece.
Mezzotint by Laurie and Whittle 1798. Not sat for and based on the Leghorn miniature with a new added background	Not a reliable source but shows an oval side ring
Oil by Charles Lucy painted in 1853. A recreation of a possible scene.	Sword handle not fully shown but appears to be an 1805 Pattern naval sword
The four paintings by Richard Westall covering Nelson at: St Vincent, Boarding in 1777, Cadiz and Tenerife. All painted in 1806.	All show an oval side ring.
Oil painting by Daniel Orme showing Nelson receiving the surrender of the *San Josef*. Painted in 1799.	Shows an oval side ring.

sword. Since both the effigy and the Rigaud painting are one-offs and do not fit with other evidence, the authors feel that they, most likely, show weapons available to the artists, rather than anything more closely associated with Nelson.

The Nelson statue at Portsmouth, sculpted by F Brook Hitch and presented by Herbert J Aldous, from whose designs the sculptor worked, also shows him wearing a five-ball sword. Furthermore, the accompanying lectern plaque asserts that: 'The Uniform is correct to the smallest detail. The sword is a copy of the one he always wore.' However, the statue dates from 1951,[35] is clearly based on the Westminster effigy and has followed its depiction of the sword. The plaque also describes the statue's original site in Pembroke Gardens as being close to his final route to the sea, but this is debateable because the actual route is unknown.

This statue generated further debate in 2005, the bicentenary of Trafalgar, when Portsmouth city council decided to move it because it was felt that, as well as the increasing isolation of the original site, Nelson could no longer see the sea. Unfortunately, he still struggles to see the sea because he is behind a wall.

Commonly, artists depicting Nelson lay great emphasis on the correct portrayal of his uniform, but do not do the same for his sword. For example, the actor who played Nelson at many of the Trafalgar Bicentenary events wore a very carefully researched uniform, but carried a post-1827 sword that was probably much later. This tendency is frustrating to the purist, but perhaps it should come as no surprise. While the swords are mired in controversy, the admiral's dress coat suffers from no such problem and hangs, undisputed, for all to see, in the National Maritime Museum.

Jean Francis Rigaud's painting showing Nelson with a slotted hilt sword. (National Maritime Museum, Greenwich, London, BHC 2901)

Statues Showing Nelson with a Sword

Nelson's Column, Trafalgar Square (statue on top and east face)	Stylised cross-hilt sword
Nelson Statue, Southsea	A five-ball sword
Nelson effigy, Westminster Abbey	Has him holding a real five-ball sword
Nelson Pillar, Dublin, which was destroyed by the IRA in 1966. The statue was designed in 1808 by William Wilkins	Unable to determine from images seen
Bridgetown, Barbados. Erected in 1813 and is supposed to reflect Nelson's image on his visit to the island	Oval side ring
Montreal. The original has been replaced and is in a museum. Erected in 1809, it remains controversial as it celebrates a British victory in a French Canadian area	Ornate knuckle guard and a solid side guard possibly representing an oval side ring type
Gibraltar erected in 2005 opposite the Trafalgar cemetery where several members of the crew of *Victory* are buried	Oval side ring
Greenwich, outside the Trafalgar Tavern on a promontory looking across the river Thames	Oval side ring
Bull Ring, Birmingham. While Nelson is not wearing a sword, he is standing next to a pile of naval equipment which includes a sword	Ornate knuckle guard, shaped as the oval side ring but without a side ring

Four statues of Nelson: (a) Southsea, showing him wearing a five-ball sword; (b) Greenwich, showing him wearing an oval side ring; (c) Birmingham, showing a sword with a hilt similar to the oval side ring; and (d) Montreal, showing an ornate knuckle and solid side ring, probably representative of an oval side ring.

CHAPTER 8

Training in Swordsmanship

The term 'fencing', referring to the use of the sword, originates from the earlier 'art of defence'. This evolved to 'art of fence' and then to 'fencing'.[1] Learning this skill requires training, ideally under the direction of a skilled practitioner. Learning to use a sword was important for both the officer and the rating and, in the days before these weapons were standardised, the training was equally varied. Then, nearly a decade after the swords had been subjected to uniform regulations, the Admiralty began to introduce uniformity in the training. This came in the form of drills which could be passed on from instructors to the men under their supervision. These drills were progressively simplified until, at the beginning of the twentieth century when the sword was ceasing to be of importance as a weapon, they were probably at their most effective. Overlapping these developments, from the middle of the nineteenth century, fencing evolved as a competitive sport. So, by the time men no longer needed to know how to use a sword in battle, there was another reason for learning to fence. But this was a different type of swordsmanship, with no danger and lighter weapons, so the training offered was very different.

Early Days

In the age of sail, both officers and ratings needed to know how to use a sword and, initially, all suffered from the same instructional lottery. There was no training syllabus and the task of ensuring the competence of the men was delegated to individual commanding officers. Naturally, not all treated this topic with equal enthusiasm, so great variety in skill with the sword resulted. However, the approach to the recruitment and training of officers was rather haphazard with a young man joining because his family had influence and serving under a captain who had agreed to take him. This concerned some of those in power and their response was the establishment of the Naval Academy in Portsmouth. This opened in 1733 and, so as not to upset the existing system of recruitment, was intended to educate about 10 per cent of potential naval officers. On the staff of this college was a fencing and firelock master.[2] Because this is the earliest known mention of formalised fencing, 1733 can be taken as the start of fencing within the Royal Navy as distinct from sword fighting. The Naval Academy continued to function under a succession of names until 1837 when it closed.

No doubt the first fencing master would have taught the young gentlemen how to use the foil, which was the practice weapon for the small-sword. Much shorter than today's fencing weapon, its length matched that of the sharp weapon very well. The method of fighting with it had been evolved by the French and the design of the weapon governed its mode of use, which was focused on the point alone. Although the edges of a small-sword's blade would have been sharpened, that was merely to discourage an opponent from grasping the blade during a fight. The stance, with the body turned to present the minimum target to the opponent, the weight placed over the rear foot and the head held well back reduced the vulnerability to the opposing blade. To reduce the risk of injury to the eye, the tip of the foil was buttoned with a ball of gutta percha, leather or cloth about the size of a musket ball but this hazard was not completely eliminated until the general adoption of the fencing mask in the early nineteenth century. Therefore, it was just as important to observe the correct position with the head held well back with the foil as with the sharp to reduce the risk of blinding still further.

The Naval Academy, Portsmouth.

Training in Swordsmanship 93

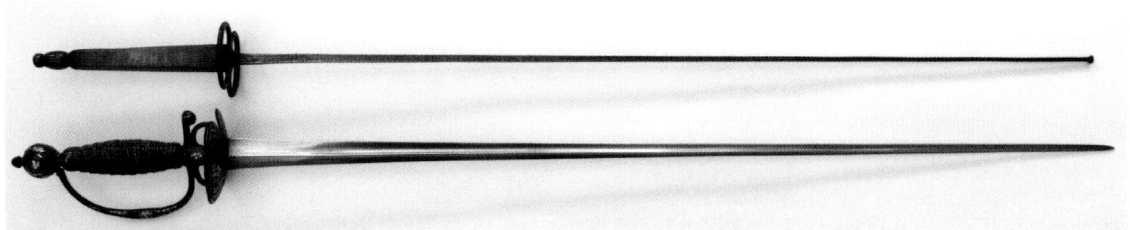

Comparison of an eighteenth-century foil with a small-sword of a similar date. Note the similarity of both the blade lengths and the dimensions of the handles. The figure of eight (lunette) guard of the foil mirrors the double shell guard of the small-sword. At this date fencing theory discouraged inserting the forefinger of the sword hand through the loop of the *pas d'âne* ring and this is reflected both in the way that this feature becomes less usable as the century progressed and its absence from the foil.

There were plenty of suitable books on the theory and practice of fencing with the small sword published in both France and Britain and, as early as 1736, a retired French naval officer had produced a text.[3] However, it was not until 1780 that one of these books had an author from the Royal Navy. In that year, John McArthur, who was serving in the Royal Navy as an Admiral's Secretary, published his *Army and Navy Gentleman's Companion*, illustrated with his own artwork. It must have been successful because two other editions were produced in 1784 and 1810. A facsimile reprint has recently been issued, which makes this text much more accessible. It seems reasonable to assume that this outlined the standard of knowledge of this weapon that was desirable for an officer towards the end of the eighteenth century. As the small sword fell into disuse, this type of fencing instruction continued, as it was deemed to provide an essential theoretical basis for learning to use the other types of swords.

With no uniformity in the cutlass until 1804, it is perhaps not surprising that no steps were taken to establish a universal system for training naval personnel in the use of the sword. However, leaving such an important function to individual commanding officers did not seem a good idea to John McArthur. He makes this very clear in a comment in the introduction to his influential book on fencing with the small sword:

> It is to be regretted, that a method is not adopted in our Royal Navy, of exercising the ships [sic] company of frigates, and such small vessels of war as are liable to be boarded, in the stile [sic] of broad-sword play (commonly called cudgelling) as it would be of the utmost utility in the offensive and defensive attacks of boarding . . . Where commanders have introduced and encouraged this exercise among their ship's company, singular advantages have ensued in the action of boarding sword in hand, both with respect to the safety of their men, and the capture of the enemy.[4]

In a footnote, he observes that: 'The guards and cuts used in broad-sword play, are the same to be used with a cutlass, hanger, &.' As he was serving as an Admiral's Secretary in the Royal Navy and was an expert swordsman, his observations carry the authority of experience.

Among those commanders notable for encouraging the

A plate from John McArthur's *Army and Navy Gentleman's Companion*.

practice of swordsmanship was Nelson. James Wallis who served as Nelson's First Lieutenant in *Boreas* from 1784 to 1786 in the West Indies wrote: 'Nelson's influence on the station [English Harbour, Antigua, July 1784] was immediate ...There were amateur theatricals, and dancing and cudgelling in the decks of the ships.'[5]

McArthur was not alone in lamenting this lack of formalised and universal training in one of the seaman's basic weapons. Others comment unfavourably on the deficiencies in swordsmanship. Unlike McArthur who mentioned only cuts, Lieutenant John Skynner recorded that the standing orders for HMS *Amazon*, his ship in 1802, advocated the use of the point, stating:

> Eagerness and heat in action, especially in a first onslaught, ought never to be the cause of a man putting himself so much off his guard ... as to lift his arm to make a blow with his cutlass ... But on the contrary, by rushing sword in hand straight out and thereby the guard maintained, and watching his opportunity of making the thrust, the slightest touch of the point is death to his enemy. [6]

Another officer writing in 1812 even went so far as to propose a method for conducting training in the use of the sword. Lieutenant William Pringle Green had seen a great deal of active service. While serving as a midshipman in HMS *Topaze* (36) in the West Indies, Green saw considerable active boat service. Still a midshipman, he was at the battle of Trafalgar in HMS *Conqueror* and took possession of Admiral Villeneuve's flagship, *Bucentaure*. He was promoted lieutenant in 1806. In 1812, he got his chance to put his ideas into practice when he was given command of the *Resolute* (14). This is the same year as the date of the manuscript now in the National Maritime Museum.[7]

Green claimed that his method was so simple that only a few days would be necessary '... to train landsmen to the use of the cutlass ...'. The training was to begin with a stick in place of a cutlass and encompassed only four guards or attacks:

> '1st Guard the Head
> 2nd Guard the Right side
> 3rd Guard the Left side
> 4th Guard Thrust or Parry
> These words serve as well for attack or defence, substituting the word Strike for Guard.

His instructions are supplemented by some naïve sketches, two of which show a pistol held along the left forearm being used to enhance the defence of the head.

The stick or cudgel mentioned in the context of cutlass training was the weapon now universally known as the singlestick. This consisted of a stout ash or hazel stick fitted with a wicker basket as a guard. Naval exponents of singlestick or cudgelling seemed happy to demonstrate their skills ashore, as this snippet by Commander A J Gardner while serving in HMS *Salisbury* between 1784 and 1785 makes clear:

'One of those fellows – Darby Collins ... did positively beat, at the back of the Point, Portsmouth, eleven men by cracking their heads at singlestick one after another. He was a tall, raw-boned Irishman, a Garry-owen boy that stood up manfully for the honour of his country.'[8] Commander Gardner also reflected on a training technique that they used on board *Edgar* while he was serving there as a midshipman (1787–9): 'We had a custom when the officers were at dinner in the wardroom, of dividing into parties; one division was to storm the other on the poop.'[9] It is clear that these were quite robust games as in one of these mock attacks he was wounded in the thigh by a bayonet and in another was hit by a broomstick which made his nose bleed off and on for several days. He commented that John Culverhouse who was serving as one of the mates at the time[10] was apparently superior to anyone in the Fleet at the singlestick at this time.[11]

One possible source of instruction during the period of the wars against France was men acting as fencing masters on board their ships. Given the wide range of occupations of those entered into naval service, by whatever means, it is entirely possible that such professionals were among them and could have supplemented their pay by teaching swordsmanship. There seems to be no specific evidence for this in the Royal Navy, but it was certainly the case with French prisoners of war held in the hulks in Portsmouth Harbour.[12]

Formalised Cutlass Training

Just one year after Green's proposal, one of the best-known fencing masters of the time, Henry Angelo, was appointed Naval Instructor in the Cutlass. He visited Portsmouth Dockyard and instructed a party of midshipmen in his method. A year later, a report appeared in *The Naval Chronicle*. (edited by McArthur) It is worth quoting in full.[13]

> The Lords of the Admiralty having determined that British seamen shall be taught the naval cutlass exercise, Mr Angelo, jun.[14] has been some time at Portsmouth,

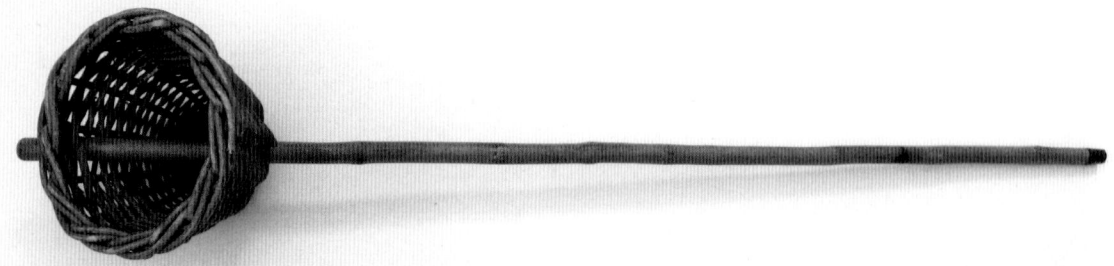

A singlestick with a wicker guard. The guard antedates the First World War but the stick is of the pattern still available from Naval Stores in the mid-1980s. Despite not having provided the guards since the end of the Second World War, some oversight in the supply organisation saw the sticks retained as Naval Stores items.

drilling the seamen there. Last week, an inspection took place in the dock-yard, before Captains Milne and Hollis, the two senior captains afloat at that port; when upwards of 60 seamen were put through the exercise, in the presence of a great number of naval and military officers: among whom were Sir A. Cochrane, Earl Northesk, and the Hon. Commissioner Grey; all of whom expressed their approbation of the measure. We understand that the same practice is also to be introduced into such parts of the army as wear the sword: the knowledge of which will give the men confidence in themselves.

A plate published in 1814 illustrates a very complex method based, as McArthur suggested, on broadsword play. It consisted of seven *cuts*, directed at left cheek, right cheek, wrist, leg, left side, right side and head and the corresponding *guards*, named respectively: inside guard, outside guard, half circle, shift, inside half hanger, outside half hanger and St George. There was also a *point* or *thrust* and a *parry*. This last was a circular movement with the blade from right through left and back, as seen from the swordsman's perspective.

Angelo did not have much work to do in formulating this exercise as it bears an uncanny resemblance to an earlier publication of his.[15] He did not even illustrate it with drawings of the cutlass it was meant to teach but instead used the 1805 Pattern sword for commanders and above. A plate differing only in the title and with infantry swords and soldiers replacing the naval swords and sailors was published in the same year to fill the need for an Army version.

This was the standard method of the fencing school dressed up for consumption by the armed forces. However suitable this training may have been for fencers, it overlooked the peculiar circumstances associated with the use of a sword at sea. It ignored the instability of the foothold and the impediment to nice blade work imposed by canvas, cordage and spars, let alone the restricted headroom that existed below decks.

While the Army persisted with versions of Angelo's sword exercise until it was replaced by a method devised by the Italian master Masiello in 1895,[16] the Royal Navy replaced it with a much-simplified routine much more akin to that proposed by Green and, just as McArthur recommended, the singlestick was used as a practice weapon. This exercise is contained in the various issues of the *Manual of Gunnery* because, unlike the Army with its separate publications for the sword exercise, the Royal Navy included its cutlass exercise under 'gunnery' a term embracing all types of drill activities. As a result of this obscurity, the cutlass exercise has been very little studied, an omission that the present authors tried to remedy in an earlier publication, *Naval Cutlass Exercise*.

Consisting of two diagonal '*Cuts*', one '*Point*', three '*Guards*' and one '*Parry*', the exercise was based on three key principles:

I. – That the 'First Guard' is the most advantageous position which a man armed with a cutlass can assume for the purpose of 'Attack' or 'Defence.'

II. – That as a point can be returned with far greater rapidity and with much more deadly effect than a cut, a point is invariably to be returned instantly after having guarded a cut,

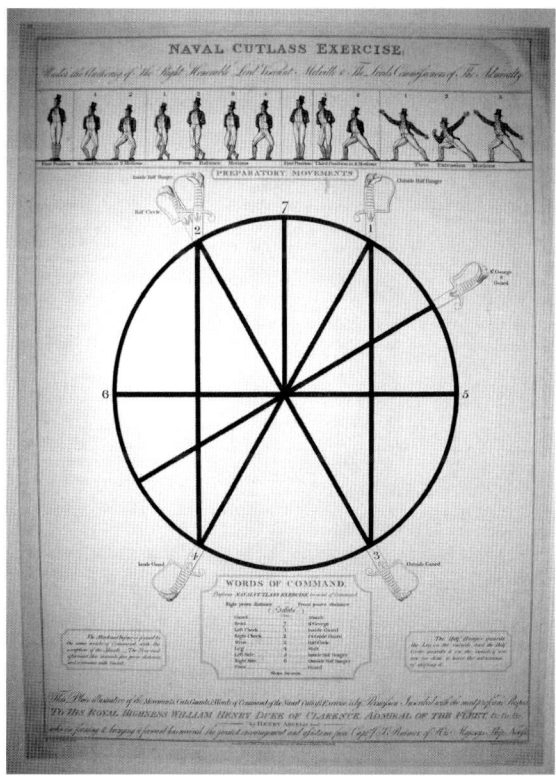

The Angelo cutlass exercise.

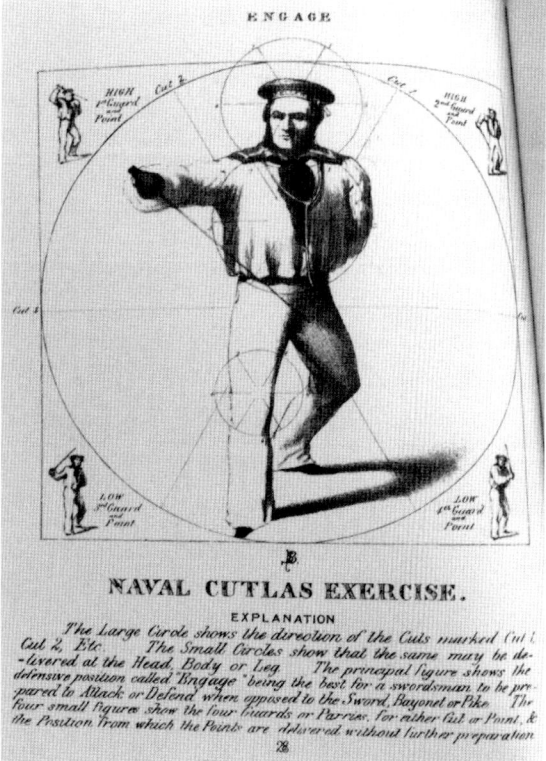

The cutlass exercise of 1859.

First Guard, stereo pair of cutlass training photographed on board HMS *Niobe* in 1900 when she formed part of the naval contribution to the Boer War. This was the basic position for attack and defence.

or parried a point delivered by an opponent.

III. – That after delivering a cut or point, the 'First Guard' is to be immediately resumed ready for instant 'Defence' or 'Attack.'

The arrival on the scene of this new cutlass drill in the middle of the nineteenth century came at about the same time as illustrated weekly papers were becoming popular. These, postcards and similar sources provide many illustrations, both engraved and photographic, of the various components of the exercise.

This 'Oilette' postcard by Raphael Tuck & Sons which illustrates the Second Guard being used to defend the head against a cut is taken from a black and white photograph of boy seamen in their second year of training on board HMS *St Vincent* moored in Portsmouth Harbour that had first appeared in *The Navy and Army Illustrated*, 3 April 1896, p 183.

Training in Swordsmanship 97

Singlestick with hide guard and fencing mask. The guard was more rugged than its wicker predecessor and the strength of the mask underlines the robust nature of this type of exercise.

Point: seamen on board a warship in the Sea of Marmora practicing thrusting with the cutlass. Quick and deadly, thrusting was the preferred method of using the cutlass. (*Extra Supplement to the Illustrated London News*, 23 March 1878)

A large amount of padding was necessary to protect the head, chest, groin and leading knee from the serious injury that could result from a stout blow or thrust in those regions. The arm could well sustain nasty bruises and a modern fencer would be surprised at the lack of an elbow guard. By this date, the wicker guard had been replaced by a more long-lasting version made of hide. The basic position for attack and defence, 'First Guard' would be recognised by modern sabreurs as the parry of second(e) and they would be puzzled at the adoption of such a high guard. However, it has to be remembered that protecting the head was a vital task and that, with a heavy weapon such as the cutlass, dropping the sword to guard against an attack against the lower part of the body would be easier and quicker than raising it to defend the head. Indeed, when the head is the principal target, as in the German student duel with the schläger or backswording with the singlestick, the guard adopted is even higher. This is a very ancient guard illustrated at least as early as 1550 by Marozzo[17] and reappearing, with minor adjustments down the succeeding centuries. This guard would have protected the upper right side.

The Second Guard is the familiar sabre parry of five (quinte).

Sailors on board HMS *Resolution* demonstrating Third Guard protecting the lower right side of the swordsman's body. (*The Navy and Army Illustrated*, 29 May 1896, p 262)

The third of the guards was intended to protect the lower right side of the swordsman's body. It, therefore, complemented the first guard, which defended the upper right side.

Green specified a guard to defend the inner, left side of the body and modern sabre fencers will be surprised at the absence of such a guard in the Cutlass Exercise. The solution given is the 'Parry'. The instructions for this are: 'Parry as quickly as possible upwards and to the left by forming the 2nd Guard and (without pausing an instant) downwards and to the right by forming the 1st Guard'. This is a type of universal defence relying on sweeping any attack directed at the chest or left side upwards and to the right. Experiments have convinced the authors that this simplified set of defensive movements is quite sufficient to meet all practical needs.

The second principle on which this exercise is predicated emphasises the importance of the point. A thrust, travelling directly to the opponent, is faster than a cut and the resulting puncture wound is far more deadly, as it is much more likely to penetrate vital organs and the damage caused is very difficult to treat. The penetration of just a few inches of blade can easily prove fatal.

The instructions for performing the two diagonal cuts are identical except that 'Cut One' is delivered from high right to low left and 'Cut Two' from high left to low right. A cut to the head is merely delivered vertically downwards, i.e. half way between cuts one and two.

Sailors were expected to be ambidextrous with the cutlass and the instructor was directed to put them through the exercise after having ordered 'Change Arms'. The cutlass is a heavy weapon and, as well as building up stamina, this helped to develop both sides of the body equally. Towards the end of the nineteenth century, to ensure continued familiarity with the weapon and to maintain fitness, cutlass drill was normally conducted on board HM Ships for an hour once a week on Wednesday afternoons.[18]

Specialised training for officer cadets began again in 1857 on board HMS *Illustrious* in Portsmouth Harbour. She was replaced by HMS *Britannia* and the new vessel moved via Portland to Dartmouth and cadets were trained with singlesticks.[19] This was important because a young officer

Above and below: Groups of sailors conducting Cutlass Drill.

It was not only the members of the RN who underwent this type of training with singlesticks. Emphasising how fundamental cutlass training was to sailors, even the schoolboys at the Royal Hospital School, Greenwich, who were being prepared for a life afloat, were taught to fence with singlesticks. (*The Graphic*, 2 July 1881, p 8)

would need to study combat with the sword, a weapon he would expect to wear in action. This training followed exactly the same methods as described for ratings and it is clear from surviving records that officers were taught the cutlass drill. This had a double function. Not only did it teach them to use their own swords but it acquainted them with the training regime for their men.

As is the way in the armed forces, such training was often the cause for some cynicism and amusement, as brought out by an article in the Magazine of the RN Engineering College which gives some idea of the form this instruction took. Entitled *Our Naval Brigade*, it describes instruction in a range of small arms including the cutlass.[20] The following extract shows the way in which this drill was received.

Part of the cutlass drill comprised practice with the single stick, and the way in which the fellows declined the instructor's invitation to 'come out and have a turn' was surprising, and even when he reduced his offer to taking any two, there was still some hesitation. Much energy was, however, displayed amongst ourselves, and legions of sticks and helmets suffered thereby. It has hitherto appeared strange that an Engineer Officer should have to provide himself with a sword and have little or no knowledge of how to use it. We hope that with the experience now acquired, and with future opportunities for instruction and practice, we shall be able to do more with a sword, on joining the Service, than fall over it, as we understand the manner of some is.

This last comment refers to the difficulty of stepping off (starting to march) when wearing a sword on slings. This necessitates throwing it up to the front and catching it at the end of the first pace. It is a trick that many officers never completely master.

It was not just formalised instruction that could provide amusement. Given the chance, young officers have always been quick to spot an opportunity and the combination of cutlasses and horses was obviously too great a temptation for two young men serving ashore during the Boer War.

Cutlass drill on horseback as tried by two of the officers one day led to a most amusing and quite unintended cavalry charge into the middle of the tents, their frightened steeds not being used to such treatment. Though we begged them to go through their interesting performance again, they were much too modest to do so.[21]

Drill itself was insufficient to develop the necessary swordsmanship skills, so practice with singlesticks, termed 'Loose Play' in the *Gunnery Manual*, was used to accustom men to attacking, parrying and hitting each other, something not possible with the cutlass itself. It was soon recognised that, as well as enhancing the professional skill of the men, this type of fencing offered great recreational benefits. Parties of bluejackets fighting with singlesticks became popular contributors to the public displays known as assaults–at-arms that were the precursors of the Royal Tournament. This loose play with the singlestick did not require too much space and

Training in Swordsmanship

Engineer cadets doing cutlass training at the Royal Naval Engineering College, Keyham, a purpose-built training facility, ca 1895.

Singlestick at sea from a postcard which is postmarked for 2 December 1906.

was, therefore, along with other robust sports such as bayonet fencing and deck hockey, a popular form of recreation while at sea.

But this is not the whole story. The Royal Navy procured two patterns of cutlass sword bayonet (see Chapter 2), the first to fit the Enfield-Snider rifle and the second for use with the Martini-Henry rifle. With these weapons, the sailors had to become proficient at a range of skills that are more often associated with soldiers. This is a fair reflection of the fact that, in the latter part of the nineteenth century, members of the Royal Navy were just as likely, if not more likely, to see action ashore as part of a naval brigade as to fight afloat.

'Prepare to receive cavalry' from *The Illustrated London News*, 20 April 1878. This is an example of the extra layer of military expertise that had to be mastered by ratings serving ashore as part of a naval brigade.

CHAPTER 9
Transition to a Sport

Towards the end of the nineteenth century, the time was fast approaching when the sword would cease to be a serious weapon worn in action. But as sword-fighting for military purposes fell into obsolescence, in Great Britain the military was responsible for preserving the skills and tricks of the trade, both as a competitive sport and as popular entertainment.

One form of popular entertainment took the form of Assaults-at-Arms. These shows involved various military skills including sword feats, such as cutting a lead bar in two, cleaving a sheep's carcass in two with one stroke, cutting a wooden pole balanced on two tumblers without breaking them or spilling their contents. For those with iron nerves, cutting apples balanced on the palm of the hand, the nape of the neck or the crown of the head were all possible. The most comprehensive instructions for performing these were written by a cavalryman, Corporal-Major J M Waite, in his book *Lessons in Sabre, Singlestick, etc.* The most notable naval exponent of such sword feats was Chief Gunner Barrett who around the beginning of the twentieth century was billed as the most expert swordsman in the navy. He added a naval flavour to his act by cutting in two a bar of lead balanced on the lighted

The etched labels on the blades of the two lead cutters.

Two lead cutter swords. These swords were modelled on the naval cutlass and were used in both service and civilian circles to perform sword feats. Typically they came in four sizes, with No 1 being the lightest and No 4 the heaviest. A swordsman would choose a lead cutter which suited his stature and strength. The left-hand image is believed to be of an early example which, although labelled Lead cutter No 2 (on the reverse side), shares all the dimensions and characteristics of the naval cutlass. It even has the same brown leather scabbard. The right-hand image is of a No 1 lead cutter believed to be later in date when these swords had evolved into items of specialised sports equipment. Both swords were manufactured by Wilkinson of Pall Mall.

Transition to a Sport 101

Sword feats: (a) cutting an apple balanced on an assistant's neck (*The Graphic*, 19 Feb 1881, p 173); (b) on the assistant's head at an athletics meeting in 1922; (c) Chief Gunner Barrett cutting a lead bar balanced on two lighted pipes; and (d) cutting mutton in half (*The Graphic* 5 Dec 1874) (e) cutting an apple (*The Illustrated Sporting and Dramatic News* 15 Dec 1883); and (f) cutting a lead bar (*The Illustrated Sporting and Dramatic News* 15 Dec 1883)

Above: Cutlass Exercise being performed by members of the Royal Naval Artillery Volunteers at the Thames Rowing Club Assault-at-Arms in 1883.

Above: Sports of the London Athletic Club, at St James's Hall: Cutlass Exercise. (*The Illustrated London News*, 2 December 1876)

pipes of two ratings.[1] The magazine of the Royal Naval College at Dartmouth, still afloat in the ships *Britannia* and *Hindoostan*, mentions Royal Marines, Sergeant Major Beckett and Sergeant Young for their performance of sword feats in 1886 and 1888 respectively.

Sword feats, along with many other athletic activities, were performed at events and shows in the Victorian period. Examples include the 1849 Scottish Fete at Holland Park witnessed by Queen Victoria and Prince Albert,[2] an Assault-at-Arms in 1865 in St James's Hall for the Royal Caledonian Asylum[3] and another in the Albert Hall in aid of the Afghan War Relief Fund in 1881.[4] There were also annual events such as the one staged by the London Athletic Club.[5] One of these started as the Grand Military Tournament and Assault-at-Arms held in Islington in 1880 and after many changes of name and venue, evolved into a military tattoo that became known as the Royal Tournament. In 1892 a group of distinguished Italian military fencers gave an exhibition of their skills and following this, the lighter Italian style of sabre became the cutting weapon of choice, and, in parallel, the Italian foil seems to have become the fashionable thrusting weapon. The first involvement of naval swordsmen in the tournament was in 1897 when a party of forty ratings from HMS *Excellent* gave a display of cutlass drill.[6]

Fencing also featured in such shows, again led by members of the Armed Forces, with foil, sabre and bayonet as the weapons contested. Bayonet fencing used a dummy rifle in which a spring-loaded plunger replaced a real bayonet. A robust sport, it was particularly popular with the Royal Marines and remained a competitive weapon in the Armed Services until 1957. Épée arrived at the Royal Tournament in 1904, the year the Royal Navy started competing as a service. The fencing épée was a development of the nineteenth-century duelling sword in which only hits with the point scored and for which the whole body was the target. The Royal Navy had some early successes, notably Lieutenant Ferdinand Fielmann who won the officers' competition at foil in 1904, at épée in 1905 and 1909 and at sabre in 1907. Lieutenant E W H Brookfield won the officers' foil event in 1913 and the officers' sabre in 1909.

Italian fencers demonstrating at the Royal Military Tournament in 1892. (*The Illustrated London News*, 4 June 1892)

Fencing in the Royal Tournament involved two preliminary qualifying events – a single-service command or area competition followed by a service championships, leading up to the final stage at the Royal Tournament itself. The Royal Navy lists its Service Champions from 1904 (see Appendix 4). These were taken to be the most highly placed individual in each weapon in the tournament, until 1921 (RN) and 1922 (RM), when they were then taken as the winner of the single-service championships.

In the early years of the Royal Tournament, officers and other ranks fenced in separate competitions. Royal Navy ratings competed from 1905 and from this date came the Navy and Army Championship which, after the advent of the RAF in 1918, evolved into the Inter-Service Championship. Chief Petty Officer Smeaton won the foil in 1907 and Lieutenant Brookfield won the foil event in 1914.[7] In 1924 the officers and other rank competitions combined and in 1966 the Royal Marines ceased to hold their own Championships and combined with the Royal Navy.

The Royal Tournament continued to include the Combined Services Championships until it ceased in 1999. Since then, each Service has hosted the Combined Services Championships in turn. Selection remains through the individual Service championships, although the original third stage of Command Championships is no longer run.

The Inter-Service Triangular Match (usually referred to as 'The Triangular') is a separate element now held immediately before the Combined Services Championships. Before the demise of the Royal Tournament, this team competition was held over a weekend, moving location between the Services and was often followed by a match between a Combined Services team against opposition such as an All-England team. The Triangular consisted of foil, épée, sabre and bayonet until 1957 when bayonet was dropped. This did not work to the advantage of the RN because the Royal Marines had been regular winners at bayonet and the loss of that element was heavily felt. The RN won the first competition under the new format, but it would be forty-seven years until their next victory. The RN finally won a weapon at the Inter Services in 2003, having been close for years, and only failed to win the overall competition on the tie-breaking mechanism. Building on this success, the RN finally became Inter-Service Champions in 2004, and they then went on to win again in 2005, and have several times won in sabre since.

The Royal Navy's Contribution to the National Sport

At the beginning of the twentieth century, British fencing began to develop as a civilian sport and move beyond the military sphere into the wider community.

In January 1902, the Amateur Fencing Association split from its parent body, the Amateur Gymnastic and Fencing Association. Among the first thirty-six individual members was the Rev G L Blake RN. The importance of fencers from the Armed Services to the sport at a national level can be seen by looking at the composition of the British fencing teams competing at the Olympic Games. In 1908, the Games were held in London and Captain H Watson RN was a member of the committee that organised the fencing competitions. Lieutenants Brookfield and Fielmann were both selected for the sabre team and were joined by Lieutenant Lockhart Leith

The RN prize winners and instructors. (Osborne Magazine Summer 1905)

in the individual event. At the next Olympiad in Stockholm, destined to be the last before the Great War, Brookfield and Fielmann again represented Great Britain in the sabre team and Brookfield also competed in the individual event. Along with Lieutenant Robin Dalglish, Fielmann was selected to fence as an individual, although neither was able to compete.

Two outstanding successes beyond the Olympics were Fielmann's victory in the British Amateur Sabre Championship in 1907 and Brookfield's performance during the 1913 Imperial Services Exhibition at Earl's Court where, out of an international entry of forty-six for the individual sabre, he tied with M Svoreik of Bohemia for first place.

The Royal Navy was also involved in establishing fencing in Canada, as Lieutenant C A Bell RN refereed the first fencing match to take place there. This took place at the James Bay Athletic Association in Victoria on 1 April 1911, and the Outpost Fencing Club of Vancouver just beat the newly formed Frontier Fencing Club of Victoria.[10]

The years of the Great War naturally disrupted organised sport so the story pauses until after the Armistice of 1918. On 10 December 1919, a general meeting of the Amateur Fencing Association was held in London and Commander Brookfield was elected to the committee. Some military figures prominent before the war resumed their positions in the first rank of British fencers. In the first post-war Olympics at Antwerp in 1920, the British team included Dalglish, now promoted Captain, Commander E W H Brookfield and Lieutenant Cecil

One of the Bayonet Teams from the 1914 Royal Tournament.

1. Quartermaster Sergeant Instructor F A Peasnell, 2. Colour Sergeant L V Clarke, 3. Sergeant P J Jerred, 4. Colour Sergeant Miller, 5. Sergeant A V Perry, 6. Sergeant R A Curtis, 7. Gunner C G Duncan, 8. Marine Jack Penfold

Royal Marines Fencers of the 1920s and 1930s

Examination of any of the Royal Tournament or Royal Navy Fencing records of the 1920s and 1930s throws up the names of a small group of Royal Marines fencers again and again. Several photographs of the same people with impressive collections of silverware also appear in journals of the period. Unfortunately, the names of those coaching and leading the training are lost to history.

This was an exceptional group of fencers – this can be seen by the fact that although some of the other Royal Marines and Navy fencers were competing at international events, the internationals were not always the strongest at Service competitions. For example, Quartermaster Sergeant Instructor F A Peasnell took part in a Dutch international fencing tournament in 1931 where he came eighth in the epée and won the sabre and then fenced in an exhibition sabre match in front of the Dutch Queen Wilhelmina. Yet he only managed to win the Royal Marines foil in 1924, the epée in 1928, sabre in 1925 and 1928 and bayonet in 1924, and never won a title at the Royal Tournament.

The most prolific winner of the Royal Marines Championships of this period was Colour Sergeant L V Clarke. Initially a Champion in the other ranks epée competition, he continued his success when officers and other ranks combined in 1924. He took the foil title eight times, only missing it once in the period 1925 to 1933.[8] He won the epée nine times, 1922–5, 1929, 1932–3 and 1935–6,[9] the sabre seven times, 1924, 1929, 1931–2 and 1934–6, but he won the bayonet only once, in 1931. A stylish fencer, he was awarded the medal for style in the sabre in the Royal Marines Championships in 1924. Clarke took the Inter Services Sabre Championships in 1934 just beating his peer QMSI Jerred, the first time for many years that the Army had not dominated. Clarke's play was described in an article in the Globe & Laurel as 'outstanding for its clarity, speed, control and though genial he was always tense and concentrated whether leading or behind in hits'. His closest rival in results was Sergeant P J Jerred who won the foil in the Royal Marines Championships in 1928, 1934, 1935 and 1936; the epée in 1927 and 1934 and the bayonet in 1933. While serving in HMS *Repulse* in 1928, Jerred won the Fleet Tournament, foil, epée and sabre without losing a single fight. In 1932, he became the Inter Services Champion-at-Arms, with a win in the Inter Services Bayonet and a second in the foil. His fencing was described as 'crisp and purposeful' and it is said he 'rarely made an error in judgement'.

Sergeant A V Perry was competing as early as 1928 when he tied for first place in bayonets at Olympia against Colour Sergeant Miller, the previous year's champion, but lost in the fight-off. The following year he reversed the position. In 1930, Perry won the Mediterranean bayonet, foil and sabre, and in 1931 again won the bayonet and sabre. In 1932 he came third in the Inter Services Bayonet and in 1933 first before slipping back to second in 1934. He finally won the Royal Marines bayonet in 1934, 1935 and 1938 having already won the Inter Services Bayonet six times, 1929, 1933 and 1935 to 1938. In 1928 and 1939 he tied for first place and had to fight off and lost.

The strength of this group is illustrated by the fact that Sergeant Perry came second equal in the Inter Services Champion-at-Arms in 1938 yet was only able to win the bayonet at the RM Championships in the same year. Similarly, Sergeant Tallent, a regular in the RM team and competitions in the 1930s, appears in placings in all four disciplines of foil, epée, sabre and bayonet. In the Portsmouth v Plymouth Inter Command in 1933, he managed to achieve a first or second in all weapons alternating with Sergeant Clarke. As Jerred and Clarke aged, Perry maintained his presence in the team, yet in 1938 he managed to come fourth equal in the Inter Services Champion-at-Arms having only achieved second place in each weapon at the RM Championships. The next two ahead of him were also Royal Marines.

Other fencers who only occasionally managed to reach the titles included Sergeant R A Curtis who won the Royal Marines Bayonet in 1930, 1936, 1937 and 1939. Gunner C G Duncan won the first Royal Marines Bayonet Championships in 1921 and was also the Bayonet Inter Services Champion that year. Duncan won the Royal Marines title again in 1925 and 1926, and in 1927 also took up the epée. Prolific fencer Marine Jack Penfold, whose 46-year career included being awarded the Russian Order of St George for his involvement in the Dardanelles, serving at the battles of Dogger Bank and Jutland and winning trophies in fencing, cross-country and boxing, but he only once took a title at the Royal Tournament, in 1922, as the Other Ranks Bayonet Champion.

Bayonet fencing on the deck of a warship.

Commander E W H Brookfield. (*Illustrated Sporting* 1913)

Kershaw. Captain Dalglish was placed sixth in the individual sabre and awarded a special prize for good sportsmanship. Kershaw deserves a special mention: not only did he represent Great Britain at foil and sabre but he was also capped sixteen times for English rugby teams at scrum half. Captain Dalglish also competed in the 1924 Olympics in Paris but was seventh in his semi-final pool, while the Amsterdam Olympiad of 1928 saw Brookfield appointed as captain of the sabre team that also included Commander Robin Jeffreys, while Sergeant Joe Field, of the Royal Marines coached the British Olympic team for the 1936 Games in Berlin.

The outbreak of war in 1939 once again put an end to most organised sport, although a team from the Royal Marines is known to have beaten teams from both the Czech Army and Cambridge University during the early 1940s.[11] When peace returned, His Excellency Vice Admiral the Earl Granville KCVO, CB, DSO was elected as President of the Amateur Fencing Association in 1946, a post he held until his death in 1953. In 1932, as the Hon William Leveson-Gower, he had won the Scottish sabre championship and represented Great Britain at the 1937 World Championships in Paris as Vice

Lieutenant C A Kershaw in a match with C R McPherson USA.

Admiral the Hon W S Leveson-Gower, probably the most senior naval officer ever to gain international honours. Surprisingly, though, he never won the Royal Navy Championships. As the Governor of Northern Ireland, he introduced fencing to the province. There was no RN representation in the fencing at the London Olympic Games in 1948 but the post of Director of Equipment was held by Captain Edward Mount-Haes.

Following the war, Joe Field, now promoted to Lieutenant, returned to competition to win the foil and epée at the 1947 Combined Services Championships, and the Ridley Martin Amateur Sabre Championships. Field represented Britain in an international competition in Paris in 1946. During this period, the Royal Navy was particularly strong in sabre: Captain Neaves and QSMI Howard-Willis and Colour Sergeant Hirst won the British Team sabre championships in 1947.

The Combined Services Championships of 1948 were

His Excellency Vice Admiral the Earl Granville, KG, KCVO, CB, DSO.

Lieutenant Joe Field RM in the centre with other fencers from a match against the Czech Army in 1944. The other fencers from left to right are N A Crow, F Tallent, R J Brooks and A A Raven. (*Tatler* 12 January 1944)

notable for the arrival on the scene of the legendary Bob Anderson, who won the sabre. This Gosport-born Royal Marines corporal, who had survived the bombing of HMS *Coventry* during the Second World War, went on to coach the British team for six Olympics and become a top Hollywood swordfight choreographer. Anderson won in foil and sabre in the Combined Services Championships every year, apart from two,[12] from 1949 to 1954, and in 1952 he even made it a clean sweep by winning in epée as well. Between 1951 and 1954, he had 103 foil bouts at the Royal Tournament without losing a single bout. He won two gold and three silver medals in the British Empire (now Commonwealth) Games in 1950 and the Corble Cup in both 1951 and 1952. He competed in the Helsinki Olympics in 1952, although an injury kept him out of the final. Following the 1953 World Championships, he turned professional and won the British professional foil sabre and epée from 1962 to 1965 as well as the European sabre championships in 1962.

Anderson succeeded his mentor and coach Roger Crosnier as National Coach in 1954 and coached the British fencing team for six Olympics from 1956 to 1976. At the first Martini epée in 1960, he demonstrated sabre rhythmic exercises and followed this with a sabre duel 'stripped to the buff' with another Royal Marine Sergeant R Thompson, who had also represented his country. In 1953, Anderson first took his skills into the film world as a coach and double for Errol Flynn in *The Master of Ballantrae*. He went on to choreograph fights for highly successful films including *Highlander, The Princess Bride, First Knight, The Mask of Zorro, The Pirates of the Caribbean*, the *Lord of the Rings* trilogy and *Die Another Day* and conducted the famous lightsabre scenes in *Star Wars*, standing in for Dave Prowse as Darth Vader in the major fight scenes. He died, aged 89, in January 2012.

Several of Anderson's protégés went on to make important contributions in their own right. Chief Petty Officer Ken Pearson fenced for England, and later coached the Irish team for the Mexican Olympics in 1968 and, once they were eliminated, assisted Bob Anderson with the GB team. Leaving the Royal Navy in 1969, he qualified as a National Coach and won a Bronze in the foil at the World Masters. Lured by the climate, Pearson emigrated to South Africa in 1981, where he had won the South African Sabre title and Master-at-Arms while still serving in the Royal Navy. He became National Coach and President of the South African Fencing Association. Colour Sergeant Jan Lacey, also an Anderson protégée, went on to become a professional coach in the Devon area.

Other Royal Navy personnel have made significant contributions to the British fencing scene at every level. Just after the Second World War, Royal Navy fencers established two fencing clubs that continue to flourish. Commander A G Olliver founded the Bath Sword Club, while Portsmouth and Southsea Fencing Club was founded by a group of RN and RM fencing instructors. Joe Field took over the coaching at Bath Sword club and Petty Officer Jacky Finch, took over from Chief Petty Officer Bill Stamper, as coach at Pangbourne School, where he stayed until 1968. The 1954 Commonwealth sabre champion Michael Amberg started Northampton Fencing Club after being demobbed from the Royal Navy. Petty Officer Ray Tiller, also a distinguished fencer, became a professional coach in the Portsmouth area on leaving the Service. In more recent years Stuart Scorgie left the Royal Navy to become a successful fencing coach at Clifton College.

Winners from the 1957 Inter Services Fencing Championships. From the left: George Thomas RM, Sticks Maker RM, Mike Howard, George Gelder Ken Pearson (RN), Bob Anderson (RM), Ray Harrison and John Evans.

AB Henry De Silva, who served for a short time in the Royal Navy in the 1950s, went on to become a coach and to establish National Veterans Fencing in 1987,[13] competing in several internationals for them. After serving as first Chairman of the National Veterans, De Silva handed over to another ex-Royal Navy fencer, Lieutenant Joe Garratt.

Royal Navy fencers have continued to contribute as competitors. Leading Wren Audrey Bennett (later Peters), Second Officer Barbara Williams (later Lyle), Warrant Officer Martin Joyce and Lieutenant Commander John McGrath represented their countries in the 1970s and 1980s, while modern pentathletes Lieutenant Tim Kennealy and Leading Physical Training Instructor Jim Nowak made the Olympic team in the same era. Captain Alasdair Baker of the Royal Marines represented Scotland at épée in the Commonwealth Championships in 1994 and 1998, and qualified for the team but was unable to attend for the 2002 and 2006 championships. He was also part of the Great Britain Olympic Squad for the Atlanta Olympics although the team narrowly failed to qualify for the Games. Lieutenant Keith Bowers Royal Navy won both a Commonwealth team and individual bronze at sabre for Scotland in 2010. As a Lieutenant Commander, Bowers was one of the officials at the London 2012 Olympics.

Fencing within Service Establishments

During the late Victorian period, naval training establishments started to move from hulks at anchor to shore establishments, and this development was paralleled by the gradual change from teaching of singlesticks as a preparation for sword-fighting to fencing as a sport.

In 1888, a gymnastic course was started at HMS *Excellent*, after which recruits were sent to the Army Gymnastic School at Aldershot. At the Royal Naval Engineering College, Keyham, Staff Instructor Garford was performing sword feats as well as teaching foil and a Mr Dupen was giving the fencing training in 1898. By 1904, Britannia Royal Naval College (BRNC) was getting its permanent buildings ashore, and this included a gymnasium where fencing was taught. Then, in 1910, a purpose-built RN School of Physical Training was opened in Pitt Street, Portsmouth, with fencing included in the curriculum. Much of the coaching was done by Royal Marines, who dominated until after the Second World War. For example, Ferdinand Fielmann was coached in foil and sabre at

Transition to a Sport

Jan Lacey, one of Anderson's protégés.

Dartmouth by Sergeant F Tyle. Fielmann won both competitions at Dartmouth in the Easter term of 1899. All the cadets received training in the cutting weapon, the sabre, and, as the instructors were Royal Marines' Warrant Officers, this training probably followed the pattern introduced to the Army by Masiello.[14] This saw the final abandonment of Angelo's method and its replacement by training based on the Italian school of sabre fencing. This taught the use of the wrist and fingers to control the sword rather than the whole arm. There was also a greater emphasis on mobility. Foil was also on the syllabus. In these pre-electric days, much fencing was done outdoors. Although Fielmann was later to dominate at épée, this weapon does not figure in any of the fencing reports from Dartmouth in these early years.

Assaults-at-Arms were also held at Dartmouth similar to those that had developed into the Royal Tournament, featuring a range of gymnastics, fencing and boxing. These would also include some unusual pairings of weapons such as in 1902 when as well as the usual events there was a competition of foil versus dagger. Surprisingly it was the dagger fencer who won. Cadet Blackman, armed with the dagger, played a waiting game but while lacking dash still defeated the foilist, Cadet Prest, with his style of low feints and rapid lunges, in a close match 5–4.

From 1904 to 1921, the magazine of the Royal Naval College, Osborne carries details of fencing at that establishment and most evenings saw cadets participating in voluntary instruction in the gymnasium in sabres, foils, boxing, or bayonet fighting.[15] Only foil and sabre were fenced and sabre seems to have attracted the greater interest with two separate competitions a year, in different terms, each with a preliminary round. The foil was part of the Assault-at-Arms held each summer term and also included horse vaulting, wall scaling displays, boxing, Swedish drill and similar gymnastic events.[16] The sabre was a stand-alone event. In 1906, the magazine proudly records a victory by eight fights to seven over Dartmouth, a success not to be repeated until 1919, just two years before the college closed. One competition that seems to have been popular at Osborne was the Dormitory Mêlée. An article and cartoon in the Summer 1919 issue of the magazine suggests that it was a dismounted version of the sport practised at the Royal Tournament. For this, each competitor had a crest attached to his mask and the winner was

The old order: engineer cadets practising singlestick in the gymnasium converted from a compartment on board the old wooden wall HMS *Marlborough*. This illustrates the last of the old facilities and training methods which were fast being superseded.

The new order: sabre practice outside the gymnasium of Britannia Royal Naval College, 1898. Here we see the type of new, purpose-designed and built shore-based physical training facilities that were being provided ashore as the hulks were abandoned. With this move came a shift from singlestick to the sports sabre.

Fencing at Dartmouth: (a) sabre in the summer of 1912; and (b) a group of the fencers and boxers from the 1901 Assault-at-Arms.

the last one to have his crest still standing. A similar competition seems to have occurred at Dartmouth in 1902 where it was described as a cockade competition.

When the German Fleet visited Portsmouth in 1907, forty of its crew were entertained at Whale Island with a display put on for entertainment which included a fencing bout as well as sword dancing, the hornpipe, ju-jitsu and chingwauloo (which is a Chinese tomahawk martial art).[17]

After the Second World War, coach Surgeon Lieutenant David Mends, later to become a regular in the Scottish national team, revitalised the club at Dartmouth. Fencing at BRNC had an upswing in 1978, when the team included Midshipman Sean O'Riley, who had already represented Britain at International level as an U20 foilist. That summer O'Riley won the Combined Services U20 Champion-at-Arms competition, the first time a midshipman had won it since it started in 1892. Another strong competitor from 1970, Meyrick Simmonds, did well in the Devon County individual events, coming third in foil and winning the épée. Fencing continues at Dartmouth to this day.

In parallel with Dartmouth, the fencing club at the Royal Naval Engineering College at Manadon, on the northern fringe of Plymouth, also played a significant role in RN fencing circles from the 1960s. During this period the two staff members most actively involved were Nigel Carter and John McGrath. Carter was best known as a sabreur, although he was fairly expert at the other two weapons as well. Fencing continued at Manadon until it closed in the mid-1990s and was home to the South-West Centre of Fencing Excellence. It also played host to an eccentric attempt to resurrect the old sport of singlesticks in the early 1980s.

The Royal Navy Amateur Fencing Association

During the early years of the twentieth century, the sport of fencing moved further from its roots as a military activity. This break was completed after the First World War when in November 1919 the Royal Navy and Royal Marines Fencing Association was formed. The first president was Brigadier General H E Blomberg CB Royal Marines with Commander F E Byrne RN as Hon Secretary and Mr H B Bain MBE as Hon Treasurer.

The creation of a formal association led in 1921 to the inauguration of a formal Service championships, fitting within the overall Royal Tournament structure. Initially, there were separate competitions for officers and ratings at foil, épée and sabre. In the first RN Officers Competitions, Kershaw swept the board, winning all three weapons, a feat almost equalled by CPO William 'Bill' Stamper for the ratings but he conceded the foil title to CPO W G Howson. In the Inter-Services Championships, Kershaw remained among the winners but a new generation was taking over and names such as Mount-Haes, Harry, Finch and Sproul-Bolton began to appear.

To reflect the greater integration between the naval and marine elements within the sport, in 1948 the Royal Navy and Royal Marines Fencing Association changed its name to The Royal Navy Amateur Fencing Association (RNAFA) by which name it is still known.

During the 1970s and 1980s, there was a real shift in the formal status of fencing within the RN. In 1975, the post of official coach supplied by the Director Naval Physical Training & Sport (DNPTS) was abolished. DNPTS had always provided the secretariat for this sport and the incumbent in the 1980s was Lieutenant Commander Bob Thompson, MBE, who had been a major driving force for naval fencing. Following his early death in 1986, the association established a secretariat from among the fencers. Lieutenant Commander Steve Orridge was appointed first Honorary Secretary. Captain Chris Walker became Chairman and another stalwart of the team Lieutenant Commander David Foster took on various roles. Foster also manufactured and presented to the RNAFA trophies for the individual weapons at the RN

Championships. In 1971 an annual match was instituted in Guernsey, which started with a triangular with Jersey. A couple of years were missed in the late 1970s and because of weather. 2011 saw the thirty-fifth match.

In 1990 the Navy's fencing salle at HMS *Nelson* was forced to close and a scheme was developed to create one in one of the empty accommodation blocks (Block D) at Whale Island. A working party was put together from HMS *Sultan* and the work was done in 1990. The decision in 1992 to close HMS *Royal Arthur* and move the Leadership facilities down to Whale Island meant that the accommodation block needed to be returned to its original use and Navy fencing lost its salle permanently.

The 1990s saw a new group of RN fencers come to the fore, with Mark Needham, Adrian Olliver, Sue Bullock and Maggie Myers dominating the titles. On the administrative side, Commander Graham Hockley acted as Chairman for a decade, with the assistance of Lieutenant Commander Paul Engeham as Vice Chairman, Lieutenant Mark Barton as Honorary Secretary and Petty Officer Louise Olliver as Captain for much of the period.

While keeping fit with fencing on the flight deck of HMS *Pretoria Castle*, Petty Officer L Burgess of Fairlie, Ayrshire scores a hit on the Physical Training Instructor Petty Officer S C Neeve, of Lowestoft. Judging in the background are Commander E A Mount-Haes, Navy Fencing Champion, and Gunner C W Tisshaw. In the foreground (right) is Gunner (T) R G V Lee, of Farnham, Hampshire.

Preparing for the Dormitory Mêlée, from the Osborne Magazine, Summer 1919.

Winning Inter Command Team from 1996 – Left to right: Commander Graham Hockley, Lieutenant Commander Steve Orridge, PO Wren Louise Olliver, Lieutenant Commander Stuart Scorgie, Lieutenant Commander Adrian Olliver, Lieutenant Commander Maggie Myers.

Wren fencers from 1956 left to right 3/O R D Joll, L/Wren J H Henning, L/Wren Butcher, 3/O S A Hales, L/Wren Nicki Jago, PO Wren P Searight, L/Wren Lanning.

Winning Inter Services Team 2005 – Back row left to right: Lieutenant Martin Russell, Lieutenant Al Baker RM, Lieutenant Ralph Coffey, Commander Barrie Cran, Lieutenant Commander David Lewis, L/Cpl Craig Merrett. Front row left to right: WO Dave Malinson, Lieutenant Keith Bowers, Commander Matt Clark, PO Mark Needham, Lieutenant Commander Mark Barton, Lieutenant Commander Chris Hendrix.

CHAPTER 10

Your Naval Sword

People can acquire a Royal Naval sword by inheritance, chance purchase or the deliberate purchase of a second-hand weapon to use in uniform. Curiosity then sets in and there is a desire to find out about the history of their sword. This chapter sets out to explain how the clues that the sword offers can be identified and interpreted to provide as much information about the history as possible. Some of the evidence is easy to acquire but other clues require some effort and detective work to unearth. This chapter directs the reader to the appropriate sources and also offers guidance on cleaning and conservation and pointers to swords that have been altered.

The Clues

The question most often asked of the authors is: 'How old is this sword?' This is the usual starting-point from which research into a weapon begins. It is easy to identify a specific pattern of uniform sword, but these tended to be used for long periods of time. Most owners and collectors would like to date their acquisitions with greater precision and find out more about their previous owners, and this can involve correlating the evidence from a number of sources. The main clues can be listed as: identified owner, inscriptions, maker or retailer, serial numbers, the coat of arms of the Sovereign, the Royal Cypher, the form of the crown associated with the fouled anchor, minor details of design and alterations to the scabbard. Unless one is very lucky, there will be no direct answer to the age of a sword; it is a matter of assembling the clues from each of the sources to minimise the time bracket from within which it dates. Some of these have been touched on in the previous text but these are now collected together with new sources of information and presented in this guide to dating and developing the history.

Identified owner

Here one is looking for inscriptions on the blade, the guard or the locket. One is in luck if it is a name but it could easily be a monogram, a coat-of-arms or a family crest. Monograms can be very difficult to decipher, especially if they are of the ornate style favoured during the Victorian era. The best work on crests is James Fairbairn's *Crests of the Families of Great Britain and Ireland* (see Bibliography), which should be available in most reference libraries, but some crests were used by many different families, so some luck with other pieces of evidence may be needed for a positive identification. Coats-of-arms can be identified by the College of Arms in Victoria Street, London, but there may well be a charge for this service. Perhaps surprisingly, even when the earlier owner has been identified, this not as definitive as may be thought. A sword may have been second-hand when purchased by this known owner and inscriptions were sometimes added to swords long after their manufacture to commemorate an event or an owner. Officers have often worn swords with family connections, again resulting in a sword older than the latest known owner. Sadly, it is not unknown for the name of a famous officer to be added to a sword to enhance its sale value.

However, provenance to a named officer is a good start and for officers of the Royal Navy, the usual beginning for any investigation is the *Navy Lists* of the appropriate periods. The early listings were a private venture by David Steel. Starting in 1780–1 as *A list of the Royal Navy, etc.*, it became *Steel's Original and Correct List of the Royal Navy, improved etc.* in 1782 and underwent further minor title changes until its issue ceased in 1816 following publication of an official version. Steel's books did not contain an alphabetical list of officers, an omission corrected, although not immediately, in the official *Navy List*. Perhaps the most useful starting point before 1815 is *The Commissioned Sea Officers of the Royal Navy, 1660-1815*, which is to be found listed in the Bibliography under its chief editor David Syrett. This lists all officers of lieutenant's rank and above. For officers serving in the Honourable East India Company's Maritime Service the book by Anthony Farrington listed in the Bibliography is the main source. None of these sources is without error, so caution must always be exercised in their use.

The records of officers who joined the RN before May 1917 are available on line from the National Archives (www.nationalarchives.gov.uk) for a small fee (£3.50 in 2011). On the home page, click on 'Records' and from that page go to 'Looking for a Person?', then to 'Royal Navy commissioned officers'. You can then download a copy of all the records held on that officer. What you will learn is a matter of some luck. The earlier the record, the less information is recorded but later records embracing service in the twentieth century tend to be much more complete. At the very least, you should get a record of all the ships in which he served with his dates of joining and leaving and of any promotions but sometimes you will be lucky with addresses and employment on leaving the RN. These records are full of abbreviations and full interpretation needs a detailed understanding of these. One always stands out: D.D. = Discharged Dead.

Makers and Retailers

Only recently, following the reintroduction of swords after the Second World War have pools of these weapons been made available from which an officer needing to wear a sword can borrow one. Before then, officers bought their own swords and many still choose to do so. Some officers bought their weapons directly from sword manufacturers such as Wilkinson or Reeves, but these were probably in the minority. The others officers obtained theirs, along with other items of uniform, from their tailors with little or no guarantee that the nice shiny weapon was really fit for service. In earlier days, there was a whole variety of traders such as hatters and lacemen who also sold swords. Many of these had their names and sometimes their addresses etched on the shoulder of the blade or engraved on the top locket of the scabbard. These retailers traded from the principal ports as well as from London and Birmingham and their names and addresses can sometimes be very helpful in limiting the dates within which a sword was sold. There is no comprehensive list of these firms, however, the listings in Volume II of May and Annis, *Swords for Sea Service*, and Bezdek, *Swords and Sword Makers of England and Scotland*, are

Proof marks

Officers always purchased their own swords and might well have looked for some kind of guarantee that the weapon was fit for purpose. At the end of the eighteenth and beginning of the nineteenth centuries, some manufacturers such as Deakin marked their sword blades with the word 'Warranted'. Gill sometimes went even further, marking some of his blades with a phrase such as 'Warranted never to fail' or 'Warranted to cut iron'. During the nineteenth century the quality assurance processes for Government supplied weapons improved and swords which had been passed as fit for issue were stamped with regulation markings (see Chapter 2). No such system existed for officers' swords so, according to John Wilkinson-Latham, in 1854 the firm of Henry Wilkinson introduced the circular brass proof mark bearing the initials 'HW' set into the shoulder of the blade to indicate that he or his assistant had personally tested the sword. This is the same date at which Wilkinson began to number his blades serially, both processes being part of the quality assurance regime. This is a neat explanation but, as pointed out by May and Annis, there are plenty of Wilkinson made swords with flat-backed blades with proof marks but no serial numbers and Henry Wilkinson himself stated that the machines to conduct the proof testing were invented by his company in 1844. This evidence suggests that the introduction of the proof mark probably antedated the numbering of blades. For naval swords this may have been coincident with the introduction of the flat-backed blade in 1846.

The procedure rapidly spread to other sword makers and Wilkinson even accuses some of forging the Wilkinson trade mark. It is impossible to know which, if any, subjected their swords to proof testing as rigorous as Wilkinson's. In many cases these proof marks are associated with retailers rather than manufacturers. In 1905, Wilkinson introduced a new style of proof mark in the form of a hexagonal brass insert bearing the letters 'HW'. This was reserved for the best swords, the circular mark being retained for swords of tailors' quality.

These marks can be useful in identifying the actual maker, who may well have been different from the retailer whose name is etched on the blade. Wilkinson Latham identifies eleven such manufacturers, other than Henry Wilkinson. May and Annis describe sixty-nine of these marks, attributing them as far as they were able to both cutlers and tailors.[1]

The early form of proof mark used by Henry Wilkinson. This is on a sword manufactured before he began the serial numbering of blades in 1854.

Before the introduction of the brass proof mark, some manufacturers inscribed words such as 'Warranted' on their blades. This example is on a blued and gilt blade by F(rancis) Deakin who traded at Suffolk Street in Birmingham from 1811 to 1839.

The hexagonal proof mark introduced in 1905 for use on Wilkinson's best blades. After that date, the round mark was used on blades of tailors' quality.

This proof mark for Thurkle appears on a sword retailed by Silver. It shows that the manufacturer and retailer were often not identical.

the best. Gardner's *Small Arms Makers* can sometimes provide a useful snippet of information. Additional information can be gained from the records of the Worshipful Company of Cutlers, which are held in the Guildhall Library, London, and through the extensive collection of trade directories also held there. The trade directories of other cities can also prove useful. Some information about the trade and private business of Robert Mole from 1903-1920 can be found in Wilkinson-Latham's book on this sword cutler. Increasingly, this type of material is being placed on the web.

Probably the best-known sword manufacturer for naval swords is Wilkinsons. This was descended from a company set up by Henry Knock which is first recorded as having a workshop in London in 1768.[2] This company was originally a manufacturer of guns and bayonets, not swords. It is probably this background that meant they were instrumental in developing fencing bayonets later. It was in 1804 that it passed to his foreman James Wilkinson who was also possibly through an adopted daughter his son in law. It was his son Henry who around 1844 first branched out into swords, publishing a pamphlet entitled *Observations on Swords* that year. At that time most British manufacturers of swords were in Birmingham although most cutting edged weapons were imported from abroad, generally from Solingen. Wilkinson developed a machine to test for both thrust and cutting on each sword and this led to the inclusion of a proof mark, a

Sword Manufacture

Swords are generally attributed to the retailer whose name appears on the weapon. This is a great simplification as comparatively few businesses could muster all the crafts necessary to make and assemble complete weapons. Some weapons would also be sold bearing the name of a tailor or other supplier who had bought the weapon in total.

The key component of the sword is the blade and its manufacture was the responsibility of a bladesmith or cutler. This challenging aspect involves producing a blade that is able to withstand hits and stresses without permanent deformation or fracture and means that a compromise has to be reached between hardness and toughness. Too hard and the blade would take sharpening to give an effective edge and point but at the same time be too brittle for use in combat. The general compromise requires a supply of good-quality steel with a carbon content of about 0.9 per cent and the availability of this raw material influenced the development of centres of production. Until the development of the open hearth and Bessemer processes for steel production in the second half of the nineteenth century, this was manufactured by a cementation process which relied on a good supply of high grade Swedish iron ore. During this period, Britain was never able to manufacture sufficient blades for its purposes and many

This illustration from the article 'Fourbisseur' in *L'Encylopédie* of Diderot and d'Alembert shows a water-powered plant for the grinding and polishing of blades. Made from natural sandstone, the large grindstones over which the workmen lay were apt to explode when a fault in the stone was encountered, leading to the death or serious injury of the operatives.

were imported from Germany, principally from Solingen.

To make a blade, a steel blank is forged at high temperature until it is close to the required dimensions. During the nineteenth century hammer forging was replaced by roll forging as the way of doing this. The blade is then soaked at a high temperature, quenched in oil and then tempered using a lower temperature to develop the optimum combination of hardness and toughness. Control of the process variables during these operations is vital to ensure that the result is a sound product. The blade is finished by grinding to the final dimensions.

The blade is now ready for decoration. A number of different crafts can be involved here. The simplest decorative effect, used on even modest weapons is to engrave the blade. More elaborate decoration in the Napoleonic period, even on fighting swords, would use a rich finish of blueing and gilding. This was the result of two processes requiring an elevated temperature and a highly polished blade. The blue was an interference colour resulting from a thin, transparent layer of oxide developed on the surface by heating. Both the colour and its intensity were time and temperature dependent. The parts to be gilded were painted with an amalgam of gold and mercury. When heated, the mercury boiled off leaving the gold firmly adhering to the metal substrate. This process of fire gilding was also used to complete the decoration of hilts and scabbard mounts. Mercury vapour is highly poisonous and gilders died young. As a result, its use declined during the nineteenth century and it became obsolete once electro-gilding of metal components was fully developed. By the middle of the nineteenth century, acid etching had effectively replaced blueing and gilding as the preferred mode of decoration. In this technique, the parts of the blade to remain brightly polished are covered with an acid-resistant varnish and the blade dipped in acid. The uncovered areas of the design are etched to a grey colour. This technique is still in use today.

Other crafts contributing to the complete sword were the handle makers and binders who shaped the grip and bound it with twisted wire. For a small-sword with its grip bound with a complex system of different sized strands and metal tapes, often secured by Turk's Head knots in wire, handle binding was a great craft. However later naval swords with a few simple helical turns of twisted wire around the grip required far less skill. The brass components of the hilt were manufactured by casting, which required the input of pattern makers, moulders and foundry men. The main techniques for embellishing hilts and components other than the blade were:

- True inlay - where silver or gold wire is worked into the base metal to give the desired design. When done in high relief this is known as encrustation.

- False-damascening – where gold or silver wire would be laid onto a roughened surface and burnished, by pressing and rubbing such that it was fixed in place.

- Damascening – where actual pieces of gold and silver are mounted on the weapon. Similar could be done with jewels.

- Enamelling – made with powdered glass and metal oxides, it gives some very highly polished almost china looking surfaces.

The leather portion of the scabbard was the preserve of the cordwainer, who would also have made the sword belt. The locket(s) and chape were worked up from sheet metal with brazed joints. These and the metallic portions of the hilt and sword belt were then either fire gilded or electro-plated with gold. A laceman would have supplied the sword knot and any sword belt with gold embroidery.

With all the components prepared, it was the turn of the furbisher to assemble the completed weapon.[4]

From the same source as the previous illustration, this shows a furbisher's shop. The workman at Fig 1 is chiselling a sword guard. At Fig 2 the prepared guard is being damascened while at Fig 3 a workman is holding a fully mounted sword. A customer, Fig 4, is testing the blade of a sword.

brass circle stamped 'HW'. Initially blades were not numbered but from 1 January 1854, his best swords were numbered, although in the early days this could be as a single number for a batch of blades. The first single sword to be recorded was 5002, with 5001 having been used for a batch of six blades. A list of these numbers up to and including the year 1974 can be found in Volume 2 of Wilkinson-Latham's book *Mr Wilkinson of Pall Mall*. Wilkinson no longer manufactures swords but the archives have survived and can be searched to provide details of the original purchaser. This service can be accessed from the website www.armsresearch.co.uk. In 2011 the fee for this search was £18.00 for EU countries and £19.00 for countries in the rest of the world.

Around 1610[3] a group of craftsman emigrated from Solingen to set up businesses based around Shotley Bridge and the border between Northumberland and County Durham where the fast-flowing River Derwent was ideal for driving the mill wheels. The local area also provided millstone grit for the grinding wheels and iron ore and charcoal for making the steel. One of these craftsmen was Hermann Mohl. This group of craftsmen initially stamped their swords 'SHOTLEY' on one side and 'BRIDG' on the other but used to the running wolf symbol that marks the swords of Solingen they adopted their own a symbol of crossed swords. When Wilkinson absorbed the firm of Robert Mole, a descendent of Mohl, into their business in 1920 they adopted its mark of crossed swords. Swords manufactured by Wilkinson after this date are marked with the crossed swords.

Royal devices

Royal Cyphers, Royal coats-of-arms and crowns are useful clues as to the date of a sword. However, it is worth noting that the representation of the St Edward's crown during Victoria's reign was very variable and often looks more like its Georgian predecessor. It should also be noted that, after Victoria took the title Empress of India in 1876, the crown on naval weapons from India is a representation of the Imperial State Crown. The space available for an etched design as complex as a royal coat of arms means that it is sometimes depicted with limited accuracy. Also, many sword blades were imported from Solingen, and that could also contribute to a less than accurate representation. However, as can be seen from the illustrations, the differences between the various versions of the royal coat-of-arms are usually sufficient for them to be told apart even in poorly rendered versions. The one exception to this concerns the arms of 1801–16 and 1816–37. Each of these displays an escutcheon of pretence in the centre of the shield and differs only with the first having a cap of maintenance above the escutcheon while the second has a crown. With the simplifications introduced to the design when decorating a blade, it is not always possible to distinguish between these versions.

Design

Minor design details can be helpful but should not be relied upon too much. For example, in 1929 Naval Dress Regulations reduced the blade width to between ⅝in and ⅞in (16mm and 22mm), however a glance at the records of both Mole and Wilkinson will show that both firms had blades 1in, ⅞in and ¾in (25mm, 22mm and 19mm) wide in simultaneous production after this date. Since the adoption of the flat-backed blade in 1846, there has been a general trend for blades to be narrower and straighter the closer they are in date to 1937, when they were finally ordered to be straight. Other useful features are the internal ring for the sword knot associated with early examples of the 1827 pipe-backed blade and the introduction of the hole and peg securing mechanism dating from about 1880.

Changes to the scabbard mounts are particularly useful and these have already been discussed. Associated sword knots and belts are of little use as these could have been changed at any time during a sword's active life and even at a later date.

This is a fascinating process and often yields dates within a very narrow time band. It is worthwhile to record carefully the evidence used in dating, as this then becomes part of the sword's history and adds to its interest for other enthusiasts.

Royal Cyphers: (a) George I, II and III; (b) George IV; (c) William IV; (d) Victoria; (e) Edward VII; (f) George V; (g) Edward VIII; (h) George VI; and (i) Elizabeth II.

Coats-of-Arms: (a) that used before 1801; (b) from 1801 to 1816; (c) from 1816 to 1837; and (d) after 1837.

Case Study of a Sword

The subject weapon is a typical levee sword with a slightly curved bade 31⅝in (803mm) long and ⅞in (22mm) broad at the shoulder. The decoration of the blade includes the Royal Arms adopted in 1837, and a fouled anchor surmounted by a Tudor crown which dates it to after the accession of Edward VII in 1901. The curved blade suggests a date before 1937 after which blades were supposed to be straight. The obverse shoulder is etched with the Royal Arms and 'BY WARRANT, HENRY WILKINSON, PALL MALL, LONDON'. On the other face, just above the shoulder are etched the Royal Arms and 'BY APPOINTMENT, GIEVES LTD, LONDON, PORTSMOUTH & DEVONPORT'. From this we can deduce that the weapon was manufactured by Henry Wilkinson and supplied to Gieves, an old-established firm of naval tailors, for their retail trade. The shoulder of this face has a hexagonal brass proof mark at the centre of a six pointed star. This hexagonal shaped mark was used by Wilkinson on best quality swords after 1905.[5] The back of the blade is stamped 'LONDON MADE' and bears the serial number 56700. This last piece of evidence gives the date of manufacture of the blade as 1919.[6] The guard has no folding inner section and is pierced by a dirk style thumb catch to retain the sword in the scabbard. The cartouche on the guard has a Tudor crown in common with that on the blade. Just inside the guard is engraved 'R.H. MANDLEY. R.N.'

This exhausts the information that can be got from the sword and The National Archives now supplies the rest of the story in the form of Mandley's service records,[7] the interpretation of which is helped by consulting the appropriate Navy Lists. From these it is learnt that Raymond Mandley was born on 31 December 1897 and his father, H Mandley Esq, was an East India Merchant. He joined Dartmouth in September 1912 as a Cadet and was promoted Midshipman with seniority of 2 August 1914. While in that rank he was appointed to HMS *Superb* on 22 September 1915, leaving her just over a year later on 23 October 1916. During this time he was at the battle of Jutland during which the ship fired fifty-four rounds from her 12in main armament but was not damaged.[8] He became an Acting Sub-Lieutenant on 15 September 1916 and a Sub-Lieutenant on 15 May in the following year. Promotion to Acting Lieutenant came on 15 September 1918 and on 15 May 1919 he became a Lieutenant. This is just the stage in his career at which a young officer would buy a sword and is consistent with the date of 1919 deduced from the evidence of the weapon itself. In May 1922, he received official thanks 'in connection with collection of intelligence during Atlantic Fleet's spring cruise'. At his own request, he was placed on the Retired List on 1 January 1923; perhaps he was a victim of the so-called 'Geddes Axe' of 1922 when the defence budget was cut by 42 per cent in one year. When he left the RN, he applied for a Board of Trade Master's Certificate and that is when he revealed that his full name was Raymond Hewitt Mandley. On his retirement he found employment with the Egyptian Ports and Lights Authority and was promoted to Lieutenant Commander on the Retired List on 15 May 1927. This might have been the end of the story but for the Second World War. He resumed his service with the RN on 19 August 1939. After an appointment to HMS *Maidstone*, he joined the Staff of Rear Admiral Commanding 3rd Cruiser Squadron at Cape Town. Then he joined HMS *Nile*, the Naval HQ in Cairo in July 1940. On 1 January 1942 he was Gazetted for a Mention in Despatches for 'zeal, patience and cheerfulness and for wholehearted devotion to duty without which the high tradition of the Royal Navy could not have been upheld'. By February 1943 he was the Chief of Intelligence Staff to the Commander-in-Chief as an Acting Commander. With his experience of the area and his earlier flair for intelligence-gathering, he must have been a square peg in a square hole. Following foreign service leave in Cyprus, he began his release routine but this was suspended for a short while for a brief spell with the Naval Intelligence Department. He was finally released on 1 May 1947 as 'medically unfit for further naval service'. His service records do not give the date of his death.

Conservation

There is always a debate about the extent to which a sword should be restored. Clearly, if it is intended for future ceremonial use, it has to be returned to as pristine a condition as possible. Otherwise, only the minimum consistent with stopping further degradation should be attempted. The main requirements are to remove deposits of dirt, metal polish and any loose and active rust. When this has been completed, the sword should receive some protection against further degradation by the atmosphere or handling. It should be emphasised that the methods outlined here are not the only ones and each individual has to decide the correct way to treat any specific weapon. There are no universal answers and the collector always faces choices. If in doubt, the safest option is to do nothing.

There are three parts of the weapon each requiring different treatments: the blade, the hilt and the scabbard. These will be dealt with in turn, although techniques are interchangeable depending on specific circumstances.

The blade is always made of steel and its main enemy is rust. Many a good sword has been ruined by the crumbs left on its blade after the wedding cake has been cut, and an equal number by careless handling. As a general rule, the use of water-based cleaning methods is to be avoided. The first stage is to inspect the blade to see if there is any particularly delicate decoration that needs to be taken into consideration before starting work. Blued and gilt blades are the most desirable but the most easily damaged. Any abrasive cleaning will cause damage and should not be used on such areas; even rubbing with a cloth can remove small particles of the gilding. Most blades have etched decoration; this is less delicate than bluing and gilding but still should not be subjected to excessive abrasion. Engraving is the most robust form of decoration but even this will lose its crispness if abraded. If you are lucky to have a blade retaining much of its original bright polish, this too should not be roughly abraded.

You may be really unlucky and find that a previous owner has varnished the blade. This invariably cracks with age, allowing corrosion to take place beneath the supposedly protective surface. Old varnish can usually be removed with an acetone-based solvent. There is no general solvent that will deal with modern varnishes; a careful trial with a range of proprietary varnish removers is the only way ahead. Blades covered in a thick layer of grease need to have this removed. This can be done by softening with a little grease-removing jelly and wiping off with a cloth.

With all those provisos in mind, start by cleaning out the muck that usually collects at the shoulder of the blade where it enters the guard. This is best done with a soft, pointed tool such as a wooden cocktail stick. The final traces of this deposit can be removed with a small, soft-bristled brush. This will have done nothing to remove any rust lurking beneath. Having completed this stage, the next operation is to remove as much soft, active rust as possible. No attempt should be made to remove hard, black rust. This is usually inactive and if the blade is properly treated will not spread, but its removal could lead to serious damage to the polished surface of the blade. On plain, engraved and etched blades, a **very fine** cutting paste can be used to clean off the active red rust. Follow the instructions, use very little and you will know you have succeeded when very little staining appears on the polishing cloth. After buffing off the cutting paste, the blade should be treated with a micro-crystalline polishing wax. The first, very sparing application will remove the final residue of the previous operation and then a second application will leave a protective coating on the blade. This will reduce the severity of any further attack by moisture and acidic gases in the air and confer a degree of protection against handling. That said, in the authors' opinion, a blade should always be handled with a clean, soft cloth or cotton gloves.

Blued and gilt blades cannot be treated with cutting paste or any such similar compound as they will cause damage to this delicate form of decoration. Polishing with micro-crystalline wax will remove dirt and leave the blade with a very thin coating that will offer some protection from handling. However, even this process should be conducted as gently as possible using the minimum amount of polish to achieve the desired result.

Dirt and metal polish tend to collect in the decoration of the hilt. They can be softened before removal using clean water applied with a cotton bud, taking care not to wet other parts of the weapon. After they have softened, dirt and metal polish can be removed with a soft, pointed instrument such as a wooden cocktail stick. A final clearing-out of this debris can be effected using a small, soft bristled brush. Then the hilt needs to be dried with a soft cloth. Remember that the metal parts of hilts were gilded and it is important to preserve all remaining traces of this. Polish with micro-crystalline wax to remove the final traces of dirt and to restore some brightness to the metalwork. The grip will usually be of ivory, bone or wood covered with fish skin, actually the skin of a ray. Micro-crystalline wax can safely be used on all these materials to remove dirt and to polish the surface of smooth grips made of bone and ivory.

The metallic parts of a scabbard should be treated in the same way as those of the weapon and the leather cleaned and polished with the micro-crystalline wax. Suitable cutting paste and micro-crystalline wax are best obtained from specialist suppliers of conservation-grade products.

Repaired Weapons

There are three types of repairs found to swords. The first was conducted during its period of use to correct damage or to conform to new regulations. These are part of the weapon's history, add to its interest and assist in dating and provenance. Indeed, sometimes the story told by such a sequence of modifications adds greatly to a weapon's interest. Examples of

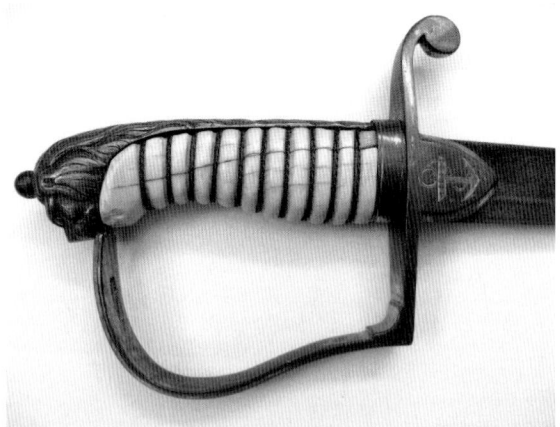

At first glance, this is a nice example of the 1805 Pattern, Ornamented sword. More careful examination shows that it is, in fact, made up from the blade, guard and grip of an 1805 sword and the back-piece/pommel of an 1827 Pattern adapted to fit the grip. Look carefully at the lion's head. Unlike the rather flattened and rounded version used with the 1805 Pattern, this is a post-1827 naturalistic representation, which has had its lower jaw cut away to fit the older grip. It also has a tang button, a feature rarely, if ever, found on 1805 swords. Although not unknown, it was unusual for the lion's mane to extend down the whole length of the back piece on 1805 Pattern swords. Examine the point where the knuckle guard enters the lion's mouth; there is a distinct shoulder on the knuckle bow which would, originally have fitted snugly to the pommel. Also, note how the ivory has been chipped at this junction. Now turn your attention to where the back-piece enters the ferrule adjacent to the cross guard. This has just been slid under the rim of the ferrule, whereas in an original mounting there would have been a stepped down tongue inserted under the ferrule leaving a smooth profile. Some repairs of this type can be old; it is only the identification of more modern parts that refines the date at which the work was undertaken. There is little doubt that this hybrid was intended to deceive an unwary collector into believing it was an example of an early and desirable sword.

Another example, this time of a later sword, appears to be the sword of a warrant officer or master-at-arms, albeit a rather battered specimen. Closer examination reveals that as well at the damage both to the quillon and to the knuckle guard, and a replacement tang button, this sword has a green-painted wooden grip bound with silver instead of gilt wires and the back piece has been hammered to make it fit. At best, it might serve to fill a gap in the collection until something better comes along.

repairs needed to keep up with changing dress regulations have already been covered by looking at scabbard conversion and these have also been shown to be useful for dating.

The second type of repair was undertaken to a damaged sword as part of its restoration. Such a repair should match as precisely as possible the materials and style of the weapon being restored but, ideally, it should also be identifiable and reversible. If it is not, it risks deceiving all but the most expert collectors and falls into the third category: the 'improvement' of a damaged weapon. Unless undertaken to enhance the sale value, even repairs in this third category are not necessarily bad; they may, after all, ensure the survival of a badly-damaged sword. Two examples are illustrated and explained.

Collecting Associated Ephemera

As well as swords and their accoutrements, the avid collector will come across all sorts of works on paper that merit inclusion in a collection because they can shed very useful light on the weapons and their use. Most obvious are the books about swords and their use written by those who served in either the RN or RM and a list of these forms one of the sections of the bibliography. From these can be learned the styles, conventions and rules pertaining at the date of publication. The illustrations are often useful sources of information about both equipment and personalities. With the exception of McArthur's book, and even that is available in facsimile, none should cost more than a few pounds, so a representative collection could be assembled very cheaply.

The visual theme can be expanded by seeking out pictures from the illustrated magazines of the late nineteenth and early twentieth centuries. Among these are *The Illustrated London News*, *The Graphic*, *The Sphere*, *The Navy and Army Illustrated*, *The Illustrated Sporting and Dramatic News*, and *Punch*. Many of these were engraved on wood blocks by well-known illustrators and often seem to capture the spirit of an event better than a photograph. This may be because the limitations of photography meant that the scenes illustrated were posed tableaux. In the later magazines, photographs were increasingly used and can provide a precision of detail absent from the sketches of the sports illustrators. Such prints can be sourced through specialist dealers or, often more cheaply, through Internet auction sites. Care needs to be taken, especially with the latter source, as some of the prints have been reproduced in recent years. It pays to at least inspect the stock of several reputable dealers, even if you decide against purchasing from these sources. Doing this will give a feel for such things as the quality and texture of the paper and the clarity of the printed line. Expect to pay between a few pounds and a few tens of pounds for this type of print, depending on date, size, medium, artist and source. One great advantage of these prints is that the date is clearly given at the head of each page. It therefore follows that a complete page is more useful as reference material than an illustrations cut from it without the dating information. This is a remarkably cost-effective way to enhance one's knowledge, build a useful reference collection and provide interesting room decoration all at the same time.

Postcards provide another great source of ephemera that can be usefully studied. There are various clues to dating of these cards but it must be remembered that images can be any date prior to that posted unless the image is dated or represents a known historical event. Picture postcards were first authorised by the Post Office in 1894 and regulations insisted that only the address could be written on the front. Any message had to be written on or around the picture on the reverse. The familiar card with the front divided for the address on one side and the correspondence on the other came on 1 January 1902. Other clues, which apply both to those cards which have been posted and to unused cards, are the form of the instruction on the front and the dimensions of the card. For cards that have been through the post, the postmark, if legible, will give the precise date of posting. Where this cannot be read, the amount paid for postage, the head of the monarch and the colour of the stamp can all be used to narrow down the date. This is not the place to go into the minutiae of these details but they are easily found in reference books on postcards and postage stamps.[9] Cards should only cost a few pounds each, again allowing the formation of an interesting collection for a very modest outlay. Other less common sources of printed ephemera are trade cards, notably for cigarettes, stereo-cards and programmes for tournaments. Many of the illustrations in this book have been taken from such sources as these, making their worth very evident.

Display

The exact form of any display of swords will reflect both the taste of the individual owner and the space available for this purpose. For display purposes, naval swords fall into two clear groups. In the first, there are all those weapons based on the 1827 pattern and in the second, all the rest. Because of the way the badge on a hilt in the first group is placed in the oval cartouche on the half-basket guard, it is important to consider the position of the viewer's eye in relation to the sword. In many cases, this will be above the sword and the design in the cartouche can only be seen if the weapon is presented with the cutting edge uppermost. This rule applies whether the sword in displayed horizontally or at an angle. Should the sword be above the viewer's eye level, then the reverse applies. One way of arranging to see the designs in the cartouches is to mount swords vertically with their points uppermost and their cutting edges facing towards the viewer. This is particularly effective where the objective is to display a range of badges.

Sword rests are available commercially, either singly or in pairs, made from clear polymethyl methacrylate. Another

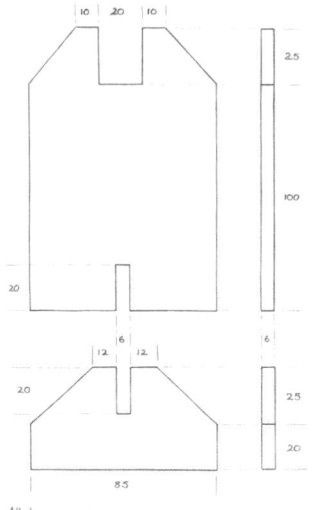

Design for a simple sword rest. The two parts slot together to give a cruciform configuration that provides a stable base. The 20mm x 25mm slot in the top comfortably accepts the top locket of a sword and also the chape if a pair of rests is used to display the weapon horizontally. Specific requirements can easily be met by adjusting the height of the large component.

All dimensions in mm

alternative is to use the stands designed for Japanese swords which accommodate either one, two or three swords displayed horizontally. Sword rests can be made to a simple basic design which can be manufactured in any height required. These can be used singly to present swords at an angle or in pairs for a horizontal display.

Some Popular Misconceptions

The error of considering dirks and midshipmen inseparable has been exposed in Chapters 2 and 4 but it bears repeating here that, until 1805, officers and midshipmen wore whatever sidearms they liked. A story concerning Prince William Henry (later William IV), while a captain in the Royal Navy, emphasises this point. The Napoleonic Admiral Sir Thomas Byam Martin describes in his memoirs while serving with Prince William Henry how the uniform conceived by his Royal Captain for his midshipman included '. . . a sword about two-thirds the length of the little body'.[10] After 1805 and until 1856, the uniform weapon for a midshipman was the sword. After 1856 and until it went into abeyance at the outbreak of the Second World War, midshipmen wore the dirk.

This is not the only myth associated with swords. Another is that the sword is carried at the trail as a mark of disgrace for ungentlemanly behaviour following a mutiny. First, there were no uniform regulations to order this at the time of the great mutinies of The Nore and Spithead. Second, the sword has been worn in three different ways (four if the Sam Browne scabbard adopted by some officers in naval brigades is included) since uniform regulations first appeared. In fact early specimens of the 1805 Pattern ornamented sword are fitted with both a frog hook and loose rings so that they can be worn in two different ways; see illustration in Chapter 3. Third, all officers' day uniforms before the advent of the 'woolly pulley' were designed to be worn on horseback (indeed there is a tale that the first uniform jacket of 1748 was modelled on the blue coat worn for riding by the Duchess of Bedford). The double vent at the back of a No. 1 (old designation No. 5) reefer jacket is the same as would be found on a hacking jacket. Until the adoption of the Sam Browne belt, Army officers wore their swords on slings; the cavalry and general officers still do. Fourth, until the sword belt disappeared under the reefer jacket, the hook was available for hitching the sword to the belt whenever that was more convenient.

Another misconception relates to the groove along each side of the blade. It is often asserted that this is a blood groove to allow the blood to escape and facilitate the withdrawal of the sword from a body. It is nothing of the sort. This groove, called a fuller, serves to lighten the blade at the same time as increasing its stiffness. It is analogous to the design of an RSJ.

The final one concerns the brass proof mark seen on the shoulder of many blades. The assertion that this indicates that the blade has been bent until the point touched the mark can be dispelled by the simplest of calculations. These show that the elastic limit of the steel would have been well and truly exceeded, resulting in, at best, a very bent weapon or, much more likely, a broken one. This fallacy has been around for a long time because it was mocked by none other than Henry Wilkinson himself.[11] Unlike cutlasses, which were tested (see Chapter 2), officers' swords were privately purchased and were not subjected to any official quality-assurance procedures. Makers and retailers placed these marks to show that the weapons had been tested in similar ways – PERHAPS! *Caveat emptor.*

Two of the different ways of wearing the sword: (*above left*) the 1847 Pattern sword carried on two equal slings; and (*above right*) the black hilted sword of non-commissioned officers on two unequal slings.

This illustrates the fact that naval officers were expected to be able to ride horses. The naval brigade from HMS *Powerful* on its return from the Boer War. (*The Graphic*, 12 May 1900)

APPENDIX 1
Patriotic Fund of Lloyd's – Swords Awarded

This list gives those swords awarded by the Patriotic Fund of Lloyd's.[1] It does not include the other awards made by the Fund, although reference is made where other awards were made for the same action. The actions have been grouped as they were when considered by the Patriotic Fund. The Fund offered the choice of taking cash instead of any other award. Sometimes only an offer of plate was made, this was usually for: events not involving commissioned officers; not in action against the enemy, or the value of the award being greater than £100. There were some occasions where officers were offered both a sword and money, or a sword and plate.

We have used the officer's rank rather than position. Previous lists reflected the inscriptions, for example:

From the Patriotic Fund at Lloyd's to John Pilford Capt of H.M.S. Ajax for his Meritorious Services In Contributing To The Signal Victory Obtained Over the Combined Fleets of France and Spain off Cape Trafalgar on the 21st October 1805.

Naval terminology uses the word 'Captain' both for a position of command and for a rank, the two not necessarily being synonymous. John Pilford was not a captain (or rather post captain) at the time, although he was in command or captaining HMS *Ajax*. He was actually a lieutenant whose captain was absent from the ship at the time of the battle, in this case to attend a court martial investigating events in a previous battle.

The post-nominal 'RM' has been used to indicate where they were members of the Royal Marines, although the abbreviation was not used at the time.

The buckle from a Patriotic Fund Sword.

The sword handle from a Patriotic Fund Sword.

The tip of a £100 Patriotic Fund Sword showing the stunning blue and gilt.

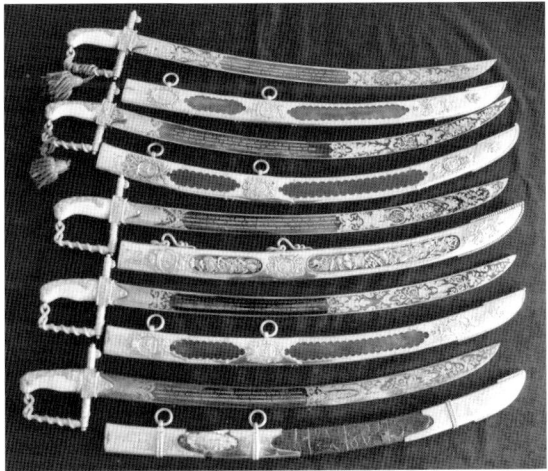
Five Patriotic Fund Swords, showing the variety within the swords. From the top: a £50 sword awarded to Captain James Pendergrass for Dance's action; a £50 sword awarded to an Army officer Major Abraham Nunn (hence the red sword knot); in the middle is a £100 awarded for an action against two French frigates to Captain Arthur Farquhar; then another £50 sword awarded to Lieutenant William Mulcaster and at the bottom is a £30 sword awarded to Master's Mate Barry Sarsfield.

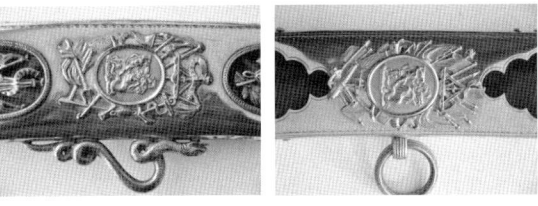
The middle lockets of (*Left*) a £100 and (*Right*) a £50 Patriotic Fund swords.

1803

27 June 1803
Cutting-out French gun brig *Venteux Isle de Bas*
Lieutenant James Bowen HMS *Loire* £50 sword
Lieutenant Francis Temple HMS *Loire* £50 sword
Midshipman Priest HMS *Loire* £30 sword

14 July 1803
Action with French privateer
Lieutenant James Wallace Gabriel HMS *Phoebe* £50 sword

12 and 17 August 1803
Actions with HMS *Niger*
Midshipman William Hillyar HMS *Niger* £30 sword

17 August 1803
Cutting-out French lugger *Messager*, Ushant
Lieutenant Watt HMS *Ville de Paris* £50 sword

18 August 1803
Cutting out five schooners and a sloop, *Machinelle*
Lieutenant George Canning HMS *Desiree* £50 sword

9 September 1803
Capture of two French *chasse-marées*
Lieutenant Henry Rowed HM Armed Cutter *Sheerness* £50 sword
A call was also awarded to the Boatswain John Marks

9 October 1803
Action in Quiberon Bay
Lieutenant George Hawkins HMS *Atalante* £50 sword

14 October 1803
Capture of French vessels off Cuba
Commander Austin Bissell HMS *Racoon* £100 sword

26 October 1803
Capture of French privateer *La Resource*
Lieutenant Robert Henderson HM Sloop *Osprey* £50 sword

31 October 1803
A French gun brig, and an armed sloop, driven ashore
Lieutenant Alexander Shippard HM Armed Cutter *Admiral Mitchell* £50 sword

5 November 1803
Cutting-out cutter, Machineel Bay
Lieutenant Hon Warwick Lake HMS *Blanche* £50 sword
Lieutenant Edward Nichols RM HMS *Blanche* £30 sword

17 November 1803
Taking of Fort Dunkirk, Martinique and French privateer *L'Harmonie*
Commander William Ferris HM Sloop *Drake* £100 sword
Lieutenant George Beatty[2] RM HMS *Blenheim* £50 sword
Lieutenant Thomas Cole HMS *Blenheim* £50 sword
Lieutenant Thomas Furber HMS *Blenheim* £50 sword
A sword was also awarded to Lieutenant Boyd RM but as he died prior to receipt his family asked for the money instead.

26 November 1803
Landing on Martinique and destruction of guns
Lieutenant James Ayscough HMS *Centaur* £50 sword
Captain Acheson Crozier RM HMS *Centaur* £50 sword
Lieutenant James Wilkes Maurice HMS *Centaur* £50 sword
Lieutenant William Walker RM HMS *Centaur* £30 sword

1804

4 February 1804
Capture of French corvette *Curieux* Martinique
Lieutenant Robert Carthew Reynolds HMS *Centaur* £50 sword
Lieutenant George Bettesworth HMS *Centaur* £50 sword
A £30 vase was awarded to Mr Tracey the Commodore's Secretary

5 February 1804
Engagement with French *Grande Decidée* off Tortola
Lieutenant William Carr HM Schooner *L'Éclair* £50 sword

9 February 1804
Destruction of batteries on Martinique
A £50 sword was awarded but not made for Lieutenant William Dommett HMS *Centaur*. It is presumed he opted for the cash equivalent

15 February 1804
Action between a division of the East India Company's fleet and a French squadron, China Sea
Captain Nathaniel Dance East India Ship *Earl Camden* £100 sword
Captain John Fann Timins East India Ship *Royal George* £50 sword
Captain Robert Hunter Brown East India Ship *Dorsetshire* £50 sword
Captain William Stanley Clarke East India Ship *Wexford* £50 sword
Captain James Farquharson East India Ship *Alfred* £50 sword
Captain William Ward Farrer East India Ship *Cumberland* £50 sword
Captain Archibald Hamilton East India Ship *Bombay Castle* £50 sword
Captain John Kirkpatrick East India Ship *Henry Addington* £50 sword
Captain Thomas Larkins East India Ship *Warren Hastings* £50 sword
Captain John Christopher Lockner East India Ship *Ocean* £50 sword
Captain Henry Meriton East India Ship *Exeter* £50 sword
Captain William Moffatt East India Ship *Ganges* £50 sword
Captain James Pendergrass East India Ship *Hope* £50 sword
Captain Robert Torin East India Ship *Coutts* £50 sword
Captain Henry Wilson East India Ship *Warley* £50 sword
Captain John jun Wordsworth East India Ship *Earl of Abergavenny* £50 sword
Lieutenant Robert Fowler RN (Passenger) East India Ship *Earl Camden* £50 sword
Captain Dance and Captain Timins were also awarded a vase

19 and 24 February 1804
Cutting-out American schooner from Trinité harbour and subsequent storming of the fort at Martinique
Lieutenant William King HM Sloop *Drake* £50 sword
Lieutenant William Compston HM Sloop *Drake* £50 sword

7–9 March 1804
Recapture of Goree
Midshipman James Hewitt HMS *Inconstant* £30 sword
A £30 sword was awarded to Midshipman Runciman but he opted to take the cash reward instead and a piece of plate was awarded to Lieutenant Pickford

13 March 1804
Cutting-out privateer schooner *Mosambique* by HM Armed Sloop *Fort Diamond*, Martinique
Lieutenant Thomas Forrest HMS *Emerald* £50 sword

23 March 1804
Capture of Dutch *Schrik*
Lieutenant James Boxer HMS *Antelope* £50 sword
Lieutenant John Martin Hanchett HMS *Antelope* £50 sword
Midshipman George Hawkins HMS *Magicienne* £30 sword
A £50 sword was awarded to but not made for Lieutenant Barber. It is presumed he opted for the cash equivalent

23 and 27 March 1804
Capture of French Frigate *L'Egyptienne*, Barbados
Commander Conway Shipley HMS *Hippomenes* £100 sword

Commander George Younghusband HM Sloop *Osprey* £100 sword

31 March 1804
Capture of Dutch *Atalante*
Commander George Nicholas Hardinge HM Sloop *Scorpion* £100 sword
Commander Charles Pelly HM Sloop *Beaver* £100 sword
Lieutenant Buckland Stirling Bluett HM Sloop *Scorpion* £50 sword
Lieutenant William Shields HM Sloop *Scorpion* £50 sword
Lieutenant Edward White HM Sloop *Beaver* £50 sword
There were two other awards of plate to Master Robert Fair and Master's Mate James Puckinghorne

1 May 1804
Capture of privateer *Veloce* in the Mediterranean
Lieutenant Robert Corner HMS *Thisbe* £50 sword

10 July 1804
Boats attacked enemy vessels, Hieres Bay
Lieutenant John Richard Lumley HMS *Seahorse* £50 sword
Lieutenant Ogle Moore HMS *Maidstone* £50 sword
Lieutenant Hyde Parker HMS *Narcissus* £50 sword
Lieutenant John Thomson HMS *Narcissus* £50 sword

31 July 1804
Capture of French privateer *Hirondelle*, St Domingo
Lieutenant Nicholas Lockyer HMS *Tartar* £50 sword
Lieutenant Henry Muller HMS *Tartar* £50 sword

18 September 1804
Action with three French vessels whilst on convoy duty in Vizagapatam Roads
Captain James Lind HMS *Centurion* £100 sword
A £50 sword was awarded to Lieutenant Philips but he opted to take the cash instead

1805

4 February 1805
Action with two French frigates whilst protecting a convoy in the Mediterranean
Commander Richard Budd Vincent HM Sloop *Arrow* 28 £100 sword
Commander Arthur Farquhar HM Bomb *Acheron* £100 sword
Commander Vincent was also awarded a piece of plate

14 February 1805
Capture of French frigate *La Psyché* and recapture of *Thetis* prize to *La Psyché* off Vizagapatam
Commander Henry Lambert HMS *St Fiorenzo* £100 sword

17 February 1805
Action against French frigate *La Ville de Milan*
Captain Sir Robert Laurie HMS *Cleopatra* £100 sword

22 February 1805
Defence of Dominica, against attempted landing by French forces
Brigadier General George Prevost £100 sword
Major Abraham Augustus Nunn 1st West Indian Regiment £50 sword
Captain Maurice Charles O'Connell 1st West Indian Regiment £50 sword
Prevost and O'Connell also received awards of plate for this action

5 April 1805
Capture of fort at Mariel, Cuba
Lieutenant James Oliver HMS *Bacchante* £50 sword

2 and 4 June 1805
Capture of privateer *Esperanza*, Bay of Camarinas (2 June) and Storming of fort/Gallant Conduct at Muros[3] (4 June)
Captain Frederick Lewis Maitland HMS *Loire* £100 sword
Lieutenant James Lucas Yeo HMS *Loire* £50 sword
Lieutenant Samuel Mallock RM HMS *Loire* £50 sword
Lieutenant Yeo also received plate and a cash reward and Master Clinch also received a cash reward.

13 June 1805
Capture of Spanish privateer schooner *Maria*
Lieutenant Hon George Alfred Crofton HMS *Cambrian* £50 sword
Lieutenant George Pigot HMS *Cambrian* £50 sword

7 July 1805
Capturing the French privateer *Matilda* and then using her to capture three more vessels
Lieutenant William Henry Masterman RM HMS *Cambrian* £50 sword
Lieutenant George Pigot received a £100 Vase for this action.

10 August 1805
Capture of French frigate *La Didon*
Captain Thomas Baker HMS *Phoenix* £100 sword

13 August 1805
Capture of Spanish schooner *La Caridad Perfecta* at Truxillo
Midshipman William Pitt Bowler HM Sloop *Swift* £30 sword

21 October 1805 Trafalgar and 4 November 1805 Action off Ferrol (also known as the battle of Cape Ortegal)

Trafalgar
Captain Henry William Baynton HMS *Leviathan* £100 sword
Captain the Hon Sir Henry Blackwood HMS *Euryalus* £100 sword
Captain Charles Bullen HMS *Britannia* £100 sword
Captain John Conn HMS *Dreadnought* £100 sword
Captain Henry Digby HMS *Africa* £100 sword
Captain Thomas Dundas HMS *Naiad* £100 sword
Captain Philip Charles Durham HMS *Defiance* £100 sword
Captain Richard Grindall HMS *Prince* £100 sword
Captain George Johnstone Hope HMS *Defence* £100 sword
Captain Richard King HMS *Achilles* £100 sword
Captain Sir Francis Laforey HMS *Spartiate* £100 sword
Captain Charles John Moore Mansfield HMS *Minotaur* £100 sword
Captain Robert Moorsom HMS *Revenge* £100 sword
Captain Israel Pellew HMS *Conqueror* £100 sword
Captain William Prowse HMS *Sirius* £100 sword
Captain Robert Redmill HMS *Polyphemus* £100 sword
Captain Edward Rotherham HMS *Royal Sovereign* £100 sword
Captain William Gordon Rutherford HMS *Swiftsure* £100 sword
Captain Charles Tyler HMS *Tonnant* £100 sword
Lieutenant John Richards Lapenotière HM Schooner *Pickle* £100 sword
Lieutenant William Pryce Cumby HMS *Bellerophon* £100 sword
Lieutenant John Pilfold[4] HMS *Ajax* £100 sword
Lieutenant John Stockham[5] HMS *Thunderer* £100 sword
Lieutenant Robert Benjamin Young HM Cutter *Entreprenante* £100 sword

Action off Ferrol
Captain the Hon Alan Gardner HMS *Hero* £100 sword
Captain Richard Lee HMS *Courageux* £100 sword
Captain Wilson Rathborne HMS *Santa Margarita* £100 sword

All captains at these two battles were awarded a sword with the exception of Captain Cooke (*Bellerophon*) and Duff (*Mars*) who died in the action and whose families were offered plate. Those not mentioned either opted for plate (Captains Hardy, Berry, Capel, Fremantle, Hargood, Morris, Baker [for Ferrol], Halstead [for Ferrol] and Lieutenant Hennah) or took cash (Captains Harvey,[6] Hotham [for Ferrol] and Fitzroy [for Ferrol]). Captain Codrington asked for his cash reward to be spent by the Fund on its main task of giving grants to those bereaved and wounded, the only known refusal of an award.[7] Admiral Nelson's family received two £500 vases, Admiral Collingwood a £500 vase. Rear Admiral the Rt Hon Earl of Northesk and Rear Admiral Sir Richard John Strachan were awarded £300 vases. The family of Lieutenant Simons (*Defiance*), who was killed at Trafalgar while hoisting the British colours on the captured *L'Aigle*, were also awarded a vase.

1806

6/7 January 1806
Cutting-out Spanish brig *Raposa*, Bay of Campeachy
Lieutenant Peter John Douglas[8] HMS *Franchise* £50 sword
Lieutenant John Fleming HMS *Franchise* £50 sword
Lieutenant Mends RM HMS *Franchise* £50 sword
Midshipman Lamb HMS *Franchise* £30 sword

10 January 1806
Capitulation of the town and garrison of the Cape of Good Hope
The two commanding officers Major Gen Sir David Baird and Commodore Sir Home Popham were formally awarded vases. Six other officers were given honorary awards two opted for plate the other four kept the sum of money or made private arrangements.

6 February 1806
Action off St Domingo
The three Admirals involved were awarded plate: Vice Admiral Sir Thomas Duckworth KB (£400), Rear Admiral the Hon Sir Alexander Cochrane (£300) and Rear Admiral Sir Thomas Louis (£300). Captains Francis William Austen (*Canopus*), Sir Edward Berry (*Agamemnon*), Richard Dalling Dunn (*Acasta*), Richard Goodwin Keats (*Superb*), Adam Mackenzie (*Magicienne*), Pultney1 Malcolm (*Donegal*), Samuel Pym (*Atlas*), the Hon Robert Stopford (*Spencer*), John Morrison (*Northumberland*) and Commander Cochrane (*Kingfisher*) were all awarded a £100 sword or plate but all opted to have a vase made. Lieutenant James Higginson (*Epervier*) was also awarded a £100 sword or plate but is presumed to have opted for cash. Captain Rutherford of the merchant vessel Helen was awarded a £100 vase for bringing intelligence of the French movements.

21 March 1806
Capture of three Spanish luggers at Avillas
Lieutenant Thomas Ussher HM Armed Brig *Colpoys* £50 sword

6 April 1806
Capture of French corvette *La Tapageuse*, River of Bordeaux
Captain Lord Cochrane HMS *Pallas* £100 sword
Lieutenant Haswell HMS *Pallas* £50 sword
Mr (Master) Sutherland HMS *Pallas* £50 sword
Mr J C Crawford HMS *Pallas* £30 sword
Edw Parkins[9] HMS *Pallas* £30 sword
Wm A Thompson HMS *Pallas* £30 sword
A vase was awarded to the gunner Hillier for his participation in the subsequent destruction of signal posts. Mr Sutherland was only awarded plate or cash, but since the sword was made by the Fund clearly requested a sword instead.

17 April 1806
Action off Tiber
Captain William Prowse HMS *Sirius* was awarded a £100 sword but opted for a vase. He had previously also been awarded a sword for Trafalgar.

4 May 1806
Cutting out the Spanish schooner *Giganta*, Vieja
Lieutenant Sir William Parker HMS *Renommee* £50 sword
Lieutenant Charles Adams HMS *Renommee* £50 sword
Lieutenant Henry John Murton RM HMS *Renommee* £30 sword

1 June 1806
Storming fort at Aguadilla, Porto Rico
Lieutenant Charles Kerr HMS *Jason* £50 sword

22 June 1806
Storming of Fort Finisterre and cutting-out five Spanish vessels
Lieutenant William Howe Mulcaster HMS *Minerva* £50 sword
Lieutenant Charles Menzies RM HMS *Minerva* £50 sword
Lieutenant Ogle Moore opted for a £50 vase having already received a sword. Lieutenant Menzies was initially awarded a £30 sword but this was amended to a £50 following his request on 22 December 1807

26 July 1806
Attack and Capture of an Enemy Squadron off Java including the destruction of Dutch brig *Christian Elizabeth*, Manado
Captain Charles Elphinstone HMS *Greyhound* £100 sword
Commander Edward Thomas Troubridge HM Sloop *Harrier* £100 sword

4 July 1806
Battle of Maida
Lieutenant Colonel J Moore 23rd Dragoons £100 sword
Major General Stuart was only offered a £300 vase, the remaining five senior officers were offered their choice of Honorary awards, two opted for plate (Lieutenant Colonel M'Leod and Major Hammill), two took the sum of money (Majors Paulett and Stuart) and Moore opted for a sword

6 July 1806
Attack on French brig *Le Caesar* and convoy, River of Bordeaux
Lieutenant Edward Reynolds Sibley HMS *Centaur* £50 sword
Lieutenant Sibley was also awarded the sum of £200

14 August 1806
Engagement with French privateer, off the Isle of Wight
Lieutenant William James Hughes HM Fire Brig *Phosphorus* £100 sword

23 August 1806
Attack on Moro Castle, Cuba and attack on the *Pomona*
Captain Charles Brisbane HMS *Arethusa* £100 Sword
Captain Lydiard was awarded a £50 sword but opted for the cash instead

12 October 1806
Action off Jersey
Awarded swords to Commander John Thicknesse HM Sloop *Sheldrake* (£100), Lieutenant Richards HMS *Constance* (£50) and Lieutenant John Nugent who was captain of HM Gun Brig *Strenuous* (£30). None of these are recorded as being made so it is presumed all took cash instead

18 October 1806
Action with Dutch ships, Batavia
Captain Peter Rainier HMS *Caroline* £100 sword

26 October 1806
Capture of French Privateer *La Superbe*, off Cape Nicholas
Lieutenant Michael Fitton HM Schooner *Pitt* £50 sword

13 December 1806
Action against three enemy ships off Gibraltar
Commander Henry Whitmarsh Pearse HM Sloop *Halycon* was awarded a £100 sword it is presumed he opted for the cash instead.

1807

1 January 1807
Taking of Curaçao
Captain William Henry Bolton HMS *Fisgard* £100 sword
Captain Brisbane was awarded a £200 vase, Captain Wood and Captain Lydiard opted for a £100 vase instead. These awards were in addition to those for Moro Castle

2 January 1807
Cutting out two vessels near St Pierre, Martinique
Lieutenant William Coote HMS *Cerberus* £50 sword
Lieutenant Bligh was awarded a £50 sword but opted for the cash instead

21 January 1807
Capture of French corvette *Le Lynx*, coast of Caraccas
Lieutenant William Coombe HMS *Galatea* £50 sword
Lieutenant Gibson HMS *Galatea* £50 sword
Master's Mate John Green HMS *Galatea* £30 sword
Master's Mate Barry Sarsfield HMS *Galatea* £30 sword
The family of Lieutenant Walker were given plate for his part in this action in which he was killed

3 February 1807
Taking of Monte Video
Lieutenant Matthias Everard 2nd or Queen's Royal Regiment of Foot £50 sword
The commanding Admiral (Stirling) and General (Auchmuty) and the three majors (Campbell, Tucker and Trotter) involved were all awarded plate. The fund subsequently received a letter recommending Everard and then awarded him a sword

14 and 16 February 1807
Capture of French schooner *Dauphin* off Cape Raphael and Destruction of Fort at Samana
Captain James Richard Dacres HMS *Bacchante* £100 sword
Captain William Furlong Wise[10] HMS *Mediator* £100 sword

8 May 1807
Cutting out Spanish packet *St Pedro*, Grand Canaria
Lieutenant George Edward Watts HMS *Comus* £50 sword

7 August 1807
Attack on fort and capture of three vessels, Begu, Catalonia
Captain George Mundy HMS *Hydra* £100 sword

Lieutenant Robert Hayes RM HMS *Hydra* £50 sword
Lieutenant Drury was also awarded a £50 sword but opted for cash instead.

1808

13 March 1808
Attack on forts in Vivero Harbour and destruction of French corvette *L'Apropos*
Lieutenant Giles Meech RM HMS *Emerald* £30 sword

8 March 1808
Capture of French frigate *La Piedmontaise*,[11] Gulf of Manaar
Lieutenant William Dawson HMS *San Fiorenzo* £100 sword
The widow of Captain Hardinge received a £100 vase for his valour in this action.

14 March 1808
Action with a Danish ship of war, coast of Norway
Commander William Henry Dillon HM Sloop *Childers* £100 sword

23 Apr 1808
Action with gunboats off Faro, Portugal
Awarded the choice of a £100 sword or vase Commander Thomas Searle HM Sloop *Grasshopper* opted for a vase

11 June 1808
Capture of Danish gunboat and three smaller vessels near the entrance of the Naskow,[12] coast of Denmark
Lieutenant Richard Head HMS *Euryalus* £50 sword

5/6 July 1808
Capture of Turkish vessel, Island of Scopolo
Awarded the choice of a £100 sword or vase Captain John Stewart HMS *Seahorse* opted for a vase

10 November 1808
Capture of French frigate *La Thetis*
Offered the choice of a £100 sword or vase Captain Michael Seymour HMS *Amethyst* opted for a vase

1809

3 January 1809 and 19 February 1807[13]
Capture of two gunboats off Corfu (1809), Burning a frigate and destroying a large battery in the Dardanelles (1807)
Captain Edward Nichols RM HMS *Standard* £100 sword

9 March, 1809
Capture of the French National ship of war *Joseph*, at St Domingo
Awarded a £50 sword Lieutenant J R Coryton RM opted for cash instead

1 April 1809
Cutting-out Venetian gun boat, Rovigno Harbour

Lieutenant Watkin Owen Pell HMS *Mercury* £50 sword

12 April 1809
Leading fire ship in attack on French Fleet, Basque Roads
Captain James Wooldridge HMS *Mediator* £100 sword
Lieutenant Nicholas Brent Clements HMS *Mediator* £50 sword

1810 and Awarded Later

The Patriotic Fund of Lloyd's ceased presenting swords in 1809 but a few officers subsequently asked permission to have a sword made with the funds they had been awarded for wounds and this was approved by the Fund, this included for actions that had taken place earlier while they were still being awarded. Captain Brenton's was paid directly by the Fund's account with Teed, Lieutenant Baynton had to make arrangements himself with Teed.

3 May 1810
Gallant action against a squadron of the enemy
Captain Jahleel Brenton HMS *Spartan* £100 sword
Lieutenant Benjamin Baynton HMS *Cambrian* £50 sword

4 January 1805
Attack on French privateer off St Vallery
Lieutenant William Cunningham Cavendish Dalyell HM Sloop *Rattler* £50 sword
Lieutenant Dalyell was awarded £100 cash so the sword was only half of his reward

21 September 1809
Attack on the Island of Bourbon
Lieutenant Thomas Robert Pye RM HMS *Boadicea* £50 sword

9 July 1810
Action off Toulon
Midshipman James Adair HMS *Alceste* £30 sword
Midshipman Adair was awarded £40 by the Fund

8 April 1811
Taking of Batavia
Commander Edward Stopford HMS *Otter* £100 sword

10 May 1811
Repulsing a sortie of the enemy, Fort St Christoval Badajoz
Colonel Thomas Turner 17th Reg of Foot Portugese £100 sword

17 November 1811
Action with French lugger, Dungeness
Captain Peter Buisey Cow Naval Transport *Chatham* £50 sword

Captain Cow was a Merchant Navy Captain.

21 July 1812
Action, coast of France
Lieutenant Thomas Warrand HM Schooner *Sealark* £50 sword

12 August 1812
Action, Valemeria
Lieutenant Dwyer HMS *Minstral* £50 sword

Three Unminuted Swords
The granting of permission to have swords made was still clearly in the mind of committee as these are from the same period as the group above. They are though not mentioned in the minutes. Perhaps it was a later decision of the individuals or asked in private and never minuted.

5 May 1804
Capture of Suriname
Lieutenant James Arnold Royal Engineers £100 sword[14]
Lieutenant Arnold was award a £100 grant by the Fund for his service in the battle in which he was wounded

23 August 1810
Isle de France
Lieutenant Thomas Sherlock Cox RM HMS *Nereide* £50 sword
Lieutenant Cox was awarded £60 from the Fund for his wounds

16 May 1811
For wounds received at the battle of Albuera
Major Edward Fleming 31st Regiment £50 sword
Major Fleming was awarded a £100 grant from the Fund

APPENDIX 2

City of London Presentation Swords

Name	Date	Service	Value
Admiral the Earl of St Vincent	1797	Cape St Vincent	200 gns
Admiral Viscount Duncan	1797	Camperdown	200 gns
Vice Admiral Sir R Onslow	1797	Camperdown	100 gns
Rear Admiral Viscount Nelson	1798	The Nile	200 gns
Vice Admiral Sir A Mitchell	1799	Coast of the Netherlands	100 gns
Captain Sir S Smith	1799	Defence of St Jean d'Acre	100 gns
Admiral Viscount Keith	1801	Egypt	100gns
Rear Admiral Lord de Saumarez	1801	Algeciras & Cape Trafalgar	100 gns
Vice Admiral Lord Collingwood	1805	Trafalgar	200 gns
Rear Admiral the Earl of Northesk	1805	Trafalgar	100 gns
Captain R Strachan	1805	Ferrol	100 gns
Captain Sir T M Hardy	1805	Trafalgar	100 gns
Vice Admiral Sir J T Duckworth	1806	Santo Domingo	200 gns
Rear Admiral Sir A F I Cochrane	1806	Santo Domingo	100 gns
Rear Admiral Sir T Louis	1806	Santo Domingo	100 gns
Commodore Sir H Popham	1806	Buenos Ayres	200 gns
Rear Admiral C Stirling	1807	Monte Video	200 gns
Captain Sir P B V Broke	1813	Capture of USS *Chesapeake*	100 gns
Admiral Viscount Exmouth	1816	Algiers & freeing of slaves	200 gns
Rear Admiral Sir D Milne	1816	Algiers & freeing of slaves	100 gns
Admiral Lord Alcester	1882	Egypt	100 gns
Admiral of the Fleet Sir D Beatty	1918	Services, First World War	100 gns
Admiral of the Fleet Viscount Jellicoe	1919	Services, First World War	100 gns
Admiral of the Fleet Viscount Cunningham	1945	Services, Second World War	£560
Admiral Lord Louis Mountbatten	1945	Services, Second World War	£500
Rear Admiral J Woodward	1982	The Falkland Islands	£898

APPENDIX 3
Naval Service Awards of the Wilkinson Swords of Peace[1]

1966 40 Commando, RM, for services in Sarawak in winning the hearts and minds of the people there.

1967 HMS *Ghurkha*, for an outstanding lifesaving operation on a badly injured Dhofari boy and other good-neighbour services in the Persian Gulf.[2]

1968 7th Mine Countermeasures Squadron, for its services during the earthquake in NW Sicily in January 1968.

1969 RFA *Ennerdale*, for assisting the South African Navy in rescue operations on Gough Island, Tristan da Cunha.

1970 HMS *Sirius*, for valuable service to the inhabitants of the British West Indies and in particular for assistance after the St Kitts ferry boat disaster.

1971 HMS *Kirkliston* for outstanding rescue work after typhoon Rose struck Hong Kong, and for many projects which helped communities in the area.

1972 40 Commando, RM, for outstanding community relations activities in Northern Ireland in particularly difficult circumstances.

1973 RNAS Culdrose, for the year round dawn-to-dusk Search and Rescue service to the local community and for longer range lifesaving missions in the Channel and Western Approaches.

1974 41 Commando, RM, for the defence of the Eastern Sovereign Base Area and the setting up of a refugee camp in Cyprus.

1975 HMS *Tiger* for work carried out in assisting local communities in the UK in particular the outstanding contribution they made to the 'Age Concern' organisation in Portsmouth.

1976 Hong Kong Squadron for its community relations with people of the Sai Kung Peninsular, the Tolo Peninsular and outlying islands.

1977 Naval Party 8901, forty-two officers and men of the RM for outstanding work in maintaining communications in the Falkland Islands.

1978 The Fishery Protection Squadron for the good and friendly relations it has established with the fishing community and the enforcement of fishery legislation.

1979 HMS *Fife* for Services to Dominica after Hurricane David.

1980 The Staff of the Senior Naval Officer, Northern Ireland, for their youth community relations work in the Province and operational maintenance of coastal security.

1981 HMS *Osprey* for their consistent effort in maintaining close links with the local community by their charitable and recreational contributions, and by their close association with the RNLI, coastguard, police and fisherman.

1982 HMS *Endurance*, for her long-standing and continuing service on behalf of those who live and work in the Falkland Islands, their Dependencies and Antarctica.

1983 HMS *Galatea* and HMNZS *Canterbury*[3] for their concerted effort in creating firm bonds of trust and friendships in and around the Indian Ocean during 1982/3.

1984 40 Commando RM, for services with the UN Peace Force in Cyprus during 1984, and in particular for helping farmers to work their land, opening up many new farms and uniting families. This was the first unit in the history of the Award to win three times.

1985 HMS *Cambridge*, the Royal Navy Gunnery School at Wembury, to mark the close links that have been forged with the local community by providing generous support and fundraising for numerous organisations, groups, schools and charities.

1986 HMS *Brazen* for re-establishing relations with Malta.

1987 RNAS Culdrose for contribution to the local community.

1988 HMS *Rooke* for taking every opportunity to improve the relationship between the Royal Navy and the people of Gibraltar.

1989 Fishery Protection Squadron for contribution to the safety of waters around the UK.

1990 Clyde Submarine Base for being an essential, part of the local community's sporting, social and fund raising life.

1991 3 Commando Brigade for humanitarian work aiding Kurdish refugees in the aftermath of the Gulf War

1992 First Mine Counter Measures Squadron (MCM 1) for assistance to the emerging Baltic States.

1993 HMS *London*, association and help to the island of Duras, and relief efforts in Albania.

1994 HMS *Fearless*, aid project in Guyana.

1995 HMS *Invincible* and HMS *Illustrious*, general high profile efforts to a variety of communities and countries.

1996 Inshore Training Squadron for high profile visits to Russia,[4] and Spain.

1997 819 Naval Air Squadron, RNAS Prestwick for Search and Rescue in the north of England and Scotland and for the Squadron's close relationship with the community in Prestwick.

1998 Task Group 326.02 (HMS *Ocean*, HMS *Somerset*, HMS *Sheffield*, RFA *Sir Tristram* and RFA *Black Rover*) for hurricane relief to Nicaragua and Honduras in the wake of Hurricane Mitch (Op TELLAR).[5]

1999 HMS *Norfolk* for delivery of humanitarian assistance to Sierra Leone in January and February 1999.

2000 RFA *Fort George* and 820 NAS for humanitarian relief effort in Mozambique following extensive flooding of the River Save in March 2000.[6]

2001 3 Commando Brigade for their work in Kosovo, August 2000 to February 2001.

2002 771 Naval Air Squadron, RNAS Culdrose for Search and Rescue in the West Country and for the Squadron's close relationship with the community.

2003 RFA *Sir Galahad* for bringing humanitarian aid to Iraq, March 2003, following the war-fighting phase of Operation TELIC.

2004 HMS *Richmond*[7] for hurricane relief in the Caribbean in the wake of Hurricanes Francis and Ivan Aug/Sep 2003.

Naval Service Awards of the Firmin Swords of Peace

2005 HMS *Chatham* for humanitarian relief to Sri Lanka and the Maldives following the Boxing Day 2004 tsunami (Operation GARRON).

2006 Not awarded.

2007 HMS *Gannet*, Prestwick, Ayrshire for Search & Rescue, and fund-raising for charity.

2008 Northern Diving Group, Faslane for ordnance disposal, diving and SAR in Scotland and Northern England, particularly in support of the seafaring community and for their contribution to the wider community.

2009 Not awarded.

2010 RFA *Largs Bay*, humanitarian relief following Haiti earthquake in Jan 2010.[8]

2011 Not awarded.

APPENDIX 4

Service Champions and Trophies

Service championships were instituted in the Royal Navy and Royal Marines in 1921. From 1904, the Service champion had been deemed to be the competitor most highly placed at the Royal Tournament. However, there was a plethora of competitions, which may be summarised as follows:

1904 Officers' Competitions at foil, épée and sabre (RN & Army); Ratings' Competitions (RN) at foil and sabre.
1905 to 1911 Officers' Competitions at foil, épée and sabre (RN & Army), Other Ranks' Competitions (RN & Regular Army) and Royal Navy and Army Championships at foil and sabre.
1912 to 1914 Officers' Competitions at foil, épée and sabre, Other Ranks' Competitions (RN, Regular Army and Territorial Forces) at foil, épée and sabre and Inter-Services Championships at foil and sabre.
1919 and 1920 Officers' Competitions and Other Ranks' Competitions at foil, épée and sabre, Inter-Services Championships at foil and sabre. The RAF competed in these competitions.

In view of the complexity of these competitions, the highest placed RN or RM competitor in each of these events has been recorded for each year. The limitation is that only the first three places in each competition are recorded in de Beaumont.[1]
There are differences between the two major sources with Binns[2] giving a single service champion for each weapon after 1921 but de Beaumont separating officers from ratings and other ranks until 1924. Here, de Beaumont has been preferred as offering more names for the record. Binns has one year (1927) missing from the records for some of Championships when no competitions were held but de Beaumont has three (1927–9). In this case, Binns has been given priority. After 1923 the RMA and RMLI amalgamated to become the RM.

1904 Officers' Competitions: Foil S/Lt F E B Fielmann (1); Sabre Lt E Fullerton (3). Royal Navy Competitions: Foil PO D Woodcock (1); Sabre PO W F Avery (1).

1905 Officers' Competitions: Epée Lt F E B Fielmann (1); Sabre Lt E J A Fullerton (1). Other Ranks' Competitions: Sabre Sgt Riddell RMA (1), PO W Avery (2).
1906 Officers' Competitions: Sabre Lt F E B Fielmann (2); Other Ranks' Competitions: Foil CPO F Smeaton (3=); Sabre Col Sgt Trott RMLI (1).
1907 Officers' Competitions: Foil Ass Paymr C C H Drake RNR (3); Epée Ass Paymr C C H Drake RNR (3); Sabre Lt F E B Fielmann (1); Other Ranks' Competitions: Foil CPO F Smeaton (1); Sabre CPO F Smeaton (2); Royal Navy and Army Championships: Foil CPO F Smeaton (2).
1908 Officers' Competitions: Foil Ass Paymr C C H Drake RNR (2); Epée Lt F E B Fielmann (3); Sabre Lt E W H Brookfield (2).
1909 Officers' Competitions; Foil Lt J C B Harbottle (3); Epée Lt F E B Fielmann (1); Other Ranks' Competitions: Foil Sgt W Riddell RMA (2), PO W Howson (3).
1910 Officers' Competitions: Foil Ass Paymr C C H Drake RN (3); Epée Ass Paymr C C H Drake (1); Sabre Capt A E Syson RMLI (2); Other Ranks' Competitions: Sabre PO Yeo (3); Royal Navy and Army Championships: Sabre Lt F E B Fielmann (2).
1911 Officers' Competitions: Foil S/Lt D Hervey MacLeary (2); Epée Lt F E B Fielmann (3); Sabre Capt A E Syson RMLI (2); Other Ranks' Competitions: Foil Sgt Crutchen RMLI (3); Royal Navy and Army Championships: Lt F E B Fielmann (2); Sabre Lt F E B Fielmann (2).
1912 Officers' Competitions: Foil Lt E W H Brookfield (2); Sabre Lt R C Dalglish (1).
1913 Officers' Competitions: Foil Lt E W H Brookfield (1); Epée Lt E W H Brookfield (3); Sabre Lt W D Phipps (2): Other Ranks' Competitions: Foil PO James; Sabre PO James; Inter-Services Championships: sabre Lt E W H Brookfield (1).
1914 Other Ranks' Competitions: Sabre Sgt F W Dash RMLI (3); Inter-Services Championships: Sabre Lt E W H Brookfield (1).
1919 Officers' Competitions: Foil Capt R C Dalglish (2); Sabre Lt Cdr R L Burnett (1); Other Ranks' Competitions: Foil CPO J Cassford; Sabre CPO J Cassford; Inter-Services Championships: Foil Cdr F E B Fielmann (3); Sabre CPO J Cassford (2).
1920 Officers' Competitions: Foil Lt C A Kershaw (2); Epée Capt R C Dalglish (1); Sabre Lt C A Kershaw; Other Ranks' Competitions: Sabre CPO W Stamper (1), Sgt M Hawes RMLI (2); Inter-Services Championships sabre Lt C A Kershaw (2).

FOIL – Royal Navy

Officers
1921	Lt C A Kershaw
1922	Cdr C B Harbottle
1923	Lt C A Kershaw

Ratings
1921	CPO W G Howson
1922	CPO W G Howson
1923	CPO Mihalop

Combined
Until 1966, the Royal Marines held a separate Corps Championship; these results are not recorded here. After that date, they amalgamated with the RN at the Service level and the Corps Championship was demoted to the status of a Command Championship.

1924	Lt C A Kershaw
1925	Lt Cdr C A Kershaw
1926	Lt Cdr C A Kershaw
1927	No competition
1928	Lt Cdr E A Mount-Haes
1929	Lt Cdr F R Baxter
1930	PO L Pack
1931	Lt E R Collins
1932	Lt R D French
1933	POI J P Finch
1934	Lt Cdr E A Mount-Haes
1935	Lt Cdr E A Mount-Haes
1936	Lt Cdr E A Mount-Haes
1937	S/Lt R A Sproul-Bolton
1938	S/Lt R A Sproul-Bolton
1939	PO J W Toft
1947	(S)CPO C G Daffey
1948	Cdr(E) A G Olliver
1949	Lt Cdr R St C Sproul-Bolton

… Appendix 4: Service Champions and Trophies 127

1950	S/Lt W Ashmole
1951	S/Lt W Ashmole
1952	S/Lt W Ashmole
1953	LS K Pearson
1954	Lt Cdr R St C Sproul-Bolton
1955	Lt Cdr R St C Sproul-Bolton
1956	LS K Pearson
1957	LS K Pearson
1958	LS K Pearson
1959	PO K Pearson
1960	Lt W Ashmole
1961	PO K Pearson
1962	PO K Pearson
1963	PO K Pearson
1964	PO K Pearson
1965	S/Lt C C Walker
1966	PO K Pearson*
1967	Sgt J T Harrison
1968	Sgt J T Harrison
1968	Sgt J T Harrison
1969	Lt C C Walker
1970	Lt C C Walker
1971	Cdt M Simmonds
1972	Lt C C Walker
1973	Sgt J T Harrison
1974	Lt Cdr C C Walker
1975	Lt M Simmonds
1976	Lt Cdr J N McGrath
1977	Lt M Simmonds*
1978	Lt Cdr J N McGrath
1979	Lt Cdr C C Walker
1980	Lt J C Gay
1981	S/Lt R Meredith
1982	S/Lt R Meredith
1983	Lt J C Gay
1984	Capt C J Baxter RM
1985	Lt Cdr J C Gay
1986	Lt Cdr J C Gay
1987	Lt A M Large
1988	Mne P Kimbley
1989	S/Lt E King
1990	Sgt P Kimbley
1991	Lt Cdr A M Large
1992	S/Lt C A S Potter RNR
1993	Sgt P Kimbley
1994	AEM M Needham
1995	Lt Cdr S O'Reilly
1996	Lt Cdr A J Olliver
1997	Cdr S A O'Reilly
1998	LAEM M Needham
1999	Lt Cdr A J Olliver
2000	Lt Cdr A J Olliver
2001	LAEM M Needham
2002	LAEM M Needham
2003	LAEM M Needham
2004	Lt Cdr A J Olliver
2005	LAEM Needham
2006	Lt Cdr A J Olliver
2007	Lt K J Bowers
2008	Cdr M Clark
2009	Lt K J Bowers
2010	Lt Cdr A J Olliver
2011	Lt K J Bowers
2012	Lt Cdr K J Bowers

EPEE – Royal Navy

Officers
1921	Lt C A Kershaw
1922	Lt C A Kershaw
1923	Lt C A Kershaw

Ratings
1921	CPO W Stamper
1922	CPO W G Howson
1923	Tel Gook

Combined
1924	Lt E A Mount-Haes
1925	Capt R C Dalglish
1926	Lt Cdr C A Kershaw
1927	Lt R C Harry
1928	Lt Cdr E A Mount-Haes
1929	Lt Cdr F R Baxter
1930	PO L Pack
1931	PO J Hawkins
1932	CPO L Pack
1933	PO J P Finch
1934	PO J P Finch
1935	Lt Cdr E A Mount-Haes
1936	Lt Cdr E A Mount-Haes
1937	PO P L Mitchell
1938	S/Lt R A Sproul-Bolton
1939	PO J W Toft
1947	Cdr(E) A G Oliver
1948	Lt G A Brooke
1949	Surg Cdr C P Collins
1950	S/Lt F Cregah-Osborne
1951	Surg Cdr C P Collins
1952	Lt Cdr R St C Sproul-Bolton
1953	Lt Cdr R St C Sproul-Bolton
1954	Lt Cdr R St C Sproul-Bolton
1955	Lt J T Spafford
1956	Lt Cdr R St C Sproul-Bolton
1957	Lt Cdr R St C Sproul-Bolton
1958	LS K Pearson
1959	Lt J T Spafford
1960	Lt C B Filmer
1961	Lt J Dougan
1962	PO K Pearson
1963	Cdr C P Jonson
1964	S/Lt L C Llewellyn
1965	PO K Pearson
1966	PO K Pearson*
1967	Sgt J T Harrison
1968	Lt C Llewellyn
1969	Lt C C Walker
1970	Lt Cdr J N McGrath
1971	CPO R Tiller*
1972	Sgt T Harrison
1973	Sgt T Harrison
1974	Sgt E Lacey
1975	Lt Cdr C C Walker
1976	Lt Cdr C C Walker
1977	Unknown
1978	Lt Cdr J N McGrath
1979	Lt J C Gay
1980	Lt J C Gay
1981	S/Lt T Kenealy
1982	S/Lt S R Meredith
1983	Lt J C Gay
1984	Lt T Kenealy
1985	Lt T Kenealy
1986	Lt T Kenealy
1987	Lt G G Trewhella
1988	WEM(O) C Whitney
1989	Lt Cdr P Engeham
1990	Capt J N McGrath
1991	Lt Cdr G G Trewhella
1992	Cpl P Kimbley
1993	Sgt P Kimbley
1994	AEM M Needham
1995	Mid W C Hale RNR
1996	LAEM M Needham
1997	Lt Cdr A J Olliver
1998	Lt Cdr A J Olliver
1999	L/Cpl A Baker
2000	Lt Cdr A J Olliver
2001	LAEM M Needham
2002	Mne W C Hale
2003	Mne W C Hale
2004	Capt A Baker
2005	LAEM M Needham
2006	Lt R Coffey
2007	LAEM M Needham
2008	Lt W C Hale RM
2009	PO M Needham
2010	Lt K J Bowers
2011	OCdt D Grant
2012	AB F Noakes

SABRE – Royal Navy

Officers
1921	Lt C A Kershaw
1922	Lt C A Kershaw
1923	Lt C A Kershaw

Ratings
1921	CPO W Stamper
1922	CPO D H S Martin
1923	CPO Barkshire

Combined
1924	Lt C A Kershaw
1925	Lt C A Kershaw
1926	Lt C A Kershaw
1927	No competition
1928	Lt Cdr E A Mount-Haes
1929	PO L Pack
1930	S/Lt H C W Head
1931	PO J Hawkins
1932	Lt Cdr R C Harry
1933	Lt Cdr R C Harry
1934	Lt Cdr E A Mount-Haes
1935	Cdr F R Baxter
1936	The Revd R J P Stewart
1937	Cdr R C Harry
1938	Cdr R C Harry

Year	Name	Year	Name	Year	Name
1939	(S)PO Daffey	2009	Lt K J Bowers	2000	Lt Cdr A J Olliver
1947	Capt R C Harry	2010	Lt K J Bowers	2001	LAEM Needham
1948	PO R G Pitt	2011	Lt K J Bowers	2002	Lt Cdr A J Olliver
1949	PO R G Pitt	2012	Lt Cdr K J Bowers	2003	S/Lt K Bowers
1950	S/Lt W Ashmole			2004	Lt Cdr A J Olliver
1951	Capt R C Harry			2005	LAEM M Needham
1952	Capt R C Harry			2006	Lt Cdr A Olliver
1953	Capt R C Harry			2007	Lt K J Bowers
1954	PO J A Sayers			2008	LAEM M Needham
1955	Mid R S Clarke			2009	LAEM M Needham
1956	Lt H A Winckles			2010	Lt K J Bowers
1957	CPO S Johnson			2011	Lt K J Bowers
1958	LS K Pearson			2012	Lt Cdr K J Bowers

RN Champion-at-Arms

In 1954 a competition was instituted for the RN Champion-at-Arms. Those placed in the first six of weapon were awarded points on the scale: 1st = 6 points; 2nd = 5 points and so on. The individual gaining the most points was to be the Champion-at-Arms. Since direct elimination without a repecharge from a last thirty-two was introduced, it moved to 1st = 8 points and so on.

1959	PO K Pearson
1960	Lt F W Ashmole
1961	CPO S Johnson
1962	PO K Pearson
1963	PO K Pearson
1964	PO K Pearson
1965	PO K Pearson
1966	PO K Pearson*
1967	SCPO(V) R Parry
1968	Lt Cdr N A Carter
1969	Lt C C Walker
1970	Lt C C Walker
1971	CPO R Tiller *
1972	Sgt J N T Harrison
1973	Sgt J N T Harrison
1974	Lt Cdr C C Walker
1975	Lt Cdr C C Walker
1976	Lt Cdr C C Walker
1977	Lt D Foster
1978	Lt J C Gay
1979	Lt J C Gay
1980	Lt Cdr C C Walker
1981	Cdr C C Walker
1982	Lt J C Gay
1983	Lt J C Gay
1984	POPTI R Hudson
1985	Lt Cdr J C Gay
1986	Lt Cdr J C Gay
1987	Lt Cdr J C Gay
1988	Capt C C Walker
1989	WOSTD C C A Siddall
1990	Seaman A P Bex RNR
1991	WOSTD C C A Siddall
1992	Capt C C Walker
1993	Capt C C Walker
1994	Lt Cdr S A O'Reilly
1995	Lt Cdr D R Fry
1996	LAEM M Needham
1997	Lt Cdr A J Olliver
1998	LAEM M Needham
1999	CSgt P A Kimbley
2000	LAEM M Needham
2001	LAEM M Needham
2002	Lt Cdr M A Barton
2003	S/Lt K J Bowers
2004	S/Lt K J Bowers
2005	S/Lt K J Bowers
2006	Lt K J Bowers
2007	Lt K J Bowers
2008	Lt K J Bowers

1954	PO J A Sayers
1955	CPO R N Tedder
1956	PO K Pearson
1957	PO K Pearson
1958	PO K Pearson
1959	PO K Pearson
1960	Lt Cdr F W Ashmole
1961	PO K Pearson
1962	PO K Pearson
1963	PO K Pearson
1964	PO K Pearson
1965	S/Lt C C Walker
1966	PO K Pearson
1967	Sgt T J Harrison
1968	Sgt T J Harrison
1969	Lt C C Walker
1970	Lt C C Walker
1971	CPO R Tiller
1972	Sgt T J Harrison
1973	Sgt T J Harrison
1974	Lt Cdr C C Walker
1975	Lt Cdr C C Walker
1976	Lt Cdr C C Walker
1977	Lt M Simmonds
1978	Lt J Gay
1979	Lt J Gay
1980	Lt J Gay
1981	S/Lt S Meredith
1982	S/Lt S Meredith
1983	Lt J Gay
1984	Capt C I J Baxter RM
1985	Lt Cdr J Gay
1986	Lt Cdr J C Gay
1987	Lt Cdr A Large
1988	WEM(O) C Whitney
1989	Lt Cdr A Large
1990	Sgt P Kimbley
1991	Lt Cdr G Trewhella
1992	Cpl P Kimbley
1993	Sgt Kimbley
1994	Lt Cdr S A O'Reilly
1995	Lt Cdr S A O'Reilly
1996	Lt Cdr A J Olliver
1997	Lt Cdr A J Olliver
1998	LAEM Needham
1999	Lt Cdr A J Olliver

FOIL – Ladies

British Fencing records[3] give top three places at the Inter Services Ladies Foil, the RN named are:

1947	2nd Wren E Renouf
1948	1st Wren A Heaton, 2nd Wren E Renouf
1949	3rd Ldg Wren B Hayer
1950–1	No WRNS in top places
1952	1st 3/O B J G Allen
1953	1st 3/O B J G Allen
1954	1st 3/O B J G Allen
1955	3rd 3/O B J G Allen
1956	3rd Ldg Wren Henney
1957	2nd 3/O R Joll, 3rd Wren S M Brooks
1958	1st Ldg Wren S M Brooks
1959	2nd 3/O R V Strong
1960	No WRNS in top places
1961	2nd Wren J S Whitehouse, 3rd 2/O R D Joll
1962	1st 3/O J A Damrel
1963–4	No WRNS in top places
1965	3rd Wren C M Horseman
1966	L/Wren R B McHugh
1967	L Wren C M Murphy
1968	Wren W M Palmer
1969	3/O F Heal[4]
1970	Wren A Bennett
1971	Wren S Waghorn*
1972	Wren B Williams*
1973	Wren B Williams*
1974	3/O B Williams
1975	3/O M Riley WRNR
1976	2/O B Williams*[5]
1977	2/O B Williams
1978	3/O M Riley WRNR
1979	2/O B Williams*
1980	3/O M Myers WRNR (née Riley)
1981	3/O M Myers WRNR
1982	C/Wren S Corbett
1983	C/Wren S Bate
1984	3/O C Frey
1985	2/O C Frey
1986	2/O M Myers WRNR
1987	2/O M Myers WRNR
1988	2/O C Pike

1989	OC C Read
1990	OC C Read
1991	Lt Cdr M Myers RNR
1992	Lt Cdr M Myers RNR
1993	S/Lt K Samuel
1994	Lt Cdr M Myers RNR
1995	Lt Cdr M Myers RNR
1996	Lt Cdr M Myers RNR
1997	Lt Cdr M Myers RNR
1998	Lt Cdr M Myers RNR
1999	Lt Cdr M Myers RNR
2000	Lt Cdr M Myers RNR
2001	Lt Cdr M Myers RNR
2002	Lt Cdr M Myers RNR
2003	S/Lt A Hale RNR
2004	S/Lt A Hale RNR
2005	Lt A Brooks RNR
2006	Lt A Hale RN
2007	Wtr R French
2008	Surg SLt (D) B Mair
2009	Surg SLt (D) B Mair
2010	LMEA G Wollaston
2011	POET(ME) G Read
2012	MA A Mills

EPEE – Ladies

1980	Wren J White
1981	L/Wren S Oldman
1982	L/Wren L McGill
1983	Wren Biggs
1984	3/O C Frey
1985	2/O C Frey
1986	Wren Davies
1987	No competition
1988	Unknown
1989	OC C Read
1990	OC C Read
1991	C/Wren C Rowing
1992	Lt S Bullock
1993	C/Wren S Bage
1994	Lt Cdr M Myers RNR
1995	Lt Cdr M Myers RNR
1996	Lt Cdr M Myers RNR
1997	Lt Cdr M Myers RNR
1998	Lt Cdr M Myers RNR
1999	A/S/Lt A Brooks RNR
2000	S/Lt A Brooks RNR
2001	LWWtr C McGillen
2002	LWWtr C McGillen
2003	Lt A Brooks RNR
2004	S/Lt A Hale RNR
2005	Lt A Brooks RNR
2006	MEM G Wollaston
2007	POMEA S Turrell
2008	LMEM G Wollaston
2009	LMEM G Wollaston
2010	LMEM G Wollaston
2011	POET(ME) G Read
2012	MA A Mills

SABRE – Ladies

1993	Mid N Hull
1994	POWETS L Olliver
1995	Lt S M Bullock
1996	Lt K Samuel
1997	S/Lt H Budden CAF
1998	Wtr C McGillen
1999	Lt Cdr M Myers RNR
2000	S/Lt A Brooks RNR
2001	S/Lt A Brooks RNR
2002	S/Lt A Brooks
2003	S/Lt A Hale RNR
2004	S/Lt A Hale RNR
2005	Lt A Brooks RNR
2006	Lt A Hale
2007	Lt Cdr H Budden RCN
2008	Lt A Glendinning
2009	Surg SLt (D) B Mair
2010	LMEA G Wollaston
2011	LNN L Parry
2012	LNN L Parry

CHAMPION-AT-ARMS – Ladies

1989	OC C Read
1990	OC C Read
1991	CWren S Bage
1992	Lt S Bullock
1993	Hon Mid N Hull RNR
1994	Lt S Bullock
1995	Lt S Bullock
1996	Lt K Samuel
1997	Lt Cdr M Myers RNR
1998	Lt Cdr M Myers RNR
1999	Lt Cdr M Myers RNR
2000	S/Lt S Brooks RNR
2001	S/Lt S Brooks RNR
2002	S/Lt S Brooks RNR
2003	S/Lt A Hale RNR
2004	S/Lt A Hale RNR
2005	Lt S Brooks RNR
2006	Lt A Hale RN
2007	Lt Cdr H Budden RCN
2008	Lt V Fane-Bailey
2009	Surg SLt (D) B Mair
2010	LMEA G Wollaston
2011	POET(ME) G Read
2012	Not awarded

Winners of the Palmer Trophy

The oldest RN fencing cup is the Palmer Trophy. The inscription on the cup reads: 'Presented by the Officers of the Gymnastic Branch of the Royal Navy as a Challenge Cup for Naval Bayonet Teams at the Royal Naval and Military Tournament 1905'. It is named after Captain Norman Craig Palmer Royal Navy who was the Superintendent of Gymnasia in Portsmouth from February 1902 to November 1904. Originally awarded to the unit which won a competition for bayonet fencing. Teams were of eight competitors with a team leader of a Petty Officer of above and containing no more than two Royal Marines. It evolved to teams of two each at foil, épée and bayonet and, following the dropping of bayonet fencing to teams of six, three at each of the remaining weapons before changing again by the mid 1960s to a team of two at each of foil, épée and sabre. From the mid-1990s ladies were permitted to be members of a unit team. The trophy for the Inter-Command three man (can include women) team competition is a cup which was, originally, awarded for boxing.

1905	RN Barracks, Portsmouth
1906	RN Barracks, Portsmouth
1907	HMS *Nelson*, Portsmouth
1908	HMS *Magnificent*, Chatham
1909	RN Physical Training School
1910	HMS *Africa*, Chatham
1911	RN Barracks, Portsmouth
1912	RN Barracks, Portsmouth
1913	RN Physical training School
1914	RN Barracks, Devonport
1919	RN Physical Training School
1920	HMS *Queen Elizabeth*
1921	HMS *Barham*
1922	HMS *Queen Elizabeth*
1923	HMS *Barham*
1924	RN Barracks, Portsmouth
1925	RN Barracks, Chatham
1926	RN Barracks, Portsmouth
1927	RN Barracks, Portsmouth
1928	RN Barracks, Portsmouth
1929	No record
1930	RN Barracks, Chatham
1931	HMS *Nelson*
1932	HMS *Nelson*
1933	HMS *Nelson*
1934	HMS *Hood*
1935	RN Physical Training School
1936	HMS *Excellent*
1937	HMS *Excellent*
1938	RN College, Dartmouth
1947	HMS *Nelson*
1948	RN Physical Training School
1949	HMS *Excellent*
1950	HMS *Daedalus*
1951	HMS *Excellent*
1952	HMS *Daedalus*
1953	HMS *Daedalus*
1954	HMS *Excellent*
1955	RN Physical Training School
1956	RN Physical Training School
1957	HMS *Victory*
1958	HMS *St Vincent*
1959	Nautical College, Pangbourne
1960	Nautical College, Pangbourne
1961	RN Barracks, Portsmouth
1962	HMS Ariel
1963	HMS Ariel
1964	BRNC
1965	HMS *Ariel*
1966	RNEC

Year	Location
1967	RNEC
1968	RNEC
1969	RNEC
1970	RNEC
1971	HMS *Daedalus*
1972	HMS *Daedalus*
1973	HMS *Daedalus*
1974	HMS *Daedalus*
1975	HMS *Collingwood*
1976	No record
1977	HMS *Collingwood*
1978	HMS *Nelson*
1979	HMS *Seahawk*
1980	HMS *Seahawk*
1981	HMS *Nelson*
1982	RNEC
1983	No competition
1984	HMS *Seahawk*
1985	HMS *Nelson*
1986	HMS *Drake*
1987	HMS *Drake*
1988	RNEC
1989	RNEC
1990	RNEC
1991	RNEC
1992	CSB Faslane
1993	HMS *Sultan*
1994	HMS *Sultan*
1995	No competition
1996	No competition
1997	No competition
1998	No competition
1999	CTCRM Lympstone
2000	No competition
2001	HMS *Sultan*
2002	HMS *Sultan*
2003	HMS *Ark Royal*
2004	No competition
2005	42 Commando RM
2006	PJHQ
2007	HMS *Sultan*
2008	HMS *Excellent*
2009	HMS *Sultan*
2010	HMS *Sultan*
2011	HMS *Sultan*
2012	MoD London

There are two other splendid bayonet trophies which are now used solely as items of table silver. These are the Royal Tournament Inter Services Bayonet Team Challenge Trophy and the Petley Trophies for the Inter Regimental Bayonet Exercise Competition, Open Army and Royal Marines.

The Silver Jubilee Fencing Cup was presented by Captain Nils Bydstrom MVO Royal Swedish Navy in 1977. Originally awarded to the person deemed to have done the most to further Navy fencing, it is now awarded for a competition between the various Commands with teams of six, two at each of foil, épée and sabre.

The cup for the Champion-at-Arms was originally a Tug-of-War trophy and has been awarded for its new purpose since the start of this competition in 1954.

Until about 1975 winners of an individual weapon competition received a miniature, silver version of the weapon and those placed second and third were given medals. After that date, medals were awarded for all places. Since 1981, trophies designed, manufactured and presented by Lt Cdr David Foster have also been awarded to be held for one year.

The lady Champion-at-Arms is awarded a trophy which was originally the RN and RM Football Association Cup. The winner of the ladies foil competition is presented with the Myers Poniard donated by Lt Cdr M Myers RNR and made from a trophy that she had won as the Combined Service Champion-at-Arms. Similarly the winner of the Ladies sabre is awarded a Quaich which is named in memory of Lieutenant Emma Douglas, a naval fencer, who died in 2004, while serving in HMS *Cornwall*.

The Julian St John trophy was donated in memory of Acting Sub Lieutenant R G I St John who died on 31 May 1937. Originally awarded to the cadet who was the best sabreur, it later became the award for an annual competition between the Royal Naval College, Dartmouth, and the Royal Naval Engineering College, Manadon. Following the closure of the latter establishment it reverted to something closer to its original purpose being awarded to the best novice at the RN Fencing Championships.

The successful competitors in all these and many other competitions have been awarded personal keepsakes of their successes. These have ranged from miniature weapons in silver, through medals in materials from silver gilt to bronze to glassware.

* Those marked with this have been deduced from other information rather than confirmed by documents or actual marked trophies.

Glossary

Back piece. In some swords the pommel is cast in one piece with a strip of metal that runs along the back of the grip up to the guard. This strip is the back piece.

Backsword, 1. Any sword where the back edge is unsharpened except towards the point.

Backsword, 2. An alternative term for singlestick.

Bayonet. In fencing terms this is a mock rifle in which a spring-loaded plunger replaces the real bayonet. It was contested in the Armed Services until the mid-1950s.

Becket. Naval term for a loop of cordage. Used to describe the attachment of a cutlass to the wrist.

Broadsword. A sword with a straight, broad, double-edged blade, often with multiple fullers.

Buckler. A small shield, typically 6–18in (150–450mm) in diameter, used in combat in the medieval and renaissance periods. It is the motion of this swashing against the sword as apprentices strutted around town that led to the term 'swashbuckling'.

Burr. A small pommel found on some patterns of cutlass.

Chape. The metal fitting at the base of the scabbard.

Claymore. The term refers to the Scottish variant of the late medieval two-handed sword. It is characterised as having a cross hilt of forward-sloping quillons with quatrefoil terminations. It was in use in combat from the fifteenth to the seventeenth centuries, but has been used for presentation weapons since then.

Cross guard. A hand guard or part of a hand guard that crosses the blade of a sword at a right angle.

Cudgel. An alternative term for singlestick.

Cut. A movement delivered with the edge or back edge of the sword.

Cutlass. A short sword with a wide, single-edged blade that may be either straight or curved, flat or grooved; now especially the sword with which sailors are armed.

Dirk, naval. A single or double-edged knife with either a straight or a curved blade which had multiple uses. In 1856 a straight bladed dirk was to become the uniform weapon of the midshipman.

Dirk, Scottish. A dagger used in combination with a targe by Highlanders.

Ecusson. The diamond-shaped central portion of the cross guard of a Mameluke-hilted sword.

Epée. A fencing weapon based on the nineteenth century duelling sword. Only thrusts with the point score and the whole body is the target.

Escutcheon of pretence. In English heraldry the husband of a heraldic heiress – a lady without any brothers – may place her father's arms in an *escutcheon of pretence* in the centre of his own shield as a *claim* ('pretence') to be the head of his wife's family. In the next generation the arms would then be quartered.

Foil, 1. The general term for a foiled or blunted practice weapon.

Foil, 2. Nowadays this term is restricted to the lightweight fencing weapon with a blade of rectangular cross-section which was originally the practice weapon for the small-sword. Only thrusts with the point score and the target is restricted to the upper part of the body excluding the head and arms.

Frog. A tube of material on a sword belt into which the sword is slipped.

Frog hook (stud). A fitting on the locket of a scabbard which retained the sword in the frog.

Fuller. A groove running longitudinally along a sword blade. Its function is to simultaneously lighten and stiffen the blade.

Guard, 1. The portion of the hilt designed to protect the hand of the swordsman.

Guard, 2. One of the positions adopted by a swordsman from which movements of attack or defence could be executed. Also one of the positions for parrying a cut or thrust.

Half-basket hilt. A style of hilt formed of interlocking bars designed to offer greater protection to the outer side of the sword hand than to the inner side. The small inner part of such a hilt generally folds down to allow the sword to sit closer to the wearer's body and to reduce chafing on his clothing. In a solid half-basket hilt, the space between the bars is filled.

Hanger. A short, curved cut-and-thrust sword; blade length typically 25–28in (635–711mm).

Hunting sword. Similar to a hanger but usually with a straight blade.

Knuckle bow. A simple guard for the knuckle consisting of a single bar in the plane of the blade.

Langet. A small, shield-shaped tongue projecting from the cross guard of a sword over the blade and the mouth of the scabbard.

Locket. A scabbard mount other than the chape. On a scabbard with only two fittings, the mount at the mouth is referred to as the locket. When a scabbard has three mounts, the one at the mouth is termed the top locket and the other the mid locket. The locket(s) carry the means for attaching the sword to the belt.

Loose play. Practicing swordsmanship using singlesticks or other training weapons.

Mameluke-hilted. A style of hilt modelled on the Indo-Persian sword hilt that became popular after the Egyptian campaigns at the beginning of the nineteenth century and among army officers, such as Wellington, who had served in India.

Marlinspike. This is a tool used for working ropes and would have been a common tool on board a sailing ship. It still often features in a seaman's toolkit. Since it is a polished metal cone tapered to a rounded or flattened point, usually 6–12in (152–304mm) long, it can make a convenient weapon.

Parry. The act of blocking or deflecting a blow from an opponent's sword.

Pas d'âne **rings.** Two loops between the shell guard and the cross guard of a small-sword. Originally they were used to increase the security of a swordsman's grip on his weapon and were of a suitably large size. As the eighteenth century progressed, they became progressively smaller until, by the end of the small-sword period, they had become degenerate, decorative features.

Pipe-backed blade. A design of blade popular from about 1820 to 1850 which was supposed to make the blade suitable for both cutting and thrusting. These slightly curved blades have a moulding in the form of a rod running the whole length of the blade to its point along the back edge. A few inches from the point, a back edge is forged above this rod giving the blade its characteristic eel like appearance. Although an efficient thrusting weapon, the pipe-back impeded the penetration of a cut through clothing and flesh. This style of blade was superseded from about 1840 by a blade with a wedge-shaped cross-section.

Point, 1. The sharp end of a sword.

Point, 2. A movement delivered with the point of a sword, also known as a thrust.

Pommel. The piece of metal in which the grip terminates. In earlier times this component was also referred to as the pummel and this reflects its possible aggressive use. Its weight also provides balance for the weight of the weapon.

Pommel cap. A form of pommel found on hangers, hunting swords and some early cutlasses in which the pommel is in the form of a socket which encloses the end of the grip.

Quill-backed blade Another name for pipe-backed blade (see above).

Quillon. A knob on the cross guard or basket guard of a sword.

Ramrod-backed blade. Another name for pipe-backed blade (see above).

Ricasso. The blunted or covered portion of the blade between the inside of the guard and the quillons of a rapier or small-sword. Although it is outside the guard, some authors also refer to the squared section of the blade at the shoulder by this name.

Riposte. The offensive action immediately following on from a successful parry.

Sabre. In fencing terms this is a lightweight sword with which both cuts and thrusts can be delivered. The target is restricted to the upper part of the body including the head and arms.

Sabre, presentation. This is curved weapon shaped as if for cutting where the large flat surface is often made use of to mark a suitable inscription.

Sabreur. A sabre fencer.

Scabbard. The protective covering for a sword. It also carries the fittings to attach the sword to the wearer's sword belt.

Schläger. A straight, double-edged sword with a massive basket guard used by German university students in their peculiar form of duel, the mensur.

Service Sword. This refers to a sword that is of the current pattern used by the military service to which the officer belongs.

Shell. A term used for the guard of a sword when it resembles a sea shell or similar.

Singlestick. A stout stick of ash or hazel provided with a wickerwork or leather basket guard and used as a practice sword.

Small-sword. A lightweight derivative of the rapier, considered an essential item of dress for a gentleman in the eighteenth century. It typically has a blade of hollow-ground, triangular cross-section with a needle-sharp point. During the earlier part of the century the guard consisted of two unequally sized shells, evolving towards the end of the century into a single oval shell. These swords were designed as thrusting weapons.

Spadroon. A sword with a straight, backsword blade and a simple guard. This term is popularly used by collectors to describe such naval and military swords from the latter half of the eighteenth into the middle of the nineteenth century.

Spring-loaded fencing musket. The weapon used for bayonet fencing.

Sword knot. A loop of cord or ribbon often terminating in a decorative tassel or moulding attached to the guard. Its original purpose was to secure the sword to the user's wrist.

Tang. That portion of a sword blade passing through the grip.

Tang button. In some instances the tang, after having passed through the pommel, is secured over a small button of spheroidal form.

Targe. A circular shield of about 18in (457mm) diameter used by Scottish Highlanders.

Thrust. A movement delivered with the point of a sword, also known as a point.

Bibliography

Naval and General History

A complete list of the Royal Navy: corrected etc. (London: printed for D Steel, 1780–1).
Adkins, Roy and Lesley, *Jack Tar* (London: Little, Brown Book Group, 2008).
A Manual of Gunnery for Her Majesty's Fleet (London; printed for HMSO by Harrison and Sons, St. Martin's Lane, 1873).
Binns, Lieut-Colonel P L, *The Story of the Royal Tournament* (Aldershot: Gale & Polden, Limited, 1952).
Blake, Admiral Robert, *The Letters of Robert Blake – Letter 314 Instructions for the Better Ordering of the Fleet in Fighting* (Naval Records Society, Volume LXXVI, 1937).
Caesar, Julius, *Commentaries on the Gallic and Civil Wars* (London: George Bell and Sons, 1885).
Clowes, W L, *The Royal Navy A History from Earliest Times to 1900*, Vol I to VII (First published in 1903; reprinted London: Chatham Publishing, 2007).
Fairbairn, James, *Crests of the Families of Great Britain and Ireland* (Rutland, Vermont: Charles E Tuttle, 1968).
Fraser, Edward, *The Sailors Whom Nelson Led: their doings described by themselves* (London: Methuen & Co Ltd, 1913).
Fraser, Edward, *The Enemy at Trafalgar* (London: Hodder and Stoughton, 1906; reprinted London: Chatham Publishing, 2004).
Frischauer, Willi and Jackson, Robert, *'The Navy's Here!' The Altmark Affair* (London: Victor Gollancz Ltd, 1970).
Gardiner, Robert, *Warships of the Napoleonic Era* (Barnsley: Seaforth Publishing, 2011).
Gawler, Jim, *Britons Strike Home: a history of Lloyd's Patriotic Fund 1803–1988* (Sanderstead: Pittot, ca 1988).
Graves, Donald E, *Lords of the Lake. The Naval War on Lake Ontario 1812-1814* (Toronto: Robin Brass Studio, 1998).
Hore, Peter (ed), *Seapower Ashore: 200 Years of Royal Navy Operations on Land* (London: Chatham Publishing, 2001).
Instruction for the Exercise of Small Arms and Field Pieces, etc, for the use of Her Majesty's Ships (London: Harrison and Sons, 1859). A modern facsimile version is available (Uckfield: The Naval & Military Press Ltd, n. d.).
James, William, *Naval History of Great Britain*, Volumes I–V (London: Richard Bentley, 1837).
Jarrett, Dudley, *British Naval Dress* (London: J M Dent & Sons, 1960).
Jeans, Surgeon T T, RN (ed), *Naval Brigades in the South African War 1899–1900* (London: Sampson, Low, Marston & Company Limited, 2nd edition, 1902).
Knight, Roger, *The Pursuit of Victory: The Life and Achievement of Horatio Nelson* (London: Allen Lane, 2005).
Lavery, Brian, *Empire of the Seas* (London: Conway Maritime Press, 2009).
Lavery, Brian, *Nelson's Navy* (London: Conway Maritime Press, 1989).
Lewis, Michael, *A Social History of the Navy 1793–1815* (London: George Allen & Unwin Ltd, 1960).
Long, W H, *Medals of the British Navy and how they were won* (London: Norrie & Wilson, 1895).
Malcomson, Robert, *Lords of the Lake, the Naval War on Lake Ontario 1812-1814* (London: Chatham Publishing, 1999).
Marsden, Peter, *Sealed by Time – The loss and recovery of the Mary Rose* (Portsmouth: The Mary Rose Trust, 2003).
McArthur, John and Clarke, James Stanier, *The Naval Chronicle* (London: 1797 to 1818).
Messenger, Charles, *Unbroken Service* (London: Lloyd's Patriotic Fund, 2003).
Miller, Amy, *Dressed to Kill, British Naval Uniform: Masculinity and Contemporary Fashion, 1748–1857* (London: National Maritime Museum, 2007).
Nicolas, Sir Nicholas Harris, *The Dispatches and Letters of Vice Admiral Lord Viscount Nelson* (London: Henry Colburn, 1845).
O'Byrne, William R, *A Naval Biographical Dictionary* (1st ed 1849; reprinted Hayward, 1986).
Perrett, Brian, *Gunboat! Small Ships at War* (London: Cassell & Co, 2000).
Pope, Dudley, *The Black Ship* (London: Maritime History Books, 2009).
Ritchie, Carson, *Q-ships* (Lavenham: Terence Dalton, 1985).
Roger, N A M, *The Wooden World* (Glasgow: Collins, 1990).
Russell, W H, *The British Expedition to the Crimea* (London: G Routledge and Co, 1858).
Sainsbury, Captain A B, VRD, MA, RNR and Phillips, Lieutenant Commander, TD, RD, RNR, *The Royal Navy Day by Day* (Stroud: Sutton Publishing Ltd, 2005).
Syrett, David, and DiNardo, R L (eds), *The Commissioned Sea Officers of the Royal Navy, 1660–1815* (Aldershot: Scolar Press for the Navy Records Society, 1994).
The Navy and Army Illustrated.
Thomas, J E, *Britain's Last Invasion: Fishguard 1797* (Stroud: Tempus Books, 2007).
Tute, Warren, *The True Glory* (London: Centurion Press, 1984).
Walker, Richard, *The Nelson Portraits* (Portsmouth: The Royal Naval Museum, 1998).
Wareham, Tom, *Frigate Commander* (Barnsley: Seaforth Publishing, 2012).
White, Colin, *The End of the Sailing Navy* (London: Mason, ca 1981).
Winton, John, *The Naval Heritage of Portsmouth* (Southampton: Ensign Publications, 1994).

Sword and Fencing History

Annis, P G W, *Naval Swords, British and American 1660 – 1815* (London: Arms and Armour Press, 1970).
Aylward, J D, *The Small-sword in England* (London: Hutchinson, 1960).
Baldick, R, *The Duel* (London: Chapman and Hall Ltd, 1965).
Beaumont, C-L de, *Modern British Fencing* (London: Hutchinson, 1949).
Beaumont, C-L de, *Modern British Fencing 1948–1956* (London: Edward Hulton, 1958).
Beaumont, C-L de, *Modern British Fencing 1957–1964* (London: Edward Hulton, 1966).
Bezdek, Richard H, *Swords and Sword Makers of England and Scotland* (Boulder, Colorado: Paladin Press, 2003).

Blair, Claude, *Three Presentation Swords* (London: Victoria and Albert Museum, 1972).
Bosanquet, Captain Henry T A, CVO, RN, FSA, *The Naval Officer's Sword* (London: Her Majesty's Stationery Office, 1955).
Cohen, Richard, *By The Sword* (London: Macmillan, 2002).
Comfort, Sim, *Naval Swords and Dirks* (London: Sim Comfort Associates, 2008).
Diderot et d'Alembert, *Encyclopédie*, vol 4, 1765, article entitled *Fourbisser*. Also see Internet Sources.
Dufty, Arthur Richard, *European Swords and Daggers in the Tower of London* (London: Her Majesty's Stationery Office, 1974).
Fare, Malcolm, *A Century of Fencing in Britain* (London: British Fencing Association, 2002).
Ffoulkes, Charles, CB, OBE, and Hopkinson, Captain E C, MC, *Sword, Lance & Bayonet* (Cambridge: Cambridge University Press, 1938).
Gardner, Col. Robert, *Small Arms Makers* (New York: Bonanza Books, 1963).
Gilkerson, William, *Boarders Away with Steel, Edged Weapons & Polearms* (Lincoln, Rhode Island: Andrew Mowbray Publishers, 1991).
Girard, Pierre Jacques François, *Nouveau Traité de la Perfection sur la Fait des Armes*, etc (Paris: Chez Moétte, 1736).
Holland, Barbara, *Gentlemen's Blood* (New York: Bloomsbury, 2003).
Holland, Sarah, Grant, Iain, Satchell, Julie, Stone, Gavin and Momber, Garry, *Warship Hazardous: Investigating a Protected Wreck* (Southampton: Hampshire & Wight Trust for Maritime Archaeology, n.d.).
Infantry Sword Exercise (London: printed for HMSO by Harrison and Sons, St Martin's Lane, 1895).
Loades, M, *Swords and Swordsmen* (Barnsley: Pen & Sword Books, 2010).
McArthur, J, *Theory and Practice of Fencing* (Uckfield: The Naval & Military Press Ltd, n.d.).
May, Commander W E, RN, *The Dress of Naval Officers* (London: HMSO, 1966).
May, Commander W E, RN, and Annis, P G W, *Swords for Sea Service* (2 Volumes) (London: HMSO, 1970).
May, W E, and Kennard, A N, *Naval Swords and Firearms* (London: HMSO, 1962).
McAleer, Kevin, *Dueling: The Cult of Honor in Fin-de-Siècle Germany* (Princeton: Princeton University Press, 1997).
Norman, A V B, *The Rapier and Small-Sword, 1460 – 1820* (London: Arms and Armour Press, 1980).
Robson, Brian, *Swords of the British Army, The regulation Patterns 1788–1914, The Revised Edition* (Uckfield: The Naval & Military Press, and London: The National Army Museum, 2011).
Silver, George, *Paradoxes of Defence* (London: Printed for Edward Blount, 1599), facsimile by The Shakespeare Association (H Milford, Oxford University Press, 1933).
Tylecote, R F, *A History of Metallurgy* (London: The Metals Society, 1976).
Verity, Liza, *Naval Weapons* (London: The National Maritime Museum, 1992).
Waite, J M, *Lessons in Sabre, Singlestick, etc* (London: Weldon & Co, 1880).
Weland, Gerald, *A Collector's Guide to Swords, Daggers & Cutlasses* (London: Grange Books, 1995).
Wilkinson, Henry, *Observations on Swords*, 18th edition (London: 27 Pall Mall, n.d.).

Wilkinson-Latham, John, *British Military Swords* (London: Hutchinson & Co, 1963).
Wilkinson-Latham, John, *British Cut and Thrust Weapons* (Newton Abbot: David & Charles, 1971).
Wilkinson-Latham, Robert, *Mr Wilkinson of Pall Mall* 2 vols (Shoreham-by-Sea: Pooley Sword Ltd, 2000).
Wilkinson-Latham, Robert, *The Swords & Records of Robert Mole & Sons 1835–1920* (Shoreham-by-Sea: Pooley Sword Ltd, 2008).
Wilkinson-Latham, Robert, *Wilkinson Sword Patterns & Blade Rubs* (Shoreham-by-Sea: Pooley Sword Ltd, 2008).
Wolfe, Sarah C, *Naval Edged Weapons* (Barnsley: Chatham Publishing, 2005).

Biographies

Allen, Joseph (under the direction of Lady Hargood), *Memoir of Admiral Sir William Hargood* (Greenwich: Henry S Richardson, 1841), Appendix E Notes of Lieutenant Nicolas RM.
Anonymous, *Tales of the Coastguard* (London: W R Chambers, 1889).
Burne, Lieutenant C R N, *With the Naval Brigade in Natal 1899–1900* (London: Edward Arnold, 1902).
Chamier, Frederick, *The Life of a Sailor* (Barnsley: Seaforth Publishing, 2011).
Charnock, John, *Biographical Memoires of Viscount Lord Nelson* (London: H D Symonds, 1806).
Chalmers, Rear Admiral W S, *The Life and Letters of David, Earl Beatty* (London: Hodder and Stoughton, 1951).
Clarke, James Stainier and McArthur, John, *The Life and Services of Horatio Viscount Nelson* (London: Fisher, Son & Co, 1840).
Cordingly, David, *Cochrane The Dauntless: The Life and Adventures of Thomas Cochrane* (London: Bloomsbury Publishing, 2007).
Crawford, Captain Abraham, *Reminiscences of a Naval Officer* (London: Chatham Publishing, 1999).
Davison, James D G, *Admiral Lord St Vincent: Saint or Tyrant - the Life of Sir John Jervis, Nelson's Patron* (Barnsley: Pen & Sword Maritime, 2006).
Fairbairn, Lt Cdr D, *The Narrative of a Naval Nobody 1907–1924* (London: John Murray, 1929).
Hoffman, Frederick, *A Sailor of King George. The Journals of Captain Frederick Hoffman 1793–1814* (edited by A Beckford Bevan and H B Wolryche-Whitmore, originally published in 1901, reprinted by Dodo Press on order).
Keyes, Admiral of the Fleet Sir Roger, *Adventures Ashore and Afloat* (London: George G Harrap and Co Ltd, 1939).
Nicol, John, *The Life and Adventures of John Nicol, Mariner* (Originally published in 1822, republished Edinburgh: Canongate Books, 2000).
Norbury, Fleet-Surgeon H F, *The Naval Brigade in South Africa* (London: Sampson, Low, Marston, Searle and Rivington, 1880).
Parsons, Lieutenant G S, RN, *Nelsonian Reminiscences* (London: Chatham Publishing, 1998), originally published 1843.
Somerville, Admiral Boyle Townsend, *Will Mariner* (London: Faber and Faber Ltd, 1936).
Southey, Robert, *The Life of Nelson* (London: John Murray, 1814).
Vesey-Hamilton, Admiral Sir Richard (ed), *Letters and Papers of Admiral Sir Byam Martin*, Vol 1 (Navy Records Society, Vol 24, 1902).

Watson, G, *A Narrative of the Adventures of a Greenwich Pensioner written by himself* (Newcastle: 1827).
Wilson, H W, *With the Flag to Pretoria* (London: Harmsworth Brothers Limited, 1900) Vol 1.

Fiction
Forester, C S, *Mr Midshipman Hornblower* (London: Penguin Books, 1968).
Lambdin, Dewey, *Havoc's Sword* (New York: Thomas Dunne Books, 2003).
O'Brian, P, *The Final Unfinished Voyage of Jack Aubrey* (London: Harper Collins, 2004)
'Taffrail', *The Watch Below* (London: C Arthur Pearson Limited, 1918).

Papers and Articles by Other Authors
Disbrey, Stuart, 'Tudor Sword salvaged from the Mary Rose', *The Sword* (January 2010), p 21.
Hutton, Captain A, 'Our Swordsmanship', *RUSI Journal*, Vol XXXVI (1893), pp 513–531
McAleer, John, '"Eminent Service": War, Slavery and the politics of public recognition in the British Caribbean and the Cape of Good Hope c 1782-1807', *The Mariner's Mirror*, Vol 95 No 1 (February 2009), pp 33–51.
Murrison, Mark, Commander, RD, MNI, RNR, 'Royal Naval Reserve 150 years young', *Marine Engineering Review* (March 2009), pp 28–9.
Southwick, Leslie, 'The Recipients, Goldsmiths and Costs of Swords presented by the Corporation of the City of London', *Journal of the Arms and Armour Society*, Vol XIII (1989–91), pp 173 et seq.
Southwick, Leslie, 'Patriotic Fund Swords (Part I and Part 2)', *Journal of the Arms and Armour Society*, Vol XII (1986–8), pp 223 et seq.
Wood, Stephen, 'In Defence of the Commerce of Great Britain . . . A group of swords presented to officers of the British Royal Navy in the 1790s', *ICOMAM 50* (2007), pp 171–205.

Internet Sources
British Library, www.bl.uk.
Collins, Alfred, *Coastguard Records*, at www.mariners-1.co.uk/UKCoastguards.
Database of Lloyds Swords, at www.Lloydsswords.com.
Diderot et d'Alembert, Fourbisser, at http://quod.lib.umich.edu/cgi/t/text/text-idx?c=did;cc=did;rgn=main;view=text;idno=did2222.0001.459.
National Maritime Museum, www.rmg.co.uk.
Oxford English Dictionary, www.oed.com.
Tuite, Peter, *British Naval Edged Weapons - an Overview*, at asoac.org/bulletins/86_tuite_naval.pdf.
Bonham Auction House, at www.bonhams.com
Thomas Del Mar Auction House, at www.thomasdelmar.com

Fencing Books Written by Serving or Former Members of the RN and RM
Anderson, Bob, *All about Fencing* (London: Stanley Paul, 1970).
Anderson, Bob, *Better Fencing – Foil* (London: Kaye and Ward, 1973).
Anderson, Bob, *Tackle Fencing* (London: Stanley Paul & Co Ltd, 1978).
De Silva, Henry, *Fencing: the Skills of the Game* (Swindon: The Crowood Press Ltd, 1991) also in paperback, 1997.
Lidstone, R A, *The Art of Fencing, a Practical Manual for Foil, Epée and Sabre* (London: H F & G Witherby, 1930).
Lidstone, R A, *Bloody Bayonets: a Complete Guide to Bayonet Fighting* (Aldershot: Gale & Polden Ltd, 1942).
Lidstone, R A, *Fencing* (London: H F & G Witherby, 1952).
McArthur, John, *The Army and Navy Gentleman's Companion* (London: Printed for James Lavers, 1780); also 2nd edition (London: J Murray, 1784) and 3rd edition (London: Marcady, 1810). This is also available as a modern facsimile edition: McArthur, John, *Theory and Practice of Fencing* (Uckfield: The Naval & Military Press Ltd).

Other Relevant Works by the Authors

John McGrath and Mark Barton (RNAFA Booklets)
Naval Cutlass Exercise.
Fencing in the Royal Navy and Royal Marines 1733?1948.
Bayonet Exercise and Bayonet Fencing.
Naval Swords.

John McGrath (RNAFA Booklet)
Swords for Officers of the Royal Navy.

John McGrath articles in *The Armourer*
'Jutland remembered' (January/February 2006), p 78.
'The abolition of swords at naval courts martial – the end of another tradition' (November/December 2006), p 90.
'Dress Swords in the Royal Navy' (May/June 2007), pp 40–2.
'Cutlass: a question of definition' (September/October 2007), pp 39–40.
'The Angelo cutlass drill in context' (March/April 2008), pp 60–3.
'Naval swords with stirrup hilts and pipe-backed blades' (May/June 2009), pp 14–15.
'One blade, two hilts and three scabbards' (January/February 2011), pp 80–1.
'Swords of the Customs and Coastguard Services' (July/August 2011) pp 49–52.
'One blade, two hilts and three scabbards, additional information' (November/December 2011), pp 65–6.
'The story of a broken sword' (July/August 2012) pp 51–5.

John McGrath articles in *Classic Arms & Militaria*
'A Pirate's Sword' (Vol XIX, Issue 2, April/May 2012), pp 26–9.
'Swords of Trinity House' (Vol XIX, Issue 6, December 2012/January 2013), pp 12–17.

Mark Barton articles
'Naval Swords', *The Review* (Spring 2005, Vol 17.4), pp 45–50.
Managing the Royal Navy during Peace and Recession – The Victorian Experience (Defence Research Paper, ACSC 13, July 2010)'
Various articles for *The Naval Review*

Mark Barton and David Hall
'Fascism and Fencing', *The Sword* (October 2011), pp 32–4.

Notes

Notes to Chapter 1

[1] Thickness of wood at waterline on HMS *Victory*.
[2] Admiral Robert Blake, *The Letters of Robert Blake* – Letter 314 Instructions for the Better Ordering of the Fleet in Fighting (Naval Records Society, Volume LXXVI, 1937), p 467.
[3] Brian Lavery, *Empire of the Seas* (London: Conway Maritime Press, 2009), p 47.
[4] Robert Gardiner, *Warships of the Napoleonic Era* (Barnsley: Seaforth Publishing, 2011), p 13 gives a total armament of 2200lbs.
[5] Napoleonic Artillery - http://napoleon-istyka.atspace.com/British_artillery.htm accessed on 15 January 2012.
[6] M Loades, *Swords and Swordsmen* (Barnsley: Pen & Sword, 2010), p 56.
[7] W H Long, *Medals of the British Navy and how they were won* (London: Norrie and Wilson, 1895), p 228.
[8] Caesar's *Commentaries on the Gallic and Civil Wars* (London: George Bell and Sons, 1885), Book IV, Chapter 33, p 101.
[9] William Gilkerson, *Boarders Away with Steel, Edged Weapons & Polearms* (Lincoln, Rhode Island: Andrew Mowbray Publishers, 1991), p 5.
[10] Edward Fraser, *The Sailors Whom Nelson Led: their doings described by themselves* (London: Methuen & Co Ltd, 1913), p 9.
[11] Admiral Boyle Townsend Somerville. *Will Mariner* (London: Faber and Faber Ltd, 1936), p 24.
[12] *Instructions for training a ships crew in the use of arms in attack and defence*, by Lieutenant William Pringle Green, Royal Navy Commander of His Majesty's Brig *Resolute, 1812*. NMM Manuscript JOD/45.
[13] David Cordingly, *Cochrane The Dauntless: The Life and Adventures of Thomas Cochrane* (London: Bloomsbury Publishing, 2007), p 58.
[14] From the French Newspaper *Le Moniteur*, published 25 October 1805.
[15] Records of the Evening Meeting of Royal United Services Institute Monday 5 May 1862. *RUSI Journal* VI p 422.
[16] Frederick Chamier, *The Life of a Sailor* (Barnsley: Seaforth Publishing, 2011), p 109.
[17] DNB online quoting *Letters and Papers of Henry VIII*, i. No. 4005
[18] DNB online quoting Ellis, *Orig. Letters*, 1st ser. i. 77
[19] This view is reinforced by the letter of Admiral Moore, quoted in Tom Wareham, *Frigate Commander* (Barnsley: Seaforth Publishing, 2012), p 70.
[20] William James, *Naval History of Great Britain* (London: Richard Bentley, 1837), Vol III, p 190.
[21] Edward Fraser, *The Enemy at Trafalgar* (London: Chatham Publishing, 2004), p 9.
[22] Fraser, *The Sailors Whom Nelson Led*, p 216.
[23] NMM manuscript MSS/77/163.
[24] Promoted 24 Dec 1805 according to *Commissioned sea officers of the RN 1660–1815*.
[25] Lieutenant James Spratt received an additional £30 from the Patriotic Fund as his wounds got worse in 1806 he had received £50 initially as recorded in the Patriotic Fund Minute Books for 1806. Spratt was also brought to the Fund's attention in June 1805 for a previous action off Gibraltar.
[26] Retired 17 July 1838 Entry for James Spratt in O'Byrne's *Dictionary of Naval Biography*, in which entries were normally provided by the individual.
[27] Joseph Allen (under the direction of Lady Hargood), *Memoir of Admiral Sir William Hargood* (Greenwich: Henry S Richardson, 1841), Appendix E p 287 Notes of Lieutenant Nicolas RM.
[28] Lieutenant G S Parsons RN, *Nelsonian Reminiscences* (London: Chatham Publishing, 1998), p 99.
[29] Ibid, p 100.
[30] Ibid, p 20.
[31] Ibid, p 85.
[32] Ibid, p 75.
[33] Chamier, *The Life of a Sailor*, p 134.
[34] British casualty figures during this period were usually given only for those killed during the battle and slight wounds were discounted as senior officers were often keen to reduce the apparent butcher's bill.
[35] *Naval Chronicle* Vol VI (1803), p 74.
[36] G Silver, *Paradoxes of Defence* (London: Printed for Edward Blount, 1599, facsimile by The Shakespeare Association, Oxford University Press, 1933), p 7.
[37] *The Newgate Calendar*, p 232 (accessed at http://www.exclassics.com/newgate/ng232.htm on 4 Feb 2012).
[38] R Baldick, *The Duel* (London: Chapman and Hall Ltd, 1965), p 74.
[39] K McAleer, *Dueling The Cult of Honor in Fin-de-Siècle Germany* (Princeton: Princeton University Press, 1997), p 64.
[40] J McArthur, *Theory and Practice of Fencing* (Uckfield: The Naval & Military Press Ltd, n.d.), p xii.
[41] From C S Forrester's *Mr Midshipman Hornblower* (London: Penguin Books, 1968) – the duel is planned to involve two pistols one loaded and one not but the Captain orders both to be unloaded. These are kept as pistols in the film "Even Chance" but a second duel is included.
[42] Dewey Lambdin's book *Havoc's Sword* (New York: Thomas Dunne Books, 2003) has a pistol duel between Beauman and Cashman.
[43] Patrick O'Brian, *The Final Unfinished Voyage of Jack Aubrey* (London: Harper Collins, 2004), 3:23a-24.
[44] Baldick, *The Duel*, pp 73–4.
[45] *The Times*, 22 May 1845.
[46] Donald E Graves. *Lords of the Lake. The Naval War on Lake Ontario 1812-1814* (Toronto: Robin Brass Studio, 1998) p 236.
[47] Chamier, *Life of a Sailor*, p 124.
[48] Anonymous, *Tales of the Coastguard*, p 76.
[49] *Instructions for training a ships crew in the use of arms in attack and defence*, by Lieutenant William Pringle Green, Royal Navy Commander of His Majesty's Brig *Resolute, 1812*. NMM Manuscript JOD/45.
[50] Frederick Hoffman, *A Sailor of King George. The Journals of Captain Frederick Hoffman 1793-1814* (Dodo Press reprint of 1901 edition), p 16.
[51] From National Archives ADM 101/120/3 pp 14–15.
[52] John Nicol, *The Life and Adventures of John Nicol, Mariner* (Originally published in 1822, republished Edinburgh: Canongate Books, 2000), p 37.
[53] *Instructions for the Exercise of Small Arms and Field Pieces for the use of Her Majesty's Ships* (London: Harrison and Sons, 1859) pp 145–7.
[54] Brian Perrett, *Gunboat! Small Ships at War* (London: Cassell & CO, 2000), p. 89.
[55] All described in detail in Peter Hore (ed), *Seapower Ashore: 200 Years of Royal Navy Operations on Land* (London: Chatham Publishing, 2001).
[56] *Navy and Army Illustrated*, Vol IV (25 June 1897), pp 68–70.
[57] Lt C R N Burne, *With the Naval Brigade in Natal 1899-1900* (London: Edward Arnold, 1902), p 9 and Fleet-Surgeon H F Norbury, *The Naval Brigade*

in South Africa (London: Sampson, Lowe, Marston, Searle and Rivington, 1880), p 190.
[58] W H Russell, *The British Expedition to the Crimea* (London: G Routledge and Co, 1858), p 191.
[59] According to *Army Staff Handbook* (2009), p 174.
[60] As confirmed by W H Russell in *The Times* Issue 14 Nov 1854 (No 21898): pp 7–8. *The Cavalry Action at Balaclava 25 October*. Discussion on issues regarding exact figures is at http://www.lawrence-crider.com/How%20Many%20Charged.html.
[61] Obituary – *Proceedings of the Royal Geographical Society and the Monthly Record of Geography*, No XL, (Nov 1882), p 697, along with the 2 memorials one erected at Fort Brockhurst, Gosport and the other at St. Marys Church, Sheet, Hampshire, along with Lieutenant General Wolseley's despatch on the battle held in the National Archives (WO 33/40 no.209 (10 Sept 1882)).
[62] Dispatch from Commodore Hewett to the Secretary of the Admiralty from HMS *Active* at Cape Coast, 3 March 1874.
[63] Perkins, R, 'Medals to the Navy', *The Review* Volume 24.2 (Naval Historical Collectors and Research Association, 2012), p 56.
[64] Letter from Captain A K Wilson, HMS *Hecla* off Trinkitat, to Captain Markham of HMS *Vernon*, dated 21 March 1884.
[65] Accession number 1979.311.
[66] W L Clowes, *The Royal Navy: A History from Earliest Times to 1900*, Volume VII (First published in 1903. Reprint London: Chatham Publishing, 2007), p 353 and *London Gazette*, 21 May 1884.
[67] *Lloyd's Weekly* dated 11 Apr 1885.
[68] *Lloyds Weekly* dated 11 Apr 1885.
[69] Cable from *Daily Mail* Omdurman Correspondent September 1898.
[70] *Te Aroha News*, dated 18 Jul 1885.
[71] Commander W E May RN and P G W Annis, *Swords for Sea Service* 2 vols (London: HMSO, 1970), Vol 1, p 88.
[72] *Lloyd's Weekly* dated 11 Apr 1885.
[73] Letter from Captain A K Wilson, HMS *Hecla* off Trinkitat, to Captain Markham of HMS *Vernon*, dated 21 March 1884.
[74] The *Vernon* sword is held by the Museum of the Royal Navy, Portsmouth, Accession No 1986/318/1. The mounts on the scabbard of the sword presented by the Ladies of Malta were updated to include the oak leaves and acorns of a Flag Officer, suggesting that this was the sword he chose to wear.
[75] *The Navy and Army Illustrated* (21 Jan 1898), p 216.
[76] *Naval Chronicle* (1799, p 444.
[77] Chamier, *The Life of a Sailor*, p 197.
[78] Parsons, *Nelsonian Reminiscences*, p 13.
[79] Ibid, p 105.
[80] *Naval Chronicle* (1799, p 81.
[81] According to James, *Naval History of Great Britain*, Vol II, p 357, the *Thetis* had on board: 333 boxes containing each 3000 dollars, four boxes containing each 2385 dollars, ninety-three boxes containing each 4000 dollars, one box containing, besides 4000 dollars, two doubloons and ninety half-doubloons, of gold ; making, altogether, 1,385,292 dollars, equal, at 4s. 6d. the dollar, to £311,690 sterling.
[82] *Naval Chronicle* (1799), p 543.
[83] Admiralty Fleet Order Number 4572 of 22 October 1936.
[84] Clowes, *The Royal Navy*, Volume VII, p 387.
[85] H W Wilson, *With the Flag to Pretoria* (London: Harmsworth Brothers, 1900), Vol 1, p 150.
[86] Clowes, *The Royal Navy*, Vol VII, pp 522–3.
[87] Beatty's diary for Friday 15 June 1900 records that the Boxers were armed with 'swords, spears and torches' but he was using gunfire but that they advanced with 'fixed bayonets'. Rear Admiral W S Chalmers *The Life and Letters of David, Earl Beatty* (London: Hodder and Stoughton, 1951), pp 54–9.
[88] Admiral of the Fleet Sir Roger Keyes, *Adventures Ashore and Afloat* (London: George G Harrap and Co Ltd, 1939), p 218. He also comments that the article on the capture of these vessels that appeared in the *Times* on 17 August 1900, has 'many absurd inaccuracies'.
[89] 'Taffrail', *The Watch Below* (London: C Arthur Pearson Ltd, 1918), p 88.
[90] The Navy Lists show that by March 1900 to July 1902, he was serving as a Midshipman with seniority 15 May 1899 in HMS *Terrible*. By November 1902 he had returned to the sail training ship HMS *Dolphin*, having been promoted Sub-Lieutenant with seniority 15 June 1902.
[91] Lt Cdr D Fairbairn, *The Narrative of a Naval Nobody 1907-1924* (London: John Murray, 1929), p 100.
[92] Ibid, p 185.
[93] Wat Tyler (6 November 2003), 'The Last Boarding Action of the Royal Navy', *WW@ People's War: An archive of World War Two memories- written by the public, gathered by the BBC*. BBC http://www.bbc.co.uk/ww2peopleswar/stories/53/a1979553.shtml accessed 7 August 2011.
[94] This double-sided sign has one side now in the Airborne Forces Museum at Aldershot, Hampshire and the other in the Royal Naval Museum at Portsmouth.
[95] Letter by Peter Harrison, Secretary of the *Cossack* Association to the *Daily Mail* 20 June 2003, also displayed on the *Cossack* Association Website.
[96] Willi Frischauer and Robert Jackson, *"The Navy's Here!" The Altmark Affair* (London: Victor Gollancz Ltd, 1970), pp 223–43.
[97] David Grant DSM (a retired CPO who was on board *Cossack* at the time) on website http://www.ankenes.no/heroes-by-chance.
[98] *Daily Telegraph* 14 November 2008, p 37
[99] *The Naval Review* (May 2009).
[100] Private Correspondence with the Naval Historical Branch.
[101] This section draws heavily on various works by J J Colledge, Captain Sainsbury, Captain Manning and David Thomas that are listed in the bibliography.
[102] Private correspondence with Robert B.D.M. Hughes-Mullock FRAS, relative of Captain Mulock.
[103] Imperial War Museum Oral History recording Frank Brewer, 1980 (IWM Ref: 4664).
[104] The sword still belongs to the family of the Japanese officer.
[105] Chamier, *Life of a Sailor*, p 44.
[106] Fraser, *The Sailors whom Nelson Led*, p 106.
[107] Case of GRIEVES v. the United Kingdom, Application no. 57067/00, Judgement, Strasbourg, 16 December 2003.
[108] *Plymouth Evening Herald*, 5 March 2004.
[109] *Lords Hansard*, 22 March 2004, Column 459.
[110] *Plymouth Evening Herald*, 1 April 2004.
[111] John McGrath, 'The abolition of swords at naval courts martial - the end of another tradition', *The Armourer*, (November/December 2006), p 90.
[112] A list of all winners is given on an honours board at the RN Submarine School.

Notes to Chapter 2
[1] *The Oxford English Dictionary* (Oxford: Clarendon Press, 1961), Vol II, p 1293. This is also the definition given in the on-line version (www.oed.com).
[2] Benerson Little, 'Eyewitness Images of Buccaneers and Their Vessels,' *The Mariner's Mirror*, Vol 98 (August 2012), p 320.
[3] May and Annis, *Swords for Sea Service*, Vol 1, p 78.
[4] Gilkerson, *Boarders Away with Steel*, p 69.
[5] *A Manual of Gunnery for Her Majesty's Fleet* (London: printed for Her Majesty's Stationery Office by Harrison and Sons, St Martin's Lane, 1873), pp 148–57.

6 Richard H Bezdek, *Swords and Sword Makers of England and Scotland* (Boulder, Colorado: Paladin Press, 2003), p 99.
7 Gilkerson, *Boarders Away with Steel*, p 82.
8 Sim Comfort, *Naval Swords and Dirks* (London: Sim Comfort Associates, 2008), Vol 1, p 34.
9 Public Records Office, W.O.47/2579, 30 May 1804, quoted in May and Annis, *Swords for Sea Service*, Vol 1, p 79.
10 H W C Semark, *The RNADs of Priddy's Hard, Elson, Frater & Bedenham* (Hampshire County Council, 1977), p 83.
11 May and Annis, *Swords for Sea Service*, Vol 1, pp 80–3.
12 Charles Ffoulkes CB, OBE, and Captain E C Hopkinson MC, *Sword, Lance & Bayonet* (Cambridge: Cambridge University Press, 1938), p 86.
13 Brian Robson, *Swords of the British Army. The Regulation Patterns 1788–1914. The Revised Edition* (Uckfield: The Naval and Military Press, 2011), p 25, Fig 20.
14 Ibid, p 31, Fig 24.
15 Mark Barton, 'Utterly Useless', *Naval Review*, Vol 96, No 4 (November 2008), pp 384–5.
16 *The Engineer* (8 March 1889).
17 Admiralty Fleet Order Number 4572 of 22 October 1936.
18 May and Annis, *Swords for Sea Service*, Vol I, p 90 and Vol II, Plates 72, 73 & 74.
19 Ibid, Vol I, pp 84 – 85.
20 Robert Wilkinson-Latham, *The Swords & Records of Robert Mole & Sons 1835?1920* (Shoreham-by-Sea: Pooley Sword Ltd, 2008), pp 68–9 and 73.
21 19 & 20 Victoriae, Cap 83.
22 Arthur Richard Dufty, *European Swords and Daggers in the Tower of London* (London: HMSO, 1974), Plate 84b.
23 Seen in a dealer's stock, April 2011.
24 Robson, *Swords of the British Army*, pp 244–5.
25 Thames Police History at http://www.thamespolicemuseum.org.uk/history.html Accessed 12 February 2013.
26 Bonhams, Sale No 19838, 31 July 2012, Lot no 142.
27 Robson, *Swords of the British Army*, pp 244 –5.
28 William Balfour Baikie, *Narrative of an Exploring Voyage up the Rivers Kwóra and Bínue (commonly known as the Niger and Tsárra) in 1854* (London: John Murray, 1856).
29 NMM, AAA2432.
30 Robert Wilkinson-Latham, *Mr Wilkinson of Pall Mall* (Shoreham-by-Sea: Pooley Sword Ltd, 2000), Vol 1, Ch 3, p 7.

Notes to Chapter 3
1 *Calendar of letters and papers of the reign of Henry VIII* (London, HMSO, n.d). A good transcription of this inventory can be found in Peter Marsden, *Sealed by Time – The Loss and Recovery of the Mary Rose* (Portsmouth: The Mary Rose Trust, 2003), p 170. The only edged weapons listed are arrows, bills and Morris pikes, suggesting that no swords were provided for use by the ship's complement. Any swords were, therefore, privately purchased, personal items, as officers' weapons remained until very recently.
2 May and Annis, *Swords for Sea Service*, Vol I, p 11, and Gilkerson, *Boarders Away with Steel*, p 110.
3 In his book *Rapiers and Small-Swords*, A V B Norman classifies this as a Type 109 hilt and traces its pedigree from the first half of the seventeenth century right through to 1816. During this time all the changes in fashionable decoration were followed and a variety of blade forms fitted. A V B Norman, *The Rapier and Small-Sword 1460–1820* (London: Arms and Armour Press, 1980), pp 189–93.
4 Sword EW 116.
5 Sarah Holland, Iain Grant, Julie Satchell, Gavin Stone and Garry Momber, *Warship Hazardous: Investigating a Protected Wreck* (Southampton: Hampshire & Wight Trust for Maritime Archaeology, n.d.), p 21.
6 Sword EW 113.
7 National Maritime Museum BHC2618.
8 Museum of the Royal Navy, Portsmouth, Accession No 1977/341.
9 Sim Comfort Collection, EW 102.
10 May and Annis, *Swords for Sea Service*, Vol II, p 302.
11 Museum of the Royal Navy, Portsmouth, Accession No 1990/327.
12 Admiralty Circular ADM/F/36 dated 4 June 1805.
13 National Maritime Museum Adm./F/36, quoted in May and Annis, *Swords for Sea Service*, Vol I, p 31.
14 The authors would surmise that it would have been the plain pattern that was adopted as this was the civil branches being moved to officer status and not seen as level with commanders upwards who wore the ornamented pattern.
15 Dudley Jarrett, *British Naval Dress* (London: J M Dent & Sons, 1960), p 73.
16 The snake was also incorporated into surgeons' uniform buttons in 1807.
17 John Latham, 'The Shape of Sword Blades', *Journal of the Royal United Services Institute*, Vol VI (1863), p 410. Latham was a key employee of Wilkinson.
18 May and Annis, *Swords for Sea Service*, Vol I, p 43.
19 Captain A B Sainsbury and Lieutenant Commander T D Phillips, *The Royal Navy Day by Day* (Stroud: Sutton Publishing Ltd, 2005), p 512.
20 National Maritime Museum, WPN 1150, May and Annis, *Swords for Sea Service*, Vol I, pp 43–4.
21 National Maritime Museum, WPN1501.
22 National Maritime Museum, WPN1417.
23 *The Navy & Army Illustrated* (17 January 1896), p 41.
24 Robson, *Swords of the British Army*, pp 159–61.
25 Admiralty Fleet Order 3/60, 1960.
26 Defence Council Instruction 85/03, 2003.
27 Both the update in positions entitled and the relative cost have been provided by Pooley Swords in correspondence with the authors.
28 Captain Henry T A Bosanquet, *The Naval Officer's Sword* (London: HMSO, 1955), pp 10–11.
29 May and Annis, *Swords for Sea Service*, Vol I, p 45. In Chapter 5, a sword of the East India Company supplied by a firm which traded under the name Goy & Co from 1861–74 is described.
30 BRD 1834, Chapter 4, *General Rules on the Wearing and Carrying of Swords b. Warrant Officer 1 (WO1) Sword*. The Warrant Officer 1 Sword differs from the Officer's Sword in that it has a rounded pommel and therefore no mane and the hilt is black in colour instead of white.
31 National Museum of the Royal Navy, Portsmouth, Accession no 1979.311.
32 Bonhams, Auction No 19854, 5 December 2012, Lot 210.
33 Admiralty Memorandum dated 2 July 1832 quoted in Jarrett, *British Naval Dress*, p 84.
34 Admiralty Memorandum dated 19 September 1832 quoted in Jarrett. *British Naval Dress*, p 85.
35 Admiralty Fleet Order 3/60, 1960.
36 John Nicol, *The life and adventures of John Nicol, mariner* as told to John Howell originally published 1822, reprint Edinburgh: Cannongate Books Ltd, 1997), p 34.
37 The similarity in swords should not be surprising as the Chinese Maritime Customs uniforms were based on British naval uniform as recorded in Robert Wilkinson-Latham, *Mr*

Wilkinson of Pall Mall, Vol 1, p 25.
[38] Keyes, *Adventures Ashore and Afloat*, p 229.
[39] Rynne, Cormac, private communication.
[40] *Defence Force Magazine*, April 1973, p 123.
[41] Rynne, Cormac, private communication.
[42] Adams Blackrock Auctioneers, Dublin, 11 March 2008, Lot 376.

Notes to Chapter 4
[1] *Oxford English Dictionary*, Second Edition, 1989, online version, March 2012.
[2] NMM MKH/17.
[3] G Watson, *A Narrative of the Adventures of a Greenwich Pensioner written by himself* (Newcastle: 1827), pp 59–60.
[4] May and Annis, *Swords for Sea Service*, Vol I, p 73.
[5] S A Cavell, 'Social Politics and the Midshipmen's Mutiny, Portsmouth 1791', *The Mariner's Mirror*, Vol 98, No 1 (February 2012), p 35.
[6] Ffoulkes and Hopkinson, *Sword, Lance and Bayonet*, p 84.
[7] C Sloane-Stanley, *Reminiscences of a Midshipman's Life. From 1850–1856* (London, private printing, 1893), p 40.
[8] Michael Lewis, *A Social History of the Navy, 1793-1815* (London: George Allen & Unwin Ltd, 1960), pp 167–70.
[9] Ibid, pp 152–3.
[10] Chamier, *The Life of a Sailor*, p 30.
[11] Hoffman *A Sailor of King George*, p 2.
[12] James D G Davison, *Admiral Lord St Vincent: Saint or Tyrant – the Life of Sir John Jervis, Nelson's Patron* (Barnsley: Pen & Sword Maritime, 2006), p 8.
[13] Hoffman, *A Sailor of King George*, p 150.
[14] Fairbairn *The Narrative of a Naval Nobody 1907-1924*, p 60.
[15] Comfort, EW 84.
[16] Bonhams, Sale no 199838, 31 July 2012, Lot 140.

Notes to Chapter 5
[1] Sim Comfort Collection, EW91.
[2] http://www.rmg.co.uk/explore/sea-and-ships/facts/faqs/people/who-were-the-royal-dockyard-volunteers.
[3] H G Hart, Major, 49th Regt, *The New Annual Army List, 1850* (London: John Murray, 1850), pp 407–10.
[4] H G Hart, Lieut.-Colonel, Unattached, *The New Annual Army List, and Militia List, for 1857* (London: John Murray, 1857), pp 481–3.
[5] H G Hart, Lieut.-Colonel, Unattached, *The New Annual Army List, and Militia List, for 1859* (London: John Murray, 1859).
[6] http://www.pembrokedock.org/h_dockyd_battn.htm.
[7] Robert Wilkinson-Latham, *Mr Wilkinson of Pall Mall*, Vol 1.
[8] NMM WPN1573.
[9] Finan's, April 2005 and Lawrence's of Crewkerne, October 2010.
[10] Robson, *Swords of the British Army*, pp 159?62.
[11] NMM WPN1036.
[12] NMM WPN1216.
[13] Bonhams Sale Number 19825, 24 April 2012, Lot 111.
[14] E.g. Bonhams Sale Number 18901, 2 August 2011, Lot 94, where a standard RN sword had the folding inner guard engraved 'A.R. Hunt R.N.V.R.'
[15] Carson Ritchie, *Q-ships* (Lavenham: Terence Hilton, 1985), pp 47–51 and Commander A T Seddon, RD★★, private communication.
[16] Jarrett, *British Naval Dress*, p 128.
[17] NMM WPN1296.
[18] NMM WPN1371.
[19] http://yourarchives.nationalarchives.gov.uk/index.php?title=Coastguard_History.
[20] Coastguard: Originally this was two words, Coast Guard. It appears in this form and in the form Coast-guard in the Coast-guard Service Act of 1856. By the time of the Coastguard Act of 1925 it had definitely become a single word. American usage is still Coast Guard.
[21] 19 & 20 Victoriae, Cap 83.
[22] J E Thomas, *Britain's Last Invasion: Fishguard 1797* (Stroud: Tempus Books, 2007), p 74.
[23] NMM WPN1221.
[24] Customs and Excise Museum, Liverpool, and Sim Comfort Collection EW154.
[25] Colonel Robert Gardner, *Small Arms Makers* (New York: Bonanza Books, 1963), p310, May and Annis, *Swords for Sea Service*, Vol II, p 302, Bezdek, *Swords and Sword Makers of England and Scotland*, p 149, and David Stroud, *A Snapshot of the Dublin Gun Trade*, Catalogue to the 34th Bisley Antique and Classic Arms Fair, Sunday 28 October 2012, reprinted from *The Irish Country Life and Country Sports Magazine*.
[26] *The Customs' Officers' Manual* (Exeter, Toker, Swetland & Spicer, 1868), pp 142–4.
[27] NMM, WPN1194.
[28] Bezdek, *Swords and Sword Makers of England and Scotland*, p 319.
[29] From a postcard published by the National Museum of Ireland.
[30] NMM WPN1096.
[31] NMM WPN1497.
[32] http://www.bris.ac.uk/history/customs/
[33] NMM WPN1322.
[34] Seen on a dealer's website.
[35] NMM WPN1322.
[36] NMM WPN 1503.
[37] NMM WPN1541.
[38] NMM WPN1603.
[39] NMM WPN1479.
[40] Sim Comfort Collection EW75 & EW76.
[41] Comfort, *Naval Swords and Dirks*, p 145.
[42] NMM WPN 1394.
[43] Sim Comfort Collection EW78.
[44] E.g. Bonhams, Sale number 18901, 2 August 2011, Lot 88.
[45] Kelly's Street Directories of London, 1859–74, yield the following information: 1859, Goy and Evans, Outfitters; 1860, Mrs Jane Goy & Co, Outfitters; 1861 and after Goy & Co, Outfitters; all at 36 Leadenhall Street.
[46] Bosanquet, *The Naval Officer's Sword*, pp 10–11.
[47] WPN1423.
[48] Bezdek, *Swords and Sword Makers of England and Scotland*, p 89.
[49] Ibid, p 205.
[50] P&O/75/1 pp 34 & 40.
[51] *The New York Times*, 1 May 1921.
[52] Hemmert, John, http://www.encyclopedia-titanica.org/white-star-line-uniform-1912.html. This is based on an article that had previously appeared in *Voyage*, the journal of the International Titanic Society.
[53] Bezdek, *Swords and Sword Makers of England and Scotland*, p 129.
[54] NMM WPN1163.
[55] NMM WPN1499.
[56] Photograph of Sir Winston Churchill in the uniform of the Lord Warden taken on the steps of 10 Downing Street on the morning of Coronation Day 1953, *Daily Telegraph*, 2 June 2012, p W11.

Notes to Chapter 6
[1] Sarah C Wolfe, *Naval Edged Weapons* (Barnsley: Chatham Publishing, 2005), pp 69–73.
[2] Victoria and Albert Museum Accession Number M.17&A-1978.
[3] National Maritime Museum, Accession Number WPN1549.
[4] Long, *Medals of the British Navy and how they were won*, p 35. May and Annis, *Swords for Sea Service*, Vol I, p 54, comment on it starting late in the eighteenth century but the earliest examples they give are all made in 1797.

A painting of this presentation is held by the National Maritime Museum and Howe's uniform sword is still being worn while he receives this impractical weapon.

5 Robert Malcomson, *Lords of the Lake, the Naval War on Lake Ontario 1812-1814* (London: Chatham Publishing, 1999), p 245.

6 Proceedings of the Meeting of the Subscribers to Lloyd's Coffee House, held 20th July, 1803.

7 Held by the RM Museum, Eastney.

8 Held by the National Army Museum.

9 Transcripts of Brisbane's despatches – *The Naval Chronicle* of 1807, pp 168–171.

10 Ibid.

11 For the most up-to-date locations of Patriotic Fund swords see Lloyd'sswords.com. The same corrections we offer in Appendix 1 would also be pertinent to the remainder of Jim Gawler's work on gifts in *Britons Strike Home: A History of Lloyd's Patriotic Fund 1803–1988* (Sandersted: Pittot, ca. 1988).

12 National Maritime Museum Accession Number WPN 1581.

13 Pelew is now known as Palau and is a group of islands in the Pacific, east of the Philippines.

14 The vessel itself cost £3000, the remainder was for fitting out. On return to Macao, Lt Snook managed to sell the vessel for £700 to recover some of the costs.

15 Dudley Pope, *The Black Ship* (London: Maritime History Books, 2009), p 326.

16 This is held by the National Maritime Museum.

Notes to Chapter 7

1 The source of both prices are as listed on the Bonhams' website for the press releases for each sale.

2 Email received by author from the auction house.

3 *The Times*, Friday December 4 1846, p. 6, Issue 19411.

4 May and Annis, *Swords for Sea Service*, Vol I, p 107.

5 Lot 510 sold at Cuttlestones' auction on 7 December 2012, for £11,000.

6 May and Annis, *Swords for Sea Service*, Vol I, p 101.

7 *Naval Chronicle* XIV (1805), p 471.

8 Biography of Captain Walpole, *Naval Chronicle* XIV (1805), p 93.

9 May and Annis, *Swords for Sea Service*, Vol I, p 22.

10 RN Trophy Centre Records for trophies 8894 and 8895.

11 NMM Accession number WPN1256.

12 Letters dated Saturday 7 November 1846 (p 7 Issue 19388), Monday 9 November 1846 (p 2 Issue 19389), Wednesday 25 November 1846 (p 3 Issue 19403), Friday 4 December 1846 (p 6 Issue 19411), Tuesday 8 December 1846 (p 7 Issue 19412), Monday 11 January 1847 (p 5 Issue 19443) and Libel case reported Wednesday 30 June 1847 (p 8 Issue 19589) all in *The Times* (London).

13 Accession number WPN 1065.

14 James, *The Naval History of Great Britain*, Vol 1, p 364.

15 NMM Accession number WPN1167.

16 Fraser, *The Sailors Whom Nelson Led*, p182.

17 NMM Accession Number WPN 1550.

18 NMM Accession Number WPN 1094.

19 Sim Comfort, *Naval Swords and Dirks* Special Supplement (London: Sim Comfort Associates, 2008).

20 Thomas Capel had only become a Lieutenant earlier in 1797, this reward of bringing back the news probably assisted him in becoming a Commander the following year and made post not long after, eventually gaining a knighthood and Admiral of the Red. David Syrett and R L DiNardo *The Commissioned Sea Officers of the Royal Navy 1660-1815* (Aldershot: Scholar Press for the Navy Records Society, 1994), p 72.

21 Comfort, *Naval Swords and Dirks*, p 162 EW 84.

22 May and Annis, *Swords for Sea Service*, Vol I, p 108.

23 Item Number 11952.

24 John Charnock, *Biographical Memoires of Viscount Lord Nelson* (London: H D Symonds, 1806), p 174.

25 Robert Southey, *The Life of Nelson* (London: John Murray, 1814), p 68.

26 The cane was passed to his Father, Edmund Nelson and then to his son-in-law George Matcham and remained in the Matcham family until 2005 and sold as Lot 7 at Sotheby in the Trafalgar: Nelson and The Napoleonic Wars, auction in October 2005.

27 National Maritime Museum Manuscript COL/15.

28 Letter from Duke of Clarence (Wm IV) to Lord Collingwood, dated 12 December 1805, NMM COL/15.

29 Fraser, *The Sailors Whom Nelson Led*, p 55.

30 Sir Nicholas Harris Nicolas, *The Dispatches and Letters of Vice Admiral Lord Viscount Nelson* (London: Henry Colbur, 1845), Vol 2, p 361.

31 Parsons, *Nelsonian Reminiscences*, p 9.

32 Fraser, *The Sailors Whom Nelson Led*, p 112.

33 Fraser, *The Enemy at Trafalgar*, p 143.

34 Richard Walker, *The Nelson Portraits* (Portsmouth: The Royal Naval Museum, 1998).

35 National maritime Museum – Memorials Websit – Memorial; M4088.

Notes to Chapter 8

1 *Oxford English Dictionary*, Second edition, on-line version, June 2012.

2 John Winton, *The Naval Heritage of Portsmouth* (Southampton: Ensign Publications, 1994), p 51.

3 Pierre Jacques François Girard, *Nouveau Traité de la Perfection sur la Fait des Armes*, etc (Paris: Chez Moétte, 1736).

4 John McArthur, *The Army and Navy Gentleman's Companion* (London, Printed for James Lavers, 1780), pp xv –xvii.

5 British Library Add. MSS 34990 25 Mar 1787 Rawson, Leeward Islands Letters, 54.

6 John Skynner, *Notebook containing standing orders for HMS AMAZON*, National Maritime Museum, JOD45.

7 Green, William Pringle, National Maritime Museum, JOD48.

8 NRS Vol XXXI *Recollections of Commander James Anthony Gardner (1775 - 1814)* Published 1906, pp 51-2.

9 NRS Vol XXXI *Recollections of Commander James Anthony Gardner (1775 - 1814)* Published 1906, pp 83-4.

10 Culverhouse went on to become a Captain before drowning in 1809.

11 NRS Vol XXXI *Recollections of Commander James Anthony Gardner (1775 - 1814)* Published 1906, p 84.

12 John McGrath, 'Fencing in Prisoner of War Hulks', *The Sword* (October 2006), pp 29–31.

13 *The Naval Chronicle*, Vol XXXI (1814), p 115.

14 Confusingly, there were two fencing masters named Henry Angelo. They were father and son. It was the son who was responsible for producing the cutlass exercise.

15 *The Guards and Lessons of the Highland Broadsword*, designed and etched by T Rowlandson and published by Mr Angelo, No. 10 Boulton Row, Berkeley Square, Jany. 20th 1799.

16 *Infantry Sword Exercise* (London, Her Majesty's Stationery Office, 1895).

17 Achille Marozzo, *Opera Nova* (Venetia: Aporesso Antonio Pinargenti, 3rd edition 1550).

18 *The Navy and Army Illustrated* (29 May 1896), p 262.

19 Colin White, *The End of the Sailing*

Navy (London: Mason, ca 1981).
[20] *Royal Naval Engineering College Annual* (1886/7), p 31.
[21] Surgeon T T Jeans, RN (ed), *Naval Brigades in the South African War 1899–1900* (London: Sampson, Low, Marston & Company Limited, 2nd edition, 1902), p 12.

Notes to Chapter 9

[1] J J Bennett, 'The Most Expert Swordsman in the Navy', *The Royal Magazine*, date unknown, and Lieut-Colonel P L Binns, *The Story of the Royal Tournament* (Aldershot: Gale & Polden Ltd, 1952), p 67.
[2] *The Illustrated London News*, 30 June 1849, p 444.
[3] *The Illustrated London News*, 3 June 1865, p 536
[4] *The Graphic*, 19 February 1881, p 173.
[5] *The Graphic*, 5 December 1874, p 640.
[6] Binns, *The Story of the Royal Tournament*, p 54
[7] Ibid, p 127.
[8] That was in 1928.
[9] His 1935 Epée trophy is in the National Fencing Museum.
[10] Reported in the *Vancouver Province* newspaper of 4 April 1911.
[11] Mrs V Gale, private communication which included a picture of the winning team showing her father, A A Raven.
[12] These were third in foil in 1950 and third in sabre in 1951. He had also won the sabre in 1948.
[13] M Fare, *A Century of Fencing in Britain* (London: British Fencing Association, 2002), p 78.
[14] *Infantry Sword Exercise* (London: Printed for HMSO by Harman and Sons, St Martin's Lane, 1895).
[15] Fairbairn, *The Narrative of a Naval Nobody 1907-1924*, p 6.
[16] Ibid, p 16.
[17] Bill Seager and Robert Mullock-Morgans 'An Assured Peace? The German visit to Whale Island', *The Review, Journal of the Naval Historical Collectors Society*, Vol 20.4 (Spring 2008), p 48.

Notes to Chapter 10

[1] Further information on this topic can be found in John Wilkinson-Latham, *British Military Swords* (London: Hutchinson & Co Ltd, 1963), pp 60–2, May and Annis, *Swords for Sea Service*, Vol II, pp 336–41 and Henry Wilkinson, *Observations on Swords*, 18th Edition (London: 27 Pall Mall, n.d.). Details of all these books can be found in the Bibliography.
[2] The full history of Wilkinson can be found in Robert Wilkinson-Latham, *Mr Wilkinson of Pall Mall*.
[3] Loades, *Swords and Swordsmen*, pp 332–3.
[4] More in-depth details can be found in the books by John and Robert Wilkinson-Latham and Diderot et d'Alembert's *Encylopédie*. The latter contains a series of 10 plates entitled *Fourbisser*, which illustrate a sword cutler's premises, blade grinding, all the machinery and tools, and the various components of swords. For those interested in the historic metal production process, the book by Tylcote remains the best general introduction. Full details and on-line internet sources are in the bibliography.
[5] John Wilkinson-Latham, *British Military Swords*, p 62.
[6] Robert Wilkinson-Latham, *Mr Wilkinson of Pall Mall*, Vol 2, 1900–1972.
[7] ADM/196/120.
[8] http://www.worldwar1.co.uk/battleship/hms-bellerophon.html
[9] For example A Byatt, *Collecting Picture Postcards; an introduction* (Malvern: Golden Age Postcard Books, 1982), and Stanley Gibbon, *Great Britain Concise Stamp Catalogue* (2011).
[10] Admiral Sir Richard Vesey-Hamilton (ed), *Letters and Papers of Admiral Sir Byam Martin*, Vol 1, NRS Vol 24 (1902), p 120.
[11] Wilkinson, *Observations on Swords*, p 13.

Notes to Appendix 1

[1] This list reflects our study of the Fund's minutes whereas earlier authors worked from the Fund's accounts of those made.
[2] Beatty's name is spelt in various ways in documents of the time also being rendered as Beat(t)ie.
[3] Captain Maitland is only recorded for the second action on 4 June.
[4] Lieutenant Pilford was in command as Captain Brown had returned for the court martial of Admiral Calder, for an earlier action off Ferrol.
[5] Lieutenant Stockham was in command as his Captain had returned for the court martial of Admiral Calder, for an earlier action off Ferrol.
[6] It is possible the Harvey did the same as Codrington and decided that the cash was used for the injured, if so it was not recorded.
[7] Charles Messenger, *Unbroken Service* (London: Lloyd's Patriotic Fund, 2003), p 40.
[8] Lieutenant Douglas initials vary from source to source P J or J P.
[9] Also spelt Perkyns in some sources.
[10] Captain Wise's sword is for the destruction of the Fort at Samana only.
[11] *La Piedmontaise* is spelt *Piémontaise* in some records.
[12] The modern spelling of this is Nakskov.
[13] The committee considered these together and decided to award a sword on 14 Feb 1809.
[14] This has not been recorded in previous lists but the medal and round presentation plaque from the box was sold as Lot 11 in an auction by Dix Noonan Webb on 23 June 2005. Colonel Arnold is mentioned in the Army List of 1841 for war service of officers of the Royal Engineers for getting a £100 Patriotic Fund swod for Surinam, p 289.

Notes to Appendix 3

[1] Except for the years 1986 to 1991 the wording of the award has been taken from the Wilkinson archives; for 1986 to 1991 it has been established as accurately as possible from *Navy News* articles and Hansard.
[2] Incorrectly stated in other sources is HMS *Fearless*, for acting as a floating 10 Downing Street (for Prime Minister Harold Wilson's talks with Ian Smith of Southern Rhodesia), embassy, exhibition hall and co-ordinating centre of civil aid projects,
[3] On display in the New Zealand Naval Museum.
[4] P2000s of the Inshore Training Squadron were the first RN ships to visit a Russian port as part of the 100th anniversary celebrations of the Russian Navy.
[5] TG number in Wilkinson archives, ship names from different sources.
[6] This sword is held by 820 NAS at RNAS Culdrose, following the paying off of RFA *Fort George* in 2011.
[7] Held onboard HMS Richmond.
[8] Since RFA *Largs Bay* was withdrawn from service prior to the presentation, the sword was presented to the RFA.

Notes to Appendix 4

[1] C-L de Beaumont, *Modern British Fencing* (London: Hutchinson, 1949) and *Modern British Fencing 1948–1956* (London: Edward Hulton, 1958)
[2] Binns, *The Story of the Royal Tournament*.
[3] C-L de Beaumont, *Modern British Fencing 1957–1964* (London: Edward Hulton, 1966).
[4] From correspondence with Bobby Thorn (née McHugh).
[5] The other possible candidate for this year was Mo Ashton.

Index

References in *italics* are to illustrations and captions.

Note: personal names appearing only in the appendices have not been indexed. Ranks quoted are the highest in which the individual appears in this book; he or she may well have been promoted further.

Abbott, Lemuel Francis, 84, 90
Aboukir, Bay of, 57
Abu Klea, 17,
Adams, Fanny, 90
Admiralty, 60, 74–5, 88, 89; and coastguard, 32, 65, 66; patterns, 45; swordsmanship training, 92, 94–5
Admiralty Surface Weapons Establishment, Fareham, 22
Afghanistan, 22
Africa, 15
Aigalliers, V Adm François-Paul Brueys d', 57
Air Pilots and Navigators, Guild of, 24, *24*
Alavas, Adm, 88
Albert, Prince (Consort), 85
Albuera, battle of, 77, 124
Aldershot, 106,
Aldous, Herbert J, 90
Alexandria, 57
Algiers, 10, 124: Dey of, 10
Amateur Fencing Association, 103, 105
Amberg, Michael, 106
Amiens, Peace of, 60, 77
Amsterdam, 105
Anderson, Bob, 106, *106*
Anderson, Sir Donald, 75
Andras, Catherine, 89–90
Angelo, Henry, 94–5, *95*, 107
Anglo-Dutch War, 36
Anglo-Japanese War, 15, *15*
Annis, P G W, 26, 29, 38, 41, 55, 82, 83, 84, 110–12
Antarctic Expedition, 23
Antigua, 94
Arctic convoys, *59*
Army Gymnastic School, Aldershot, 106
Army Hospital Corps, 33
Army & Navy Gentleman's Companion, *93*, 93–4
Arnold, Lt James, 77, 124
Aruba, island of, 78
Ashanti War, 15
Atlanta, 106
Australia, 25, 36
axe, 7, 8, 15

Bach, Lord, 24
Baikie, Dr William, 33–4
Bailey, E H, 88
Bain, H B, 108
Bairnsfather, Bruce, 20
Baker, Capt Alasdair, RM, 106, 109
Balaclava, battle of, 16
Barbados, 91

Barfleur, battle of, 7
Barham, Lord, 76
Barnard (artist), 90
Baron, Hugh, 39
Barrett, Chief Gunner, 100–2
Barrett, Corney & Corney, 84
Barton, Mark, 109, *109*, 128
Bath Sword Club, 106
bayonet, 7, *13*, 18, 20, 21, 94: *Altmark* incident, 21; Crimean War, 16; cutlass sword, 17, 31–2, *31–2*, 34, 99; fencing, *104*, 107; manufacture, 112
Beasley, Capt Thomas, 73
Beatty, Adm Lord, 16, 20, 22, 78, *79*, 124
becket, 11
Bedford, Duchess of, 118
Beechy, Sir William, *86*, 89, *89*
Bengal Marine, 69; see also Bombay Marine, Indian Navy
Benin (Brohemie), 15
Bennett, L/Wren Audrey (Peters), 106, 128
Berlin, 105
Berry, Capt, 88, 122
Bezdek, Richard H, 110–12
Bidoux, Chevalier Prégent de, 9
Birmingham, 34, 91, *91*, 110, *111*, 112
Blackman, Cadet, 107
Blake, Rev G L, 103
Blake, Adm Robert, 7
Blomberg, Brig Gen H E, 108
Bodill, William, 72, *72*
Boer War, 15, 19, 96, 98, 118
Bohemia, 103
Bolton, Capt William Henry, 78, *78*, 123
Bombay, 79: Bombay [and Bengal] Marine, 69, 72, 79; see also East India Company, Indian Navy
Bonhams, 63
Bosanquet, Capt Henry T A, 71, 85
Bowers, Lt Cdr Keith, 106, *109*, 127, 128
Boxer Rebellion, 19–20, 53
Boyd, Lt, 77, 120
Brackenbury, Lt Cdr John Boileau Fabian, 59, *59*
Brassey, Thomas, MP, 63
Brenton, Capt Jahleel, 82, 123
Brest, 11
Bridgetown, 91
Bridport: 2nd Baron, 86; family, 87
Brisbane, Capt Charles, 78, 122, 123
Bristol, 63
Britannia Royal Naval College, Dartmouth (BRNC), 25, 57, 58–9, 102, 106–9, *108*, 115, 129, 130
broadsword, 17, 53, 68, 95–6
Broke, Capt P B V, 14, 124
Brookfield, Cdr E W H,

102, 103, *105*, 126
Brooks, R J, *105*
Brown, Mr, 12
Brown, Capt Angus, 73
Brownfield, Capt William, 60, 72
Brownrigg, Capt Charles, 15
Buller, General Redvers, 17
Bullock, Lt Sue, 109, 129
Burnham Thorpe, 84
Butcher, L/Wren *109*
Byrne, Cdr F E, 108
Byron, Lord, 13

Cadiz, 88, 90
Caesar, Julius, 7
Cairo, 115
Calcutta, 44
Cambridge, Duke of, 58
Cambridge University, 105
Cameret Bay, 11–12
Cameronians (Scottish Rifles), 2nd Batt'n, 20
Campbell, Gen Sir Colin, 16
Campbell, V Adm Sir Patrick, 38
Canada, 13, 25, 52, 91
Canton, 20, 77
Cape François, 83
Cape St Vincent, battle of, 9, 10, 19, 78, *79*, 84, 87–8, *87–8*, 90, 124
Cape Town, 115
Capel, Adm Thomas, 86–7, 122
Carreg Wastad Bay, 65
Carrington, Viscount, 73
Carter, Nigel, 108
Cary, Adj, 62
cavalry swords, 30, 31
Cawdor, Lord, 65
Ceylon: Naval Volunteer Force, 69; Royal Ceylon Navy, 69; Royal Naval Volunteer Reserve, 69
Chamier, Capt Frederick, 9, 11, 13, 18, 56
Charles II, 36
Charlotte, Queen, *76*
Chatham, 60
Chaworth, Mr, 13
Chayla, R Adm A S M Blanquet du, 8, 90
Chichester, Sir Francis, 36
China, *19*, 19–20, 21, *53*, 68: Maritime Customs Service, 53, 68, 68–9
Christies, 84, 88
Cinque Ports, Lord Warden of the, 75, 75
Circello, Marquis, 87
Cisneros, Adm, 88
Clarence, Duke of, 87
Clark, Capt, 13
Clark, Cdr Matt, *109*, 127
Clarke, James Stanier, 83
Clarke, Col Sgt L V, 104, *104*
claymore, 24–5
Clifton College, 106
Clyde, 63, 125
Coast Blockade Service, 18, 65, 65–6
Coastguard Service, 18, 45, 65–8, *67*, 80: cutlass, 32, 32–3; Act (1856), 65
Cochrane, Adm Lord, 8, 122, 124

Cockburn, V Adm Sir George, 38, *40*, 86, *86*
Codrington, Capt Edward, 77, 122
Coffey, Lt Ralph, *109*
Coffin, Capt Isaac, 56
College of Arms, 110
Collingwood, Adm Lord, 44, 88, 122, 124
Collins, Darby, 94
Comfort, Sim, 27, 38: collection, 38, 39, 41, 69–70, 87
Commando Brigade (3), 22, 125
Conquet Bay, 9
conservation, 115–17
Cook, Capt James, *35*, 36
Cornwallis, Adm Sir William, *80*
court-martial, 23–4
Cox, Lt Thomas Sherlock, 77, 124
Craddock, Cdr, 20
Cran, Cdr Barrie, *109*
Crickhowell, 85, 87
Crimean War, 14, *44*, 61
Crosnier, Roger, 106
Crow, N A, *105*
Crowley, Hon Lt Sidney, 63
Cruikshank, George, *7*
Culverhouse, John, 94
Cunningham, Adm Lord, 16, 124
Curaçao, 78, *78*, 123
Curtis, Sgt R A, 104, *104*
Customs, Board of, 65
Customs Service, 65–6, 66
Cuthbert, Lt, 86
cutlass, *7*, 8, *13*, 25–34, *100*, 118: Coast Blockade, 18: at court-martial, 23; hybrid, 63, *63*; last use, 18–21; use by midshipmen, 18; in Napoleonic Wars, 11, 12; pistol and, 14; pre-1804, 26; sword bayonet, 17, 31–2, *31–32*, 34, 99; at Trafalgar, 9–10; training, 93, *95*, 94–9
Cutlers, Worshipful Company of, 112
cutting-out actions, 11–12, 38, 80, 83, 120, 122, 123
Cyprus, 115
Czech Army, 105

DSO (Distinguished Service Order), 20
Dacca, 19
dagger, 8, 55, 107; see also dirk
Daily Telegraph, 17, 21
Dalglish, Capt Robin, 103–5, 126, 127
Darby, V Adm George, 55, 57
Dardanelles, 73, 104
Dartmouth, *24*, 25, 97, *107*, 106–8; see also Britannia Royal Naval College
Davison, Alexander, 83, 87
De Silva, AB Henry, 106
Defence Force Magazine, 54
Dennington, Mr, 84
Deptford, 60
Derwent, River, 114
Devonport, 13: battalion,

60, 61, 62
Dictionary of National Biography, 82
Dimbleby, Richard, 87
dirks, 7, 18, *49*, 55, 55–9: Chinese, 68; crocodile, 76, 87; midshipmen and, 23, 36, 45, 47, 48, 52, 56–9, 118; Nelson, 82, 83, 84; presentation, 80; propeller, 56, 57; uniform, 58–9
display swords, *see* presentation swords
display of swords, 117–8
Dobbin, Lt, 65, 65–6
Dogger Bank, battle of, 104
Dominica, 39
Dominique, 14
Dorling, Capt Henry Taprell, 20
Drake, Sir Francis, *35*, 35–6,
dress regulations, 43, 48, *48*, 56, 66
dress swords, 38, 42, *42*, 46, 52, 83, 84
drills, sword: Admiralty, 92; cutlass, *98*; naval, 8–9; military, 8; *see also* training
Dublin, 66, 91
Dunbury, Mr, 14
Duncan, Gunner C G, 104, *104*
Dungeness, 65, 123
Dunn, Air Cdre Wilfrid Henry, 64
Dupen, Mr, 106
Durham, Capt Philip, 9

East India Company, [The Honourable], 77, 79, 110, 120: Mercantile Marine, 70, 71; swords, 69–72, *71*, 74, 76
East Indies, *80*
Edinburgh, HRH the Duke of, 75, *75*
Edridge, Henry, 90
Edward VII, *114*, 115
Edward VIII, *114*
Egypt, 45, 57, 115, 124
Egyptian Club, 57, *57*, 86, 87
El Teb, 16, 17, *17*, 50
Elizabeth I, 13, 35–6
Elizabeth II, 25, 36, 75, *114*
Ellenborough, Lord, 60
Elliot, Mid, 23
Ellis, 2nd Lt, 9
Enfield, 32, 34: rifle, 31; cutlass sword bayonet, 31, *31*, 34
Enfield-Snider, 31–2, 99
Engeham, Lt Cdr Paul, 109, 127
Engineer, The, 29
Enslin, battle of, *see* Graspan
epée, *see* fencing
Ethelston, Cdr, 19
European Court of Human Rights, 24
Evans, John, *106*
Evans, Thomas, 85
Evans-Nicholas sword, 85
exercise, *see* drill, training
Exmouth, Adm Lord, 10, 41, 124

Fairbairn, Lt Cdr Douglas, 20–21, 57
Fairbairn, James, 110
Falkland Islands, 79, 124, 125
Fane, Capt, *80*
Farrington, Anthony, 110
Fearney, William, 10, 87
Fegen, Lt Frederick Fogarty, 19
Fencibles: River and Sea, 60, 72
fencing, 92, 100–9, *104*, 112, 126–30
Ferrers, Major E B, 20
Field, Lt Joe, RM, *105*, *105*, 106
Fielmann, Lt Ferdinand, 102, 103, 106–7, 126
Finch, Petty Officer Jacky, 106, 108, 126, 127
First World War, 19, 20–1, 23, 64, 72, 73, 78, *94*, 124
Fisher, Adm John 'Jacky', 16
Fishguard, 65, 66
Fleet Air Arm, 24: FAA sword, 24, *24*
Fleming, Major Edward, 77, 124
Flynn, Errol, 106
foil, *see* fencing
Fort Louis, *12*
Foster, Lt Cdr David, 108–9
France, 39, 60, 77, 93
France, Isle de, 77, 124
Fraser, Edward, 9, 87, 88
Fraser, River Insp William Donald, 68, *69*

Galfridus Walpole-Suckling sword, 83; *see also* Walpole, Galfridus
Gallipoli, 23
Galwey, Lt, 88
Gardner, Capt James Anthony, 94
Gardner, Col Robert, 112
Garford, Staff Instructor, 106
Garratt, Lt Joe, 106
Garter, Order of the, 74, *75*
Gate Pah, 15
Gelder, George, *106*
Genoa, 83
George I, *114*
George II, *114*
George III, 76, *76*, *114*
George IV, *114*
George V, *49*, 59, *59*, 72, *114*
Geraldino, Capt Don Thomas, 88
Germany, 17, 113: *Altmark* incident, 21; navy, 75, 108; *schläger* tradition, 13
Gibraltar, 91
Gieves, 45, 53, 54, 75, 115
Gilkerson, William, 26, 27
Gladstone, W E, 75
Glorious First of June, battle of the, 76, 78
Gosport, 13
Granville, V Adm the Earl, 105, *105*
Graspan, battle of, *18*, 19, 20
Graves, R Adm Thomas, 86
Gravesend, *68*

Index

Gravina, Adm, 88
Gray, Edwyn, 22
Great Exhibition (1851), *66*
Great Lakes Campaign, 13, 76–7
Greece, 87
Green, V, 39
Green, Lt William Pringle, 14–15, *94*, 95, 97
Greenwich, 85, 86, 91, *91*, *98*: Royal Hospital, 87; RH School, *98*
Grindlay, Capt Robert Melville, 70
Guantanamo, 24
Guernsey, 109: Castle Cornet Museum, 37, 86,
Guichen, Adm de, 39
Guildhall Library, 112
Gunnery, Manual of, 95, 98
Guy, Mid, 20
Guzzardi, Leonardo, 88, *89*

Hales, 3/O S A, *109*
Halewood, Cdre John, 76
Hamburg, 87
Hamilton, Capt Archibald, 69, 70, 120
Hamilton, Sir Edward, 80
Hamilton, Lady [Emma], 83, 89
Hamilton, Sir William, 85, 88
Hamish Ashley Ripper Memorial sword, 73
Hamlet, Thomas, 79
hanger, 25, 36, 37, 38, 55, 84, *84*, 93; *see also* hunting sword
Hardy, Capt Thomas Masterman, 83, 122, 124
Harrison, Ray, *106*
Harry, Capt R C, 108, 127, 128
Hart's Army Lists, 60
Head, Sir Guy, 90
Helsinki, 106
Hendrix, Lt Cdr Chris, *109*
Henning, L/Wren J H, *109*
Henry VIII, 9, 35, 73
hilt: 1845 pattern, *28*; brass, 26; crocodile, 57–8, 76; cross, 91; Customs Service, 66; double disc (figure of eight), *27*; dragon, 53; Gothic, 62; half-basket, *43*, 43–6, 62, 65, 67; light cavalry, *41*; Mameluke, 45–6, *46*, 50, 88; slotted, 36, *36*, *90*; stirrup, 32, 37, 65, 66, 67, 70, 72, 84; Type A and B, 29; *see also* knuckle guard
Hirst, Col Sgt, 105
Hitch, F Brook, 90
Hockley, Cdr Graham, 109, *109*
Hoffman, Capt Frederick, 14, 56–7
Hollis, Capt, 95
Hollywood, 106
Holy Trinity, Guild of the, 73; *see also* Trinity House
Hong Kong, 20
Hood, Alexander, 55
Hood, Adm Sir Samuel, 55, 76, *76*, 86, 86
Hopes, Gunner Stephen, 15
Hopkins, Lt, 65
Hoppner, John, 89, 90
Hore, Capt Peter, 15–16
House of Lords, 42
Howard, Sir Edward, 9, *9*
Howard, Mike, *106*
Howard-Johnston, Adm C D, 25
Howard-Johnston, Sub Lt R G, 25
Howard-Willis, QSMI, 105
Howe, Adm Lord, 76, 78
Howson, CPO W G, 108, 126, 127
Hskiu, *19*
hunting sword, *35*, 36, 38, 55, 83; *see also* hanger
Hussars, 7th, 17
Hyde, Chief Officer F W, 67–8

Illustrated London News, 88, *99*, 117
India, 16, 19, 72, 77: Indian Marine, 69, *see also* East India Company; Indian Marine, HM, 69, 72; Indian Mutiny, 15, *15*, 16, *44*, 45, 69, 70; Indian Navy, 69; Indian Navy, HM, 70, *71*, 72
Inkerman, battle of, *44*
Innis, Capt, 13
Ireland, *65*, 77, 91, 105, 106, 125; Irish: Code, 13, Defence Force, 54, Marine Service, 54, Maritime Inscription, 54, Naval Service, 54, *54*, Revenue Police, 67
Isandlwana, battle of, 16
Italy, 102

Jack, Alex, 14
Jago, L/Wren Nicki, *109*
Jamaica, 76, 80, *81*
James IV, of Scotland, 9
Jeffrey, Cdr Robin, 105
Jellicoe, Adm Lord, 16, 19, 124
Jerred, Sgt P J, 104, *104*
Jersey, 109
Jervis, Adm Sir John, *see* St Vincent, Earl of
Joll, 3/O R D, *109*
Jøssingfjord, 21
Joyce, W/O Martin, 106
Jutland, battle of, *59*, 80, *80*, 104, 115

Kennealy, Lt Tim, 106, 127
Kent, 18, 65
Keppel, Adm Sir Charles, *46*, 46, 50
Kershaw, Lt Cecil A, 103–5, *105*, *108*, 126, 127
Keyes, Adm Sir Roger, 20, 53
Kinsey, John, 83, 85
knives, 7
Knock, Henry, 112
knuckle guard, 26–7, 58: 1889, *30*; bow, 36, *40*; bowl, *28*, 29, 31; brass, 32, *33*; crocodile, 58; double disc, 33; double shell, 27, *34*, 93; half-basket, *43*, 43–4, 45, 54, 61, *61*, 70, *72*, 117; openwork, 67; RNAV, 62; stirrup, 60, 69, 70, 72; winged victory, *80*; *see also* hilt
Krupp guns, 16
Kyd, Thomas, 25

La Hougue, battle of, 11
Lacey, Col Sgt Jan, 106, *107*
Ladysmith, relief of, 20
Laird, Macgregor, 33
Lambert, V Adm Sir George Robert, 84, *84*
landings, 11–12
Lanning, L/Wren, *109*
Latham, John Wilkinson, *see* Wilkinson-Latham, John
Laurie, Robert, 90
Lawry, Lt, 55
Le Bair, Capt James, 37, 72
lead cutter swords, 100
Lebanon, 86
Lee, Gunner (T) R G V, *109*
Leith, 64
Leith, Lt Lockhart, 103
Lessons in Sabre, Singlestick, etc, 100
levee sword, 52, *52*, 115
Leveson-Gower, Hon William S, *see* Granville, Earl
Lewis, Lt Cdr David, *109*
Lewisham, 27
Light Brigade, 16
Linois, Contre Adm Charles-Alexandre Durand, 77
Liverpool, 63, 64, 73
Llangattock, Lady, 85, 87
Lloyd's of London, 77–8, 79
Loades, Michael, 7
Lock, Lt Walter, 38
London, 63, 73, 74, 77–9, 88, 91, 103, 110: Athletic Club, 102, *102*; City of, 80, 88: Modern Galleries, 87, swords, 78–9, 77, 87, 124; *Gazette*, 78; Museum of, 88
Long, Adj, 62

Lossack, Lt, 12
Lucas, John, *44*
Lucknow, 16, *44*
Lucy, Charles, 90
Lynch, John, *81*
Lytham, 67

McArthur, John, 13, 83, 84, 93–5, 117
McCulloch, Capt Joseph, 65
McGrath, John, 106, 108, 127
McKenna, Cdre, 54
McPherson, C R, *105*
Macao, 79
Madrid, Museo Naval, 88
Malinson, WO Dave, *109*
Malta, 17, 80: Battalion, *61*, 61–2; Maritime Museum, 62
Mandley, H, 115
Mandley, Lt Cdr Raymond Hewitt, 115
Maria II, of Spain, 19
Marines, 7: in Napoleonic Wars, 11; and naval discipline, 23; Sudan, 16; Harbour Volunteer, 60; Royal, 62, 64, 77, 125: duelling, 13, fencing, 102–4, *104*, 106–8, 126–30, at Trafalgar, 10
Maritime Warfare School, 25
Markham, Capt, 16
marlinspikes, 7
Marmora, sea of, 97
Marozzo, Achille, 97
Martin, Capt George Bohun, 45
Martin, Adm Sir Thomas Byam, 118
Martini-Henry rifle, 32, *32*, 99
Martinique, *12*
Masiello, 95, 107
Maxwell, Lt, 12
May, Cdr W E, 26, 29, 38, 41, 55, 82, 83, 84, 110–12
Mends, Surgeon Lt David, 108
Menzies, Lt, 77
Merchant, Marine, 33–4; Navy, 60, 69, 72–3
Merlin (helicopter), 25
Merrett, Lt/Lcpl Craig, *109*
Meteren, 20
Mexico, 106
Middleton, Capt, 76
Miller, Capt, 13
Miller, Capt Ralph, 88
Miller, Col Sgt, 104, *104*
Milne, Capt, 95
Mitchell, PO Samuel, 15
Monmouth, 85
Moresby, Capt Fairfax, 80
Mortimer, H W, 82
Mount-Haes, Capt Edward, 105, 108, *109*, 126, 127
Mulock, Capt George F A, 23, *23*
Muntok, 23
Muros Bay, 7
Museum of the Royal Navy, *see* Royal Naval Museum
muskets, 11, 13
Myers, Lt Cdr Maggie, 109, *109*, 128, 129, 130

Napier, Charles, 19
Napoleonic Wars, 9, 15, 18, 45, 84: landings, 11, 12; Patriotic Fund, 77–8; sea service pistol, 14
National Archives, The, 110, 115
National Army Museum, 79, *79*
National Maritime Museum, 34, 45, 60, 63, 64, 66, 67, 69–70, 73, 74: Nelson, 84, 85, 87, 88, 90
Naval Academy, Portsmouth, 92, *92*
Naval Brigade, 19–20
Naval Chronicle, The, 12, 83, 94–5
Naval Cutlass Exercise, 95, 95–6

Naval General Service medal, 19
Naval Review, The, 20
Navy & Army Illustrated, 65, 68, 96, 117
Neaves, Capt, 105
Needham, PO Mark, 109, *109*, 127, 128
Neeve, PO PT Instructor, *109*
Nelson, Adm Lord Horatio, 7, *8*, *82*, 122: Cape St Vincent, 9, 10, 78; depictions of, 88–91, *88–91*; *Nelsonian Reminiscences*, 11; Nile, 57, 76; swords, 37, 38, 42, 82–91, *84*, 124; swordsmanship, 94; Trafalgar, 8
Nelson, Horatia, 83, 85
Nelson, Lady, 88
Nelson Museum: Great Yarmouth, 87; Monmouth, 85
Nelson, Walter, 84
Nesbitts, 84
Neuve Chapelle, battle of, 20
Neville, Lt, 12
New York Times, 73
New Zealand wars, 15, *16*
Nicholas, Lt, RM, 10
Nichols, Capt Edward, 77, 120, 123
Nicol, John, 15, 52
Nicolas, Sir Nicholas Harris, 82, 85
Niger, River, 33
Nile, battle of, 17, 57–8, 76, 86: dirks 57, 57–8, swords, *86*, 86–7, 88, 90, 124
Nore, The, 77, 118
Northampton Fencing Club, 106
Northesk, Earl, 95, 124
Norway, 21
Norwich, 88, 89: Castle Museum, 88
Nowak, Leading PT Instructor Jim, 106

O'Brian, Patrick, 13
O'Riley, Mid Sean, 108
officers' swords, 35–54
Olliver, Cdr A G, 106, 126
Olliver, Lt Cdr Adrian J, 109, *109*, 127, 128
Olliver, PO Wren Louise, 109, *109*, 129
Olympic Games, 103–6
Ontario, Lake, 76–7
Ord, Adm Sir John, 13
Ordnance, Board of, 27, 34
Orford, Robert, 1st Earl of, 83
Orford, 3rd Earl of, 83
Orme, Daniel, 90
Orridge, Lt Cdr Steve, *109*

P&O (Peninsular & Oriental Steam Navigation Co), 72–3
Pakistan Navy, 69
Palembang, 23
Palmer, Lt Edward Gascoine, 82
Paris, 105
Parkes, Chief Officer, *68*
Parry, R Adm Sir William, 42–3
Parsons, Lt G S, 11, 18, 88
Patriotic Fund of Lloyd's, 77–8, 79, 82, 87, 119–24
Pearson AB, 19
Pearson CPO Ken, 106, *106*, 127, 128
Peasnell, QSI F A, 104, *104*
Pedro IV, Dom, 19
Peel, Capt Sir William, 16, *44*, 45
Peitsang, 19
Peiyang, 19
Peking, *19*, 20
Pelew Islands, 77–9
Pemba, island of, 25
Pembroke, 60; Royal Dockyard Battalion, 60, 62
Penfold, Marine Jack, 104, *104*
Perrés, R Adm, 88
Perry, Sgt A W, 104, *104*
Philippines, 79
pike, 7: boarding, 8;

Napoleonic wars, 11; method of use, 15
pistols, 8, 11, 13, 16, 18
Pitt, William , 13, 60
Plumbe, Major, *18*, 19
Plymouth, 18
pommel: acanthus, 45; burr, *28*; crocodile, *57*, 57–8, 76, 86, 87; cushion-shaped, 38, *56*, 57, 70; dragon's head, 68, *68*; eagle, 64; helmet-shaped, 79, *79*; lion: head, 39, 40, 42, 42–5, 48, 58, 61, *61*, 63, 66, 67, *67–8*, *71*, 72, 72, recumbent, 74, *74*; stepped, 62, 67; urn-shaped, 38, 69
Pooley: Robert, 24; swords, 24–5
Popham, Adm Home, 76, 122, 124
Portland, 97
Portsmouth, 38, 90, 94, 96, 97, 106, 108: Naval Academy, 92, *92*; Royal Dockyard Battalion, 60, 62; RN Museum, 20, 42–3, 84; & Southsea Fencing Club, 106
Portugal, 39, 123
presentation swords, 73, 76–81, 119–25; *see also* Patriotic Fund of Lloyd's; London, City of
Prest, Cadet, 107
Prettyman, Lt T George, *80*
Preventative Waterguard, 65
Princess Royal, HRH the, 24
prize swords, 24; *see also* presentation swords
procurement (sword), 17, 34
proof marks, 111–14
Prosser, John, 77, 84
Prowse, Dave, 106

Queen's Sword, 24
Quint, Gunner Stephen, 15

RUSI (Royal United Services Institute), 8, 84, *84*, 87
rapier, 13, 38
Raven, A A, *105*
Rawson, Cdr Wyatt, 16, *16*
Read, George, 67
Reserves, 60–75
Revenue Service, 33, *34*
revolver: cartridge, 14; flintlock, 14
Rice, Capt, *23*
Rickard, Lt T P, *61*, *62*
rifles, 16, 20: Enfield, 31; Enfield-Snider 31, 32, 99; Martini-Henry 32, 99; Minié, 34
Rigaud, Jean Francis, 89–90, *90*
Riquelme, Don Francisco, 88
Rising, John, 90
Rodney, Adm Sir George Brydges, 39, *39*
Romney, George, 55, *55*
Rosebery, Lord, 75
Rowland, Dr, 14
Royal Academy, 89
Royal Ceylon Navy, 69
Royal Dockyard Battalion (RDB), 50, 60–2, *60–1*
Royal Fleet Reserve, 64
Royal Flying Corps, 64
Royal Hospital, Greenwich, 85
Royal Hospital School, Greenwich, *98*
Royal Indian Marine, 69, *71*, 72; *see also* Indian Navy
Royal Indian Navy, 69, *71*, 72; *see also* Indian Navy
Royal Mail Line, 73
Royal Marines, *see* Marines
Royal Naval Air Service (RNAS), 64, 64, 125
Royal Naval Artillery Volunteers (RNAV), 61, 63, *63*, 102
Royal Naval College, Osborne, 107, *109*; *see also* Britannia Royal Naval College
Royal Naval Division (RND), 64–5
Royal Naval Engineering College: Keyham, 98, 99,

106; Manadon, 108, 130
Royal Naval Exhibition, 84
Royal Naval Museum (Museum of the Royal Navy), Portsmouth, 16, 20, 42–3, 84
Royal Naval Reserves (RNR), 63–4, *64*, 67, 68, 72, 73
Royal Naval Trophy Centre, 84
Royal Naval Volunteer Reserve (RNVR), 63–4, *64*
Royal Naval Volunteer (Supplementary) Reserve (RNV(S)R), 63
Royal Navy Amateur Fencing Association, 108–9
Royal Navy & Royal Marines Fencing Association, 108
Royal Navy School of Physical Training, Portsmouth, 106
Royal Pakistan Navy, 69
Royal Small Arms Factory, 32
Royal Tournament, 15, 98, *102*, 102–4, 106, 107, 108, 126
Royal Warwickshire Regiment, 20
Runciman, Walter, 1st Viscount, 75
Russell, Adm, 11
Russell, Lt Martin, *109*
Russell, W H, 16

sabre, 14, *80*, 83, 97; *see also* fencing
St Anne, 78
St George, Order of, 104
St Vincent, Admiral the Earl, 13, 57, 78, 79, *81*, 87, 124
Salter, John, 42, 66, 77, 83, 85; *see also* sword makers and retailers
Saumarez, James, 86, 124
scabbard, 25, 28, 47–50, *48–9*, *61*, 61–2: Army pattern, 62; dirk *56–8*, 57, 58; leather: black, 30–3, 40–2, 61, 66, 67, 69–70, brown, 29, 32, 38; manufacture, 113; mounts, 44; punishment using, 23; Sam Browne, 20, 64, 118; seal, 37; *see also* sword patterns
scimitar, 82, 87
Scorgie, Lt Cdr Stuart, 106, *109*
Scotland, 53:fighting methods, 8; regiments, 53, 63
Searight, PO Wren, *109*
Second World War, 51, 54, 59, 63, 73, 78–9, *94*, 106, 108, 110, 118, 124
Seddon, Col, 88
Selwyn, Capt, 8
Seven Years War, 39
Seymour, Adm, *19*
Shah Najif, 16
shako, 61
Shee, Sir Martin Archer, *74*
Sheerness, 60
Shetland Islands, 73
ships, British: *Affray*, 25; *Agamemnon*, 83, 122; *Ajax*, 9, 119, 121; *Anson*, 78; *Arethusa*, 78, 122; *Ark Royal*, 73; *Armada*, 22; *Bellisle*, 10; *Berengaria*, 72; *Blanche*, 86, 120; *Boreas*, 94; *Britannia*, 58–9, 97, 102, 121; *Captain*, 83, 88; *Centurion*, *19*, 121; *Collingwood*, 25: Officers' Association, 25; *Conqueror*, 14, 15, 121; *Cornwall*, 59; *Cossack*, 21, *21*: Association, 21; *Coventry*, 106; *Cumberland*, 59, 120; *Defiance*, 9–10, *10*, 121, 122; *Diamante*, 121; *Diligence*, 6; *Drake*, 23, 120; *Dreadnought*, 83, 121; *Eclipse*, 15; *Edgar*, 94; *Endymion*, *19*; *Esk*, 15; *Excellent*, 106; *Fame*, 20; *Fisgard*, 77, 77, 78, 123; *Golden Hind*, 35; *Goliath*, 23; *Harrier*, 15; *Hazardous*, 38; *Hebe*, 38; *Hecla*, 16, 42–3; *Hermione*, 79; *Hindoustan*, 102; *Illustrious*, 97, 125;

Latona, 78; *Lion*, 83; *London*, 15, 56; *Maidstone*, 115, 121; *Majestic*, 86; *Malaya*, 80, *80*; *Marlborough*, *107*; *Mary Rose*, 23, 35, *35*, 36; *Mayflower*, 37, 72; *Menai*, *81*; *Minerva*, 86; *Mutine*, 86; *Nelson*, 109; *Nile*, 115; *Niobe*, 96; *Norma*, 73; *Northumberland*, 88; *Orion*, 86; *Pelican*, *80*; *Pelorus*, 15; *Pickle*, 86, 121; *Pleiad*, 33–4; *Port-au-Prince*, 8; *Powerful*, 19, *118*; *Pretoria Castle*, *109*; *Prince Charles*, 64; *Queen Charlotte*, 76; *Racoon*, 9, 120; *Raisonnable*, 84; *Repulse*, 104; *Resolute*, 94; *Resolution*, 97; *Royal Arthur*, 109; *St Vincent*, 96; *Salisbury*, 80, 94; *Saturn*, 18; *Shannon*, 7–8, 14, 16, *44*; *Spartiate*, 88, 121; *Speedwell*, 65; *Speedy*, 8; *Success*, 88; *Sultan*, 23, 109; *Superb*, 59, 115; *Terrible*, 20; *Tonnant*, 10, 82, 121; *Topaze*, 94; *Triumph*, 84, *84*; *Turquoise*, 19; *Vernon*, 16, 17; *Victoria*, 15, 86; *Victory*, 83, 84; *Warley*, 79, 120; *Wasp*, 80; *Whiting*, 20; *Wizard*, 80; *Zealous*, 86, 86; ships, foreign: *Adm Graf Spee*, 21; *Aigle*, 9; *Altmark*, 21, *21*; *Aquilon*, 88; *Argus*, 80; *Bucentaure*, 94; *Chesapeake*, 7–8, 14, 124; *Chevrette*, 11–12; *Desiree*, 38; *El Gamo*, 8; *Kenan Hasselaar*, 78; *L'Amelie*, 9; *L'Intrepide*, *10*; *La Jeune Adele*, 9; *La Mutine*, 9; *La Petite Fille*, 9; *Le Généreux*, 88; *President*, 19; *Sabina*, 86; *San Josef*, 9, 118, 87, 88, 89, 89, 90; *San Nicolas*, 9, 10, 87, *87*; *Santa Ana*, 88; *Santa-Brigida*, 18; *Suriname*, 78; *Thetis*, 18, 121; *Troisième Ferailleur*, 37; *U36*, 64; *Urain*, 12
Shore, Cdr Thetton Henry N, 65
Shotley Bridge, 114
Sicily, King of, 87
Silver: George, 13; & Co, 48, 63, 73, *111*
Simmonds, Lt Meyrick, 108, 127
Sinclair, Arthur, 76–7
Singapore, 23
singlestick, 94, *94*, 95, 97–9, 97–9, 106, *107–8*, 108
Skynner, Lt John, 94
Sloane-Stanley, C G, 56
small-swords, 38–9, 76, *80*, 83, 85, 87, 88; 90: oval side ring, *84*; and foil, 92, *93*; manufacture, 113
Smeaton, CPO, 102, 126
Smith, Alderman Joshua, 83, 85
Smith & Wesson, 14
Snook, Lt Samuel, 79, *79*
Solent, 35
Solingen, 17, 34, 54, 112–14
Sotheby's 84, 87
South Africa, 106: Fencing Association, 106
South Foreland, 65
Southampton, 13
Southsea, 91, *91*
Southwark, 83, 85
spadroon, 37, 38, 39–40, 41
Spain, 9, 77; sword, 64
Spencer, Lt John George, 64
Spencer, John Poyntz, 5th Earl, 74–5, *75*
Spithead, 77, 118
Spratt, James, 9–10
Sproul-Bolton, Lt Cdr R St C, 108, 126, 127
Sri Lankan Navy, 69
Stamper, CPO William 'Bill', 106, 108, 126, 127
Starbuck: Revd F, 84; sword, 84
Steel, David, 110
Steuart, Capt Don Jacobo, 86
Stewart, Adm Sir Houston, *80*
Stilwell, Maj Michael, 21

Stockholm, 103
Stokes, Lt Geoffrey Durham, 80, *80*
Stokes, Phillip, 86
Stopford, Adm Sir Robert. 85
Strasbourg, 24
Street, Lt, 38
Suckling: Capt, 84, *84*; Mid Benjamin William, 83; Maurice, 83; Lt Maurice William, 83; family sword, 83
Sudan, 16, 17
Sulivan, Adm Sir Bartholomew, 60–1
Sumatra, *23*
Surat, 69
Suriname, capture of, 77, 124
Sussex, HRH the Duke of, 42, 58
Sutherland, Mr, 77
Suvali, 69
Svoreik, M, 103
sword-bayonet, *see* cutlass, bayonet, sword patterns
sword belt, 25, 28, 43, 49–51, *50*, *52*, 61–2, 62, 69; Cinque Ports, 75; coastguard, 66–7; dirk, 58, *59*; Patriotic Fund, 78; manufacture, 113; RNR, *64*
sword dancing, 108
sword design, 114: Army influence, 27, 30, 31; *see also* sword patterns, sword makers
sword drills: Admiralty, 92; cutlass, 98; naval, 8–9; military, 8; *see also* training
sword feats, 100–3, *101–2*, 108
sword knot, 25, 28, 43–5, *46*, 49–50, *50*, 61, 62–3, *63*, 68, 70, *70*: 1859, 31; Cinque Ports, 75; cord, 42; dirk, 58; Irish, 54; manufacture, 113; Patriotic Fund, 78; post-1891, 68; RNR, 64; slot, 40; Trinity House, 75; sword conservation, 115–17
sword makers & retailers, 110–15: Aston, 34; Bate, 34; Chavasse, 34; Clauberg, 34; Cooper, 34; Craven, 34; Davies, E M, 63; Dawes, 34; Deakin, Francis, 111, *111*; Firmin & Son, 24, 125; Goy & Co, 71, *71*; Greaves, 34; Grindlay & Co, 71; Hadley, 34; Höller, 34; Hollier, Thos, 27; Kenning, G, 64; Kirschbaum, 34; *see also* Weyersberg; Klönne, 34; Lambert & Brown, 67; Lawrence, 34; Makepeace, Robert, 87; Mohl, Hermann, 114; Mole, 34: Robert, 112, 114, & Sons, 32; Morisset, James, 87; Moxham, 34; Nelson, Thos, 27; Odell, *74*: Bennet, T, J & B, 74, John, 74, & Atherley, 74; Reddell, 34, 58; Reeves, 34, 110; Rigby: William & John, 66, & Salter, 66; Robinson: 34, & Watts, 34; Salter: 34, John, 42, 66, 77, 83, 85, Rigby &, 66; Schnitzler & Kirschbaum, 34; Starkey, Joseph, 54; Swinburn, 34; Teed, Richard, 77; Thurkle, *111*; Weyersberg, 34: W, Kirschbaum & Co (WKC), 25, WKC Stahl- und Metallwarenfabrik, 52; Woolley, 34; *see also* Enfield, Gieves, Pooley, Silver & Co, Wilkinson Sword Company
sword manufacture, 26, 112–14, *112*; *see also* sword makers
sword, oval side ring, 83–4, *84*, 90
sword patterns: 1796: Army, 39, infantry, 40, light cavalry, 40–1, *41*; 1803: Army, 37, 38, 39, grenadier and light infantry, 41; 1804 cutlass, *27*, 27–8, 33, 34, 39; 1805: 39–43, 45, 66, 66, 70, 72, 74,

82–5, *85*, 88, *88*, 95: plain, *40–1*, 41, 42–3, 56, ornamented, *39*, 39–41, *40*, *42*, 44, 70, 118, *116*; 1814 Norwegian cutlass, 27; 1822 infantry, 67; 1825 civil branches, 43, *50*; 1825–32 purser's, *43*; 1827, 41, *43–4*, 45, *50*, 66, 70, 70–1, *116*, 117; 1845 cutlass, 28–9, *28–9*, 34; 1846, 47, 52, *72*, 1847, 48, *48*, 52, 61, *118*; 1856, *50*, 58, 61; 1859 Enfield-Snider cutlass sword bayonet, 31–2, 34; 1871 Martini-Henry cutlass sword bayonet, 32, *32*; post-1879 dirk, *59*; 1882 cavalry, 30; 1887 cutlass, 29, 34; 1889 cutlass, 29, 30, *30*; 1890 cavalry trooper, 30; 1891, *52*, 63, 74; 1900 cutlass, 31, *31*; sword of peace, 24, 125
sword-pistol, 82
sword procurement, 17, 34
Swordfish (aircraft), 25
swords, displaying, 117–8
symbolism, 22
Syrett, David, 110

Taku forts, 20
Tallent, Sgt, 104, *105*
Tamai, 17
targe, 8
Taylor's auction house, 60
Tel-el-Kebir, 16, 16
Tenerife, battle of (Santa Cruz de), 83, 84, 87, 90
Thames River Police, *32*, *33*
Thames Rowing Club, *102*
Thomas, George, *106*
Thomas, Lord, of Gresford, 24
Thompson, Lt Cdr Bob, 108
Thompson, Sgt R, 106
Tientsin, *19*, 20
Tierney, George, MP, 13
Tilbury, 68
Tiller, PO Ray, 106, 127, 128
Times, The, 16, 82, 85
Tisshaw, Gunner C W, *109*
tomahawk, 15, 108; *see also* axe
Tomkinson, 20
Tourville, Adm, 11
Trafalgar, battle of, 7, 8, 9–10, *10*, 14, 60, 82, 83, 88, 94: bicentenary, 90; signalling, 76; Spanish ships, 9; swords, 77, 79, 85, 86–7, 119, 121–2, 124
Trafalgar House, 87
training, 15, 28, 92–9; *see also* drills
Treaty of Paris, 39
Trigger, Boatswain Richard, 15
Trinity House, 64, 70, 73–5, 75: Artillery Volunteers, 60
Trowbridge, R Adm Sir R J, *52*
Tryon, Adm George, 86
Tuck, Raphael, & Sons, 96
Turkey, Sultan of, 87; *see also* scimitars
Tyle, Sgt F, 106
Tyler, Capt Charles, 82, 121
Tyrason, Don Miguel, 88

Ukraine Defence College, 25
United States: Navy, 9, 53, 76, 80; Revolutionary War, 76; War of 1812, 11, 15
Ushant, 76

Vado Bay, 83
Venezuela, 78
Vian, Capt Philip, 21
Victoria, Queen, 72, 102, 114
Victoria & Albert Museum, 76
Victoria Cross, 15, 16–17, *17*, 20, *44*, 50
Villeneuve, Adm, 8, 83, 88, 94
Vittoriosa, 62
Volunteers: 1st Class, 56, 58, *58*; 2nd Class, 56; *see also* Ceylon, Harbour V Marines, Reserves, Trinity House

Waite, Corporal-Major J M, 100

Wakefield, Lord, 87
Waldegrave, V Adm, 87
Walker, Capt, 66
Walker, Capt Chris, 108, 127, 128
Wallis, H, 12
Wallis, Lt James, 94
Walpole, Capt Galfridus, 83
War Department, 27
War of 1812, 11, 15, 76–7
Ward, Horatia, *see* Nelson, Horatia
Warsash Maritime Academy, 73
Waterloo, battle of, 7, 60
Watkins, Capt, 18
Watson, Capt H, 103
West, Lord, of Spithead, 48
West India Merchants, 33
West Indies, 11, 39, 76, 78, 83, 89, 91, 94
Westall, Richard, 90
Westcott, Capt, 86
Westminster Abbey, 89, 91
White Star, 73
Whitechapel, 27
Whitsand Bay, 9
Whittle (artist), 90
Wight, Isle of, 22, 84, 122
Wilhelmina, Queen, 106
Wilkinson, Henry, 61, 111, *111*, 115, 118; *see also* Wilkinson Sword Company
Wilkinson, James, 112
Wilkinson-Latham, John, 8, 43, 111, 112, 114
Wilkinson, Norman, *21*
Wilkinson Sword Company, 8, 34, 46, 48, 53, 62, 79, *100*, 110, 115: closure, 25, 54; coastguard, 66, 67; history, 112, 114; mark, 34; RDB, *60*; RNAV, 63
Wilkinson Sword of Peace, 24, 125
William IV, 32, 38, 87, 114, 118
Williams, 2/O Barbara (Lyle), 106, 128
Wilson, Adm Sir Arthur Knyvet, 16–17, *17*, 50
Wilson, H W, 19
Wimbledon Common, 74
Winthuysen, Adm Don Francisco, 88, 89, 89
Wodehouse, Hon P, 14
Wolfe, Sarah C, 76
Wolseley, Lt Gen, 16
Wood, Lt Ebenezer, 62
Woodward, Adm Sir John, 79, 124
Woolmore, Capt Sir John, 73–4, *74*
Woolwich, 60
Wormald, Lt, 17
wounds, 14

Yangtze River, 68
Yarmouth (IOW), 22
Yeo, Cdre Sir James Lucas, 7, 13, 121
York, Cardinal, 87
Yorke, Lt George Cockburn, 86
Ypres, 20

Zante, island of, 87
Zanzibar, 19